EXCLUSION AND EXTREMISM

The question of how people develop extreme, radical, or even terrorist ideas and behaviors is one that is attracting more and more scientific attention. There are many factors that contribute to such extremist attitudes. This book focuses on one specific contributor that has received only little attention in the past: social exclusion. Recent research shows that being kept apart from others, physically or emotionally, is a powerful event in people's lives. The chapters provide an overview of the existing body of research for the first time and explore the exclusion–extremism link in depth by gathering together a seminal collection of essays, written by leading social psychologists. Timely, novel, and highly instructive, this volume delivers an expert understanding of psychological underpinnings of such behavior and offers inspiration for future research.

MICHAELA PFUNDMAIR is Professor of Intelligence Psychology at the Federal University of Administrative Sciences in Berlin, Germany. Her research focuses on the consequences of social exclusion and the psychology of terrorist radicalization.

ANDREW H. HALES is Professor of Psychology at the University of Mississippi, USA. He researches the many ways people influence one another, including social ostracism.

KIPLING D. WILLIAMS is Distinguished Professor of Psychological Sciences at Purdue University, USA. An expert on ostracism and social influence, he has authored and coedited numerous books on the subject.

T0384952

EXCLUSION AND EXTREMISM

A Psychological Perspective

Edited by

MICHAELA PFUNDMAIR
Federal University of Administrative Sciences

ANDREW H. HALES
University of Mississippi

KIPLING D. WILLIAMS
Purdue University

CAMBRIDGE
UNIVERSITY PRESS

Shaftesbury Road, Cambridge CB2 8EA, United Kingdom

One Liberty Plaza, 20th Floor, New York, NY 10006, USA

477 Williamstown Road, Port Melbourne, VIC 3207, Australia

314–321, 3rd Floor, Plot 3, Splendor Forum, Jasola District Centre,
New Delhi – 110025, India

103 Penang Road, #05–06/07, Visioncrest Commercial, Singapore 238467

Cambridge University Press is part of Cambridge University Press & Assessment,
a department of the University of Cambridge.

We share the University's mission to contribute to society through the pursuit of
education, learning and research at the highest international levels of excellence.

www.cambridge.org
Information on this title: www.cambridge.org/9781009408134

DOI: 10.1017/9781009408165

First published 2024

A catalogue record for this publication is available from the British Library

Library of Congress Cataloging-in-Publication Data
Names: Pfundmair, Michaela, 1984– author. | Hales, Andrew, 1989– author. | Williams,
Kipling D., 1953– author.
Title: Exclusion and extremism : a psychological perspective / Michaela Pfundmair, Federal
University of Administrative Sciences, Germany, Andrew Hales, University of Mississippi,
Kipling D. Williams, Purdue University.
Description: 1 edition. | New York, NY : Cambridge University Press, 2024. |
Includes bibliographical references and index.
Identifiers: LCCN 2024001535 | ISBN 9781009408134 (hardback) |
ISBN 9781009408127 (paperback) | ISBN 9781009408165 (ebook)
Subjects: LCSH: Social isolation – Psychological aspects. | Extreme behavior
(Psychology) | Social psychology.
Classification: LCC HM1131 .P48 2024 | DDC 302.5/45–dc23/eng/20240304
LC record available at https://lccn.loc.gov/2024001535

ISBN 978-1-009-40813-4 Hardback
ISBN 978-1-009-40812-7 Paperback

This book is for the people who always make us feel included.

CONTENTS

vii

CONTRIBUTORS

HANNA BÄCK, Lund University

JUANA CHINCHILLA, Universidad Nacional de Educación a Distancia

BERTJAN DOOSJE, University of Amsterdam

MOLLY ELLENBERG, University of Maryland

ALLARD R. FEDDES, University of Amsterdam

VERENA GRAUPMANN, DePaul University

ANDREW H. HALES, University of Mississippi

MICHAEL A. HOGG, Claremont Graduate University

ROLAND IMHOFF, Johannes Gutenberg-University Mainz

ÁNGEL GÓMEZ, Universidad Nacional de Educación a Distancia and ARTIS International

ROBIN M. KOWALSKI, Clemson University

ARIE W. KRUGLANSKI, University of Maryland

MARK R. LEARY, Duke University

LIESBETH MANN, University of Amsterdam

MARCO MARINUCCI, University of Milano-Bicocca

MICHAELA PFUNDMAIR, Federal University of Administrative Sciences

FELICIA PRATTO, University of Connecticut

J. N. RASMUS MÖRING, University of Kaiserslautern Landau and University of Connecticut

EMMA A. RENSTRÖM, Kristianstad University

PAOLO RIVA, University of Milano-Bicocca

GREGORY J. ROUSIS, University of South Florida

WILLIAM B. SWANN, JR., The University of Texas–Austin

JOSEPH A. WAGONER, University of Colorado

ERIC D. WESSELMANN, Illinois State University

KIPLING D. WILLIAMS, Purdue University

NATASHA R. WOOD, University of Mississippi

~

Introduction

MICHAELA PFUNDMAIR, ANDREW H. HALES, AND
KIPLING D. WILLIAMS

Extremism has recently been described as one of the most pressing problems in contemporary society (Litter & Lee, 2023). The burst of extremism in today's world has happened as the hodgepodge of different ideologies replaced the hegemonic ideological blocks of the Cold War (Ugarriza, 2009) and the rise of digital technologies catalyzed this change (Litter & Lee, 2020). In order to propose policies or interventions to reduce or eliminate extremism, it is necessary to understand its causes. What is clear is that extremism results from a multitude of causes, not just one. In this volume, we will focus on one specific contributor which has received relatively little attention in the past: social exclusion.

Social exclusion – being kept apart from others physically or emotionally – is a powerful event per se. It is known from previous research that social exclusion can be an extremely painful experience associated with threats to fundamental human needs like control and meaningful existence (see Williams, 2009). That extremism can be triggered as a result from this threatening event does not seem implausible. At the same time, social exclusion is very common. A diary study, for example, recorded about an ostracism episode a day for the average person (Nezlek et al., 2012), and other research also shows that exclusion is something we all experience (Bernstein et al., 2021). Because of this fact alone, it should not be assumed that every excluded person will become extremized. Instead, exclusion seems to be one ingredient in a lethal cocktail that contributes to the likelihood of extremism. Thus, moderators are likely to be at work, driving the connection between exclusion and extremism in certain constellations.

To explore the exclusion–extremism link in depth and gather empirical evidence, this volume will provide an overview of the existing body of research for the first time. The book is organized into three parts, spanning the core effect, underlying mechanisms, and associated concepts.

In Part I, we look at the basic link between exclusion and extremism. Hales, Wood and Williams (Chapter 1) review the temporal need-threat model of ostracism and apply it to the question of how ostracism could lead to extremism: Various needs that are threatened by ostracism could be met through extreme groups. They also examine empirical investigations of this possibility and consider whether participating in extreme groups might lead to further ostracism. Renström and Bäck (Chapter 2) address exclusion and radicalization, and here specifically the role of individual differences. They show that exclusion-related traits such as rejection sensitivity and need to belong are relevant moderators of the relationship between exclusion and radicalization. Pfundmair (Chapter 3) focuses on terrorism, the violent endpoint of radicalization that will not occur in every case of radicalization but is associated with the most serious consequences. She presents theories and findings that outline how exclusion and terrorism are linked. The remaining chapters of Part I look at two special cases of extremism and how they relate to exclusion: White extremism and extremism among incels. Graupmann and Wesselmann (Chapter 4) examine how perceived threats of marginalized status among White individuals has led to White extremism. They emphasize the role of social identity and the self in understanding the psychology behind this process, and through this lens, they consider possible productive ways to promote more healthy racial identity. Rousis and Swann (Chapter 5) deal with incels, the so-called involuntary celibates, men who aspire to romantic or sexual partners but fail to obtain them. They outline their radicalization processes, including the role of exclusion.

In Part II, we explore factors that drive the exclusion–extremism link. The first chapters deal with important mediators of the link between exclusion and extremism. Ellenberg and Kruglanski (Chapter 6) examine how extremism could arise from a motivational imbalance. They examine how a quest for significance – which could be activated by exclusion – can motivate individuals to make extreme sacrifices and engage in otherwise unacceptable actions to fulfill that need. Wagoner and Hogg (Chapter 7) take a detailed look at the influence of identity uncertainty, that is, the feeling of being uncertain about oneself and one's own identity, how this feeling can be potentiated under exclusion and contribute to joining extremist groups. Doosje, Feddes, and Mann (Chapter 8), on the other hand, address the group as an important driver of extremism. They show how social identity processes – processes known to be elevated under exclusion – promote nonnormative developments. The remaining chapters of Part II look at relevant moderators of the link between exclusion and extremism. Möring and Pratto (Chapter 9) elaborate status indignity, i.e., the resentment that one's own group is perceived to be lower than it deserves and that can be linked to perceptions of social exclusion. Chinchilla and Gómez (Chapter 10) investigate how these processes could play out across different cultural and psychological contexts. They examine in particular the process of identity fusion, in which people become profoundly identified with a group or ideology, and how this could motivate fighting on its behalf.

The final part of the book, Part III, explores related concepts that are relevant to better understand the link between exclusion and extremism.

Kowalski and Leary (Chapter 11) explore how people react to interpersonal rejection and examine five forms of extreme aggression that sometimes result (school and mass shootings, intimate partner violence, hazing, retaliative suicide, and cyberbullying). Riva and Marinucci (Chapter 12) address how chronic exclusion, which has already led to resignation, can fuel the radicalization process. And, finally, Imhoff (Chapter 13) presents an overview of the psychology of conspiracy beliefs and examines the evidence for a possible link between social exclusion experiences and increased belief in conspiracies.

All in all, the findings presented in this volume can be integrated into a comprehensive framework (see Figure 0.1). According to this, extremism – i.e., the development into a norm deviation – arises from certain antecedents, for example, in the case of terrorist radicalization, a cognitive opening for radical ideas, and ends with certain outcomes. It should be borne in mind that a violent endpoint like terrorism is a possible outcome; however, it is not inevitable. Most people who embrace extreme or even extremist ideas act accordingly only in the rarest of cases (Borum, 2011). Both the antecedents for and a progression into extremism are driven by a wide variety of factors. One of these factors is social exclusion. The pathway from exclusion to extremism is likely not direct, but occurs indirectly through the consequences of exclusion – such as an increased search for significance, the avoidance of uncertainty, or intensified group processes. Moreover, the link between exclusion and extremism is made more likely by certain boosters – for example, increased rejection sensitivity, a sense of status indignity, or a particular cultural context.

In gathering together a collection of chapters written by leading social psychologists, we not only aim to shed further light on the theoretical concepts

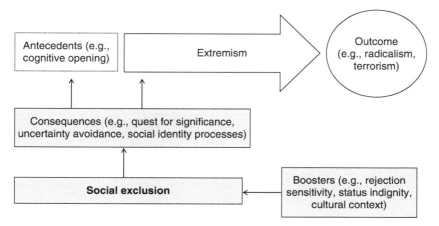

Figure 0.1 Integrative framework on the link between exclusion and extremism.

of extremism and social exclusion but would also like to contribute to the development of preventive and interventive measures that could take a potent starting point in the promotion of social inclusion. Because, as Jesse Jackson said, "inclusion is not a matter of political correctness, it is the key to growth" (Daniels, 2007).

Bernstein, M. J., Neubauer, A. B., Benfield, J. A., Potter, L., & Smyth, J. M. (2021). Within-person effects of inclusion and exclusion on well-being in daily life. *Personal Relationships*, 28(4), 940–960. https://doi.org/10.1111/pere.12399

Borum, R. (2011). Radicalization into violent extremism I: A review of social science theories. *Journal of Strategic Security*, 4(4), 7–36. https://doi.org/10.5038/1944-0472.4.4.1

Daniels, S. (2007, May 15). Allstate, Jackson to discuss using minority firms more. *Crain's Chicago Business*. www.chicagobusiness.com/article/20070515/NEWS01/200024995/allstate-jackson-to-discuss-using-minority-firms-more

Littler, M., & Lee, B. (2020). *Digital extremisms: Readings in violence, radicalization and extremism in the online space*. Palgrave Macmillan. https://doi.org/10.1007/978-3-030-30138-5

Littler, M., & Lee, B. (2023). Studying extremism in the 21st century: The past, a path, & some proposals. *Studies in Conflict & Terrorism*, 1–3. https://doi.org/10.1080/1057610X.2023.2195056

Nezlek, J. B., Wesselmann, E. D., Wheeler, L., & Williams, K. D. (2012). Ostracism in everyday life. *Group Dynamics: Theory, Research, and Practice*, 16(2), 91–104. https://doi.org/10.1037/a0028029

Ugarriza, J. E. (2009). Ideologies and conflict in the post-Cold War. *International Journal of Conflict Management*, 20(1), 82–104. https://doi.org/10.1108/10444060910931620

Williams, K. D. (2009). Ostracism: A temporal need-threat model. *Advances in Experimental Social Psychology*, 41, 275–314. https://doi.org/10.1016/S0065-2601(08)00406-1

PART I

The Link between Exclusion and Extremism

Ostracism and Extremism

How Extreme Groups Can Address Threatened Needs

ANDREW H. HALES, NATASHA R. WOOD,
AND KIPLING D. WILLIAMS

1.1   Introduction

Humans are fundamentally social, so it is not surprising that people are drawn to associating with groups. Typically, the groups people seek out are ordinary organizations or loose associations that serve good ends in reasonable ways. However, some groups are morally questionable, and others may even be extreme. Be it in their beliefs (say, that the Earth is flat), their advocacy (say, overthrowing the government), or the requirements imposed on their members (say, strict dress codes or heavy monetary contribution), some groups are just *out there*. Why, then, would humans want to participate in such non-normative and extreme organizations?

There is, of course, no single answer to this question. However, a number of critically important factors have been identified. One factor that appears to play an important role in motivating people to explore, and perhaps join, extreme groups is the experience of having been recently (or chronically) *ostracized*. The fact that humans are fundamentally social not only drives group affiliation in the first place but may also cause people to feel especially hurt in response to even minor signs of exclusion, which could cause them to entertain participating in groups that would otherwise be unappealing.

In this chapter, we address the relationship between social ostracism and extremism. We first review the temporal need-threat model of ostracism and examine its predictions for why ostracism could stoke in its targets a desire to affiliate with extreme groups. We then review the existing empirical evidence for the effect of ostracism on openness to extremism. This tendency for ostracism to open people up to extremism likely depends on many factors, so we also consider some important potential moderating factors and the theoretical reasons to expect them to affect when and how ostracism leads to extremism. Finally, we switch perspective and consider the possibility – and corresponding evidence – that participating in extremism may, unhelpfully, lead one to encounter yet more ostracism from nonextremists.

1.2   Temporal Need-Threat Model of Ostracism

To understand how ostracism can motivate interest in extremism, it is helpful to review a theoretical framework that explains how people respond to ostracism in general. The temporal need-threat model of ostracism provides a complete and coherent framework for understanding how responses to ostracism unfold following ostracism (Williams, 2009). The model defines ostracism as any instance of being ignored and excluded by an individual or group, and outlines how reactions to ostracism unfold over three stages. Ostracism can be thought of as a type of social exclusion, in which people are kept apart from others (Wesselmann et al., 2016). It has similarities to related experiences like being explicitly rejected, but its core feature is that it entails being ignored and excluded. In this chapter we focus specifically on social ostracism, as it is known specifically to threaten a cluster of needs that are relevant to the radicalization process.

First, in the *reflexive stage*, individuals become aware of the ostracism and experience immediate pain, negative emotions, and threats to their fundamental psychological needs, including belonging, self-esteem, control, meaningful existence, and certainty (Hales & Williams, 2021). As the name of the stage suggests, this ostracism-induced pain signal is reflexive and automatic, detected quickly and crudely (Zadro et al., 2004). As such, ostracism is experienced as painful – at least initially – in a variety of situations in which one would logically expect it not to hurt. Being ostracized hurts even when it is delivered by entirely unknown strangers online for a period of just a few minutes (Williams et al., 2000). It hurts even when it is delivered from a despised out-group (Fayant et al., 2014; Gonsalkorale & Williams, 2007), when it costs money to be included (van Beest & Williams, 2006), and when the agent of exclusion is nonhuman such as a computer or a pet (Jauch et al., 2022; Richman, 2020; Zadro et al., 2004). And people feel negatively in response to not only everyday forms of ostracism such as being explicitly excluded (e.g., Bernstein et al., 2021) but also subtle ignoring such as not being looked in the eye (Wesselmann, Cardoso, et al., 2012; Wirth et al., 2010), or being ignored while people look at their phones (Hales et al., 2018). This hyperresponsive tendency is understandable from an evolutionary perspective. Being an outcast would have had devastating effects on the survival and reproductive fitness of ancestral humans; it would cut them off from the cooperative benefits of group living and from potential mating partners. So there is adaptive value in a strong and unignorable signal that one is being left out, as it could alert one to the need to repair relations with the ostracizing group, or to find a new group with which to affiliate (Kerr & Levine, 2008; Wesselmann, Nairne, et al., 2012). The cost of under-detecting ostracism by not recognizing when one is being left out could have been ultimately fatal. In contrast, the cost of over-detecting ostracism would have been relatively minimal. For these reasons, ostracism in the *reflexive* stage is strongly painful and indiscriminate to specific details of the exclusion.

Second, in the *reflective stage*, individuals consider the causes and implications of the ostracism and are motivated to restore their threatened psychological needs. In this stage, people tend to seek out attributions for why the ostracism occurred and engage in the process of recovering their threatened psychological needs (Williams, 2009). In contrast to the immediate reflexive stage – in which responses to ostracism tend to be indiscriminately strong – people's speed of recovery in the reflective stage may be more variable and depend on individual difference variables (e.g., dispositional anxiety; Zadro et al., 2006), situational variables (e.g., whether an audience witnesses the exclusion; Hales et al., 2021), and behavioral variables (e.g., rumination, self-affirmation; Hales et al., 2016; Wesselmann et al., 2013). A key element of the reflective stage is that individuals are *motivated* to restore their basic needs. This may take the form of engaging in behaviors that restore liking and belonging from others (i.e., behaving prosocially to be reincluded; e.g., Riva et al., 2014) or engaging in behaviors that bestow a sense of power, significance, and control (i.e., behaving provocatively even if antisocially; e.g., Maner et al., 2007; Ren et al., 2018). We will see that this motivated state induced by ostracism can have the potential to leave people more open to extremism.

Third, in the final *resignation stage*, if ostracism persists, and if individuals are unable to restore their basic psychological needs, they are theorized to experience alienation, unworthiness, helplessness, and depression. Correlational evidence indicates that people who are chronically ostracized report higher levels of these negative outcomes (Riva et al., 2017). Longitudinal studies further indicate that experiencing ostracism predicts subsequent diagnoses of depression (Rudert et al., 2021) and also more lasting feelings of alienation, unworthiness, and helplessness (Marinucci & Riva, 2021).

1.3   Ostracism and Extremism

To address the question of whether ostracism can leave people more susceptible to extremism, we first address the theoretical rationale for such a connection, and then the empirical evidence for such a link. In this chapter, we refer to extremism as a belief, attitude, intention, or behavior that is rare (i.e., numerically uncommon) and nonnormative (i.e., the opposite of moderation). Furthermore, extremism is motivational, suggesting that there is an end goal to the belief, attitude, intention, or behavior.

1.3.1   *Theoretical Rationale*

As outlined earlier, the temporal need-threat model posits a *motivational* response to ostracism. When people experience the threat to basic needs that is caused by ostracism, they are then motivated to restore those needs. It follows that if extreme groups offer a pathway to restore these needs, they will be especially attractive to those who have been ostracized. And indeed, theorists have reasoned this is the case (Knapton, 2014; Pfundmair et al., 2022; Wesselmann & Williams, 2010; Williams et al., 2019).

Just as a state of food deprivation (hunger) could cause someone to be open to a wider range of foods than they would ordinarily find appetizing, so could a state of social deprivation (ostracism) lead people to be open to a wider range of social connections than they would ordinarily entertain (an analogy that is helpfully suggested by the concept of *social snacking*; Gardner et al., 2005). From this perspective, being ostracized may induce a sort of social indiscrimination, in which people affiliate with any group that will have them, even if it is an extreme group (Williams et al., 2019).

However, there are also reasons to think that extreme groups are not just sufficient to people who have been ostracized but perhaps even especially appealing. Extreme groups have many properties that could make them especially well suited to address each of the basic needs threatened by ostracism.

1.3.1.1   Belonging

Extreme groups may be an especially powerful source of belonging for a variety of reasons. They may be seen as more selective, such that when one is included, the sense of belonging is felt more powerfully (and cognitive dissonance processes may cause greater loyalty to the group, justifying the effort one had to endure to be accepted). This dynamic may operate in groups such as small extreme religious organizations that shower members with positive affection when they conform to norms but harshly punish them when they deviate, producing a cycle where the group serves as a powerful, but monopolistic, source of belonging (Parsons, 1986; Venter, 1998). Basic research has experimentally documented an analogous effect: When individuals initially experience ostracism by a group before being welcomed into it, they ultimately identified more strongly with the group and were more willing to take risks on its behalf than those who were initially included (i.e., without the selective ordeal at the beginning; Dahl et al., 2019). Moreover, because extreme groups are often more entitative (i.e., seen as more cohesive and uniform; see Section 1.3.1.5), they may offer an especially powerful sense of belonging. In sum, extreme groups can be seen as a potent source of belonging – at least provided the individual is able to gain inclusion.

1.3.1.2   Self-Esteem

People want to belong to groups. But they also often want to belong to not just any group, but ones that allow them to identify as having a sense of optimal distinctiveness (Brewer, 1991; Leonardelli et al., 2010). One way this can be achieved is by identifying with groups that are numerically distinct, or that are "strongly differentiated from the mainstream" (Hornsey & Jetten, 2004, p. 251). By definition, extreme groups are distinctive and separate from the mainstream, so they could be a powerful source of feeling positively distinctive. And, indeed, political extremists tend to endorse a form of high self-esteem: the belief that their political views are *superior* to the views of others (Toner et al., 2013). Likewise, extreme groups may project a sense that they are superior to more moderate counterparts, and such superiority could be an attractive source of self-esteem. Extreme groups could thus induce in people a sense of positive distinctiveness, relative to more moderate groups that hold similar views, but in less extreme ways.

1.3.1.3 Control

Extreme groups tend to be not just numerically distinct but also are often willing to engage in a wider range of actions to achieve their goals. Thus, they might be seen as more capable of realizing the changes that they would like to see, making them especially well suited to providing a sense of control. In short, extreme groups may be seen as more likely to make a difference. This may be especially operative in a political context – if people sense the prior, more moderate methods of social engagement have not produced the desired outcome, they could be drawn to groups that endorse more extreme methods, even if these methods are ultimately counterproductive (Simpson et al., 2018). Recent research attests to the operative role of *control* specifically in understanding the appeal of extremism, as it was found to mediate the link between ostracism and endorsement of the use of violence to support a cause (Pfundmair, 2019).

1.3.1.4 Meaningful Existence

One reason ostracism is so distressing is that it causes one to experience a moment of invisibility, a glimpse of what the world would be like if they did not exist at all, as if they were socially dead (Hales, 2018). This is a surreal feeling of nonexistence, and it motivates people to feel as if they matter to the world, and that things are different because they are here. In short, it makes people feel insignificant and provokes the need to matter. The significance quest theory (Ellenberg & Kruglanski, this volume; Kruglanski et al., 2014; Webber & Kruglanski, 2018) articulates that this can be a driving factor in what motivates extremism: people become extreme to realize a more significant impact on the world around them, and to have this significance recognized in the eyes of others. Compared to moderate groups, extreme groups are more likely to engage in the sort of provocative and impactful actions that bestow a sense of significance (in the sense of being noticed by others).

1.3.1.5 Certainty

Ostracism has been shown to make people feel uncertain about the situation and themselves (Hales & Williams, 2018; Williams et al., 2019). Extreme groups are theorized to be especially effective at helping people restore a sense of certainty. According to uncertainty-identity theory (Hogg, 2007), people are motivated to identify with groups not only for a sense of belonging and esteem but also to provide a sense of certainty. Groups, in general, can provide a prototypical template of what is normal and expected. Extreme groups, in particular, tend to be especially well suited for this, at least in part because they are highly *entitative*. That is, they are perceived as an entity, and one that has clear boundaries and behavior prescriptions for its members. Because of this, extreme groups may be especially capable of providing a sense of certainty (Gaffney et al., 2014; Hogg, 2014; Wagoner & Hogg, this volume) and thus especially attractive following ostracism.

1.3.2 Empirical Evidence

Experimental investigations of ostracism and its effects often use a paradigm known as Cyberball (Williams et al., 2000; Williams & Jarvis, 2006). In Cyberball, participants are led to believe that they are playing an online ball tossing game with (typically) two other real players; however, in reality they are virtual confederates programmed to behave in a certain way. For participants randomly assigned to an inclusion condition, the other two players include the participant in the game evenly. In the ostracism condition, the other two players throw the ball to the participant a few times early on but then, without explanation, leave the participant out of the rest of the game. Cyberball reliably induces feelings of ostracism, pain, negative affect, and threats to the fundamental needs (Hartgerink et al., 2015).

Research using Cyberball has shown that being ostracized can increase interest in extreme groups. In one direct test of this hypothesis, researchers first experimentally manipulated ostracism using Cyberball and then measured participants' openness to an extreme group on campus: an advocacy group pushing for reducing tuition (Hales & Williams, 2018). This group used legal but extreme means to pursue its cause (e.g., blockading campus). Participants who had been ostracized indicated greater openness to attending a meeting of this group. A second study – again manipulating ostracism with Cyberball – measured participants' openness to joining a gang, which was defined for them as "A group of people who spend a lot of time together, normally engaged in delinquent acts. They have a strong sense of identity and are affiliated with a specific cause." Again, participants who had been ostracized indicated a greater openness to the idea of participating in a gang (Hales & Williams, 2018).

Additional research also finds evidence for an effect of ostracism on openness to extremism in general (Pfundmair, 2019). For example, following

Cyberball, when asked directly which actions participants would support in favor of an endorsed cause, ostracism elicited greater endorsements of more extreme actions (e.g., threats of violence). In a second study (using a different, but related, ostracism paradigm in which participants are ostracized via video call), ostracism led to greater willingness to commit property damage on behalf of animal rights advocacy – an effect that was mediated by ostracized participants' threatened sense of control (Pfundmair, 2019).

Other studies have also found evidence for such a connection between ostracism and extremism, though looking specifically at attitudes and beliefs. When participants were ostracized in Cyberball, they subsequently reported attitudes more consistent with those of a radical left-wing group they had read about (Bäck et al., 2018), and this effect was especially strong for those who are highly sensitive to rejection. Ostracism also caused religious participants to endorse more fundamentalist beliefs (Schaafsma & Williams, 2012), but only when they were ostracized specifically by religious in-group members (not out-group members who presumably would not have shared those beliefs). These findings emphasize the importance of moderators in understanding the ostracism extremism link, which we turn to now.

1.4 Unexplored Moderators

As discussed throughout this chapter so far, there is evidence that ostracism can elicit extremism *on average* (i.e., as an overall main effect). Recently, researchers have begun to explore moderators effecting this effect, such as rejection sensitivity (Knapton et al., 2015; Renström et al., 2020; Renström & Bäck, this volume). However, there are many potential individual and contextual factors that could influence the effect of ostracism on extremism that have yet to be investigated. One unresearched variable that we finding particularly interesting is the identity of the ostracism source, specifically their relationship to the target. This section explores the potential of this moderator and gives examples of how it may play out in ostracism/extremism research.

Ostracism research suggests that the identity of the source of the ostracism and its relationship with the target matters, particularly when examining ostracism recovery/coping (Williams, 2009). For example, while ostracism is still painful when the source is an out-group member – even a despised out-group (Gonsalkorale & Williams, 2007) – the experience hurts more when being ostracized by an in-group member (Bernstein et al., 2010). Past empirical work suggests that while nearly all experiences of ostracism hurt, relationship dynamics between the source and target could further influence this effect.

Furthermore, this factor may be influential when examining how ostracism can lead to aggression in general. After experiencing ostracism, people who need to continue interacting with the ostracism source in the future are more likely to act antisocially, whereas those who will interact with someone who is not the ostracism source may choose to act prosocially in order to be included (Ren et al., 2018). Ostracism may elicit aggression only toward the source, usually through experimental aggression paradigms like administering a loud noise blast (e.g., Chen et al., 2012) or giving hot sauce to their interaction partner (e.g., Warburton et al., 2006). However, a more extreme reaction of ostracism would be to view the source as a prototype and to react aggressively toward those whom the target sees as a representation of the source. School shootings are an example of this occurrence. In an examination of school shootings between 1995 and 2001, Leary and colleagues (2003) found that most of the perpetrators were teased/bullied (e.g., ostracized; also see Kowalski & Leary, this volume). While the bullies were often targeted victims in the shootings, sometimes the victims were other students, maybe those who reminded the shooter of the bullies.

But would this factor influence the effect of ostracism on extremism? Theorizing about extremism suggests this would be the case. For example, people may radicalize due to grievances, such as personal victimization or victimization from a group (e.g., ostracism; McCauley & Moskalenko, 2008). Furthermore, Borum (2014) highlights how people may over-detect grievous intent (i.e., hostile attribution bias), which may lead them to react more antisocially and perhaps even extremely so. Extreme narratives may justify grievances and provide a road map for how they should be avenged. Indeed, believing that terrorists have valid grievances is associated with support for violence (Cherney & Murphy, 2019).

Thus, we could hypothesize that the source identity and relationship to the target could influence the effect of ostracism on extremism. Perhaps the type of source could affect the dimension of one's radicalization or affect the extent to which one radicalizes. In the following subsections we consider a couple of examples of this unexplored moderator that we find most promising.

1.4.1   Potential Romantic versus Platonic Ostracism Source

People approach social interactions expecting to be included (Wesselmann et al., 2017). And when one is included, relationship partners help satisfy our psychological needs and achieve our goals (Baumeister & Leary, 1995; Orehek & Forest, 2016). However, ostracism is a painful experience even when the source is a stranger – and most ostracism experiences are by acquaintances or strangers (Nezlek et al., 2015). Furthermore, the majority of the ostracism literature involves ostracism by strangers whom the target will never see again – perhaps because it is easy to study in a lab – and little research has investigated the effect of being ostracized by current close others, although the results of research examining exclusion by a close other versus stranger are mixed (Blackhart et al., 2009; Snapp & Leary, 2001). Some lines of research suggest that ostracism hurts more when the source and target are close (Nezlek et al., 2012), maybe because they do not have the defense of uncertainty as they would with a stranger. Others suggest that being ostracized by a stranger hurts just as much as being ostracized by a romantic partner, though being ostracized by a romantic partner causes people to feel less close, less satisfied, and to perceive better alternatives (Arriaga et al., 2014). Others suggest that being ostracized by a stranger threatens needs more than being ostracized by a current friend (Iannone et al., 2014), maybe because there is not an existing relationship available to be a buffer and allow people to devalue rejection because of established good feelings within the relationship.

Research has yet to examine the effect of being ostracized by a *potential* new close other – either a new potential romantic partner or friend. Because being ostracized by friends is more common than being ostracized by a romantic partner (Nezlek et al., 2012), people may expect to be ostracized by acquaintances more so than romantic partners. Similarly, people have more to lose when rejected by a potential romantic partner because a romantic partner typically fulfills more goals and needs than friends or acquaintances (Orehek et al., 2018). Thus, we would hypothesize that being excluded by a potential romantic partner has more negative effects than being excluded by a potential platonic partner, such as reacting with greater aggression/extremism.

This possibility could be extended to examine how being excluded by a potential romantic or platonic partner influences extremism, especially if the exclusion is experienced chronically. In a recent study that used a simulated online dating paradigm, men who were rejected reported greater aggressive tendencies against the potential romantic partners who rejected them (Andrighetto et al., 2019). They also reported greater rape myth beliefs and positive attitudes toward dating violence. Furthermore, people who are high in rejection sensitivity react hostilely after being romantically rejected (Romero-Canyas et al., 2010), and men who are high in rejection sensitivity are more likely to use violence against dating partners (Downey et al., 2000). Thus, being rejected by potential romantic partners (particularly men being rejected by women) could manifest as interest in or support of male supremacy groups (Southern Poverty Law Center, n.d.) or similar groups such as incels (see Rousis & Swann, this volume). Romantic rejection can also result in extreme violence, like school shootings (Farr, 2019), though peer/platonic rejection is also common among school shooters (Kowalski et al., 2021; Leary et al., 2003). In a study that examined the presence of significance loss in a sample of people who committed ideological crimes, 22 percent of perpetrators had experienced romantic troubles (e.g., rejection) and 12 percent had experienced platonic troubles (Jasko et al., 2017). Both romantic and platonic troubles were significantly associated with extreme violence. Therefore, being excluded by a potential close other – particularly a potential romantic partner – may lead people to radicalize against that ostracizing identity and potentially commit extreme violence.

1.4.2 Higher versus Lower Status Ostracism Source

People have a fundamental need for status – holding respect and good reputation from others (Anderson et al., 2015). Ostracism, as a threatening social experience, may thwart a target's status. In most ostracism experiences, the source and target are of equal social status (Nezlek et al., 2012, 2015), although, anecdotally, ostracizing someone of lower (versus equal or higher) status is easier (Williams et al., 2000). There are many reasons as to why someone may use ostracism as a tool against someone of a different status. Ostracism can be used as a tactic to maintain/protect one's status (e.g., control over the target; Zadro et al., 2014) or to reduce someone else's – even to the point of being less human (Bastian & Haslam, 2010). It can also be used obliviously, in which a high-status person ostracizes someone with lower status because they do not deem that person worthy of their attention (Williams, 2009). Furthermore, ostracism can be used as a means to feeling more powerful, both when a higher status person ostracizes a lower status person (Zadro et al., 2008) and vice versa (Williams et al., 2000). Past research suggests that when people experience socially threatening experiences, those with low or high status are more likely to act aggressively than those with average status (Åslund et al., 2009).

To our knowledge, no research has thoroughly examined the antisocial responses of being ostracized by someone with a lower status. It is thus difficult to establish the effect of this occurrence on extremism. Therefore, we will focus on the experience of being ostracized by a source with a higher status than the target. There is mixed theorizing about the result of a low-status person being ostracized. Perhaps they may act prosocially in order to be reincluded, particularly by those who have higher status (Robinson et al., 2013), or they may be worried about potential repercussions if they enacted revenge (Aquino et al., 2001). On the other hand, research shows that when someone is ostracized by someone of a higher status than their own, they support deviance toward others (Fiset et al., 2017). In general, people often react aggressively when they experience a threat to their social status (e.g., Bosson & Vandello, 2011), which could be further exacerbated by the status of the ostracism source. Perhaps the target acts aggressively in order to restore their threatened status, or as a means of justice/retaliation/revenge for the perceived wrongdoing (Aquino & Douglas, 2003). Furthermore, when people display anger (such as in response to ostracism), they are seen as more competent and given greater social status (Tiedens, 2001), suggesting that this effect may be cyclical.

Lower social status is associated with greater extremism, even extreme violence (Jasko et al., 2017). People may radicalize to see extremism as a means to increase one's social status. Thus, if someone is ostracized by a source that is of a higher status, their own status may be threatened, particularly if status was made salient as the reason for the ostracism. For example, a jihadist may feel that that they are being excluded by Western society, perhaps via Americans' cruel treatment of Muslim immigrants post-9/11. In turn, the target may see they have nothing to lose and view extremism as a way to restore their status needs (i.e., gain status). In this example, this may look like the jihadist committing an anti-West terrorist attack to gain status from other jihadists. Extremism theories would recognize this type of radicalization as a "status-seeker" (Venhaus, 2010). The target may also radicalize to a worldview in which the enemy is the identity of the ostracism source. For example, a low-income person may feel that they are being excluded from opportunities and institutions because they do not make enough money to be included (e.g., college, loans). If so, they could become radically anti-capitalist and hold extreme beliefs – maybe even commit extreme action – against the people/groups from which they were excluded. Furthermore, someone may join an extremist group as a protective factor against future experiences of being ostracized by a higher status source. Sometimes, extremist groups hold great power within a community, and being a member of the group can not only increase the lower status person's social status but also make them figuratively untouchable within the community (McCauley & Moskalenko, 2008). Overall, the social status of the ostracizer, specifically in reference to the target's social status, may influence one's radicalization. It does seem likely that ostracism can motivate extremism, to some degree, regardless of the status of the ostracizer, but future research should examine whether the strength of this effect depends on status.

1.5 The Reverse Effect: Can Extremism Lead to Ostracism?

Throughout this chapter, we have explored the possibility that ostracism can lead people to engage with extremist and radical ideologies. It is important to note, however, that an effect of ostracism on extremism in no way rules out the possibility of the reverse causal path: perhaps people who engage in extremism are more likely to be ostracized (at least by outsiders who are not associated with the extremist group).

From the perspective of potential ostracizers – or sources – ostracism can be used for a variety of reasons (Hales, Ren, et al., 2016), including motivating individuals to conform to group norms and potentially removing individuals who are both deviant and resistant to conforming. Classic and contemporary research indicates that people with stubbornly atypical opinions are more likely to encounter social rejection (Eidelman et al., 2006; Schachter, 1951; Wesselmann et al., 2014). It is reasonable to expect, then, that becoming known as someone who engages with extreme groups and ideologies could lead one to become ostracized.

Recent research finds direct evidence for this effect (Hales & Williams, 2020). In this research, participants read descriptions of forty different individuals, and for each one learned that the person belongs to a group that either does or does not engage in extreme actions. Participants reported that they were substantially more willing to ignore and exclude people who were affiliated with groups engaged in extreme actions. Interestingly, this was the case even when the group engaged in extreme actions in support of a prosocial goal such as increasing funding for education (this is because when the group is antisocial, people are more willing to ostracize the target regardless of how the group pursues its goals).

Together with what we have seen in the rest of the chapter, this finding hints at the possibility of a negative spiral in which people may engage with extremism because they are ostracized but, having become more extreme, encounter more ostracism. This could create a negative situation where people become increasingly dependent on extremist groups for their social needs. To our knowledge, no evidence exists showing this process directly. And it is possible that in most cases intervening forces step in before a negative cascade is realized (e.g., close family members notice alarming signals and provide social support). However, given the consequences of this possibility, it is important to understand empirically. Future research should address this question dynamically by studying ostracism and extremist tendencies both over time (to measure downward cascades) and also in networks (to corroborate that ostracism is occurring from the perspective of both sources and targets).

1.6   Conclusion

Ostracism is a painful experience that threatens several fundamental human needs. It is not entirely surprising that it can produce severe outcomes, such as engagement with extremism. In this chapter, we investigated the theoretical and empirical bases for this connection and suggested looking at types of relationships and status as important potential factors influencing ostracism and extremism. Finally, we considered whether extremism can lead to ostracism. Together, the existing research suggests that ostracism is an important factor in extremism dynamics and continues to require further research.

References

Anderson, C., Hildreth, J. A. D., & Howland, L. (2015). Is the desire for status a fundamental human motive? A review of the empirical literature. *Psychological Bulletin, 141*(3), 574–601. https://doi.org/10.1037/a0038781

Andrighetto, L., Riva, P., & Gabbiadini, A. (2019). Lonely hearts and angry minds: Online dating rejection increases male (but not female) hostility. *Aggressive Behavior, 45*(5), 571–581. https://doi.org/10.1002/ab.21852

Aquino, K., & Douglas, S. (2003). Identity threat and antisocial behavior in organizations: The moderating effects of individual differences, aggressive modeling, and hierarchical status. *Organizational Behavior and Human Decision Processes*, *90*(1), 195–208. https://doi.org/10.1016/S0749-5978(02)00517-4

Aquino, K., Tripp, T. M., & Bies, R. J. (2001). How employees respond to personal offense: The effects of blame attribution, victim status, and offender status on revenge and reconciliation in the workplace. *Journal of Applied Psychology*, *86*(1), 52–59. https://doi.org/10.1037/0021-9010.86.1.52

Arriaga, X. B., Capezza, N. M., Reed, J. T., Wesselmann, E. D., & Williams, K. D. (2014). With partners like you, who needs strangers? Ostracism involving a romantic partner. *Personal Relationships*, *21*(4), 557–569. https://doi.org/10.1111/pere.12048

Åslund, C., Starrin, B., Leppert, J., & Nilsson, K. W. (2009). Social status and shaming experiences related to adolescent overt aggression at school. *Aggressive Behavior: Official Journal of the International Society for Research on Aggression*, *35*(1), 1–13. https://doi.org/10.1002/ab.20286

Bäck, E. A., Bäck, H., Altermark, N., & Knapton, H. (2018). The quest for significance: Attitude adaption to a radical group following social exclusion. *International Journal of Developmental Science*, *12*(1–2), 25–36. https://doi.org/10.3233/DEV-170230

Bastian, B., & Haslam, N. (2010). Excluded from humanity: The dehumanizing effects of social ostracism. *Journal of Experimental Social Psychology*, *46*(1), 107–113. https://doi.org/10.1016/j.jesp.2009.06.022

Baumeister, R. F., & Leary, M. R. (1995). The need to belong: Desire for interpersonal attachments as a fundamental human motivation. *Psychological Bulletin*, *117*(3), 497–529. https://doi.org/10.1037/0033-2909.117.3.497

Bernstein, M. J., Neubauer, A. B., Benfield, J. A., Potter, L., & Smyth, J. M. (2021). Within-person effects of inclusion and exclusion on well-being in daily life. *Personal Relationships*, *28*(4), 940–960. https://doi.org/10.1111/pere.12399

Bernstein, M. J., Sacco, D. F., Young, S. G., Hugenberg, K., & Cook, E. (2010). Being "in" with the in-crowd: The effects of social exclusion and inclusion are enhanced by the perceived essentialism of ingroups and outgroups. *Personality and Social Psychology Bulletin*, *36*(8), 999–1009. https://doi.org/10.1177/0146167210376059

Blackhart, G. C., Nelson, B. C., Knowles, M. L., & Baumeister, R. F. (2009). Rejection elicits emotional reactions but neither causes immediate distress nor lowers self-esteem: A meta-analytic review of 192 studies on social exclusion. *Personality and Social Psychology Review*, *13*(4), 269–309. https://doi.org/10.1177/1088868309346065

Borum, R. (2014). Psychological vulnerabilities and propensities for involvement in violent extremism. *Behavioral Sciences & The Law*, *32*(3), 286–305. https://doi.org/10.1002/bsl.2110

Bosson, J. K., & Vandello, J. A. (2011). Precarious manhood and its links to action and aggression. *Current Directions in Psychological Science*, *20*(2), 82–86. https://doi.org/10.1177/0963721411402669

Brewer, M. B. (1991). The social self: On being the same and different at the same time. *Personality and Social Psychology Bulletin, 17*(5), 475–482. https://doi.org/10.1177/0146167291175001

Chen, Z., DeWall, C. N., Poon, K. T., & Chen, E. W. (2012). When destiny hurts: Implicit theories of relationships moderate aggressive responses to ostracism. *Journal of Experimental Social Psychology, 48*(5), 1029–1036. https://doi.org/10.1016/j.jesp.2012.04.002

Cherney, A., & Murphy, K. (2019). Support for terrorism: The role of beliefs in jihad and institutional responses to terrorism. *Terrorism and Political Violence, 31*(5), 1049–1069. https://doi.org/10.1080/09546553.2017.1313735

Dahl, E., Niedbala, E. M., & Hohman, Z. P. (2019). Loving the group that denies you first: Social identity effects of ostracism before inclusion. *Personality and Social Psychology Bulletin, 45*(2), 284–299. https://doi.org/10.1177/0146167218784901

Downey, G., Feldman, S., & Ayduk, O. (2000). Rejection sensitivity and male violence in romantic relationships. *Personal Relationships, 7*(1), 45–61. https://doi.org/10.1111/j.1475-6811.2000.tb00003.x

Eidelman, S., Silvia, P. J., & Biernat, M. (2006). Responding to deviance: Target exclusion and differential devaluation. *Personality and Social Psychology Bulletin, 32*(9), 1153–1164. https://doi.org/10.1177/0146167206288720

Farr, K. (2019). Trouble with the other: The role of romantic rejection in rampage school shootings by adolescent males. *Violence and Gender, 6*(3), 147–153. https://doi.org/10.1089/vio.2018.0046

Fayant, M.-P., Muller, D., Hartgerink, C. H. J., & Lantian, A. (2014). Is ostracism by a despised outgroup really hurtful? *Social Psychology, 45*(6), 489–494.

Fiset, J., Al Hajj, R., & Vongas, J. G. (2017). Workplace ostracism seen through the lens of power. *Frontiers in Psychology, 8*, 1528. https://doi.org/10.3389/fpsyg.2017.01528

Gaffney, A. M., Rast, D. E., Hackett, J. D., & Hogg, M. A. (2014). Further to the right: Uncertainty, political polarization and the American "Tea Party" movement. *Social Influence, 9*(4), 272–288. https://doi.org/10.1080/15534510.2013.842495

Gardner, W. L., Pickett, C. L., & Knowles, M. (2005). Social snacking and shielding: Using social symbols, selves, and surrogates in the service of belonging needs. In K. D. Williams, J. P. Forgas, & W. von Hippel (Eds.), *The social outcast: Ostracism, social exclusion, rejection, and bullying* (pp. 227–241). Psychology Press.

Gonsalkorale, K., & Williams, K. D. (2007). The KKK won't let me play: Ostracism even by a despised outgroup hurts. *European Journal of Social Psychology, 37*(6), 1176–1186. https://doi.org/10.1002/ejsp.392

Hales, A. H. (2018). Death as a metaphor for ostracism: Social invincibility, autopsy, necromancy, and resurrection. *Mortality, 23*(4), 366–380. https://doi.org/10.1080/13576275.2017.1382462

Hales, A. H., Dvir, M., Wesselmann, E. D., Kruger, D. J., & Finkenauer, C. (2018). Cell phone-induced ostracism threatens fundamental needs. *The Journal of*

Social Psychology, *158*(4), 460–473. https://doi.org/10.1080/00224545.2018.1439877

Hales, A. H., McIntyre, M. M., Rudert, S. C., Williams, K. D., & Thomas, H. (2021). Ostracized and observed: The presence of an audience affects the experience of being excluded. *Self and Identity*, *20*(1), 94–115. https://doi.org/10.1080/15298868.2020.1807403

Hales, A. H., Ren, D., & Williams, K. D. (2016). *Protect, correct, and eject* (S. G. Harkins, K. D. Williams, & J. Burger, Eds.; Vol. 1). Oxford University Press. https://doi.org/10.1093/oxfordhb/9780199859870.013.26

Hales, A. H., Wesselmann, E. D., & Williams, K. D. (2016). Prayer, self-affirmation, and distraction improve recovery from short-term ostracism. *Journal of Experimental Social Psychology*, *64*, 8–20. https://doi.org/10.1016/j.jesp.2016.01.002

Hales, A. H., & Williams, K. D. (2018). Marginalized individuals and extremism: The role of ostracism in openness to extreme groups. *Journal of Social Issues, 74* (1), 75–92. https://doi.org/10.1111/josi.12257

Hales, A. H., & Williams, K. D. (2020). Extremism leads to ostracism. *Social Psychology*, *51*(3), 149–156. https://doi.org/10.1027/1864-9335/a000406

Hales, A. H., & Williams, K. D. (2021). Social ostracism: Theoretical foundations and basic principles. In P. A. M. Van Lange, E. T. Higgins, & A. W. Kruglanski (Eds.), *Social psychology: Handbook of basic principles* (3rd ed.; pp. 337–349). Guilford Press.

Hartgerink, C. H. J., van Beest, I., Wicherts, J. M., & Williams, K. D. (2015). The ordinal effects of ostracism: A meta-analysis of 120 Cyberball studies. *PLoS ONE*, *10*(5), e0127002. https://doi.org/10.1371/journal.pone.0127002

Hogg, M. A. (2007). Uncertainty–identity theory. In M. P. Zanna (Ed.), *Advances in Experimental Social Psychology* (Vol. 39, pp. 69–126). Elsevier. https://doi.org/10.1016/S0065-2601(06)39002-8

Hogg, M. A. (2014). From uncertainty to extremism: Social categorization and identity processes. *Current Directions in Psychological Science*, *23*(5), 338–342. https://doi.org/10.1177/0963721414540168

Hornsey, M. J., & Jetten, J. (2004). The individual within the group: Balancing the need to belong with the need to be different. *Personality and Social Psychology Review*, *8*(3), 248–264. https://doi.org/10.1207/s15327957pspr0803_2

Iannone, N. E., McCarty, M. K., Kelly, J. R., & Williams, K. D. (2014). Friends with each other but strangers to you: Source relationship softens ostracism's blow. *Group Dynamics: Theory, Research, and Practice*, *18*(4), 349–356. https://doi.org/10.1037/gdn0000018

Jasko, K., LaFree, G., & Kruglanski, A. (2017). Quest for significance and violent extremism: The case of domestic radicalization. *Political Psychology*, *38*(5), 815–831. https://doi.org/10.1111/pops.12376

Jauch, M., Rudert, S. C., & Greifeneder, R. (2022). Social pain by non-social agents: Exclusion hurts and provokes punishment even if the excluding source is a computer. *Acta Psychologica, 230,* 103753. https://doi.org/10.1016/j.actpsy.2022.103753

Kerr, N. L., & Levine, J. M. (2008). The detection of social exclusion: Evolution and beyond. *Group Dynamics: Theory, Research, and Practice, 12*(1), 39–52. https://doi.org/10.1037/1089-2699.12.1.39

Knapton, H. M. (2014). The recruitment and radicalisation of western citizens: Does ostracism have a role in homegrown terrorism? *Journal of European Psychology Students, 5*(1), 38–48. https://doi.org/10.5334/jeps.bo

Knapton, H. M., Bäck, H., & Bäck, E. A. (2015). The social activist: Conformity to the ingroup following rejection as a predictor of political participation. *Social Influence, 10*(2), 97–108. https://doi.org/10.1080/15534510.2014.966856

Kowalski, R. M., Leary, M., Hendley, T., et al. (2021). K–12, college/university, and mass shootings: Similarities and differences. *The Journal of Social Psychology, 161*(6), 753–778. https://doi.org/10.1080/00224545.2021.1900047

Kruglanski, A. W., Gelfand, M. J., Bélanger, J. J., et al. (2014). The psychology of radicalization and deradicalization: How significance quest impacts violent extremism: Processes of radicalization and deradicalization. *Political Psychology, 35,* 69–93. https://doi.org/10.1111/pops.12163

Leary, M. R., Kowalski, R. M., Smith, L., & Phillips, S. (2003). Teasing, rejection, and violence: Case studies of the school shootings. *Aggressive Behavior: Official Journal of the International Society for Research on Aggression, 29*(3), 202–214. https://doi.org/10.1002/ab.10061

Leonardelli, G. J., Pickett, C. L., & Brewer, M. B. (2010). Optimal distinctiveness theory. In M. P. Zanna & J. M. Olson (Eds.), *Advances in Experimental Social Psychology* (Vol. 43, pp. 63–113). Elsevier. https://doi.org/10.1016/S0065-2601(10)43002-6

Maner, J. K., DeWall, C. N., Baumeister, R. F., & Schaller, M. (2007). Does social exclusion motivate interpersonal reconnection? Resolving the "porcupine problem." *Journal of Personality and Social Psychology, 92*(1), 42–55. https://doi.org/10.1037/0022-3514.92.1.42

Marinucci, M., & Riva, P. (2021). Surrendering to social emptiness: Chronic social exclusion longitudinally predicts resignation in asylum seekers. *British Journal of Social Psychology, 60*(2), 429–447. https://doi.org/10.1111/bjso.12410

McCauley, C., & Moskalenko, S. (2008). Mechanisms of political radicalization: Pathways toward terrorism. *Terrorism and Political Violence, 20*(3), 415–433. https://doi.org/10.1080/09546550802073367

Nezlek, J. B., Wesselmann, E. D., Wheeler, L., & Williams, K. D. (2012). Ostracism in everyday life. *Group Dynamics: Theory, Research, and Practice, 16*(2), 91–104. https://doi.org/10.1037/a0028029

Nezlek, J. B., Wesselmann, E. D., Wheeler, L., & Williams, K. D. (2015). Ostracism in everyday life: The effects of ostracism on those who ostracize. *The Journal of Social Psychology, 155*(5), 432–451. https://doi.org/10.1080/00224545.2015.1062351

Orehek, E., & Forest, A. L. (2016). When people serve as means to goals: Implications of a motivational account of close relationships. *Current*

Directions in Psychological Science, 25(2), 79–84. https://doi.org/10.1177/0963721415623536

Orehek, E., Forest, A. L., & Barbaro, N. (2018). A people-as-means approach to interpersonal relationships. *Perspectives on Psychological Science*, 13(3), 373–389. https://doi.org/10.1177/1745691617744522

Parsons, A. S. (1986). Messianic personalism: A role analysis of the Unification Church. *Journal for the Scientific Study of Religion*, 25, 141–161.

Pfundmair, M. (2019). Ostracism promotes a terroristic mindset. *Behavioral Sciences of Terrorism and Political Aggression*, 11(2), 134–148. https://doi.org/10.1080/19434472.2018.1443965

Pfundmair, M., Wood, N. R., Hales, A., & Wesselmann, E. D. (2022). How social exclusion makes radicalism flourish: A review of empirical evidence. *Journal of Social Issues*, josi.12520. https://doi.org/10.1111/josi.12520

Ren, D., Wesselmann, E. D., & Williams, K. D. (2018). Hurt people hurt people: Ostracism and aggression. *Current Opinion in Psychology*, 19, 34–38. https://doi.org/10.1016/j.copsyc.2017.03.026

Renström, E. A., Bäck, H., & Knapton, H. M. (2020). Exploring a pathway to radicalization: The effects of social exclusion and rejection sensitivity. *Group Processes & Intergroup Relations*, 23(8), 1204–1229. https://doi.org/10.1177/1368430220917215

Richman, S. B. (2020). Man's Best Friend? The Effects of Being Rejected by a Pet. *Journal of Social and Clinical Psychology*, 39(6), 498–522. https://doi.org/10.1521/jscp.2020.39.6.498

Riva, P., Montali, L., Wirth, J. H., Curioni, S., & Williams, K. D. (2017). Chronic social exclusion and evidence for the resignation stage: An empirical investigation. *Journal of Social and Personal Relationships*, 34(4), 541–564. https://doi.org/10.1177/0265407516644348

Riva, P., Williams, K. D., Torstrick, A. M., & Montali, L. (2014). Orders to shoot (a camera): Effects of ostracism on obedience. *The Journal of Social Psychology*, 154(3), 208–216. https://doi.org/10.1080/00224545.2014.883354

Robinson, S. L., O'Reilly, J., & Wang, W. (2013). Invisible at work: An integrated model of workplace ostracism. *Journal of Management*, 39(1), 203–231. https://doi.org/10.1177/0149206312466141

Romero-Canyas, R., Downey, G., Berenson, K., Ayduk, O., & Kang, N. J. (2010). Rejection sensitivity and the rejection–hostility link in romantic relationships. *Journal of Personality*, 78(1), 119–148. https://doi.org/10.1111/j.1467-6494.2009.00611.x

Rudert, S. C., Janke, S., & Greifeneder, R. (2021). Ostracism breeds depression: Longitudinal associations between ostracism and depression over a three-year-period. *Journal of Affective Disorders Reports*, 4, 100118. https://doi.org/10.1016/j.jadr.2021.100118

Schaafsma, J., & Williams, K. D. (2012). Exclusion, intergroup hostility, and religious fundamentalism. *Journal of Experimental Social Psychology*, 48(4), 829–837. https://doi.org/10.1016/j.jesp.2012.02.015

Schachter, S. (1951). Deviation, rejection, and communication. *Journal of Abnormal and Social Psychology*, 46, 190–207.

Simpson, B., Willer, R., & Feinberg, M. (2018). Does violent protest backfire? Testing a theory of public reactions to activist violence. *Socius*, 4, 2378023118803189. https://doi.org/10.1177/2378023118803189

Snapp, C. M., & Leary, M. R. (2001). Hurt feelings among new acquaintances: Moderating effects of interpersonal familiarity. *Journal of Social and Personal Relationships*, 18(3), 315–326. https://doi.org/10.1177/0265407501183001

Southern Poverty Law Center (n.d.). *Male supremacy*. www.splcenter.org/fighting-hate/extremist-files/ideology/male-supremacy

Tiedens, L. Z. (2001). Anger and advancement versus sadness and subjugation: The effect of negative emotion expressions on social status conferral. *Journal of Personality and Social Psychology*, 80(1), 86–94. https://doi.org/10.1037/0022-3514.80.1.86

Toner, K., Leary, M. R., Asher, M. W., & Jongman-Sereno, K. P. (2013). Feeling superior is a bipartisan issue: Extremity (not direction) of political views predicts perceived belief superiority. *Psychological Science*, 24(12), 2454–2462. https://doi.org/10.1177/0956797613494848

van Beest, I., & Williams, K. D. (2006). When inclusion costs and ostracism pays, ostracism still hurts. *Journal of Personality and Social Psychology*, 91(5), 918–928. https://doi.org/10.1037/0022-3514.91.5.918

Venhaus, J. M. (2010). Why youth join al-Qaeda. United States Institute of Peace. www.usip.org/sites/default/files/resources/SR236Venhaus.pdf

Venter, M. A. (1998). Susceptibility of adolescents to cults. *Southern African Journal of Child and Adolescent Mental Health*, 10, 93–106.

Warburton, W. A., Williams, K. D., & Cairns, D. R. (2006). When ostracism leads to aggression: The moderating effects of control deprivation. *Journal of Experimental Social Psychology*, 42(2), 213–220. https://doi.org/10.1016/j.jesp.2005.03.005

Webber, D., & Kruglanski, A. W. (2018). The social psychological makings of a terrorist. *Current Opinion in Psychology*, 19, 131–134. https://doi.org/10.1016/j.copsyc.2017.03.024

Wesselmann, E. D., Cardoso, F. D., Slater, S., & Williams, K. D. (2012). To be looked at as though air: Civil attention matters. *Psychological Science*, 23(2), 166–168. https://doi.org/10.1177/0956797611427921

Wesselmann, E. D., Grzybowski, M. R., Steakley-Freeman, D. M., et al. (2016). Social exclusion in everyday life. In P. Riva & J. Eck (Eds.), *Social exclusion* (pp. 3–23). Springer International Publishing. https://doi.org/10.1007/978-3-319-33033-4_1

Wesselmann, E. D., Nairne, J. S., & Williams, K. D. (2012). An evolutionary social psychological approach to studying the effects of ostracism. *Journal of Social, Evolutionary, and Cultural Psychology*, 6(3), 309–328. https://doi.org/10.1037/h0099249

Wesselmann, E. D., Ren, D., Swim, E., & Williams, K. D. (2013). Rumination hinders recovery from ostracism. *International Journal of Developmental Science*, 7(1), 33–39.

Wesselmann, E. D., & Williams, K. D. (2010). The potential balm of religion and spirituality for recovering from ostracism. *Journal of Management, Spirituality & Religion*, 7(1), 31–49. https://doi.org/10.1080/14766080903497623

Wesselmann, E. D., Williams, K. D., Pryor, J. B., et al. (2014). Revisiting Schachter's research on rejection, deviance, and communication (1951). *Social Psychology*, 45(3), 164–169. https://doi.org/10.1027/1864-9335/a000180

Wesselmann, E. D., Wirth, J. H., & Bernstein, M. J. (2017). Expectations of social inclusion and exclusion. *Frontiers in Psychology*, 8, 112. https://doi.org/10.3389/fpsyg.2017.00112

Williams, K. D. (2009). Ostracism: A temporal need-threat model. In M. P. Zanna (Ed.), *Advances in Experimental Social Psychology* (Vol. 41, pp. 275–314). Elsevier. https://doi.org/10.1016/S0065-2601(08)00406-1

Williams, K. D., Bernieri, F. J., Faulkner, S. L., Gada-Jain, N., & Grahe, J. E. (2000). The Scarlet Letter study: Five days of social ostracism. *Journal of Personal & Interpersonal Loss*, 5(1), 19–63. https://doi.org/10.1080/10811440008407846

Williams, K. D., Cheung, C. K. T., & Choi, W. (2000). Cyberostracism: Effects of being ignored over the internet. *Journal of Personality and Social Psychology*, 79 (5), 748–762.

Williams, K. D., Hales, A. H., & Michels, C. (2019). Social ostracism as a factor motivating interest in extreme groups. In S. C. Rudert, R. Greifeneder, & K. D. Williams (Eds.), *Current directions in ostracism, social exclusion and rejection research* (pp. 17–30). Routledge.

Williams, K. D., & Jarvis, B. (2006). Cyberball: A program for use in research on interpersonal ostracism and acceptance. *Behavior Research Methods*, 38(1), 174–180. https://doi.org/10.3758/BF03192765

Wirth, J. H., Sacco, D. F., Hugenberg, K., & Williams, K. D. (2010). Eye gaze as relational evaluation: Averted eye gaze leads to feelings of ostracism and relational devaluation. *Personality and Social Psychology Bulletin*, 36(7), 869–882. https://doi.org/10.1177/0146167210370032

Zadro, L., Arriaga, X. B., & Williams, K. D. (2008). Relational ostracism. In J. P. Forgas & J. Fitness (Eds.), *Social relationships: Cognitive, affective, and motivational processes* (pp. 305–320). Psychology Press.

Zadro, L., Boland, C., & Richardson, R. (2006). How long does it last? The persistence of the effects of ostracism in the socially anxious. *Journal of Experimental Social Psychology*, 42(5), 692–697. https://doi.org/10.1016/j.jesp.2005.10.007

Zadro, L., Godwin, A., & Gonsalkorale, K. (2014). "It is better to give than to receive": The role of motivation and self-control in determining the consequences of ostracism for targets and sources. In J. P. Forgas & E. Harmon-Jones (Eds.), *Motivation and its regulation: The control within* (pp. 351–366). Psychology Press.

Zadro, L., Williams, K. D., & Richardson, R. (2004). How low can you go? Ostracism by a computer is sufficient to lower self-reported levels of belonging, control, self-esteem, and meaningful existence. *Journal of Experimental Social Psychology*, *40*(4), 560–567.

Exclusion and Radicalization

The Role of Individual Differences in the Relation between Exclusion and Radicalization

EMMA A. RENSTRÖM AND HANNA BÄCK

2.1 Introduction

This chapter focuses on the role of social exclusion in the radicalization process. Several theoretical approaches discuss variations of exclusion or feelings related to exclusion (e.g., deprivation, significance loss) as a potential part in the radicalization process. This idea is based on the assumption that humans have an innate need to seek out belongingness and meaning. When faced with social exclusion, such needs are threatened, leading individuals to seek out ways to reestablish a sense of value and belongingness. One way to do this is by associating with radical goals and ideals and adapting to radical groups. In this chapter, we zoom in on individual differences as moderators of exclusion in the radicalization process.

While social exclusion is painful for most, not all individuals react in a similar manner. Individual-level features, such as rejection sensitivity, must also be considered when explaining how social exclusion may lead to radicalization. This chapter goes through the empirical evidence of such a mechanism and discusses how various types of radical behavior can be explained by social exclusion, for example, misogynistic violence related to the so-called incel movement. In this chapter we discuss social exclusion in a broad sense, ranging from interindividual social exclusion and intergroup social exclusion, to general feelings or perceptions of being excluded, marginalized, or "left behind" in a changing societal structure.

2.2 Models of Radicalization

Radicalization is the process by which an individual comes to adopt attitudes and/or behaviors related to extreme ideologies or religious beliefs (McCauley & Moskalenko, 2008). Kruglanski and Webber (2014, p. 379) define radicalization as "a process whereby one moves to support or adopt radical means to address a specific problem or goal. A radical means is a means that moves one toward fulfilling his or her focal goal while simultaneously undermining other goals and concerns." This entails that radicalization is a matter of degrees, and a low degree of radicalization may involve support for radical groups/violence, while a high degree is the act of committing violence (Kruglanski et al., 2019). McCauley and Moskelenko (2008, p. 416) define political radicalization: "Functionally, political radicalization is increased preparation for and commitment to intergroup conflict. Descriptively, radicalization means change in beliefs, feelings, and behaviors in directions that increasingly justify intergroup violence and demand sacrifice in defense of the ingroup." This radicalization process may or may not result in extreme behavior, that is, the presence of violent action is not a fundament of radicalization (McCauley & Moskalenko, 2017). Thus, radicalization is not synonymous with terrorism, the violent act, although it *can* result in terrorism. McCauley and Moskalenko (2017) even discuss that radicalization can be a process of opinion radicalization only, separate from action radicalization.

The process approach has important consequences for the study of radicalization. From the outset, individuals that have been radicalized may not be extreme at all, but rather should in many cases be seen as "unremarkable" individuals (Silber & Bhatt, 2007). Therefore, it is relevant to study mechanisms of radicalization among the normal population (Renström et al., 2020).

2.2.1   Exemplary Models of Radicalization

Many theories concerning radicalization have been put forth, starting as early as 1981 by Crenshaw, but research on radicalization spurred after 9/11 and has since mainly focused on religious and political radicalization (McCauley & Moskalenko, 2017). As noted earlier, a common feature in many of the radicalization theories is the view of radicalization as a process that starts out with "ordinary people" (Silber & Bhatt, 2007). For instance, Moghaddam (2005) suggests that the radicalization process should be understood as a stairway where the ground floor is the perception of unfairness or relative deprivation, the first floor is the search for options, the second floor is anger at perceived perpetrators of injustice, the third floor is moral engagement that justifies terrorism, the fourth floor is joining a terrorist group, and the fifth and last floor is the dehumanization of enemy targets and legitimization of violence against them.

Horgan (2014) presents three themes in the progression to terrorist acts – injustice, identity, and belonging. Again, a gradual progression is emphasized. First, perceived injustice, such as perceptions of wrongdoing, or grievances, is a triggering factor. Injustices, such as feeling discriminated against, may influence identification with different groups (Knapton et al., 2022). Hence, a second theme is that an individual's search for identity may draw them into extremist organizations. Extremist ideas are often absolutist and "black and White," which may be appealing to individuals who feel overwhelmed by the complexity and stress of navigating a complicated world (Borum, 2011). Third, belongingness is a recurring theme in the radicalization literature. Radical groups provide a sense of meaning, connectedness, and affiliation. The theme belonging also entails that there is community support for violent actions.

In a report by Silber and Bhatt (2007), another stage approach was presented in relation to homegrown jihadization specifically. The first stage is labeled pre-radicalization, where they suggest that most terrorists start out as unremarkable individuals before the radicalization process begins. The second stage is self-identification, in which individuals start to explore the new identity and gradually move away from their old identity. In line with other models, this phase is assumed to be evoked by some event that has made the individual question their previously held ideas. Examples of such triggering events are economic (losing a job), social (discrimination or racism), or political (international conflicts involving Muslims). In the following indoctrination phase, the individual becomes increasingly progressive in their beliefs and concludes that action is needed. This action is militant jihad. Here, we also see the group and belongingness ideas. While the self-identification may be an individual process, in the indoctrination phase the group becomes increasingly important to encourage and reinforce radical views. The final phase is labeled jihadization, in which individuals engage in terrorism in the name of jihad. While this model was specifically developed to account for jihadization, the same elements and progressional ideas are present as in other models of radicalization.

McCauley and Moskalenko (2008) present a pyramid model where the base of the pyramid consists of individuals who have certain ideological sympathies, and the apex consists of terrorists. They present eleven mechanisms that are involved in the radicalization of individuals, groups, and masses moving from the base to the apex of the pyramid. For instance, individual-level radicalization can occur through personal victimization, political grievance, and the joining of a radical group. In a more recent version of this model (McCauley & Moskalenko, 2017), they separate the pyramids into two: one for radicalization of opinions and one for radicalization of actions. The idea is that most of the previous models end with engagement in terrorism. However, most people who become radicalized never engage. Moreover, some people who do commit terrorist deeds do not possess the radical opinions. Thus, McCauley and Moskalenko (2017) suggest that radicalization into opinions is psychologically different from radicalization to extremist action.

The significance quest theory (Kruglanski et al., 2019; see also Ellenberg & Kruglanski, this volume) identifies three key components that create the foundation for the radicalization process. Again, radicalization is described as a gradual shift toward goals that run contrary to goals and values commonly held in the population. *Need* is the motivational element, referring to a fundamental need to feel valued, to "be someone," and to be respected – to feel significance (Kruglanski et al., 2009). Significance can be lost (Kruglanski et al., 2019), such as through rejection by others. Significance can also be socially based, meaning that the experience of significance loss is rooted in one's social identity (Knapton et al., 2022). *Narrative* refers to how the means to reach a goal is narrated, for instance, by justifying violence (Webber & Kruglanski, 2018). The *network* part refers to the networks that serve as "conduits through which individuals get acquainted with, and embrace, the ideological narrative that the network espouses" (Kruglanski et al., 2019, p. 51).

As should be clear by now, most theories of radicalization start out with "ordinary people," and even though most people in the early stages of the radicalization process will not go on to become terrorists, we argue that it is important to explore these early processes of radicalization. Hence, while we do not aim to predict who will end up performing terrorist deeds, we do aim to contribute with a better understanding of the factors involved in the radicalization process.

2.2.2   Social Exclusion as Part of the Radicalization Process

Social exclusion is generally referred to simply as exclusion and used as an umbrella term encompassing both ostracism (being ignored) and rejection (being explicitly unwanted). People may also *feel* excluded, rejected, or deprived, even though this is not actually the case. For instance, if an individual believes that an out-group and its members can threaten their job security, this belief will influence how that individual feel about the other group, even if their job situation is unaffected by members of the out-group (Esses et al., 1998; Esses et al., 2001; Stephan et al., 2009). The focus on perceived exclusion is important. First, it adds to our understanding of why many individuals that are societally marginalized do not become radicals – they may not feel excluded due to having relevant group memberships, and why some that come from stable middle-class backgrounds do; there are individual variations in perceptions of exclusion. We elaborate on this later in this chapter.

There is much research on the negative consequences of social exclusion. The immediate negative reactions are often seen as evolutionary based (Williams, 2007, 2009). To be included in a group would imply life or death in early human history. Belongingness is therefore assumed to be a basic motivational force grounded in survival (Baumeister & Leary, 1995). Exclusion, or threats thereof, can therefore be used to modify behaviors so people fit with the group and ensures that group members are cohesive norm-followers (Ouwerkerk et al., 2005). Reactions to exclusion are thus swift and strong. It has even been suggested that exclusion results in a "social pain" of similar magnitude to extreme physical pain (Eisenberger, 2013; Eisenberger et al., 2003).

Four fundamental needs are threatened by social exclusion (Williams, 2007): the need to belong, the need for self-esteem, the need for a meaningful existence, and the need for control. These needs are important to well-being, and when an individual is exposed to an episode of social exclusion, self-estimates of these needs are lowered (e.g., Carter-Sowell et al., 2008; Williams, 2007; Williams & Zadro, 2005; Zadro et al., 2004).

In most radicalization models some contextual change, or perception of a change, related to exclusion or feelings thereof is the igniting factor. Moghaddam (2005) describes this contextual change as relative deprivation or perceptions of unfairness, McCauley and Moskalenko (2017) mention personal victimization, Kruglanski and colleagues (2014) discuss various factors such as failure, loss, humiliation, and discrimination, and Renström et al. (2020) describe social exclusion.

In relation to the newest terrorist threat, the incel movement (Hoffman et al., 2020), episodes of exclusion are clearly an important factor explaining why these men seek out the online communities where they risk becoming radicalized (see also Rousis & Swann, this volume). While one form of exclusion that these men experience is the explicit rejection by women, they also feel societally excluded in a new world order where women and other minority groups are gaining rights associated with possibilities for choice, which means that some men feel "left behind" or excluded from this modern society (Renström et al., 2024). The status of the White man has been lost, as has some men's individual feelings of significance.

Social exclusion and associated concepts therefore constitute an important part of the radicalization process, which has also been shown empirically (Hales & Williams, 2018; Pfundmair, 2019; Pfundmair et al., 2022; Pfundmair, this volume). Yet, there are important boundary conditions to this process. First, individuals' own leanings will decide in what direction their radicalization process will go. That means that it is unlikely that an individual with preexisting left-leaning political views would become attracted to a right-wing extremist organization simply by experiencing social exclusion. We would, however, expect a left-leaning individual to become attracted to a left-wing extremist organization, if such an opportunity for inclusion presented itself, and potential other boundary conditions are fulfilled (Renström et al., 2020). In the search to regain belongingness and meaningfulness following social exclusion, the ideological context in which the individual is situated will define the perceived acceptable ways to regain significance (Jasko et al., 2017; Kruglanski & Webber, 2014).

One reason for this boundary condition is that after experiencing social exclusion, individuals become motivated to search for opportunities for inclusion, and the group that represents a possible inclusion must be in the form of a realistic inclusion opportunity (Maner et al., 2007). A group that completely contradicts their own views does not represent such a realistic inclusion opportunity. Another reason is that exclusion may increase identification with an in-group to lessen the damage of the exclusion experience.

A second boundary condition is other potential individual differences that may moderate the effect of the exclusion experience (Pfundmair et al., 2022), on which we elaborate next.

2.3   The Role of Individual Differences Related to Exclusion in the Radicalization Process

In the early stages of radicalization research in the 1970s, the general idea about extremists and terrorists was that these were psychologically disturbed individuals, which spurred research into finding a "terrorist profile." The point of departure in this research was the use of cases with extremists and trying to figure out their commonalities (e.g., Ferracuti & Bruno, 1981), and in such a way "backtracking" the radicalization process. Such attempts turned out to be futile, and Horgan (2005, 2008) suggested that research should focus on explaining how individuals become radicalized instead of who becomes radicalized.

In most of the major radicalization models, individual differences are mentioned but not discussed in depth. There are some indicators that individual differences could be important (Kruglanski et al., 2019), but in general studies examining the link between personality traits and extremism are notably absent in the literature, and those that exist often present contradictory findings (Corner et al., 2021). In this chapter we focus mainly on individual differences connected to a desire for inclusion and belongingness, which can be connected to the idea that exclusion is an igniting factor in the radicalization process.

We here argue that the answer to the question of who and how individuals become radicalized most likely lies in the intersection of the who and the how – individuals with certain characteristics will react to a context and the way they react is contingent upon their individual characteristics. Hence, it is important to remember that personality is an important aspect in the explanation of radicalization, but there does not seem to be one specific terrorist profile made up of a specific set of personality traits.

In our attempts at incorporating individual differences into radicalization research, our point of departure is that the traits must have relevance for how people may react to (perceptions of) the changing context, and/or the possibility for redemption upon experiencing exclusion. One such trait that is clearly connected to the experience of social exclusion is rejection sensitivity.

2.3.1   Rejection Sensitivity and Processes of Radicalization

The desire for acceptance and to avoid rejection has long been acknowledged as a universal human motivation (Baumeister & Leary, 1995; Downey & Feldman, 1996; Horney, 1937; Maslow, 1987). While this motivation is fundamental and universal, individuals differ in readiness to perceive rejection and in how they respond to episodes of rejection (Downey & Feldman, 1996). Some people respond to potential indications of rejection as intentional, while others retain equanimity. Some react to every potential instance of rejection with strong emotions that even compromise health and relationships (Downey & Feldman, 1996).

Rejection sensitivity is an individual difference in attention to rejection cues and in how people respond to ostracism, rejection, or similar experiences, which may or may not in fact occur (Downey et al., 2004). Rejection sensitivity may help explain why some people, more than others, seem to adapt more readily to a new group following social exclusion. Rejection sensitivity has been defined as a disposition to anxiously expect, readily perceive, and intensely react to rejection (Berenson et al., 2009; Downey et al., 1997). Early research on rejection sensitivity has established a link between rejection sensitivity and exposure to rejecting parenting in childhood (Feldman & Downey, 1994), meaning that this is a learned feature. Ideas about the origins of rejection sensitivity date back as far as to Karen Horney (1937) and John Bowlby (1969). For instance, Horney (1937) attributed maladaptive orientations to relationships to "basic anxiety" about desertion, abuse, humiliation, and betrayal. Bowlby's attachment theory (Bowlby, 1969, 1980) is one of the most elaborated models about how early childhood experiences influence later adult relationships and general well-being. Research on attachment is vast and the ideas have received extensive empirical support (Cassidy et al., 2013).

Individuals who are sensitive to rejection have usually experienced rejection from close others previously and have learned to expect rejection in different situations (Downey et al., 1997). Highly rejection-sensitive individuals more readily adapt to a group following an identity threat (Romero-Canyas et al., 2010). Rejection sensitivity has been shown to foster difficulties in romantic relationships such as dissatisfaction due to a heightened perception of rejection and the assumption that it is intentional (Downey & Feldman, 1996). Rejection sensitivity has also been shown to influence the desire for retaliation following an episode of rejection. In one study, individuals high in rejection sensitivity were more likely to punish the perpetrator of rejection given the opportunity (Ayduk et al., 2008).

In a radicalization context, rejection sensitivity may influence not only the way an individual experiences social exclusion but also how they experience other forms of significance loss (Kruglanski et al., 2014). Our research shows that individuals experiencing social exclusion tend to be more attracted to a radical group, in line with their preexisting ideology, contingent upon their level of rejection sensitivity (Bäck et al., 2018; Renström et al., 2020).

In a series of experiments (Bäck et al., 2018; Renström et al., 2020), participants who self-identified to the left or right on the political spectrum were exposed to either an episode of social exclusion or not. In these studies, the social exclusion manipulation was either Cyberball (Hartgerink et al., 2015;

Williams, 2007; Williams et al., 2000) or the Ostracism Online paradigm (Wolf et al., 2015). Cyberball is an extensively used method for manipulating feelings of exclusion (Williams, 2007). Participants are presented to an online ball tossing game where they are supposedly connected to other participants (preprogrammed avatars). They are then asked to play a game where they toss a ball to each other for a few minutes. In the beginning, the participant receives the ball a couple of times, but after that, participants in the exclusion condition do not receive the ball at all, while participants in the inclusion condition continue to receive the ball about as often as the other players. While this might sound trivial, a huge body of literature indicates that it successfully manipulates experiences of social exclusion and that these experiences are strong and have strong impact on the participants. Another variation of social exclusion is the Online Ostracism paradigm (Wolf et al., 2015). This method takes the shape of a social media platform, where participants can interact with other people (preprogrammed avatars). The paradigm makes use of the inclusion cues that constitute "likes" (or similar) on many social media platforms. The participant chooses an avatar and writes a short text about themselves. They are then hooked up to a social media platform and can see other peoples' profiles. They can then "like" these others' profiles and receive "likes" from the others. In the exclusion condition, participants receive only one like, while in the inclusion condition they receive about six likes – an average comparable to the other profiles.

After experiencing the exclusion episode, participants were invited by one of the other (fictive) participants to read about a new activist group. This group was designed to align with the participants' original political leaning (Bäck et al., 2018; Renström et al., 2020). The inviting, fictive participant presented themselves as a representative of a group engaged in radical actions. Participants were given a brief description of the group. While the presentations of the groups were similar in style and content, the cause differed. For the right-wing group, the main cause was presented as decreased immigration, while for the left-wing group the main cause was increased inclusion of all forms of minority groups. In both group descriptions, the means with which they aimed to advance their cause was presented to be fairly extreme. For instance, the group had hosted previous events that had culminated in violence. After having read the group description, the participant was asked questions, still supposedly from the group representative, about their attitudes toward the group, their goals, and identification with the group. We found that individuals who were highly rejection-sensitive reacted stronger to the exclusion episode and adapted their attitudes more to an including group (Bäck et al., 2018), and they identified more strongly with the group (Renström et al., 2020). Moreover, these individuals were more willing to engage in extreme actions with the group and endorse extreme actions (Renström et al., 2020).

To further extend on these results, we tested if rejection would influence adaption in a nonpolitical setting. Most of the theories on radicalization aim to be content-free, that is, the basic mechanism relating to human nature should be the same regardless of content of the cause (be it ideological or religious or something else). In this study, we also changed setting to inter-individual face-to-face rejection. The study was presented as a study about a possible implementation of tuition fees at higher education institutions in Sweden. Because higher education is subsidized by the government, most students oppose tuition fees. Participants were asked to write a short statement about their feelings toward the implementation of tuition fees. This text was supposed to be used as a "proposal" to join a student organization working against the implementation of tuition fees. The experimenter took the statement and left the room, supposedly checking with an organization representative if the participant could be included in the organization. Upon arrival back to the lab, the participant was informed that they were either included in the organization, or that the organization representative did not feel that they were compatible with the standards of the organization, that the participant's beliefs and values did not match those of the organization, and thus they could not be part of the organization. The rejected participants were then informed that on the way back, the experimenter had run into another organization's representative who had read their statement and who thought they should be part of this organization instead. Hence, participants were first excluded and then included, which should be seen as a necessary sequence to study radicalization which entails the loss of significance and the inclusion in a radical group (Bäck & Altermark, 2016). Following this, all participants were provided with a fictive article describing the including organization's previous actions, which, among other actions, depicted violence. They were then asked to what extent they thought the actions of the group and more extreme actions were acceptable, justified, and if they would be willing to participate in such actions as described in the fictive article and more extreme actions. Rejected individuals, high in rejection sensitivity, were found to be more positively inclined to extremism, such that they were more likely to accept and justify the organization's actions, and they were more willing to participate themselves in extreme actions with the organization (Renström et al., 2020). Important to note here is that in this study, we found a main effect of rejection on endorsement of extremism (acceptance, justification, and willingness to participate in extreme actions with the group), which was not present in the other studies that were performed online. In this study, student participants were explicitly told they were unwanted. Hence, the form of rejection in this study was quite extreme. This differs from the online settings, where the exclusion rather takes the form of being ignored, and it could be argued that the effect is weaker in online settings due to the artificial format in general. Of course, both forms are present in everyday life, indicating that in some situations rejection sensitivity may constitute enhanced vulnerability to be drawn into radical groups, but in some cases, rejection might be so strong that virtually anybody would react to it.

One conclusion from these studies is that people may adapt to radical ideas and engage in radical behaviors due to a desire for inclusion and fitting in. This idea is supported in a study by Knapton and colleagues (2015). In this study, student participants were again rejected or included in a laboratory setting. The setup followed that described earlier regarding tuition fees, but participants were also asked about action intentions against the excluding organization (or for the included participants, against an opposing organization). All participants were provided with a similar fictive article as described previously, detailing the including organization's previous actions, which, among other actions, depicted violence. The results showed that participants who had experienced rejection were more willing to engage in actions against an opposing organization compared to those who had not experienced rejection. Moreover, this effect was fully mediated by inclusionary needs. Hence, participants who experienced rejection and whose inclusionary needs were damaged were more willing to retaliate. Finally, participants that had experienced rejection and were high in rejection sensitivity were more willing to engage in actions against the other organization. This tells us that actions directed against a group could be motivated by belongingness needs to the in-group. If the norm prescribed by the in-group is violence, then people may conform to this norm simply because they want to be included rather than actually opposing the other group. This research speaks to the prosocial nature of violence (Bäck & Altermark, 2016). Somewhat ironically, individuals endorsing extremism are also more likely to be ostracized by the general public (Hales & Williams, 2020; Hales et al., this volume), leading to a negative spiral where they become increasingly dependent on the radical group to provide the tenacious social support they so strongly desire.

2.3.2   Other Individual Differences Related to Exclusion that Influence the Radicalization Process

Which individual differences are important may differ depending on the content of the radical goal. While the general radicalization models aim to be generally applicable to different content, the specific individual-level variables that influence the radicalization process may differ. We are not making an exhaustive list of individual features that may be relevant but discuss a few that we believe need to be further explored.

2.3.2.1   Need to Belong

Like rejection sensitivity, need to belong is an individual difference feature connected to inclusion needs and therefore makes a good candidate to play a role in the radicalization process. As discussed extensively already, humans have a strong fundamental need to belong (Baumeister & Leary, 1995), but the strength of the need to belong varies between individuals (Leary et al., 2013).

To date, not much empirical research has focused on the need to belong in a radicalization setting. Therefore, we here include research on political activism in general. While activism is not radicalism, some scholars discuss activism as a potential precursor to radicalism in a sort of conveyor belt analogy (Moskalenko & McCauley, 2009). Moreover, most of the radicalization models discussed earlier conceptualize radicalization as a gradual process that may start out with more normative actions (e.g., Kruglanski et al., 2019; McCauley & Moskalenko, 2008, 2017; Moghaddam, 2005).

Social incentives to political participation have long since been acknowledged (Riker & Ordeshook 1968), and studies show that protest activity can fulfill the need for social group belongingness (Bäck et al., 2013; Bäck et al., 2015; Bäck et al., 2018). In one study, participants from a smaller suburban college, indicative of marginalization (compared to a large university in the city), and participants experimentally excluded were more likely to express intent to engage in collective action against the implementation of tuition fees when they were high in need to belong (Bäck et al., 2015). In another study, we found that when rejection cues are made salient in the form of participants writing words associated with rejection, compared to neutral words, participants become increasingly willing to conform to a political engagement norm. Moreover, this relationship was moderated by need to belong, such that participants who were primed with rejection cues and high in need to belong displayed higher willingness to conform to the engagement norm (Renström et al., 2018).

Young people seem to be more strongly motivated by need to belong in their choice to take part in protest activities (Renström et al., 2021). In a representative survey of the Swedish population, young participants' (as defined by the mean minus one standard deviation ≈ 20 years) engagement in protests was explained by their level of need to belong, while there was no such relationship for medium-aged or older participants (as defined by the mean, ≈ 40 years plus one standard deviation ≈ 60 years). The protest activity engagement included signing petitions, collecting petition signatures, wearing a badge or other symbol, boycotting or buying a certain product, or participating in a legal demonstration or strike. Participants rated if they had done any of this within the last twelve months, longer ago, or not at all.

In another study, ostracized participants high in need to belong perceived their own group to be morally superior, which in turn led them to endorse extreme behaviors (Pfundmair & Wetherell, 2019).

2.3.2.2 Sex/Gender and Masculinity

Sex/gender is usually not explicitly mentioned as a risk factor (although see, e.g., Kebbell & Porter, 2012; Pfundmair & Lefort-Besnard, 2020). However, it is widely known that most terror deeds are committed by men and that masculinity may be an important contributing aspect for radicalization (Agius, 2022; Ferber & Kimmel, 2008). Recently, a new terrorist threat has emerged, which necessitates greater scrutiny of sex/gender in the radicalization process – that of misogynistic radicalization (Hoffman et al., 2020).

In the early 2000s, the so-called manosphere – a misogynistic and antifeminist online milieu said to promote masculinity and men's rights – moved from the fringes of the internet into mainstream spotlight (Ging, 2019; Jane, 2018; Jones et al., 2020). The manosphere is a collection of websites, blogs, and online forums that are readily available online (Ging, 2019). Core ideas in such forums focus on the societal relations between women and men, and the general position is that feminism is to blame for the (White) man's fall from the most privileged societal position. Gender, that is, gender roles, structures, and relations, is at the core of the misogynistic ideology and (White) male supremacism (Cottee, 2022). Manhood has been described as precarious and something that needs to be performed to be maintained (Vandello & Bosson, 2013). Such precarity leads men, compared to women, to more easily experience gender identity threats (Vandello et al., 2008). Masculinity, the need and expression of it, should be conceptualized as an individual difference variable with consequences for radicalization.

The concept of hegemonic masculinity entails the existence of multiple variations of masculinities, which vary across time and social context (Connell et al., 2005). Importantly, hegemonic masculinity can be seen as the enactment of behaviors and ideas that aim to legitimize men's dominant societal position (Connell, 2005). If this position is threatened, for instance by progress in women's liberation, which changes the gender hierarchy, men may experience aggrieved entitlement (Kalish & Kimmel, 2010). Reactions to aggrieved entitlement include anger, which could be manifested as violence (against women) or involvement in White supremacist, White male supremacist, or other misogynistic groups (Kimmel, 2018).

When faced with a masculine identity threat, men may overcompensate their masculinity by displaying hypermasculine behaviors and traits (Bosson et al., 2009; Willer et al., 2013). Consequently, outwardly extreme enactment of masculinity (e.g., violence, extreme misogyny) could signal individual insecurity (Vandello et al., 2008; Willer et al., 2013). This idea is directly applicable to the incel community, where insecurity about one's appearance is a major motivation for joining misogynistic forums, which then translates into ideas about violence (see also Rousis & Swann, this volume). Moreover, threats to masculinity have been shown to decrease appearance satisfaction (Frederick et al., 2017), indicating a negative spiral.

In relation to radicalization theories, such as the 3-N model, the manosphere constitutes almost a textbook example. People may experience significance loss due to personal failure, rejection, and humiliation (Dugas et al.,

2016; Kruglanski et al., 2019; Renström et al., 2020), which are all common themes in the manosphere and have been pointed to as reasons why men seek out the manosphere. Rejection experiences may be personal, such as repeated rejections by women, but significance may also be lost to those men who feel themselves to be the victims of a changing gender structure. One way to restore significance is to retaliate against the source of the threat or to seek out new groups that can provide camaraderie and purpose, which may lead them to the manosphere. The type of co-rumination of loneliness that bonds together members of the movement on the manosphere forums can create a spiral with increased feelings of isolation and repression and potentially set forth a radicalization process (Rose, 2002; Rose et al., 2017). What may start as a desire to overcome social isolation by joining an online community (Burgess et al., 2001) may instead lead to a cementation of loneliness, and eventually an adoption of toxic beliefs about masculinity, dominance, and violence (Ging, 2019). The changing societal structures of Western, progressive, more inclusive societies imply that some individuals may feel left behind – the White men (Kalish & Kimmel, 2010).

In manosphere forums, means to reach a goal is narrated by justifying violence. Narrative serves two important roles. First, ideologies are shared systems of beliefs (Jost et al., 2008) that identify the actions required to achieve significance, which typically involve violence against perceived enemies of one's group (Bélanger et al., 2019). Second, ideological narratives provide the moral justifications rendering violence an acceptable option to use against the out-group(s) (Kruglanski et al., 2014). Research on moral disengagement has shown that people may engage in cognitive maneuvers so that they can "safely" proceed with unethical behaviors without self-blame (Bandura, 1999). For instance, harming others feels justified when the others are dehumanized, and when violence is portrayed as morally justified to reach a higher goal. Such rationalizations are also common in the manosphere. For instance, women are often referred to as fundamentally different and less human than men, referred to using derogatory labels such as "femoid," "foid" (female humanoid), or just "it" (Bates, 2020), or even as instruments for sex, seen in labels such as "sex machine." Such dehumanization and objectification of women has been related to violence against women (Morris et al., 2018).

By joining groups of like-minded others, one is less exposed to further possibilities of significance loss, and the epistemic and relational motives of attaining a mutual understanding and a shared reality in a predictable and controlled environment are obtained (Echterhoff et al., 2009; Hardin & Higgins, 1996; Kruglanski et al., 2006). In such groups, or networks, violence is socially condoned and encouraged, and individuals that defend the group are bestowed with significance and referred to as martyrs (Horgan, 2008; Kruglanski et al., 2014), increasing individuals' motives to radicalize. A prominent example from the manosphere is the incel mass murderer

Elliot Rodger, who explicitly targeted young women because they rejected him and is often depicted as a martyr.

2.3.2.3   Entitlement and the Dark Triad

Entitlement is an aspect of narcissism, which is part of the so-called dark triad. The dark triad refers to a set of three interrelated dark traits: Machiavellianism, psychopathy, and narcissism (Furnham et al., 2013; Paulhus & Williams, 2002). Machiavellianism is the tendency to be manipulative, calculating, instrumental, and detached from moral qualms (Jones & Paulhus, 2009). Psychopathy refers to expressions of antisocial behaviors, lacking inhibition, empathy, and remorse (Stone & Brucato, 2019). On the individual level, narcissism encompasses a need for being admired, relevant, the center of attention, and more deserving than others (APA, 2021; Krizan & Herlache, 2018). As such, narcissism includes aspects of entitlement, which is sometimes considered a sub-trait of narcissism (Miller et al., 2009). Entitlement is considered a stable personality trait encompassing the idea that one is more deserving and entitled to more, compared to other people (Campbell et al., 2004). When it comes to narcissism and entitlement, it could be argued that these are connected to a desire for inclusion and fear of exclusion.

Research on the dark triad traits and radicalization shows mixed results but in general there seems to be weak to moderate associations between the dark traits and radicalization or extremism (Chabrol et al., 2019; Corner et al., 2021; Duspara & Greitemeyer, 2017; Mededovic & Knezevic, 2019; Mordages-Bamba et al., 2018; Pavlovic & Wertag, 2021). One reason for the varying results is that some traits may be more relevant than others, and, moreover, all three traits contain sub-facets that may contribute to varying degrees of explanation. Of relevance to the present chapter, research that focuses on entitlement is of particular interest since entitlement is connected to exclusion/inclusion.

While research on radicalization often aims to find universality in explaining factors, there may also be variations in the content of the radicalized ideas. For instance, regarding misogynistic radicalization, entitlement is clearly an important and explicit driving force (see also the concept of status indignity in Möring & Pratto, this volume). Psychological entitlement captures rigid beliefs about a very inflated sense of deservingness, being special and privileged, having exaggerated expectations of others, and the view of oneself as well as exploitative tendencies (Grubbs & Exline, 2016; Moeller et al., 2009). If one is denied this, say for instance by being rejected by the object of desire, or by the general feeling that one's social group is left behind, a radicalization process may begin. In one study, we found that entitlement moderated the effect of a masculinity threat on misogynistic attitudes (Renström et al., 2023). Participants in this study, heterosexual men, were exposed to either a fictional tweet highlighting women's progress, and that men risk losing status in the future, or to a neutral control condition. Men who were high in entitlement reacted with stronger negative emotions, especially anger and disgust, to the threatening tweet. However, only disgust mediated the effect on misogynistic attitudes and willingness to join a misogynistic group. This makes sense since disgust has also been presented as an important emotion when it comes to the ability and justification of harming others (Staub, 1990). Both disgust and contempt have been related to dehumanization (Esses et al., 2008). Matsumoto and colleagues (2012) propose that disgust has different effects from anger in intergroup dynamics, being more connected to judgments of other people being bad in themselves rather than a certain action being bad. As an emotion related to avoidance or elimination, they suggest that it could set apart the dangerous and violent groups from the merely angry groups. Harming others feels justified when the others are dehumanized (Staub, 1990), and when violence is portrayed as morally justified to reach a higher goal.

In another study, entitlement was related to the drive for achieving status (Lange et al., 2019). As such, entitlement may be relevant in radicalization in general, given that status is part of the significance concept. Hence, it can be assumed that individuals high in entitlement may react differently to significance threats such as exclusion than those with lower levels of entitlement. Moreover, entitlement is gendered in the sense that men, compared to women, in patriarchal societies have higher entitlement. Taking entitlement into consideration when explaining radicalization may thus also contribute to the understanding of gender differences in radicalization and extremism.

Narcissism as defined as one of the traits in the dark triad refers to individual narcissism, but narcissism may also be collective (de Zavala et al., 2020). As such, it refers to the idea that one's group is superior compared to other groups and should hence also be entitled to more than other groups. Moreover, individuals high in collective narcissism also experience the feeling that others do not recognize the group's superiority enough (de Zavala et al., 2020). According to de Zavala and colleagues, collective narcissism is related to a heightened sensitivity to group-based provocation, such as when traditional group hierarchies in society are challenged. Moreover, hostile revenge may often be seen as the appropriate response. Such reasoning has clear implications for radicalization.

2.4 Conclusions

In this chapter we have focused mainly on individual differences connected to a desire for inclusion and belongingness, which can be connected to the idea that exclusion is an igniting factor in the radicalization process. In our attempts at incorporating individual differences into radicalization research, our point of departure is that traits must have relevance for how people may react to (the perceptions of) changing context, and/or the possibility for redemption upon experiencing exclusion. One important trait that is clearly connected to the experience of social exclusion is rejection sensitivity. In a radicalization context, rejection sensitivity may influence not only the way an individual experiences social exclusion but also how they experience other forms of significance loss (Kruglanski et al., 2014). Our research shows that individuals experiencing social exclusion tend to be more attracted to a radical group, in line with their preexisting ideology, contingent upon their level of rejection sensitivity (Bäck et al., 2018; Renström et al., 2020).

We have also discussed some other individual difference features that may be relevant to the radicalization process. Even though many models of radicalization are of a general nature, we suggest that which individual differences are important may differ depending on the content of the radical goal. Sex/gender is not often explicitly mentioned as a risk factor, even though it is widely known that most terror deeds are committed by men, and that masculinity may be an important contributing aspect to radicalization processes. The fact that misogynistic violence has become more prevalent in recent years stresses the importance of analyzing the role of gender in the radicalization process.

References

Agius, C., Edney-Browne, A., Nicholas, L., & Cook, K. (2022). Anti-feminism, gender and the far-right gap in C/PVE measures. *Critical Studies on Terrorism*, *15*(3), 681–705. https://doi.org/10.1080/17539153.2021.1967299

American Psychiatric Association (2013). *Diagnostic and statistical manual of mental disorders* (5th ed.). American Psychiatric Publishing.

Ayduk, Ö., Gyurak, A., & Luerssen, A. (2008). Individual differences in the rejection–aggression link in the hot sauce paradigm: The case of rejection sensitivity. *Journal of Experimental Social Psychology*, *44*(3), 775–782. https://doi.org/10.1016/j.jesp.2007.07.004

Bäck, E. A., & Altermark, N. (2016). Gemenskap och utstötning: Socialpsykologiska perspektiv på politiskt våld. In C. Edling & A. Rostami (Eds.), *Våldets sociala dimensioner*. Studentlitteratur.

Bäck, E. A., Bäck, H., Altermark, N., & Knapton, H. M. (2018). The quest for significance: Attitude adaption to a radical group following social exclusion. *International Journal of Developmental Science*, *12*(1–2), 25–36. https://psycnet.apa.org/doi/10.3233/DEV-170230

Bäck, E. A., Bäck, H., & Garcia Albacete, G. (2013). Protest activity, social incentives, and rejection sensitivity: Results from a survey experiment about tuition fees. *Contention*, *1*, 1–15. https://doi.org/10.3167/cont.2013.010101

Bäck, E. A., Bäck, H., & Knapton, H. M (2015). Group belongingness and collective action: Effects of need to belong and rejection sensitivity on willingness to participate in protests activities. *Scandinavian Journal of Psychology*, 56(5), 537–544. https://doi.org/10.1111/sjop.12225

Bandura, A. (1999). Moral disengagement in the perpetration of inhumanities. *Personality and Social Psychology Review*, 3(3),193–209. https://doi.org/10.1207/s15327957pspr0303_3

Bates, L. (2020) *Men who hate women: From incels to pickup artists, the truth about extreme misogyny and how it affects us all*. Simon & Schuster UK.

Baumeister, R. F., & Leary, M. R. (1995). The need to belong: Desire for interpersonal attachments as a fundamental human motivation. *Psychological Bulletin*, 117(3), 497–529. https://doi.org/10.1037/0033-2909.117.3.497

Bélanger, J. J., Moyano, M., Muhammad, H., et al. (2019). Radicalization leading to violence: A test of the 3 N Model. *Frontiers in Psychiatry*, 10, 42. https://doi.org/10.3389/fpsyt.2019.00042

Berenson, K. R., Gyurak, A., Ayduk, Ö., et al. (2009). Rejection sensitivity and disruption of attention by social threat cues. *Journal of Research in Personality*, 43(6), 1064–1072. https://doi.org/10.1016/j.jrp.2009.07.007

Borum, R. (2011). Radicalization into violent extremism I: A review of social science theories. *Journal of Strategic Security*, 4(4), 7–36. https://doi.org/10.5038/1944-0472.4.4.1

Bosson, J. K., Vandello, J. A., Burnaford, R. M., Weaver, J. R., & Arzu Wasti, S. (2009). Precarious manhood and displays of physical aggression. *Personality and Social Psychology Bulletin*, 35(5), 623–634. https://doi.org/10.1177/0146167208331161

Bowlby, J. (1969). *Attachment and loss*, Volume 1: *Attachment*. Basic Books.

Bowlby, J. (1980). *Attachment and loss*, Volume 3: *Loss, sadness, and depression*. Basic Books.

Burgess, E. O., Donnelly, D., Dillard, J., & Davis, R. (2001). Surfing for sex: Studying involuntary celibacy using the internet. *Sexuality & Culture*, 5, 5–30. https://doi.org/10.1007/s12119-001-1028-x

Campbell, W. K., Bonacci, A. M., Shelton, J., Exline, J. J., & Bushman, B. J. (2004). Psychological entitlement: Interpersonal consequences and validation of a self-report measure. *Journal of Personality Assessment*, 83(1), 29–45. https://doi.org/10.1207/s15327752jpa8301_04

Carter-Sowell, A. R., Chen, Z., & Williams, K. D. (2008). Ostracism increases social susceptibility. *Social Influence*, 3(3), 143–153. https://doi.org/10.1080/15534510802204868

Cassidy, J., Jones, J. D., & Shaver, P. R. (2013). Contributions of attachment theory and research: A framework for future research, translation, and policy. *Development and Psychopathology*, 25(4, Pt 2), 1415–1434. https://doi.org/10.1017/S0954579413000692

Chabrol, H., Bronchain, J., Morgades Bamba, C. I., & Raynal, P. (2019). The Dark Tetrad and radicalization: Personality profiles in young women. *Behavioral*

Sciences of Terrorism and Political Aggression, 12(3), 1–12. http://doi.org/10.1080/19434472.2019.1646301.

Connell, R. W. (2005). *Masculinities* (2nd ed.). University of California Press.

Corner, E., Taylor, H., Van Der Vegt, I., et al. (2021) Reviewing the links between violent extremism and personality, personality disorders, and psychopathy. *The Journal of Forensic Psychiatry & Psychology, 32*(3), 378–407. https://doi.org/10.1080/14789949.2021.1884736

Cottee, S. (2022). Incel (e)motives: Resentment, shame and revenge. *Studies in Conflict & Terrorism, 44*(2), 93–114 https://doi.org/10.1080/1057610X.2020.1822589

Downey, G., & Feldman, S. I. (1996). Implications of rejection sensitivity for intimate relationships. *Journal of Personality and Social Psychology 70* (6),1327–1343. https://doi.org/10.1037/0022-3514.70.6.1327

Downey, G., Khouri, H., & Feldman, S. (1997). Early interpersonal trauma and adult adjustment: The mediational role of rejection sensitivity. In D. Cicchetti & S. Toth (Eds.), *Rochester symposium on developmental psychopathology, Volume 8: The effects of trauma on the developmental process* (pp. 85–114). University of Rochester Press.

Downey, G., Mugious, V., Ayduk, O., London, B., & Shoda, Y. (2004). Rejection sensitivity and the defensive motivational system: Insights from the startle response to rejection cues. *Psychological Science, 15*, 668–673. https://doi.org/10.1111/j.0956-7976.2004.00738.x

Dugas, M., Bélanger, J. J., Moyano, M., et al. (2016). The quest for significance motivates self-sacrifice. *Motivation Science, 2*(1), 15–32. https://doi.org/10.1037/mot0000030

Duspara, B., & Greitemeyer, T. (2017). The impact of dark tetrad traits on political orientation and extremism: An analysis in the course of a presidential election. *Heliyon, 3*(10), e00425. https://doi.org/10.1016/j.heliyon.2017.e00425

Echterhoff, G., Higgins, E. T., & Levine, J. M. (2009). Shared reality: Experiencing commonality with others' inner states about the world. *Perspectives on Psychological Science, 4*, 496–521. https://doi.org/10.1111/j.1745-6924.2009.01161.x

Eisenberger, N. I. (2013). Why rejection hurts: The neuroscience of social pain. In C. N. DeWall (Ed.), *The Oxford handbook of social exclusion* (pp. 152–162). Oxford University Press. https://doi.org/10.1093/oxfordhb/9780195398700.013.0015

Eisenberger, N. I., Lieberman, M. D., & Williams, K. D. (2003). Does rejection hurt? An fMRI study of social exclusion. *Science, 302*(5643), 290–292. https://doi.org/10.1126/science.1089134

Esses, V. M., Dovidio, J. F., Jackson, L. M., & Armstrong, T. L. (2001). The immigration dilemma: The role of perceived competition, ethnic prejudice, and national identity. *Journal of Social Issues, 57*(3), 389–412. https://doi.org/10.1111/0022-4537.00220

Esses, V. M., Jackson, L. M., & Armstrong, T. L. (1998). Intergroup competition and attitudes toward immigrants and immigration: An instrumental model. *Journal of Social Issues, 54*(4), 699–724. https://doi.org/10.1111/j.1540-4560.1998.tb01244.x

Esses, V. M., Veenvliet, S., Hodson, G., & Milic, L. (2008). Justice, morality, and the dehumanization of refugees. *Social Justice Research*, *21*, 4–25. https://doi.org/10.1007/s11211-007-0058-4

Feldman, S., & Downey, G. (1994). Rejection sensitivity as a mediator of the impact of childhood exposure to family violence on adult attachment behavior. *Development and Psychopathology*, *6*, 231–247. https://doi.org/10.1017/S0954579400005976

Ferber, A. L., & Kimmel, M. S. (2008). The gendered face of terrorism. *Sociology Compass*, *2*(3), 870–887. https://doi.org/10.1111/j.1751-9020.2008.00096.x

Ferrucati, F., & Bruno, F. (1981). Psychiatric aspects of terrorism in Italy. In I. Barak-Glanatz & C. R. Huff (Eds.), *The mad, the bad and the different: Essays in honor of Simon Dinitz* (pp. 199–213). Lexington Books.

Frederick, D. A., Shapiro, L. M., Williams, T. R., et al. (2017). Precarious manhood and muscularity: Effects of threatening men's masculinity on reported strength and muscle dissatisfaction. *Body Image*, *22*, 156–165. https://doi.org/10.1016/j.bodyim.2017.07.002

Furnham, A., Richards, S. C., & Paulhus, D. L. (2013). The dark triad of personality: A 10 year review. *Social and Personality Psychology Compass*, *7*(3), 199–216. https://doi.org/10.1111/spc3.12018

Ging, D. (2019). Alphas, betas, and incels: Theorizing the masculinities of the manosphere. *Men and Masculinities*, *22*(4), 638–657. https://psycnet.apa.org/doi/10.1177/1097184X17706401

Golec de Zavala, A., & Lantos, D. (2020). Collective narcissism and its social consequences: The bad and the ugly. *Current Directions in Psychological Science*, *29*(3), 273–278. https://doi.org/10.1177/0963721420917703

Grubbs, J. B., & Exline, J. J. (2016). Trait entitlement: A cognitive-personality source of vulnerability to psychological distress. *Psychological Bulletin*, *142*(11), 1204–1226. https://psycnet.apa.org/doi/10.1037/bul0000063

Hales, A. H., & Williams, K. D. (2018). Marginalized individuals and extremism: The role of ostracism in openness to extreme groups. *Journal of Social Issues*, *74*(1), 75–92. https://psycnet.apa.org/doi/10.1111/josi.12257

Hales, A. H., & Williams, K. D. (2020). Extremism leads to ostracism. *Social Psychology*, *51*(3), 149–156. https://psycnet.apa.org/doi/10.1027/1864-9335/a000406

Hardin, C. D., & Higgins, E. T. (1996). Shared reality: How social verification makes the subjective objective. In E. T. Higgins & R. M. Sorrentino (Eds.), *Handbook of motivation and cognition: The interpersonal context* (pp. 28–84). Guilford Press.

Hartgerink, C. H., van Beest, I., Wicherts, J. M., & Williams, K. D. (2015). The ordinal effects of ostracism: A meta-analysis of 120 Cyberball studies. *PLoS ONE*, *10*(5), e0127002. https://doi.org/10.1371/journal.pone.0127002

Hoffman, B., Ware, J., & Shapiro, E. (2020). Assessing the threat of incel violence. *Studies in Conflict & Terrorism*, *43*(7), 565–587. https://doi.org/10.1080/1057610X.2020.1751459

Horgan, J. (2005). *The psychology of terrorism*. Routledge. https://doi.org/10.4324/9780203496961

Horgan, J. (2008). From profiles to pathways and roots to routes: Perspectives from psychology on radicalization into terrorism. *The Annals of the American Academy of Political and Social Science, 618*(1), 80–94. https://doi.org/10.1177/0002716208317539

Horgan, J. G. (2014). *The psychology of terrorism* (2nd ed.). Routledge. https://doi.org/10.4324/9781315882246

Horney, K. (1937). *The neurotic personality of our time*. Norton.

Huddy, L., Feldman, S., & Cassese, E. (2007). On the distinct political effects of anxiety and anger. In W. R. Neuman, G. E. Marcus, A. N. Crigler, & M. MacKuen (Eds.), *The affect effect: Dynamics of emotion in political thinking and behavior* (pp. 202–230). University of Chicago Press.

Jane, E. A. (2018). Systemic misogyny exposed: Translating rapeglish from the manosphere with a random rape threat generator. *International Journal of Cultural Studies, 21*, 661–680. https://doi.org/10.1177/1367877917734042

Jasko, K., LaFree, G., & Kruglanski, A. (2017). Quest for significance and violent extremism: The case of domestic radicalization. *Political Psychology, 38*(5), 815–831. https://psycnet.apa.org/doi/10.1111/pops.12376

Jones, C., Trott, V., & Wright, S. (2020). Sluts and soyboys: MGTOW and the production of misogynistic online harassment. *New Media & Society, 22*(10), 1903–1921. https://doi.org/10.1177/1461444819887141

Jones, D. N., & Paulhus, D. L. (2009). Machiavellianism. In M. R. Leary & R. H. Hoyle (Eds.), *Handbook of individual differences in social behavior* (pp. 93–108). Guilford Press.

Jost, J. T., Ledgerwood, A., & Hardin, C. D. (2008). Shared reality, system justification, and the relational basis of ideological beliefs. *Social and Personality Psychology Compass, 2*, 171–86. https://doi.org/10.1111/j.1751-9004.2007.00056.x

Kalish, R., & Kimmel, M. (2010). Suicide by mass murder: Masculinity, aggrieved entitlement, and rampage school shootings. *Health Sociology Review, 19*(4), 451–464. https://doi.org/10.5172/hesr.2010.19.4.451

Kebbell, M. R., & Porter, L. (2012). An intelligence assessment framework for identifying individuals at risk of committing acts of violent extremism against the West. *Security Journal, 25*(3), 212–228. https://doi.org/10.1057/sj.2011.19

Kimmel, M. (2018). *Healing from hate: How young men get into – and out of – violent extremism*. University of California Press. https://doi.org/10.1525/9780520966086

Knapton, H. M., Bäck, H., & Bäck, E. A. (2015). The social activist: Conformity to the ingroup following rejection as a predictor of political participation. *Social Influence, 10*(2), 97–108. https://doi.org/10.1080/15534510.2014.966856

Knapton, H., Renström, E. A., & Bäck, H. (2022). Outgroup exclusion, identity, and collective action in the Brexit context. *Journal of Applied Social Psychology, 52*(9), 912–927. https://doi.org/10.1111/jasp.12898

Krizan, Z., & Herlache, A. D. (2018). The narcissism spectrum model: A synthetic view of narcissistic personality. *Personality and Social Psychology Review, 22*(1), 3–31. https://doi.org/10.1177/1088868316685018

Kruglanski, A. W., Bélanger, J. J., & Gunaratna, R. (2019). *The three pillars of radicalization: Needs, narratives, and networks.* Oxford University Press. https://doi.org/10.1093/oso/9780190851125.001.0001

Kruglanski, A. W., Chen, X., Dechesne, M., Fishman, S., & Orehek, E. (2009). Fully committed: Suicide bombers' motivation and the quest for personal significance. *Political Psychology, 30*(3), 331–357. https://doi.org/10.1111/j.1467-9221.2009.00698.x

Kruglanski, A. W., & Fishman, S. (2009). Psychological factors in terrorism and counterterrorism: Individual, group, and organizational levels of analysis. *Social Issues and Policy Review, 3*(1), 1–44. https://doi.org/10.1111/j.1751-2409.2009.01009.x

Kruglanski, A. W., Gelfand, M. J., Bélanger, J. J., et al. (2014). The psychology of radicalization and deradicalization: How significance quest impacts violent extremism. *Political Psychology, 35*, 69–93. https://doi.org/10.1111/pops.12163

Kruglanski, A. W., Pierro, A., Mannetti, L., & De Grada, E. (2006). Groups as epistemic providers: Need for closure and the unfolding of group-centrism. *Psychological Review, 113*, 84–100. https://doi.org/10.1037/0033-295X.113.1.84

Kruglanski, A. W., & Webber, D. (2014). The psychology of radicalization. *Zeitschrift für Internationale Strafrechtsdogmatik 9*, 379–388. https://zis-online.com/dat/artikel/2014_9_843.pdf

Lange, J., Redford, L., & Crusius, J. (2019). A status-seeking account of psychological entitlement. *Personality and Social Psychology Bulletin, 45*(7), 1113–1128. https://psycnet.apa.org/doi/10.1177/0146167218808501

Leary, M. R. (2013). *Need to belong scale (NTBS).* APA PsycTests.

Lerner, J. S., & Keltner, D. (2001). Fear, anger, and risk. *Journal of Personality and Social Psychology, 81*(1), 146–159. https://doi.org/10.1037/0022-3514.81.1.146

Maner, J. K., DeWall, C. N., Baumeister, R. F., & Schaller, M. (2007). Does social exclusion motivate interpersonal reconnection? Resolving the "porcupine problem." *Journal of Personality and Social Psychology, 92*(1), 42–55. https://doi.org/10.1037/0022-3514.92.1.42

Maslow, A. (1987). *Motivation and personality* (3rd ed.). Harper & Row.

Matsumoto, D., Hwang, H., & Frank, M. (2012). The role of emotion in predicting violence. *FBI Law Enforcement Bulletin, 81*(1), 1.

McCauley, C., & Moskalenko, S. (2008). Mechanisms of political radicalization: Pathways toward terrorism. *Terrorism and Political Violence, 20*(3), 415–433. https://doi.org/10.1080/09546550802073367

McCauley, C., & Moskalenko, S. (2017). Understanding political radicalization: The two-pyramids model. *American Psychologist, 72*(3), 205–216. https://doi.org/10.1037/amp0000062

Međedović, J., & Knežević, G. (2019). Dark and peculiar. *Journal of Individual Differences, 40*(2), 92–103. https://doi.org/10.1027/1614-0001/a000280

Miller, J. D., Campbell, W. K., Young, D. L., et al. (2009). Examining the relations among narcissism, impulsivity, and self-defeating behaviors. *Journal of Personality*, *77*(3), 761–794. https://doi.org/10.1111/j.1467-6494.2009.00564.x

Moeller, S. J., Crocker, J., & Bushman, B. J. (2009). Creating hostility and conflict: Effects of entitlement and self-Image goals. *Journal of Experimental Social Psychology*, *45*(2), 448–452. https://doi.org/10.1016/j.jesp.2008.11.005

Moghaddam, F. M. (2005). The staircase to terrorism: A psychological exploration. *American Psychologist*, *60*(2), 161–169. https://doi.org/10.1037/0003-066X.60.2.161

Morgades-Bamba, C. I., Raynal, P., & Chabrol, H. (2018). Exploring the radicalization process in young women. *Terrorism and Political Violence*, *32*(7), 1–19. https://doi.org/10.1080/09546553.2018.1481051

Morris, K. L., Goldenberg, J., & Boyd, P. (2018). Women as animals, women as objects: Evidence for two forms of objectification. *Personality & Social Psychology Bulletin*, *44*(9), 1302–1314. https://doi.org/10.1177/0146167218765739

Moskalenko, S., & McCauley, C. (2009). Measuring political mobilization: The distinction between activism and radicalism. *Terrorism and Political Violence*, *21*(2), 239–260. https://doi.org/10.1080/09546550902765508

Ouwerkerk, J. W., Kerr, N. L., Gallucci, M., & van Lange, P. A. M. (2005). Avoiding the social death penalty: Ostracism and cooperation in social dilemmas. In K. D. Williams, J. P. Forgas, & W. von Hippel (Eds.), *The social outcast: Ostracism, social exclusion, rejection, and bullying* (pp. 321–332). Psychology Press.

Paulhus, D. L., & Williams, K. M. (2002). The Dark Triad of personality: Narcissism, Machiavellianism, and psychopathy. *Journal of Research in Personality*, *36*(6), 556–563. https://doi.org/10.1016/s0092-6566(02)00505-6

Pavlović, T., & Wertag, A. (2021). Proviolence as a mediator in the relationship between the dark personality traits and support for extremism. *Personality and Individual Differences*, *168*, 110374. https://doi.org/10.1016/j.paid.2020.110374

Pfundmair, M., Aßmann, E., Kiver, E., et al. (2022). Path-ways toward Jihadism in Western Europe: An empirical exploration of a comprehensive model of terrorist radicalization. *Terrorism and Political Violence*, *34*(1), 48–70. https://doi.org/10.1080/09546553.2019.1663828

Pfundmair, M., & Lefort-Besnard, J. (2020). An attempt to identify predictive features among Islamist radicals: Evidence from machine learning. https://hal.science/hal-03042809/

Pfundmair, M., & Wetherell, G. (2019) Ostracism drives group moralization and extreme group behavior. *The Journal of Social Psychology*, *159*(5), 518–530. https://psycnet.apa.org/doi/10.1080/00224545.2018.1512947

Renström, E. A., Aspernäs, J., & Bäck, H. (2021). The young protester: The impact of, belongingness needs on political engagement. *Journal of Youth Studies*, *24*(6), 781–798. https://doi.org/10.1080/13676261.2020.1768229

Renström, E. A., & Bäck, H. (2021a). Anxiety, compassion and pride: How emotions elicited by the government's handling of Covid-19 influences health-promoting behaviors. *Psychologica Belgica*, *61*(1), 224–237. https://doi.org/10.5334/pb.1053

Renström, E. A., & Bäck, H. (2021b). Emotions during the Covid-19 pandemic: Fear, anxiety and anger as mediators between threats and policy support and political actions. Journal of Applied Social Psychology, *51*(8), 861–877. https://doi.org/10.1111/jasp.12806

Renström, E. A., Holm, K., Plume, M., & Bäck, H. (2024). *Becoming misogynistic. The role of entitlement and negative emotions in men's adaption to misogynistic ideas and actions.* [Manuscript in preparation].

Renström, E. A., Bäck, H., & Knapton, H. M. (2018). Conforming to collective action: The impact of rejection, personality and norms on participation in protest activity. *Social Psychological Bulletin*, *13*(4), 1–17. https://doi.org/10.32872/spb.v13i4.26427

Renström, E. A., Bäck, H., & Knapton, H. M. (2020). Exploring a pathway to radicalization: The effects of social exclusion and rejection sensitivity. *Group Processes & Intergroup Relations*, *23*(8), 1204–1229. https://doi.org/10.1177/1368430220917215

Riker, W. H., & Ordeshook, P. C. (1968). A theory of the calculus of voting. *American Political Science Review*, *62*(1), 25–42. https://doi.org/10.2307/1953324

Romero-Canyas, R., Downey, G., Berenson, K., Ayduk, O., & Kang N. J. (2010). Rejection sensitivity and the rejection–hostility link in romantic relationships. *Journal of Personality*, *78*, 119–148. https://doi.org/10.1111/j.1467-6494.2009.00611.x

Rose, A. J. (2002). Co-rumination in the friendships of girls and boys. *Child Development*, *73*(6), 1830–1843. https://doi.org/10.1111/1467-8624.00509

Rose, A. J., Glick, G. C., Smith, R. L., Schwartz-Mette, R. A., & Borowski, S. K. (2017). Co-rumination exacerbates stress generation among adolescents with depressive symptoms. *Journal of Abnormal Child Psychology*, *45*(5), 985–995. https://doi.org/10.1007/s10802-016-0205-1

Silber, M. D., & Bhatt, A. K. (2007). *Radicalization in the west: The homegrown threat.* NYPD Intelligence Division.

Staub, E. (1989). *The roots of evil: The origins of genocide and other group violence.* Cambridge University Press.

Stephan, W. G., Ybarra, O., & Morrison, K. R. (2009). Intergroup threat theory. In T. D. Nelson (Ed.), *Handbook of prejudice, stereotyping, and discrimination* (pp. 43–59). Psychology Press.

Stone, M. H., & Brucato, G. (2019). *The new evil: Understanding the emergence of modern violent crime.* Prometheus Books.

Vandello, J. A., & Bosson, J. K. (2013). Hard won and easily lost: A review and synthesis of theory and research on precarious manhood. *Psychology of Men & Masculinity*, *14*(2), 101–113. https://psycnet.apa.org/doi/10.1037/a0029826

Vandello, J. A., Bosson, J. K., Cohen, D., Burnaford, R. M., & Weaver, J. R. (2008). Precarious manhood. *Journal of Personality and Social Psychology*, *95*(6), 1325–1339. https://psycnet.apa.org/doi/10.1037/a0012453

Webber, D., & Kruglanski, A. W. (2018). The social psychological makings of a terrorist. *Current Opinion in Psychology*, *19*, 131–134. https://doi.org/10.1016/j .copsyc.2017.03.024

Weber, H. (2004). Explorations in the social construction of anger. *Motivation and Emotion*, *28*, 197–219. https://doi.org/10.1023/B:MOEM.0000032314.29291.d4

Willer, R., Rogalin, C. L., Conlon, B., & Wojnowicz, M. T. (2013). Overdoing gender: A test of the masculine overcompensation thesis. *American Journal of Sociology*, *118*(4), 980–1022. https://doi.org/10.1086/668417

Williams, K. D. (2007). Ostracism. *Annual Review of Psychology*, *58*, 425–452. https://doi.org/10.1146/annurev.psych.58.110405.085641

Williams, K. D. (2009). Ostracism: A temporal need–threat model. In M. P. Zanna (Ed.), *Advances in experimental social psychology* (pp. 275–314). Elsevier Academic Press. https://doi.org/10.1016/S0065-2601(08)00406-1

Williams, K. D., Cheung, C. K. T., & Choi, W. (2000). Cyberostracism: Effects of being ignored over the Internet. *Journal of Personality and Social Psychology*, *79* (5), 748–762. https://doi.org/10.1037/0022-3514.79.5.748

Williams, K. D., & Zadro, L. (2005). Ostracism: The indiscriminate early detection system. In K. D. Williams, J. P. Forgas, & W. von Hippel (Eds.), *The social outcast: Ostracism, social exclusion, rejection, and bullying* (pp. 19–34). Psychology Press.

Wolf, W., Levordashka, A., Ruff, J. R., et al. (2015). Ostracism Online: A social media ostracism paradigm. *Behavior Research Methods*, *47*(2), 361–373. https:// doi.org/10.3758/s13428-014-0475-x

Zadro, L., Williams, K. D., & Richardson, R. (2004). How low can you go? Ostracism by a computer is sufficient to lower self-reported levels of belonging, control, self-esteem, and meaningful existence. *Journal of Experimental Social Psychology*, *40*(4), 560–567.

In the Realm of Action

Social Exclusion as a Catalyst for Terrorism

MICHAELA PFUNDMAIR

3.1   Introduction

In July 2011, the 32-year-old Anders Breivik murdered eight people in the government district of Oslo and then carried out a massacre at a vacation camp on the island of Utøya, dressed in a police uniform. In total, seventy-seven people died. Only hours before the attack, he had sent out his manifesto to a thousand recipients, in which he had outlined his antifeminist, Islamophobic, and xenophobic attitude. Breivik had an unstable childhood. He was bullied in his youth and not accepted in the Progress Party of which he was a member for ten years. Eventually, he was excluded by the far-right on the Internet who did not read his manifesto or respond to his emails. A journalist later wrote: "Whatever he tried in his previous life, he was rejected" (Graf, 2016).

About ten years later: The 22-year-old Fabian D. was arrested in February 2020 as the result of a tip from the internal intelligence authority in Germany. He had come across the right-wing extremist chat group "Fire War Division" a year earlier, where its members exchanged dehumanizing ideas. They shared extreme dislike about women, Jews, and foreigners. Prompted by the responses of the group, Fabian became more and more radicalized in his statements and militaristic self-presentation until he decided to obtain firearms. According to his statements in the chat group, his plan was to commit an attack at a place of worship. In the group, he had already asked about particularly perfidious places of attack. Different from that was how he lived offline: He had been teased from childhood for being overweight and had been bullied during his school years. He lived in a basement-like mansion in his mother's house and had neither friends nor a girlfriend. He felt humiliated and met rejection everywhere he went. The ultra-racist chat partners from all over the world had been the only ones who had given him the feeling of "being someone" (Przybilla, 2020a, 2020b).

These two cases differ in many important points, from the basic conditions of their lives to the final outcome. However, in one point, they intriguingly overlap: Both men had experienced social exclusion in their lives repeatedly. In this chapter, I will address whether this observation goes beyond individual cases and whether social exclusion is systematically involved in terrorism.

3.2   Terrorism

3.2.1   Terminology

As a first step, it is vital to differentiate between the core terms radicalization, extremism, and terrorism.

Radicalization can be defined as a process by which people come to adopt increasingly extreme ideals and aspirations that reject or undermine the status quo or contemporary ideas of freedom of choice (Wilner & Dubouloz, 2010). This gradual process makes them ready to use violence, although the use of violence is not inevitable (Hafez & Mullins, 2015). This is an important point because most people who radicalize do not become terrorists (Borum, 2011). This is also why many established radicalization theories differentiate between opinions and actions (e.g., McCauley & Moskalenko, 2017). Moreover, radicalization is one possible (and in Western cultures probably the predominant) pathway into terrorism involvement but it is not the only one. Somewhat less clearly defined is the term *radicalism*. Whereas radicalization is a process, radicalism is a structure. However, there are different approaches how to understand this structure. Some define radicalism as a way of thinking that tends toward the extreme and seeks to tackle social problems and conflicts "from the root" (radicalism derives from the Latin word "radix," meaning root), but within the fundamental values of liberal democracy (Dienstbühl, 2019). Others define radicalism as readiness to participate in illegal or violent political action (as opposed to activism, the readiness to participate in legal and nonviolent political action; Moskalenko & McCauley, 2009).

Extremism is often understood as opposition to fundamental values, including democracy, the rule of law, individual liberty, and mutual tolerance of different faiths and beliefs (e.g., Backes & Jesse, 1996; HM Government, 2011). In this sense, extremism strives to overcome the system (Dienstbühl, 2019). Some researchers additionally differ between cognitive and violent extremism. Cognitive extremism means that people only have an attitude opposing fundamental democratic values, while violent extremism means they are ready to use violence for this attitude (Richards, 2015). Notably, extremism can also be understood much more broadly: Extremism is also conceptualized as an infrequent phenomenon whose rarity results from a pronounced intensity or magnitude of its underlying motivation (Kruglanski et al., 2021). This is more consistent with the term "extreme," which simply refers to deviations from the norm.

As soon as violence is actually used to achieve one's own (political or ideological) goals, extremism turns to terrorism. *Terrorism* can be defined as an act of violence, usually committed against civilians, aimed at achieving behavioral change and political objectives by creating fear in a larger population (Doosje et al., 2016). Laqueur (1987) has argued that "one man's terrorist is another man's freedom fighter" (pp. 7, 302) and referred to a school of thought according to which it depends entirely on the subjective outlook of the definer who is viewed as a terrorist. However, more recent definitions draw a clearer boundary, categorizing freedom fighters as people who fight for legal rights in conformity with the law of armed conflict, while terrorists fight to achieve illegal advantages by means of targeting civilians (Bahman, 2023).

3.2.2 Phenomena of Terrorism

Because terrorism always relates to a specific goal, phenomena of terrorism can be differentiated along their underlying ideology. Currently, there are five main ideologies: right-wing (concern: safeguarding the high-status position of the "White race"), left-wing (concern: achieving a just distribution of wealth), religiously motivated (concern: adhering to a strict interpretation of religion), nationalistic or separatist (concern: securing a territory), and single issues (focusing on one particular topic, e.g., environment or climate; Doosje et al., 2016). According to an influential theory, ideologies can be used to understand the history of modern terrorism, which came in waves: The first anarchist wave started in the 1880s and continued into the early decades of the twentieth century. This was followed by the anti-colonial wave from the 1920s to the 1960s. The third wave was the new left wave, happening from the 1960s until the end of the twentieth century. A religious wave began in 1979 and still continues (Rapoport, 2001, 2012). Notably, this theory has also been extended and criticized: Some researchers argue that, at the moment, we are on the cusp of a fifth extreme right wave (Hart, 2021), while others suggest that it could be more useful to think about different types of terrorism as strains rather than waves (Parker & Sitter, 2016).

Beyond these considerations, terrorism can also be differentiated according to organizational structures. For a long time, a larger (usually more than ten people), hierarchically structured group was dominant in terrorism. The fact that such groups were more likely to be identified by security authorities gave rise to a new form of organization: smaller cells linked more by ideological attitude and less by an organizational structure. Indicating its flat hierarchies, the term "leaderless resistance" became relevant. In addition, there are also so-called lone actors or lone wolves. These individuals do not follow any group and their actions are self-determined. However, this does not rule out the possibility that they are influenced by a particular scene or group (Pfahl-Traughber, 2020, 2023).

3.2.3   Explanatory Approaches for Terrorism

As noted earlier, one possible route to become a terrorist is radicalization. Importantly, radicalization is less a product of specific profiles or even a "terrorist personality". Instead, it involves specific pathways (Horgan, 2008). Research from different disciplines has developed a plethora of work to illuminate the process of terrorist radicalization. These research efforts can be divided into studies that have identified single factors of radicalization and studies that have established full models of radicalization.

Factors of radicalization can be classified as intra- and interpersonal as well as situational. Important *intrapersonal factors* are the wish to pursue personal significance (Kruglanski et al., 2019; Ellenberg & Kruglanski, this volume) and the need to reduce uncertainties about oneself or the world (Hogg, 2014; Wagoner & Hogg, this volume). These factors are not specific for radicalization but occur universally. However, extreme ideas can be particularly suitable to fulfill them. Most terrorist attacks are planned and executed in groups (Spaaj, 2010). Thus, factors related to the group – *interpersonal factors* – are also important drivers for radicalization. Researchers even argue that nearly all mechanisms of radicalization occur in the context of group identification (McCauley & Moskalenko, 2008; Doosje et al., this volume). Indeed, processes such as identity fusion, a state in which the group is becoming equivalent to the personal self (Gómez et al., 2021; Chinchilla & Gómez, this volume), and perceived group threat, the subjective feeling that an imminent threat to the group is present (Doosje et al., 2013), fuel the radicalization process. Finally, research has identified a set of *situations* that make individuals particularly vulnerable to radicalization. One of these factors is prison (LaFree et al., 2020). However, conditions that occur on a regular basis can also be drivers for radicalization. Specifically, the state of social exclusion has been found to promote a terrorist mindset (Pfundmair, 2019). Intriguingly, these situations appear to deprive intrapersonal needs – such as a need for control and significance – and, at the same time, make those concerned more susceptible to approaching groups, tapping directly into the known intra- and interpersonal risk factors for radicalization.

Models of radicalization usually follow either a puzzle or process structure. The "radicalization puzzle," for example, suggests that four factors have to come together to produce terrorist radicalization: personal and collective grievances, networks and interpersonal ties, political and religious ideologies, and enabling environments and support structures (Hafez & Mullins, 2015). Doosje et al. (2016), on the other hand, suggests that individuals follow three phases during the radicalization process: a sensitivity phase in which psychological processes within the individual drive radicalization, a group membership phase in which the radical group fuels the radicalization process, and an action phase in which people turn to using violence. These models have been

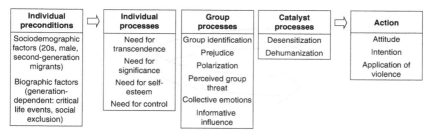

Figure 3.1 Model of radicalization (Pfundmair, Aßmann, et al., 2022).

developed by a synthesis of empirical literature and are compact in understanding radicalization; however, they are quite abstract. A more extensive model that is not only based on a combination of previous findings but also empirically tested postulates the following (Pfundmair, Aßmann, et al., 2022): Individual preconditions such as biographical breaking points (like social exclusion or critical life events) lay the groundwork for radicalization. Three processes then fuel radicalization: individual processes (e.g., the psychological needs for significance and control), group processes (e.g., group polarization and perceived group threat), and cognitive processes (e.g., desensitization and dehumanization). The model assumes that these processes may occur in a staggered manner during radicalization (e.g., individual before cognitive processes), but that they also reinforce each other and are particularly explosive in their interaction. This model is displayed in Figure 3.1.

A whole range of research in recent decades has thus come close to answering the question of how terrorism arises. However, it should be noted that individual trajectories toward terrorism are highly individual. Radicalization is an individual process: Its beginning is often difficult to identify and its ending is neither inevitable nor predictable. Even though many factors are now known that can potentially lead to radicalization, there is no guarantee that it will take place, even if all problematic constellations come together. Thus, in a certain sense, radicalization remains a random event (Sageman, 2009).

3.3   Social Exclusion

3.3.1   *Terminology and Phenomena*

The need to belong is a fundamental human motivation (Baumeister & Leary, 1995; Bowlby, 1969; Maslow, 1968): Humans have a pervasive drive to form and maintain lasting, positive, and significant interpersonal relationships. This need has probably evolved from the evolutionary necessity of inclusion in groups that offered their members more security and reproductive opportunities (Gruter & Masters, 1986). Excluding burdensome or deviating members, on the other hand, made a group more cohesive. Thus, not only the need to belong but also exclusion probably evolved for reasons of functionality (Barner-Barry, 1986).

Social exclusion, being kept apart from others physically or emotionally, is a universal phenomenon: It takes place in diverse cultures and contexts, both institutionalized like excommunication and, to a greater extent, informally. It also is an event that people experience in minimal forms daily and in meaningful ways at least once in their lives (Wesselmann et al., 2015). It can be split in two phenomena: rejection (an incidence of social exclusion with negative attention) and ostracism (an incidence of social exclusion with a lack of attention; Wesselmann et al., 2016). Thus, social exclusion involves both very explicit statements that someone is unwanted by others (e.g., Twenge et al., 2001) and instances in which someone is treated with disinterest (e.g., Wirth et al., 2010) or in which important information is withheld (e.g., Jones et al., 2009). Notably, any kind of social exclusion stimulates a physical and psychological alarm system that can detect such social threats quickly.

3.3.2   Response Patterns

The temporal need-threat model proposed by Williams (2009) is often used to systematically describe reactions to social exclusion (see Hales et al., this volume). The model proposes three stages: an immediate reflexive stage, a delayed reflective stage, and a long-term resignation stage. According to the model, as soon as ostracism is detected, the excluded reflexively feel pain and negative affect as well as a deprivation of basic needs such as belonging, self-esteem, control, meaningful existence, and certainty (reflexive stage). After they had time to reflect on the motives, meaning, and relevance of the experience, they try to fortify their deprived needs (reflective stage). This can be in the form of either prosocial or antisocial behaviors. The model specifically assumes that prosocial behaviors help to fortify inclusionary needs such as belonging and self-esteem, whereas antisocial behaviors help to fortify power/provocation needs such as meaningful existence and control. If ostracism persists over extended time, people react with alienation, depression, helplessness, and unworthiness (resignation stage).

This model has been validated by a large number of empirical studies. For example, referring to the reflexive stage, social exclusion induced activity in the dorsal region of the anterior cingulate cortex (dACC), a region involved in the distressing component of pain (see Lieberman & Eisenberger, 2006), and deprived basic needs for belonging, self-esteem, control, and meaningful existence, even when the instance of social exclusion was seemingly trivial (e.g., when people were excluded by despised others, Fayant et al., 2014; or by a computer, Zadro et al., 2004). Validating the reflective stage, excluded participants engaged in hostile cognitions and aggressive behaviors (e.g.,

DeWall et al., 2009; Warburton et al., 2006), but also behaved highly prosocially, for example, in the form conformity, compliance, and even obedience (e.g., Carter-Sowell et al., 2008; Riva et al., 2014; Williams et al., 2000). Supporting the assumptions of the resignation stage, exclusion fostered the development of depressive symptomatology (Rudert et al., 2021). Research also found exclusion-induced effects beyond the model's predictions. For example, instances of exclusion negatively affected cognitive performances (e.g., Xu et al., 2018) and led to the perception of oneself as less human (Bastian & Haslam, 2010).

Although these findings reveal devastating consequences of social exclusion, research also suggests that the initial pain of exclusion may dissipate after some time (e.g., Zadro et al., 2006) and that coping – for example, by parasocial attachments with media figures (Knowles, 2013) or prayer (Hales et al., 2016) – is possible.

3.4 The Relationship between Social Exclusion and Terrorism

3.4.1 Theoretical Overlaps

The previous sections have outlined that personal deprivation and receptiveness to social influences are important factors – both to understand how terrorism evolves and to predict how people respond to exclusion. Thus, there seems to be an overlap between motivators for terrorism and consequences of exclusion. The following points in particular reveal an intriguing convergence:

- Uncertainty, the feeling of being unable to predict and plan behavior, comparable to a sense of low control, has been argued to be a root of extremism because it triggers a desire to identify with strong and clearly defined groups to resolve this uncertainty (Hogg, 2014; Hogg, Kruglanski, et al., 2013; also see Wagoner & Hogg, this volume).
- The quest for personal significance, constituting diverse human motivations like esteem and meaning, has been suggested to motivate terrorism (Kruglanski et al., 2014; Kruglanski & Orehek, 2011; also see Ellenberg & Kruglanski, this volume).
- The need to belong has been posited to be a focal point of becoming a terrorist (Sageman, 2004). For example, studies with left-wing terrorists have revealed that close personal relationships with terrorists were a better predictor of joining a terrorist group than political orientations (Della Porta, 1988).

These components overlap with the basic needs regularly threatened by social exclusion: Being kept apart from others causes people to feel uncertain (deprived control), insignificant (deprived meaningful existence), and disconnected (deprived belonging; see Williams, 2009).

- Furthermore, most of the mechanisms of radicalization are argued to occur in the context of group identification and accompanied processes (McCauley & Moskalenko, 2008). "Fused" people, that is, those who not only feel as a unit with their group but whose self–other barrier is blurred to the point where they are ready to fight and die for their group (Swann et al., 2009), are especially vulnerable to recruitment into terrorist groups (Atran et al., 2014). Group processes that may follow such intense group identification – like conformity, group polarization, and perceived group threat (Doosje et al., 2013; Moghaddam, 2005; Sunstein, 2001) – are known to play significant roles in boosting terrorist radicalization (also see Doosje et al., this volume).

Likewise, social exclusion strongly affects sociality up to the point of extreme in-group loyalty (e.g., Gómez et al., 2011) and also increases group-serving processes such as compliance, conformity, and obedience (e.g., Carter-Sowell et al., 2008; Riva et al., 2014; Williams et al., 2000).

All in all, consequences of social exclusion overlap with motivations for becoming a terrorist. Thus, although the underlying idea of terrorism (achieving behavioral change and political goals) does not directly aid the excluded individual, its underlying motivators do. In other words, in embracing terrorist ideas, excluded individuals may feel personally significant and self-certain again, and in joining a highly cohesive terrorist group, they may fortify their threatened need for belonging. Therefore, theoretically, a relationship between exclusion and terrorism seems likely.

3.4.2 Empirical Evidence

3.4.2.1 The Exclusion–Terrorism Relationship: Related Research

Although there seems to be a clear theoretical overlap between social exclusion and terrorism, controlled empirical research on this topic is at its beginning (for an overview, see Pfundmair, Wood, et al., 2022). Nonetheless, research has produced rich data on related issues, specifically, social exclusion and its link to general extremism and political activism.

A number of papers find a relationship between exclusion and extreme antisocial behaviors. For example, previous work has revealed that social exclusion is linked with alarming events such as mass shootings (Kowalski et al., 2021; Leary et al., 2003; Kowalski & Leary, this volume). Experimental work has also shown that a short instance of exclusion is enough to make its victims indicate a greater openness toward membership in a gang that engaged in delinquent acts (Hales & Williams, 2018; Hales et al., this volume). Further research has demonstrated that exclusion can make people increase their willingness to engage in fight-and-die behaviors on behalf of important others or important causes (Gómez et al., 2011; Pfundmair & Wetherell, 2018; Pretus et al., 2018).

Other work has revealed a link between social exclusion and susceptibility to social influences related to extreme political opinions. Specifically, exclusion made people adapt their attitude to and indicate support for groups that provided them re-inclusion, although these groups were extreme political organizations (Bäck et al., 2018; Knapton et al., 2015; Renström et al., 2020; Renström & Bäck, this volume). This relationship was particularly pronounced among participants high in rejection sensitivity, a tendency to anxiously expect, readily perceive, and overreact to rejection (Downey & Feldman, 1996).

3.4.2.2   The Exclusion–Terrorism Relationship: A Direct Link

Beyond this work, there are initial studies providing a more direct link between exclusion and terrorism, that is, the violence used to achieve a specific ideological goal. One set of studies has approached the core concepts by investigating this relationship in the normal population. Here, of course, it is not real terrorists that are studied but instead a terrorist mindset, that is, the reported willingness to engage in violence used to reach a political goal.

A first study (Treistman, 2021) examined the exclusion–terrorism link in a large and random sample of individuals across forty-nine countries using data obtained from the World Values Survey. This work specifically focused on two variables: sociopolitical exclusion (here defined as the denial of services or inability to participate in government institutions) and a terrorist mindset (defined as the extent to which individuals experienced terrorism as political, ideological, or religious mean is justifiable). The study revealed that high levels of exclusion within a state were associated with the belief that terrorism is a justifiable means to achieve political objectives, providing initial support for the exclusion–terrorism link.

Another field study (Pfundmair & Mahr, 2022a) explored the relationship between social exclusion and a terrorist mindset during the last period of restrictions of the COVID-19 pandemic in Germany. Here, only individuals who opposed the COVID-19 measures were investigated. The study showed that social exclusion induced by the pandemic containment policies was a meaningful predictor for radicalism intentions. In other words, the more people felt excluded due to the state's measures taken to contain the spread of the virus, the more willingness they reported to use illegal and violent behaviors to fight for their opinion on how to deal with the pandemic. Interestingly, this was not specific to a political subsample; the pattern emerged for both more leftist and more right-leaning participants. Moreover, feelings of exclusion were associated with lower control; the reported radicalism, on the other hand, increased perceived control.

Another study (Pfundmair, 2019) investigated the general relationship between exclusion and a terrorist mindset using an experimental approach.

Therefore, participants were excluded or included using the Cyberball or the O-Cam paradigm. In the Cyberball paradigm (Williams & Jarvis, 2006), participants are asked to play a virtual ball tossing game with other players. Unbeknownst to the participants, these players are computerized and programmed to either throw the ball only twice at the beginning at the game to the actual participant (exclusion condition) or fairly distributed over all players (inclusion condition). In the O-Cam paradigm (Goodacre & Zadro, 2010), participants are asked to take part in a web conference with other participants. Again, these other participants are not real but actors whose actions are prerecorded. While the actual participant gives a presentation about themselves, the fake participants briefly listen but then turn to each other, begin having a conversation and ignore the participant (exclusion condition) – or they listen attentively to them (inclusion condition). After that, a terrorist group was presented to the participants. This was either a (fictitious) terrorist organization that was described as defending democracy and fighting right-wing extremists, or the "Animal Liberation Front," an existing animal protection terrorist organization. Participants were asked how far they would go to support this organization and whether they would join it or commit property or even personal damage on behalf of it. For the "Animal Liberation Front," this read as follows:

> The "Animal Liberation Front" is an international organization founded in 1976 and dedicated to animal rights. Its goal is to prevent animal testing and the killing of animals. In doing so, it goes further than traditional animal rights organizations: It conducts animal liberations, destroys animal testing labs and fur facilities, organizes veterinary care, and finds safe homes for animals. The organization does whatever it takes to save animal lives.
>
> "Huntingdon Life Sciences" (since 2015 under the name "Envigo") is a research organization with two laboratories in the UK and one laboratory in the US. It conducts animal experiments on behalf of pharmaceutical and chemical companies. According to information from animal activists, about 500 animals die in these experiments every day (182,500 animals per year). A few years ago, footage was released from a few infiltrated activists showing how employees systematically mistreated animals. For example, there was a video of a beagle puppy being pulled up by the neck and repeatedly punched in the face. There was also video of a monkey being dissected alive and fully conscious. "Huntingdon Life Sciences" obtained a ban on speaking in the US, so further incriminating footage from animal rights activists cannot be released to authorities. On March 13, 2008, activists mailed a letter poisoned with Ricin to the then CEO of "Huntingdon Life Sciences." He was in a coma for two weeks but survived the poisoning.

The study found that excluded participants reliably favored more extreme options than included participants or participants in a control condition to support the pro-democracy terrorist organization. Moreover, excluded (compared to included) participants indicated greater willingness to commit property damage on behalf of the "Animal Liberation Front." Interestingly, this effect was mediated by the deprived need for control. Thus, as in Pfundmair and Mahr (2022a), it was again control acting as a mediator for the exclusion–terrorism link.

Another experimental study (Pfundmair & Mahr, 2022b) also investigated the link between social exclusion and a terrorist mindset, this time, however, with a focus on group processes as mediators of this relationship. Again, participants were experimentally excluded or included using the Cyberball or the O-Cam paradigm. As in Pfundmair (2019), excluded (vs. included) participants reported a greater willingness to join and/or to commit property damage on behalf of either an existing environmental terrorist organization (the "Earth Liberation Front"), the existing "Animal Liberation Front", or a new (fictitious) animal protection terrorist organization called "Animal Rights First – Go." (In one of the three studies, this pattern was only found among female participants.) The studies also implemented a minimal group paradigm to create controlled in-groups related to the terrorist organizations and to investigate the impact of these in the exclusion–terrorism link. To do so, participants were assigned to a new group based on their alleged preferences, about which they later learned that the group members were environmental or animal advocates. Interestingly, the relationship between exclusion and a terrorist mindset was mediated by sympathy for the in-group and group processes such as perceived group threat and group polarization. Furthermore, these mediators boosted the exclusion–terrorism link in such a way that excluded participants were even willing to commit personal damage as soon as group processes were interposed. In other words, excluded individuals showed a greater in-group love and this increased their involvement in violent ideological acts. To investigate this pattern also in real cases, the study reanalyzed coded qualitative data of a sample of Islamists. Here, no evidence for a direct association between exclusion and the assessed catalysts for terrorism was found. However, more excluded subjects were associated with higher levels of perceived group threat, and this translated to more pronounced catalysts for terrorism. This pattern may map genuine radicalization trajectories more realistically because in real cases, these effects are likely to occur staggered. That is, excluded people might search for a new group and, having overcome social exclusion in this way, ultimately follow the group into terrorism.

This work studied the link between exclusion and terrorist mindset (mostly) in the normal population. Another set of studies explored this relationship among real extremists and terrorists. Notably, these studies could only provide correlational evidence. However, supporting experimental evidence with real-world data, they provide a more comprehensive picture of the exclusion–terrorism link.

In one of these studies (Pfundmair, Aßmann, et al., 2022), the goal was to test a full model of radicalization using two samples of Islamists. One of these samples consisted of people currently in the radicalization process who had not (yet) executed a terrorist criminal act; they were investigated by a special unit of the German state office of criminal police. The other sample consisted of people who had completed the radicalization process and had been reported in newspapers for reasons such as planning or committing a terrorist attack or joining the Islamic State. Data on these individuals came from police reports (depicting the first sample with an *n* of 75 target persons) or a larger collection of newspaper articles (depicting the second sample with an *n* of 86 target persons). These qualitative data were coded by either the police professionals who had personally known the subjects or three independent psychologists, each along a specific coding scheme. Notably, social exclusion was only one out of several variables investigated. However, two intriguing patterns related to exclusion emerged: First, in the sample in which individuals were studied who were at the beginning of the radicalization process, there was no person who was associated with only low levels of exclusion. Instead, 55.8 percent had experienced medium and 44.2 percent high extent of social exclusion in their lives. Exclusion was also a factor that differentiated them statistically from non-radical subjects. Second, in the sample in which individuals had completed the radicalization process, this pattern was much more washed out: Now, 41.7 percent of all target persons were associated with low levels of exclusion, whereas 36.7 percent had medium and 21.7 percent high levels of social exclusion. This indicates that exclusion takes on a more important role at the beginning of terrorist radicalization, when it might function as cognitive opener to extreme ideas or extreme groups. Later, the need to belong might be fulfilled by the new terrorist group.

In work by Chermak and Gruenewald (2015), sociodemographic characteristics of three types of domestic extremists were examined: far right-wing offenders, members of Al-Qaida affiliated movements, and environmental and animal rights extremists. The database used to compare these individuals' sociodemographics was the Extremist Crime Database, an open-source database including detailed information on crimes committed by domestic extremists in the United States. Again, this study was not limited to social exclusion but investigated a larger quantity of variables. Of interest for the exclusion–terrorism link, however, the study showed that in particular far-right and religiously motivated offenders were excluded from society in different ways: Whereas far-right offenders had less success in the labor market, members of Al-Qaida-affiliated movements remained cultural outsiders.

A very recent work (Pfundmair, Pachurka, et al., 2022; Pfundmair et al., 2024) investigated systematically whether social exclusion is an incident that occurs more frequently in the lives of right-wing and religiously motivated terrorists. Therefore, interviews with terrorism experts were conducted and, as in Pfundmair, Aßmann, et al. (2022), qualitative data about terrorists were coded. The latter were taken from either newspaper articles or judicial decisions. These data showed that social exclusion appeared to accumulate in terrorist biographies. For right-wing terrorists, it was particularly exclusion due to the lack of peer group and explicit rejection experiences; for religiously motivated terrorism, it was particularly exclusion due to sociocultural background and nonextremist criminality. The study also showed that the more exclusion individuals had suffered, the more severe was their extremist crime or the more radical their attitude.

Another study (Hansen et al., 2020) explored the relationship between exclusion and terrorism on not an individual but a societal level. Underlying data were domestic terrorist incidences documented in the Global Terrorism Database. This data was merged into the PRIO-GRID cellular structure, which divides the world into a collection of cells. The study found that the more an ethnic group was excluded from power, the more incidences of domestic terrorism had occurred. Specifically, a cell with an excluded group had a 45.3 percent higher chance of a domestic terrorist attack, replicating the exclusion–terrorism link with a different approach.

3.4.3   An Exclusion–Terrorism Model

On the whole, empirical evidence has revealed a causal relationship between social exclusion and a terrorist mindset and, probably, also terrorism. However, the link between exclusion and terrorism is not likely to be direct; rather, it works indirectly, presumably through processes such as deprived needs (especially the need for control) and higher social susceptibility. Other factors, like hostile cognitions or dehumanizing tendencies, which are known consequences of social exclusion (Bastian & Haslam, 2010; DeWall et al., 2009), could also play mediating roles, although these specific links have not yet been empirically investigated. Ultimately, social exclusion is likely to act as an early cognitive opener for terrorism through its individual- and group-level consequences. The role of social exclusion in the process of terrorist radicalization is displayed in Figure 3.2.

When considering the influence of social exclusion in the process of terrorist radicalization, two points should be taken into account. First, in terrorist radicalization, a number of different factors push and pull people into becoming radicalized (Horgan, 2014). Thus, in the vast majority of cases, terrorism is a product of mutual interrelationships, and social exclusion might be only one of several risk factors. Second, if a person is excluded, there is no guarantee that

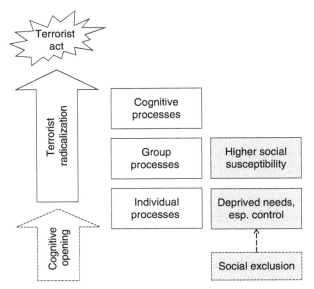

Figure 3.2 An exclusion–terrorism model: Social exclusion is likely to act as cognitive opener for terrorist radicalization via deprived needs and higher social susceptibility, factors known to fuel the radicalization process.

they will become a terrorist. Instead, it is quite possible that this person will manage the social threat in other ways since other coping mechanisms are well known, and terrorist radicalization and, in particular, terrorism are rare, albeit terrifying, events. Nevertheless, terrorism *can* be a consequence of exclusion, which is why it should not be neglected.

3.5   Discussion

3.5.1   Future Research

There are several open questions about the exclusion–terrorism link that future research should address. First, research needs to investigate under which circumstances people adopt a terrorist mindset in the aftermath of exclusion rather than dealing with exclusion in different ways. Extreme ideas and groups are especially well equipped to resolve people's uncertainty (Hogg & Adelman, 2013), which is why it could be the strength of the social injury that moderates extreme (vs. nonextreme) reactions. This reasoning could be supported by findings showing that people high in rejection sensitivity are particularly vulnerable to extreme political groups (Bäck et al., 2018; Knapton et al., 2015; Renström et al., 2020). On the other hand, whether one adopts a terrorist mindset or not could also be a random event, as other researchers have suggested (Sageman, 2009), and simply depend on the availability of an extreme (vs. nonextreme) group.

Second, it is to be investigated to which ideologies the exclusion–terrorism link applies. Whereas the experimental studies mainly used eco- and animal rights terrorism as a proxy to explore the relationship between social exclusion and a terrorist mindset (an ideology generally supported by most people and, thus, particularly suitable to be investigated in the normal population), the studies analyzing real extremists and terrorists focused on right-wing and religiously motivated ideologies. Although the empirical approaches were different, this could indicate that the exclusion–terrorism link is independent of ideology. Indeed, there is more and more evidence that terrorist radicalization is psychologically similar across different phenomena (Van Prooijen & Krouwel, 2019). However, whether this also applies for exclusion needs to be explored in future research.

Furthermore, future research would benefit from taking a deeper look at the mediators of the exclusion–terrorism link that appear to play powerful roles. So far, deprived needs, in particular control and group processes, have emerged as driving factors. However, it is quite possible that there are more than these. One promising future account are cognitive processes. Terrorism usually has to be justified by those responsible because they seek to legitimize behavior that transgresses certain norms, such as injuring or killing innocent others (Koomen & Van der Pligt, 2016). This is, for example, done by dehumanization (e.g., Saucier et al., 2009), which entails the conviction that a person or a group lacks certain human characteristics. Placing someone outside moral values, in turn, can justify violence. Social exclusion, on the other hand, is known to affect cognitive processes – from a decrease of simple cognitive performances (e.g., Xu et al., 2018) to cognitions of oneself as less human (Bastian & Haslam, 2010). Thus, a relationship between exclusion and radicalizing cognitions appears plausible.

Finally, to investigate a phenomenon like terrorism, it appears fruitful to combine different empirical approaches: on the one hand, experimental designs to break down cause-and-effect relationships, which have been underdeveloped in terrorism research so far (Schuurman, 2020) but can only approach the core concepts; on the other hand, field research to combine such insights with real-life cases and increase external validity. Moreover, longitudinal studies examining a potential radicalization process over time could yield valuable findings, combining benefits of both approaches.

3.5.2 Practical Implications

Although the specific profiles of radicalized individuals ultimately differ and it is therefore difficult to predict a phenomenon such as terrorist radicalization, research on the exclusion–terrorism link provides clues as to how terrorism can possibly be prevented. These could be used to shape both secondary (i.e., measures for specific risk groups) and tertiary (i.e., deradicalization) prevention measures.

One important aspect is social inclusion. Historic deradicalization programs have already made strategic use of (re-)inclusion: For example, in the course of the demobilization of the "Black September" of the Palestine Liberation Organization (the terrorist group that committed the 1972 Munich Olympic bombing), incentives to start a family were created. Members of the Black September were offered the prospect of marrying a "carefully selected" woman and receiving $8,000 for their wedding and first child (Dechesne, 2011). Modern projects also use inclusion as core measure: For example, a German program called "Social City" attempts to support integration at the societal level. Urban development investments in housing and infrastructure in disadvantaged neighborhoods are used to promote opportunities for participation and integration (BMI, 2019) – an approach to secondary prevention.

Another important aspect is to serve basic needs among people who could be susceptible to a terrorist mindset. The need for control, for example, could be met by providing support systems or assisting with professional developments. Such approaches are already applied in various programs. For instance, the deradicalization program of the LKA Bavaria, a program specifically designed for people at the beginning of the radicalization process, provides individually tailored support to vulnerable persons – for example, by providing contact persons for the Muslim faith or by helping them to achieve their school-leaving qualifications (Pfundmair & Schmidt, 2019). In a deradicalization program composed of seven different elements (e.g., educational, vocational, spiritual), developed for former members of the Liberation Tigers of Tamil Eelam in Sri Lanka, strategies that empowered the former terrorists were specifically successful in reducing extremism (Webber et al., 2018).

3.5.3 Conclusion

Although rare, terrorism is one of the most frightening and destructive human accomplishments. We know that a number of different factors push and pull someone into becoming a terrorist. Current research has revealed that social exclusion is one of those factors.

According to Malala Yousafzai, "With guns you can kill terrorists, with education you can kill terrorism" (Yousafzai, n.d.). Thus, increasing our knowledge of the processes of radicalization, we might also be able to prevent terrorism.

References

Atran, S., Sheikh, H., & Gomez, A. (2014). Devoted actors sacrifice for close comrades and sacred cause. *Proceedings of the National Academy of Sciences*, *111*(50), 17702–17703. https://doi.org/10.1073/pnas.1420474111

Bäck, E. A., Bäck, H., Altermark, N., & Knapton, H. (2018). The quest for significance: Attitude adaption to a radical group following social exclusion. *International Journal of Developmental Science*, *12*(1–2), 25–36. https://doi.org/10.3233/DEV-170230

Backes, U., & Jesse, E. (1996). *Politischer Extremismus in der Bundesrepublik Deutschland [Political extremism in the Federal Republic of Germany]*. Schriftreihe Band (4. Ausg.). Bundeszentrale für politische Bildung.

Bahman, A. (2023). Freedom fighter or terrorist? *International Law Research, 12* (1), 76–86. https://doi.org/10.5539/ilr.v12n1p76

Barner-Barry, C. (1986). Rob: Children's tacit use of peer ostracism to control aggressive behavior. *Ethology and Sociobiology*, *7*(3–4), 281–293. https://doi.org/10.1016/0162-3095(86)90054-3

Bastian, B., & Haslam, N. (2010). Excluded from humanity: The dehumanizing effects of social ostracism. *Journal of Experimental Social Psychology*, *46*(1), 107–113. https://doi.org/10.1016/j.jesp.2009.06.022

Baumeister, R. F., & Leary, M. R. (1995). The need to belong: Desire for interpersonal attachments as a fundamental human motivation. *Psychological Bulletin*, *117*, 497–529. https://doi.org/10.1037/0033-2909.117.3.497

BMI. (2019). *Soziale Stadt [Social City]*. Städtebauförderung. www.staedtebaufoer derung.info/DE/ProgrammeVor2020/SozialeStadt/sozialestadt_node.html

Borum, R. (2011). Radicalization into violent extremism I: A review of social science theories. *Journal of Strategic Security*, *4*(4), 7–36. https://doi.org/10.5038/1944-0472.4.4.1

Bowlby, J. (1969). *Attachment and loss*, Volume 1: *Attachment*. Basic Books.

Carter-Sowell, A. R., Chen, Z., & Williams, K. D. (2008). Ostracism increases social susceptibility. *Social Influence*, *3*(3), 143–153. https://doi.org/10.1080/15534510802204868

Chermak, S., & Gruenewald, J. A. (2015). Laying a foundation for the criminological examination of right-wing, left-wing, and Al Qaeda-inspired extremism in the United States. *Terrorism and Political Violence*, *27*(1), 133–159. https://doi.org/10.1080/09546553.2014.975646

Dechesne, M. (2011). Deradicalization: Not soft, but strategic. *Crime, Law and Social Change*, *55*(4), 287–292. https://doi.org/10.1007/s10611-011-9283-8

Della Porta, D. (1988). Recruitment processes in clandestine political organizations: Italian left-wing terrorism. *International Social Movement Research, 1*, 155–69.

DeWall, C. N., Twenge, J. M., Gitter, S. A., & Baumeister, R. F. (2009). It's the thought that counts: The role of hostile cognition in shaping aggressive responses to social exclusion. *Journal of Personality and Social Psychology*, *96* (1), 45–49. https://doi.org/10.1037/a0013196

Dienstbühl, D. (2019). *Extremismus und Radikalisierung: Kriminologisches Handbuch zur aktuellen Sicherheitslage [Extremism and radicalization: Criminological handbook on the current security situation].* Boorberg.

Doosje, B., Loseman, A., & Van Den Bos, K. (2013). Determinants of radicalization of Islamic youth in the Netherlands: Personal uncertainty, perceived injustice, and perceived group threat. *Journal of Social Issues, 69*(3), 586–604. https://doi .org/10.1111/josi.12030

Doosje, B., Moghaddam, F. M., Kruglanski, A. W., et al. (2016). Terrorism, radicalization and de-radicalization. *Current Opinion in Psychology, 11,* 79–84. https://doi.org/10.1016/j.copsyc.2016.06.008

Downey, G., & Feldman, S. I. (1996). Implications of rejection sensitivity for intimate relationships. *Journal of Personality and Social Psychology, 70*(6), 1327–1343. https://doi.org/10.1037/0022-3514.70.6.1327

Fayant, M. P., Muller, D., Hartgerink, C. H. J., & Lantian, A. (2014). Is ostracism by a despised outgroup really hurtful? *Social Psychology, 45*(6), 489–494. https:// doi.org/10.1027/1864-9335/a000209

Gómez, Á., Bélanger, J. J., Chinchilla, J., et al. (2021). Admiration for Islamist groups encourages self-sacrifice through identity fusion. *Humanities and Social Sciences Communications, 8*(1), 1–12. https://doi.org/10.1057/s41599-021-00734-9

Gómez, Á., Morales, J. F., Hart, S., Vázquez, A., & Swann Jr, W. B. (2011). Rejected and excluded forevermore, but even more devoted: Irrevocable ostracism intensifies loyalty to the group among identity-fused persons. *Personality and Social Psychology Bulletin, 37*(12), 1574–1586. https://doi.org/10.1177/ 0146167211424580

Goodacre, R., & Zadro, L. (2010). O-Cam: A new paradigm for investigating the effects of ostracism. *Behavior Research Methods, 42*(3), 768–774. https://doi .org/10.3758/BRM.42.3.768

Graf, J. (2016, July 22). *"Er wurde zurückgewiesen – überall": Wie Breivik zum Massenmörder wurde [He was rejected – everywhere": How Breivik became a mass murderer].* n-tv. www.n-tv.de/politik/Wie-Breivik-zum-Massenmoerder-wurde-article18245816.html

Gruter, M., & Masters, R. D. (1986). Ostracism: A social and biological phenomenon. *Ethnology and Sociobiology, 7,* 149–395. https://doi.org/ 10.1016/0162-3095(86)90043-9

Hafez, M., & Mullins, C. (2015). The radicalization puzzle: A theoretical synthesis of empirical approaches to homegrown extremism. *Studies in Conflict & Terrorism, 38*(11), 958–975. https://doi.org/10.1080/1057610X.2015.1051375

Hales, A. H., Wesselmann, E. D., & Williams, K. D. (2016). Prayer, self-affirmation, and distraction improve recovery from short-term ostracism. *Journal of Experimental Social Psychology, 64,* 8–20. https://doi.org/10.1016/j.jesp.2016 .01.002

Hales, A. H., & Williams, K. D. (2018). Marginalized individuals and extremism: The role of ostracism in openness to extreme groups. *Journal of Social Issues, 74* (1), 75–92. https://doi.org/10.1111/josi.12257

Hansen, H. E., Nemeth, S. C., & Mauslein, J. A. (2020). Ethnic political exclusion and terrorism: Analyzing the local conditions for violence. *Conflict Management and Peace Science, 37*(3), 280–300. https://doi.org/10.1177/0738894218782160

Hart, A. (2021). Right-wing waves: Applying the four waves theory to transnational and transhistorical right-wing threat trends. *Terrorism and Political Violence, 35*, 1–16. https://doi.org/10.1080/09546553.2020.1856818

HM Government (2011). *PREVENT Strategy; PREVENT Programme.* The Stationery Office Limited.

Hogg, M. A. (2014). From uncertainty to extremism: Social categorization and identity processes. *Current Directions in Psychological Science, 23*(5), 338–342. https://doi.org/10.1177/0963721414540168

Hogg, M. A., & Adelman, J. (2013). Uncertainty-identity theory: Extreme groups, radical behavior, and authoritarian leadership. *Journal of Social Issues, 69*(3), 436–454. https://doi.org/10.1111/josi.12023

Hogg, M. A., Kruglanski, A., & Bos, K. (2013). Uncertainty and the roots of extremism. *Journal of Social Issues, 69*(3), 407–418. https://doi.org/10.1111/josi.12021

Horgan, J. (2008). From profiles to pathways and roots to routes: Perspectives from psychology on radicalization into terrorism. *The ANNALS of the American Academy of Political and Social Science, 618*(1), 80–94. https://doi.org/10.1177/0002716208317539

Horgan, J. G. (2014). *The psychology of terrorism.* Routledge. https://doi.org/10.4324/9781315882246

Jones, E. E., Carter-Sowell, A. R., Kelly, J. R., & Williams, K. D. (2009). "I'm out of the loop": Ostracism through information exclusion. *Group Processes & Intergroup Relations, 12*(2), 157–174. https://doi.org/10.1177/2F1368430208101054

Knapton, H. M., Bäck, H., & Bäck, E. A. (2015). The social activist: Conformity to the ingroup following rejection as a predictor of political participation. *Social Influence, 10*(2), 97–108. https://doi.org/10.1080/15534510.2014.966856

Knowles, M. L. (2013). Belonging regulation through the use of (para)social surrogates. In C. N. DeWall (Ed.), *The Oxford handbook of social exclusion* (pp. 275–285). Oxford University Press. https://doi.org/10.1093/oxfordhb/9780195398700.013.0026

Koomen W., & Van der Pligt, J. (2016). *The psychology of radicalization and terrorism.* Routledge. https://doi.org/10.4324/9781315771984

Kowalski, R. M., Leary, M., Hendley, T., et al. (2021). K–12, college/university, and mass shootings: Similarities and differences. *The Journal of Social Psychology, 161*(6), 753–778. https://doi.org/10.1080/00224545.2021.1900047

Kruglanski, A. W., Bélanger, J. J., & Gunaratna, R. (Eds.) (2019). *The three pillars of radicalization.* Oxford University Press. https://doi.org/10.1093/oso/9780190851125.001.0001

Kruglanski, A. W., Gelfand, M. J., Bélanger, J. J., et al. (2014). The psychology of radicalization and deradicalization: How significance quest impacts violent extremism. *Political Psychology, 35*, 69–93. https://doi.org/10.1111/pops.12163

Kruglanski, A. W., & Orehek, E. (2011). The role of the quest for personal significance in motivating terrorism. In J. Forgas, A. Kruglanski & K. Williams (Eds.), *The psychology of social conflict and aggression* (pp. 153–166). Psychology Press.

Kruglanski, A. W., Szumowska, E., Kopetz, C. H., Vallerand, R. J., & Pierro, A. (2021). On the psychology of extremism: How motivational imbalance breeds intemperance. *Psychological Review, 128*(2), 264–289. https://doi.org/10.1037/rev0000260

LaFree, G., Jiang, B., & Porter, L. C. (2020). Prison and violent political extremism in the United States. *Journal of Quantitative Criminology, 36*(3), 473–498. https://doi.org/10.1007/s10940-019-09412-1

Laqueur, W. (1987). *The age of terrorism*. Little, Brown and Company.

Leary, M. R., Kowalski, R. M., Smith, L., & Phillips, S. (2003). Teasing, rejection, and violence: Case studies of the school shootings. *Aggressive Behavior, 29*(3), 202–214. https://doi.org/10.1002/ab.10061

Lieberman, M. D., & Eisenberger, N. I. (2006). A pain by any other name (rejection, exclusion, ostracism) still hurts the same: The role of dorsal anterior cingulate cortex in social and physical pain. In J. T. Cacioppo, P. S. Visser & C. L. Pickett (Eds.), *Social neuroscience: People thinking about thinking people* (pp. 167–187). The MIT Press.

Maslow, A. H. (1968). *Toward a psychology of being*. Van Nostrand.

McCauley, C., & Moskalenko, S. (2008). Mechanisms of political radicalization: Pathways toward terrorism. *Terrorism and Political Violence, 20*(3), 415–433. https://doi.org/10.1080/09546550802073367

McCauley, C., & Moskalenko, S. (2017). Understanding political radicalization: The two-pyramids model. *American Psychologist, 72*(3), 205–216. https://doi.org/10.1037/amp0000062

Moghaddam, F. M. (2005). The staircase to terrorism: A psychological exploration. *American Psychologist, 60*(2), 161–169. https://doi.org/10.1037/0003-066X.60.2.161

Moskalenko, S., & McCauley, C. (2009). Measuring political mobilization: The distinction between activism and radicalism. *Terrorism and Political Violence, 21*(2), 239–260. https://doi.org/10.1080/09546550902765508

Parker, T., & Sitter, N. (2016). The four horsemen of terrorism: It's not waves, it's strains. *Terrorism and Political Violence, 28*(2), 197–216. https://doi.org/10.1080/09546553.2015.1112277

Pfahl-Traughber, A. (2020). Der Einzeltäter ist ein einzelner Täter: Eine Analyse von Fällen und deren Kontext im Rechtsterrorismus [The lone perpetrator is a single offender: An analysis of cases and their context in right-wing terrorism]. *Kriminalistik, 74*(2), 74–80.

Pfahl-Traughber, A. (2023). Rechtsterrorismus als Terminus und Untersuchungskonzept [Right-wing terrorism as a term and concept of investigation]. Zeitschrift für Polizeiwissenschaft und polizeiliche Praxis, 20(2), 36–46.

Pfundmair, M. (2019). Ostracism promotes a terroristic mindset. *Behavioral Sciences of Terrorism and Political Aggression, 11*(2), 134–148. https://doi.org/10.1080/19434472.2018.1443965

Pfundmair, M., Aßmann, E., Kiver, B., et al. (2022). Pathways toward Jihadism in Western Europe: An empirical exploration of a comprehensive model of terrorist radicalization. *Terrorism and Political Violence, 34*(1), 48–70. https://doi.org/10.1080/09546553.2019.1663828

Pfundmair, M., & Mahr, L. A. (2022a). Regaining power: How feelings of exclusion during COVID-19 are associated with radicalism among critics of containment policies. *Frontiers in Psychology, 13*. https://doi.org/10.3389/fpsyg.2022.952760

Pfundmair, M., & Mahr, L. A. (2022b). How group processes push excluded people into a radical mindset: An experimental investigation. *Group Processes & Intergroup Relations, 26*(6), 1289–1309. http://doi.org/10.1177/13684302221107782

Pfundmair, M., Pachurka, R., Späth, P., & Witiska, T. (2022, February). Social exclusion in the life of terrorists [Presentation]. Twenty-third Meeting of the Society for Personality and Social Psychology, San Francisco, CA, USA.

Pfundmair, M., Pachurka, R., Späth, P., & Witiska, T. (2024). *Empirical evidence on the accumulation of social exclusion in the lives of terrorists* [Manuscript submitted for publication]. Faculty of Intelligence, Federal University of Administrative Sciences.

Pfundmair, M., & Schmidt, H. (2019). Der Weg zur Radikalisierung und zurück: Deradikalisierung und seine psychologischen Mechanismen in der Praxis [The path to radicalization and back: Deradicalization and its psychological mechanisms in practice]. *Praxis der Rechtspsychologie, 29*(1), 23–39.

Pfundmair, M., & Wetherell, G. (2019). Ostracism drives group moralization and extreme group behavior. *The Journal of Social Psychology, 159*(5), 518–530. https://doi.org/10.1080/00224545.2018.1512947

Pfundmair, M., Wood, N. R., Hales, A., & Wesselmann, E. D. (2022). How social exclusion makes radicalism flourish: A review of empirical evidence. *Journal of Social Issues*, 1–19. https://doi.org/10.1111/josi.12520

Pretus, C., Hamid, N., Sheikh, H., et al. (2018). Neural and behavioral correlates of sacred values and vulnerability to violent extremism. *Frontiers in Psychology, 9*, 2462. https://doi.org/10.3389/fpsyg.2018.02462

Przybilla, O. (2020a, November 26). *Rechtsterrorismus in Cham: "Wie ein Soldat, der ins Leere schaut" [Right-wing terrorism in Cham: "Like a soldier looking into the void"]*. Süddeutsche Zeitung. www.sueddeutsche.de/bayern/rechtsterror-cham-prozess-nuernberg-angeklagter-1.5128303

Przybilla, O. (2020b, November 27). *Prozess in Nürnberg: Zuhause in einer Welt aus Hass [Trial in Nuremberg: At home in a world of hate]*. Süddeutsche Zeitung. www.sueddeutsche.de/bayern/rechtsterror-cham-prozess-nuernberg-plaedoyer-1.5129702

Rapoport, D. C. (2001). The fourth wave: September 11 in the history of terrorism. *Current History, 100*(650), 419–429. https://doi.org/10.1525/curh.2001.100.650.419

Rapoport, D. C. (2012). The four waves of modern terrorism. In J. Horgan & K. Braddock (Eds.), *Terrorism studies: A reader* (pp. 3–30). Routledge.

Renström, E. A., Bäck, H., & Knapton, H. M. (2020). Exploring a pathway to radicalization: The effects of social exclusion and rejection sensitivity. *Group Processes & Intergroup Relations*, *23*(8), 1204–1229. https://doi.org/10.1177/1368430220917215

Richards, A. (2015). From terrorism to "radicalization" to "extremism": Counterterrorism imperative or loss of focus? *International Affairs*, *91*(2), 371–380. https://doi.org/10.1111/1468-2346.12240

Riva, P., Williams, K. D., Torstrick, A. M., & Montali, L. (2014). Orders to shoot (a camera): Effects of ostracism on obedience. *The Journal of Social Psychology*, *154*(3), 208–216. https://doi.org/10.1080/00224545.2014.883354

Rudert, S. C., Janke, S., & Greifeneder, R. (2021). Ostracism breeds depression: Longitudinal associations between ostracism and depression over a three-year-period. *Journal of Affective Disorders Reports*, *4*, 100118. https://doi.org/10.1016/j.jadr.2021.100118

Sageman, M. (2004). *Understanding terror networks*. University of Pennsylvania Press. https://doi.org/10.9783/9780812206791

Sageman, M. (2009). *Hofstad case study & the Blob Theory: Theoretical frames on pathways to violent radicalization*, ARTIS Research and Risk Modeling.

Saucier, G., Akers, L. G., Shen-Miller, S., Knežević, G., & Stankov, L. (2009). Patterns of thinking in militant extremism. *Perspectives on Psychological Science*, *4*(3), 256–271. https://doi.org/10.1111/j.1745-6924.2009.01123

Schuurman, B. (2020). Research on terrorism, 2007–2016: A review of data, methods, and authorship. *Terrorism and Political Violence*, *32*(5), 1011–1026. https://doi.org/10.1080/09546553.2018.1439023

Spaaij, R. (2010). The enigma of lone wolf terrorism: An assessment. *Studies in Conflict & Terrorism*, *33*(9), 854–870. https://doi.org/10.1080/1057610X.2010.501426

Sunstein, C. R. (2001). Why they hate us: The role of social dynamics. *Harvard Journal of Law & Public Policy*, *25*, 429–440.

Swann Jr, W. B., Gómez, A., Seyle, D. C., Morales, J., & Huici, C. (2009). Identity fusion: the interplay of personal and social identities in extreme group behavior. *Journal of Personality and Social Psychology*, *96*(5), 995–1011. https://doi.org/10.1037/a0013668

Treistman, J. (2021). Social exclusion and political violence: Multilevel analysis of the justification of terrorism. *Studies in Conflict & Terrorism*, 1–24. https://doi.org/10.1080/1057610X.2021.2007244

Twenge, J. M., Baumeister, R. F., Tice, D. M., & Stucke, T. S. (2001). If you can't join them, beat them: Effects of social exclusion on aggressive behavior. *Journal of Personality and Social Psychology*, *81*(6), 1058–1069. https://doi.org/10.1037/0022-3514.81.6.1058

Van Prooijen, J. W., & Krouwel, A. P. (2019). Psychological features of extreme political ideologies. *Current Directions in Psychological Science*, *28*(2), 159–163. https://doi.org/10.1177/0963721418817755

Warburton, W. A., Williams, K. D., & Cairns, D. R. (2006). When ostracism leads to aggression: The moderating effects of control deprivation. *Journal of Experimental Social Psychology*, *42*(2), 213–220. https://doi.org/10.1016/j.jesp.2005.03.005

Webber, D., Chernikova, M., Kruglanski, A. W., et al. (2018). Deradicalizing detained terrorists. *Political Psychology*, *39*(3), 539–556. https://doi.org/10.1111/pops.12428

Wesselmann, E. D., Grzybowski, M. R., Steakley-Freeman, D. M., et al. (2016). Social exclusion in everyday life. In P. Riva & J. Eck (Eds.) *Social exclusion: Psychological approaches to understanding and reducing its impact* (pp. 3–23). Springer International Publishing. https://doi.org/10.1007/978-3-319-33033-4_1

Wesselmann, E. D., Hales, A. H., Ren, D., & Williams, K. D. (2015). Ostracism threatens personal security: A temporal need threat framework. In P. J. Carroll, R. M. Arkin, & A. L. Wichman (Eds.), *The handbook of personal security* (pp. 191–206). Routledge.

Williams, K. D. (2009). Ostracism: A temporal need-threat model. *Advances in Experimental Social Psychology*, *41*, 275–314. https://doi.org/10.1016/S0065-2601(08)00406-1

Williams, K. D., Cheung, C. K., & Choi, W. (2000). Cyberostracism: effects of being ignored over the Internet. *Journal of Personality and Social Psychology*, *79*(5), 748–762. https://doi.org/10.1037/0022-3514.79.5.748

Williams, K. D., & Jarvis, B. (2006). Cyberball: A program for use in research on interpersonal ostracism and acceptance. *Behavior Research Methods*, *38*(1), 174–180. https://doi.org/10.3758/BF03192765

Wilner, A. S., & Dubouloz, C. J. (2010). Homegrown terrorism and transformative learning: An interdisciplinary approach to understanding radicalization. *Global Change, Peace & Security*, *22*(1), 33–51. https://doi.org/10.1080/14781150903487956

Wirth, J. H., Sacco, D. F., Hugenberg, K., & Williams, K. D. (2010). Eye gaze as relational evaluation: Averted eye gaze leads to feelings of ostracism and relational devaluation. *Personality and Social Psychology Bulletin*, *36*(7), 869–882. https://doi.org/10.1177/0146167210370032

Xu, M., Qiao, L., Qi, S., et al. (2018). Social exclusion weakens storage capacity and attentional filtering ability in visual working memory. *Social Cognitive and Affective Neuroscience*, *13*(1), 92–101. https://doi.org/10.1093/scan/nsx139

Yousafzai, M. (n.d.). *Quotes*. Moab Valley Multicultural Center. https://moabmc.org/malala-yousafzai

Zadro, L., Boland, C., & Richardson, R. (2006). How long does it last? The persistence of the effects of ostracism in the socially anxious. *Journal of Experimental Social Psychology*, *42*(5), 692–697. https://doi.org/10.1016/j.jesp.2005.10.007

Zadro, L., Williams, K. D., & Richardson, R. (2004). How low can you go? Ostracism by a computer is sufficient to lower self-reported levels of belonging, control, self-esteem, and meaningful existence. *Journal of Experimental Social Psychology*, *40*(4), 560–567. https://doi.org/10.1016/j.jesp.2003.11.006

4

Seeking the Self in the Extreme

White Extremism, Exclusion, and Threat to Self

VERENA GRAUPMANN AND ERIC D. WESSELMANN

4.1 Introduction

"Although this is probably a lone-wolf incident, this is not the first mass shooting we have seen, and sadly it will not be the last." This quote is taken from State Senator James Sanders' response to the shooting committed by a 19-year-old White male that killed ten Black Americans in a grocery store in Buffalo, NY, in 2022. The shooter seemed to have been motivated by online hate-related rhetoric claiming that communities of color are slowly replacing White communities, which will eventually become extinct (Katersky & Hutchinson, 2022). This rhetoric is often called the great replacement theory and pushed on White extremist websites and recruitment materials. Senator Sanders' quote highlights a strange paradox: people engaging in violent hate crimes, seemingly driven by *both* personal isolation and alienation ("lone wolf") and social connection with an observably growing ideological White extremist movement (inspired by racially motivated mass shootings/identified with radicalized online community). In most cases, individuals do not seem to jump to violence immediately nor do they adopt extremist philosophies overnight. Radicalization is a social process by nature, whether the social interactions occur in person, online, or a combination.

Most psychological research on radicalization focuses on racial, ethnic, or religious minoritized groups in the United States or European countries. However, there have been increasing incidents of terrorist violence perpetrated by individuals who otherwise fit identity categories of the majority cultures – White, male, Christian citizens of the countries in which they stage their attacks. These individuals often have couched their violent actions within identity-related motivations, such as protecting their racial, ethnic, religious, or national groups from contamination or even existential destruction by "outsiders" – members of the social groups that they ultimately target in their attacks. Rhetoric that these White terrorists have used, such as fear of replacement and "White genocide," was once found only in fringe sociopolitical movements (Dobratz & Shanks-Meile, 2000). However, in the United States elements of this rhetoric have become normalized, even showing up in speeches from prominent elected officials, political candidates, and major media outlets (Bond, 2023; Castle et al., 2020; Jaffe & Siemaszko, 2016; Yousef, 2022). US intelligence agencies now consider White extremism the top domestic threat to national security (Neidig & Beitsch, 2021; Sullivan & Benner, 2021; Walters & Chang, 2021). These trends likely are not unique to the United States and thus may become a global problem (Ekman, 2022; King's College London, 2023; Rose, 2022).

Given that psychologists interested in extremism and radicalization have focused largely on assessing individuals from other identity groups (e.g., Muslims, animal rights enthusiasts), it is unclear how applicable this research is to these phenomena among groups categorized as "White extremists." In this chapter, we provide a brief review of key psychological models of extremism and radicalization. We then argue that future models and research should intentionally consider the construct of "self" and self-related theories. We then use White extremism and related literature as a case study that has self-related implications, both for understanding the radicalization process and potentially for short-circuiting this process.

4.2 The Scope of White Extremism and Related Constructs

Political extremism can be defined as the organized rejection of democratic values and the institutions of a given democratic society. This type of extremism often dovetails with other aspects of members' identity beyond just their specific political orientation (e.g., conservative or liberal), such as religion or race/ethnicity. Extremist ideology is often the cause of group-based violence and terrorism. Any rise in extremist ideology (left- or right-wing) is therefore of natural concern to those invested in individual liberty, equality, and a democratic legal system.

When people discuss "White extremists," whether in popular media or in research, they also use other descriptors such as "White supremacist," "White nationalist," and "White separatist." Though these terms are interrelated, they have ideological nuances that can be important to separate, at least in terms of understanding the identities of those who subscribe to these terms (Dobratz & Shanks-Meile, 2000). For example, though all movements center members' White racial identity, "supremacists" explicitly believe that White individuals are superior to all other non-White racial and ethnic categories. This definition distinguishes between individuals who explicitly endorse a race-based hierarchical power structure from individuals who endorse and benefit from White supremacy-based systems, yet may not explicitly recognize the institutionalized aspects of racism (old-fashioned versus modern/symbolic racism, endorsing a color-blind racial ideology, etc.; Neville et al., 2013; Swim et al., 1995).

The terms "White nationalist" and "White separatist" tend to refer to their political goals as far as race, ethnicity, and geographic region within their country of origin. White "nationalists" tend to focus on ensuring that only White individuals live in their country, whereas "separatists" typically argue that individuals of all races and ethnicities can live within their country, but these groups should live separately in localized homogenous communities. Though one may argue individuals in either group endorse White supremacist beliefs implicitly, at least some individuals may not espouse such beliefs explicitly (especially among those who focus on separation, rather than complete expulsion from one's country; Dobratz & Shanks-Meile, 2000).

These various identity groups tend to share an emphasis on the centrality of their racial identity, pseudoscientific ideas around racial genetics as justification for racial separation and/or supremacy, and a general opposition to multiculturalism. Many, though not all, interpret specific passages from religious texts to provide justification for their beliefs (Berlet & Vysotsky, 2006; Dobratz & Shanks-Meile, 2000; Hoffman, 1995; Ornstein & Ornstein, 2016; Tourist & Wohlforth, 2000). Finally, many of them believe in some version of the great replacement theory and other conspiracy theories about "White genocide," which argue non-White immigration policies are concerted efforts to change the racial and ethnic demographic makeup of North America and Europe to culturally dominate and eventually extinguish those identifying as White (Dobratz & Shanks-Meile, 2000). For our purposes, we will focus on what unites these groups ideologically and use the term "extremist/ism" as an umbrella term, only making specific distinctions when they are theoretically relevant or in direct quotes when individual members or scholars use those terms meaningfully. We choose "extremity" to indicate that the attitudes, beliefs, and behaviors in question exist beyond the pale for most individuals within democratic societies such as the United States.

In the United States, there has been a renewed rise in White extremism since the 2016 election presidential election of Donald Trump (Reyna et al. 2022), observable in both the number of hate groups documented (Wilson, 2020) and the amount of violent hate crimes committed against people of color (e.g., 6,643 hate crimes were committed on the basis of race or ethnicity in 2021, compared to 5,227 in 2020 and 3,963 in 2019; US Department of Justice, 2021, 2023). There is some consensus in the literature that among the many reasons for this rise in White extremism, fear of being "replaced" plays a leading role (Davey & Ebner, 2019; Obaidi et al. 2022). From a psychological perspective, the rhetoric around the great replacement theory points to underlying fears of being excluded from a changing society as well as concerns of status related to social identities concerning race and ethnicity. As one White extremist noted:

> im starting to understand that I am a white guy working hard and a vet and tired of being screwed by this country and all of the bull*** diversity and political correctness that seem to favor all the minorities and leave white men with the shaft.   (Schafer et al., 2014, p. 183)

Along with the rise in prominence of White extremism comes an increase in dissemination of White extremist ideology through traditional and social media outlets that have created echo chambers of right-wing messaging leading to what appears to be a parallel "reality" when perceived from the outside. Importantly, this echo chamber has expanded its reach into the mainstream media. The following of Tucker Carlson – a former Fox News television host known for his vocal support of many far-right ideas, including replacement, as well as his emphasis on an us-versus-them view of society, pitting White conservatives against a leftist "ruling class" (NPR 1A, 2023) – is just one indicator that people receive constant reminders of the supposed threat of being excluded because of their White identity.

4.3 Understanding Extremism and the Radicalization Process

There are various theoretical models focused on the psychological dynamics of extremism and the processes by which one is radicalized into an extremist position. These processes are complex, involving an interplay between individual proclivities and contextual factors (Doosje et al., 2016; Pfundmair et al., this volume). The models focus on perceived threats, often both to oneself personally and to one's group broadly (Beelmann, 2020; Beller & Kröger, 2021; Jasko et al., 2017; Pfundmair, 2019; Pfundmair et al., 2022). These perceived threats can be tangible (such as a loss of job opportunities or resources), interpersonal (discrimination or social exclusion), or symbolic (such as perceived racial replacement). After perceiving the threat(s), these individuals experience deprivation in physical or psychological needs. These needs may be for a sense of personal control (Pfundmair & Mahr, 2022a), compensatory control (Kay & Eibach, 2013), or general sense of meaning and personal significance (Bäck et al., 2018; Ellenberg & Kruglanski, this volume; Jasko et al., 2017; Kruglanski et al., 2009; Renström & Bäck, this volume).

4.3.1 Need for Belonging

Regardless of the specific needs, targets of radicalization are promised that their threatened needs will be satisfied only through joining the extremist group. In many cases, individuals are brought into these groups by friends or acquaintances, which leverages the need for belonging as an overarching persuasion factor (Jasko et al., 2017). Ironically, extremism tends to make individuals more likely to be socially excluded by people outside of the extremist group (Hales & Williams, 2020). Thus, as individuals become more radicalized, they are likely to become more dependent upon the extremist group to sustain a general sense of belonging and perhaps even safety, given that social exclusion can increase people's perceived vulnerability to harm (Dean et al., 2019). Such dependence may be one reason why group dynamics such as in-group love and polarization are important factors in the later stages of the radicalization process (Pfundmair & Mohr, 2022b; Pfundmair et al., 2022).

4.3.2   Threat-Based Rhetoric

Historically, White extremist members, leaders, and their recruitment propaganda have employed threat-based rhetoric, whether it be focused on the individual safety level by highlighting the potential dangers of racial integration (utilizing danger-based stereotypes about persons of color; Dixon & Maddox, 2005; Donders et al., 2008), or highlighting group-level threats by focusing on the perceived discrimination of White individuals by Affirmative Action or social safety-net ("welfare") programs and "racial genocide" (i.e., the perceived elimination of the White demographic group via demographic shifts) by pro-immigration polices (Balzak, 2001; Berbrier, 1998; Dobratz, 2001; Dobratz & Shanks-Meile, 2000; Ornstein & Ornstein, 2016; Schafer et al., 2014). As previously stated, similar rhetoric has leaked into mainstream right-wing media personalities like Tucker Carlson. Carlson's great replacement theory-related rhetoric focuses on a threat to electoral power, such as when he argued that such replacement was a liberal "electoral strategy" (Harvey, 2022) that gives him (and presumably his audience) "less political power" (Michel, 2021). Further, Carlson's rhetoric channels broader existential concerns both symbolically and literally, arguing that modern immigration policies have "changed America completely and forever" (Tucker Carlson [@TuckerCarlson], 2022a) and that these changes will lead to "social collapse" (Tucker Carlson [@TuckerCarlson], 2022b). Similar threat-based rhetoric has occurred in the purported manifestos of racially motivated mass shooters, using words such as "invasion" to describe non-White immigration (Arango et al., 2019).

Some of this rhetoric seems focused on how the sources define – and identify with – the United States, such as Carlson's argument that the country has been negatively changed "completely and forever" by people immigrating "who have no connection to America . . . who don't speak our language and have no idea what the Constitution says and don't care" (Tucker Carlson [@TuckerCarlson], 2022a, 2022b), the mass shooter who argued the country is "rotting from the inside out" (Arango et al., 2019), or American Nazi Party founder George Lincoln Rockwell, who argued "Too many Americans are doing everything possible to hasten the death of our civilization . . . all in the name of 'Brotherhood' and 'Freedom'" (Rockwell, 1972, as cited in Dobratz & Shanks-Meile, 2000, p. 58). Indeed, many individuals involved in White extremist movements argue that their activities focus less on hating out-group members and more on loving and safeguarding the existence of their own in-group, the White (Aryan) race (Berbrier, 1998; Dobratz & Shanks-Meile, 2000; Ornstein &

Ornstein, 2016; Schafer et al., 2014; Vysotsky & McCarthy, 2017). As one White extremist argued, "We are not saying we are better than anybody else. We believe in all races sustaining their own identity" (Anonymous #5, 1989, as cited in Berbrier, 1998, p. 509).

These rhetorical shifts are important for both recruitment and overall group image management to the outside world (Berbrier, 1998). For example, fighting for "White racial freedom" ("The Cause," 1994, as cited in Dobratz & Shanks-Meile, 2000, p. 64) likely sounds more positive to others (and perhaps oneself) than fighting for White supremacy, even if ultimately these two foci amount to the same thing. There are even White extremist groups such as Identity Evropa (later renamed the American Identity Movement), the Identitarian Movement, and Christian identity-based religious groups who use the term "identity" in their titles. Finally, one social-developmental approach to understanding the radicalization process identifies identity problems as a key factor in predicting an orientation toward extremist groups (Beelmann, 2020). All these examples provide evidence that psychologists interested in radicalization and extremism need to be intentional about including the concepts (and related theories) of "self" and "identity" in their theory-building and hypotheses.

4.4   Self, Identity, and Threat

One's sense of "self" can be defined as a system of awareness and agency (Markus & Kitayama, 2010) that allows one efficient navigation of their social, physical, and mental world. This is achieved by monitoring and regulating self-integrity, i.e. being responsive to anything that threatens the idea of the person as "competent, good, coherent, unitary, stable, capable of free choice, capable of controlling important outcomes, and so on" (Steele, 1988, p. 263). There are many ways to conceptualize how a sense of self relates to the idea of "identity." Here we define identity as the ways individuals describe themselves in a given context. A person's self typically contains multiple identities related to personal, relational, and collective mental representations (Brewer & Gardner, 1996; Forgas & Williams, 2002), all of which are social in nature (Sedikides & Brewer, 2001).

Self-esteem, one's general affect for themselves, is a central pillar of a functioning sense of self. It is an inherently social construct, generally derived from perceived evaluation by others (Leary, 1999). Consequently, self-esteem is closely tied to belongingness needs and threatened by experiences of exclusion (Williams, 2009). Importantly, self-esteem is associated with social identity, the part of our self-concept defined by the various groups we belong to. Social identity theory (Tajfel, 1978) holds that identity derived from group memberships fulfills belongingness needs and is associated with self-esteem and pride. Attaching one's individual sense of self to a group's identity is therefore a way to boost self-esteem. In other words, group identity is set up for sense of self to thrive – this allows a person to be in a setting that already provides group-based self-esteem and provides resources for connection and well-being.

Generally, people seek a state of equilibrium for having both personal and social identity goals fulfilled (Kumashiro et al., 2008). Optimal distinctiveness theory (Brewer, 2003) in particular explains how it is functional for humans to be sensitive to both levels of being included in a social group and being distinct as an individual to sustain personal motives to thrive (control, choice). Therefore, people tend to choose large groups to identify with when feeling isolated or otherwise socially vulnerable and instead focus more on distinct identities when needs for protection and inclusion are fulfilled (Brewer, 2003).

People vacillate between these poles when they feel depleted in the fulfillment of their self and identity needs, whether these are personal or relational. A person's sense of self becomes particularly tangible when it emerges under threat (Graupmann, 2018). Threat to the self, in turn, can be defined as whatever hinders or diminishes the maintenance of a positive, functioning self-view embedded in social acceptance. Using the metaphor of a fortress (Graupmann et al., 2013), different self-related motivations can be seen as parts of a larger structure to maintain a person's balance between individual goals and goals relating to remaining a valued partner for social interaction to others (in other words: being socially included).

4.4.1   The Appeal of White Extremism under Identity Threat

In the larger societal discourse, race – despite being a social construct without a biological basis (Smedley & Smedley, 2005) – has been increasingly acknowledged as an identity category that shapes the lived experience for people of color in the United States in the form of transgenerational trauma, as well as in current experience and anticipation of future racist oppression and racist violence. As a consequence, Black identity in particular can be a resource of pride and resilience for Black people living in a racist world (Romero et al., 2014). In contrast, not having to pay attention to race (color-blindness; Ferber, 2012) or not identifying with one's race is often described as being an integral part of White privilege (Hardiman & Keehn, 2011). Consequently, an emphasis on and interest in White identity and White pride can be understood as a reaction to the acknowledgment of race as a meaningful category for people of color in the United States, as well as perceived victimhood (e.g., being the target of "reverse discrimination" or the fear of one's race being "replaced"; Berbrier, 1998; Castle et al., 2018; Dobratz & Shanks-Meile, 2000).

However, Whiteness by itself as an identity – as opposed to identities based on ethnic heritage (e.g. Polish, Italian) – bears little substance until it is imbued with meaning. Such meaning is derived by creating an in-group–out-group dynamic typically characterized by a reciprocal relationship between in-group love and out-group hostility (Brewer, 1999), here based on racial category, distinguishing it from Black identity. Tapping into pseudoscientific ideas related to racial hierarchy and genetic superiority, Whiteness is erected as an ideal that is under threat and needs to be protected (Dobratz & Shanks-Meile, 2000). White extremists infuse even their children's entertainment with such rhetoric, as evidenced in a "White TV" program that involves child actors arguing "if all the races mix, there won't be any more White kids" (Ornstein & Ornstein, 2016).

The models of extremism and radicalization described earlier give reason to assume that understanding the specifics of the motivations surrounding a psychological sense of self, especially in light of its social foundations, can provide rich insight into what psychological needs are being fulfilled through identification with extremist groups in general, but perhaps more so for White extremism, due to its unique role as an extremism movement around a privileged/majority identity.

4.4.2   Self-related Motives and White Extremism

In 2017 the former White extremist turned antiradicalism advocate Christian Picciolini observed, "The allure of power, identity, and purpose is inherent in extremist culture" (Picciolini, 2017a, pp. xxiii–xxiv). These psychological themes, as well as others, are apparent in the research on self-related motives and White extremism. We now will review the research on these themes in detail.

4.4.2.1   Self-esteem, Belonging, and Identity

Economic hardship and insecurity can be experienced as physical pain (Chou et al., 2016). Physical pain, in turn, can negatively impact an individual's basic psychological needs such as self-esteem (Riva et al., 2011). Given previous research finding a connection between these experiences and radicalization among religious and ethnic minoritized communities (Doosje et al., 2013; Obaidi et al., 2019), it is reasonable to expect that these factors would increase radicalization tendencies among White extremists as well. Consequently, White extremist rhetoric appeals to people who have a heightened need for individual and collective self-esteem, which can be provided by larger group identity based on racial categorization (Picciolini, 2017a, 2017b). For example, one White extremist described their increasing racial identification in terms of pride: "I realized how much I loved my ancestry. It made me more proud than ever" (Schafer et al., 2014, p. 185). Sometimes this boosted self-esteem – due to identification with a large group identity – comes with a downward comparison to the racial out-group: "It opened my eyes to how proud I should be to be

White, and how we are so much more powerful and intelligent than any other race" (Schafer et al., 2014, p. 186).

4.4.2.2   Sense of Control and Agency

Having perceived agency or control in one's life is another aspect of a functioning sense of self. One's sense of control is an integral part of psychological well-being. Even an illusory perception of control predicts mental health, particularly in comparison with people suffering from depression, who tend to have more realistic perceptions of the extent of control they have (Alloy et al., 1979; Taylor & Brown, 1988). Direct/primary control is distinguished from indirect/secondary control, with the latter describing attributions of individually uncontrollable outcomes to causes that will explain them (Rothbaum et al., 1982). Secondary control thereby allows for predictability and meaning and preserves motivation toward the exertion of primary control throughout the lifespan (Heckhausen & Schultz, 1995). Threats to control and agency usually are met with attempts toward restoration (Brehm, 1966). White extremism provides a way to reassert a sense of symbolic agency, as one White extremist notes: "[minoritized individuals] CAN express their pride but when people like us [whites] do it, we're racist and all. I think its stupid that they're allowed to voice they're [sic] heritage and we're not" (Schafer et al., 2014, p. 186).

One way in which the desire to maintain control relates to identification with extremist groups and ideologies is conceptualized in uncertainty-identity theory (Hogg, 2014; Wagoner & Hogg, this volume). When people feel uncertain about the world, their status, and their relationships with others, planning behavior, exerting control, and predicting outcomes (secondary control) becomes difficult, and often this uncertainty results in anxiety and the motivation to decrease uncertainty. One efficient way to reduce uncertainty about a complex and changing social environment is through social categorization. Identifying with a social group and categorizing others into that same or a different group identity drastically reduces the complexity of one's social world, as in/out-group categorization provides one a heuristic to predict someone's perceived loyalty and expected behavior (Hogg, 2014).

Highly distinctive and entitative groups, like groups that promote extremist ideas about race, lend themselves well to reducing uncertainty, which is why people may be likely to identify even with low-status groups the greater their perceived uncertainty is (Reid & Hogg, 2005). Former Fox News host Tucker Carlson focused on a hybrid of political and working-class identity, arguing that liberally oriented rich individuals had stacked the deck against working-class US citizens: "They want to control you" (New York Times, August 30, 2022); "This is too much change" (Tucker Carlson [@TuckerCarlson], 2022a). Whereas some may argue that Carlson added race into this identity mix by suggesting ideas related to the great replacement theory (NPR 1A, 2023),

US-based White extremists have directly advocated for racial supremacy as a means of survival and flourishing framed simply as in-group preservation: "Loving your own race – our Aryan race – and putting the survival and self preservation of our 'folk' above all else. The White Race First!" (Dobratz, 2001, p. 288).

4.4.2.3 Self-continuity

Perceiving one's self as continuous over time is another important aspect of ensuring self-integrity and efficient navigation in a highly complex social world. Research on terror management theory suggests that threats to a person's *self-continuity* in the form of death reminders can increase identification with one's in-group's culture (cultural worldview defense; Solomon et al., 1991) for the purpose of symbolic immortality as a coping mechanism for dealing with existential anxiety. Indeed, research demonstrates that reminding White individuals of their mortality increases their support for White extremism (Greenberg et al., 2001). Thus, White extremist rhetoric in the vein of the great replacement theory seems particularly well suited to activate existential threat on the group level and to heighten defensive coping imbuing White racial identity with life-transcending meaning. For example, perception of demographic shifts toward a decline in the non-Hispanic White population has been associated with greater collective existential threat (measured with items such as "My racial group faces a threat to its existence"), which has been shown to mediate an increase of support for far-right political groups (Bai & Federico, 2021). The White extremist organization SS Action Group (n.d.) further illustrates this perceived existential threat in their promotional material when stating: "We believe that this country was built by White people, and that minorities, non-White crime, and racial treason are ruining this nation. We are witnessing the virtual destruction of our White Aryan culture and heritage in every aspect of daily living" (as cited in Dobratz & Shanks-Meile, 2000, p. 62).

4.4.2.4 Consistency

Cognitive dissonance occurs when one's attitudes, values, beliefs, and behaviors are not compatible with each other. When individuals become aware of such incongruence, they generally seek ways to reduce or eliminate the dissonance (Festinger, 1957) and restore a general sense of self-integrity (Steele, 1988). Further, perceived consistency in oneself and in others is a key component of interpersonal trust (Cialdini et al., 1995). Inequity, racism, and oppression, when clearly visible in a society, can be seen as large inconsistencies for individuals, especially when they experience a certain amount of privilege. It is difficult to think of oneself as a genuinely good person when faced with the reality that one lives in and benefits from a society with a disproportionate distribution of poverty, lack of access to education, subjection to police violence, and other injustices toward people of color. One way to reduce the resulting dissonance is to seek confirmation for this status quo through ideas around racial superiority and deservedness as provided by White extremist ideology. As one White extremist publication argues:

> Our people have explored the frontier, have conquered diseases, have tamped wilderness, have looked deep into the heavens ... Our people have given much to the advancement of civilization and what a pity it would be if our people should cease to exist.
>
> (Dobratz & Shanks-Meile, 2000, p. 124)

4.5   A Self-Threat-Informed Perspective on White Racial Identity

The inherently social nature of one's sense of self emerges in the ways self-related motives are tied evolutionarily to how one is treated by others. To ensure inclusion for survival, humans theoretically evolved to perceive the smallest cues of exclusion (Spoor & Williams, 2007; Wesselmann et al., 2012). US demographic trends suggest that eventually people who identify as racially White will be a minority, and this perception leads to greater racial bias in those White individuals who view this trend as threatening (Craig & Richeson, 2014). Given the rhetoric of the great replacement theory and White extremist literature, these demographic shifts likely provided the biggest threat toward individuals who center Whiteness at the center of their identity.

White individuals often receive information about this demographic shift, yet many of these individuals do not become White extremists. As such, how does one identify and forestall the radicalization process into White extremism? Qualitative analyses demonstrate that White extremists often identify key moments in which they become aware of their racial identity and the importance that race often plays in US society, and that these moments propelled them on their path of radicalization (Berbrier, 1998; Blee, 1996; Dobratz & Shanks-Meile, 2000; Schafer et al., 2014). But does racial identification have to be yoked to racial extremism? Does racial in-group love need to involve outgroup hate?

4.5.1   Racial Identity Development

Clinicians studying racial identity have developed models focused on facilitating the development of a "healthy" racial identity across various racial and ethnic groups (Atkinson et al., 1997; Cross, Jr. & Vandiver, 2001; Hardiman & Keehn, 2011; Helms, 1997; Phinney, 1996; Ruiz, 1990; Sabnani et al., 1991; Scott & Robinson, 2001; Sellers et al., 1998). Though each model contains culturally specific nuances, collectively these models define a "healthy" racial identity as a centering of one's racial identity as a key part of the self but at the same time recognizes it is only one part of one's overall identity, as well as celebrating the racial and ethnic diversity of others who are included in one's broader in-group, such as one's national identity (Schwarzbaum & Thomas, 2013). In other words, whether one is Black, White, and so on, each person can celebrate all racial heritages equally with no group subsuming another.

4.5.1.1 White Identity Dissonance

Collectively, these models note that a key tension occurs when people become aware of their racial identity and how it relates to the racial imbalance inherent in US society. For White individuals, this awareness often involves moving from a privileged state of color-blindness to one of recognizing that race is an important sociopolitical variable (Hardiman & Keehn, 2011; Helms, 1997; Sabnani et al., 1991; Scott & Robinson, 2001). Typically, the recognition that one has benefited from a systemic racial hierarchy can produce cognitive dissonance in White individuals – an unpleasant emotional state that one needs to reduce to tolerable levels. Such dissonance may be intensely acute for individuals who have internalized a "just world" worldview or for those who have an idealized view of egalitarianism in US history, perhaps increasing their likelihood of reducing it by doubling down on support for White supremacy-based systems and resisting attempts to dismantle these systems (Hughes, 2018; Wilkins & Wenger, 2014).

One White racial identity development model (Helms, 1997) posits a few key ways for White individuals to reduce this dissonance. First, one can retreat into a state of color-blindness and deny their newfound awareness of the importance of race in individuals' daily lives. Indeed, such retreat can be linked to the general concept of White fragility and the desire to ensure one's racial identity is invulnerable to threatening information (Applebaum, 2017; Ford et al., 2022). Second, one can acknowledge the racialized aspects of US society and develop further beliefs to justify the imbalance favoring one's racial in-group. These beliefs often involve both positive views of one's in-group, negative views of one's out-groups, and sometimes a desire to avoid out-groups completely. This second option fits with research on charting White individuals' radicalization process, regardless of whether they identify as a White "supremacist," "nationalist," or "separatist" (Blee, 1996; Dobratz & Shanks-Meile, 2000; Schafer et al., 2014). Other research suggests that endorsing a White identity correlates with endorsement for White extremism and political leaders aligned with these efforts (Long, 2022). Thus, how White individuals respond to this race-based cognitive dissonance is crucial to understanding how to short-circuit the White extremist radicalization process.

White racial identity development models typically argue that individuals can develop a healthy racial identity by engaging in the difficult process of overcoming this dissonance in such a way that they fully recognize the history of systemic racism in the United States, feel positive self-respect regarding their White racial identity, and celebrating non-White identities as part of their broader in-group (Helms, 1997; Rowe et al., 1994). This goal converges with identity complexity theory (Brewer & Pierce 2005; Roccas & Brewer, 2002), which argues that the more people are aware of their own set of social identities being distinct from each other while crosscutting with identities of people they might consider as out-group on the basis of just one of their identities, the less prejudiced and the more accepting they are of minoritized groups.

4.5.1.2   Toward a Healthy White Identity

Still, the key question is, how does one provide White individuals the framework to move from an initial state of color-blind obliviousness to an advocate of antiracism who works toward a future where everyone feels appreciation and respect for their own and each other's racial heritage? How can people attain identification with Whiteness that is positive and does not operate from a place of being threatened, and thus can be accepting and valuing of other racial identities? Such a process is challenging given that terms such as "White pride" have been weaponized by White extremists groups (Berbrier, 1998; Dobratz & Shanks-Meile, 2000), making them controversial concepts in general society that may be tough to reclaim. Further, many recent challenges to antiracist educational efforts hinge on the fear that such efforts may make White individuals (especially children) feel guilty about their White identity (Farrington, 2022; Scully, 2022).

Importantly, guilt and other stressful emotions are a key part of moving beyond a color-blind identity stage (Hardiman & Keehn, 2011; Helms, 1997). Perhaps one way to harness these emotions toward healthy identity development for White individuals who are in this portion of the identity process is to encourage them to draw on the self-compassion literature (Germer & Neff, 2013; MacBeth & Gumley, 2012; Neff, 2011). This literature encourages sitting with these uncomfortable emotions in a way that encourages growth-focused self-reflection.

Additionally, centering historian Ibram X. Kendi's (2019) argument that antiracism is a daily process with which those committed to antiracism (himself included) struggle might be a way to surpass ego-defense motivations in White people when engaging with issues around social justice and equity.

Research suggests that a key reason why White individuals may push back against diversity, equity, and inclusion (DEI) initiatives is because they perceive these initiatives as threatening, especially to their identity (Iyer, 2022; Kachanoff et al., 2022). Here, Kendi's (2019) antiracism framework provides the potential to mitigate the self-related threat inherent in the acceptance of the notion of living in an unequal, racist society. By emphasizing that "racist" is not a "permanent label" reserved for specific individuals, but instead something inherent in the systemic inequities in a racist *society*, leaving *everyone* responsible for engaging in antiracist behaviors, it provides individuals a way to acknowledge their previous failings in a growth-focused mindset and emphasizes their ability to change in ways that preserve their overall sense of self-consistency with the egalitarian desires toward most people aspire. Preliminary research (Graupmann et al., 2023) has explored Kendi's (2019) antiracism framework as a DEI framing device experimentally. Predominantly White college students who read about Kendi's framework indicated more agreement with uncomfortable truths about racism and racial inequities (e.g. "The justice system favors Whiteness") than those in the control condition (who read a neutral passage). Further, these students showed no correlation between perceived self-related threat and their endorsement of those truths. While those in the control condition indicated more self-related threat the more they agreed with the statements about racial inequities, there was no such association between self-related threat and the acknowledgment of racial inequities for those who had read Kendi's antiracism passage. This may indicate that Kendi's antiracism framework allows people to engage with antiracism without getting defensive regarding their own identity.

There may be other potential ways to facilitate White individuals' identity transition from color-blind to being a proud White antiracist immune to the lure of White extremism. Social psychologist Marilynn Brewer (1999) has argued that the transition from in-group love to out-group hate is a slippery slope that individuals of various identity categories fall down too easily. There are key factors that contribute to this process, however, and thus viable solutions involve addressing these factors. These factors are multifaceted and present complex challenges, though one key approach may be to encourage White individuals to recognize that as they are finding pride in their racial identity, it is only one part of their self-concept and need not be the only (or most important) facet on which to focus (Brewer, 1999). Further, taking pride in one's racial in-group does not need to come at the expense of out-groups. People can and do have concentric loyalties to various in-groups, all of which they can be proud of while also celebrating other group members' pride in their diverse identities.

4.6 Conclusion

Extremism is a threat to living safely in culturally diverse communities everywhere. The palpable racial inequities that systemically and disproportionately disadvantage people of color in the United States (Ipsos Survey, 2023) make racial categorizations salient also because there is a growing momentum in the general population to attain social justice. White extremism has increasingly entered mainstream communication channels over the last decade and is weaponizing the salience of racial identity via threat-based rhetoric. White extremist groups have used this rhetoric to imbue Whiteness with idolized meaning (Reyna et al. 2022). We argue that these groups tap into threatened areas of the psychological sense of self and offer a seemingly simple narrative solution for potential recruits to regain a sense of esteem, control, continuity, and belonging.

In light of this, we argue that merging racial identity models from counseling psychology with social-psychological theories of self and identity can help researchers interested in understanding and defusing White extremism to develop potential intervention approaches. Specifically, White individuals are most vulnerable to White extremist rhetoric when they are experiencing threats to their sense of self, whether at the individual, relational, and/or collective level, especially if these threats are experienced as being racially oriented. Strategies that likely will be most effective in providing pathways to healthy racial identity development are ones that provide an opportunity for positive feelings toward one's own race as well as others. Importantly, they should fulfill various psychological needs (e.g., self-integrity and belonging) while sustaining complex cross-racial cultural identities. If our society wishes to continue the necessary and important work of dismantling White supremacy-based systems and encouraging White individuals to engage actively in antiracism efforts, we need to make sure that – when challenging White individuals who are in the color-blind stage of identity development – we do not leave a self-related void that White extremist groups will be happy to fill.

References

Alloy, L. B., & Abramson, L. Y. (1979). Judgment of contingency in depressed and nondepressed students: Sadder but wiser? *Journal of Experimental Psychology: General, 108*(4), 441–485. https://doi.org/10.1037/0022-3514.41.6.1129

Anonymous #5 (1989). Notes of interest: White power. *The Populist Observer, 36* (Jan.), 17–19.

Applebaum, B. (2017). Comforting discomfort as complicity: White fragility and the pursuit of invulnerability. *Hypatia, 32*(4), 862–875. https://doi.org/10.1111/hypa.12352

Arango, T., Bogel-Burroughs, N., & Benner, K. (2019, August 3). Minutes before El Paso killing, hate-filled manifesto appears online. *New York Times.* www.nytimes.com/2019/08/03/us/patrick-crusius-el-paso-shooter-manifesto.html

Atkinson, D. R., Morten, G., & Sue, D. W. (1997). A minority identity development model. In K. Arnold & I. C. King (Eds.), *College student development and academic life: Psychological, intellectual, social, and moral issues* (pp. 193–205). Garland Publishing.

Bäck, E. A., Bäck, H., Altermark, N., & Knapton, H. (2018). The quest for significance: Attitude adaption to a radical group following social exclusion. *International Journal of Developmental Science, 12*(1–2), 25–36. https://doi.org/10.3233/DEV-170230

Bai, H., & Federico, C. M. (2021). White and minority demographic shifts, intergroup threat, and right-wing extremism. *Journal of Experimental Social Psychology, 94*, 104–114. https://doi.org/10.1016/j.jesp.2021.104114

Beelmann, A. (2020). A social-developmental model of radicalization: A systematic integration of existing theories and empirical research. *International Journal of Conflict and Violence, 14*(1), 1–14. https://doi.org/10.4119/ijcv-3778

Beller, J., & Kröger, C. (2021). Religiosity and perceived religious discrimination as predictors of support for suicide attacks among Muslim Americans. *Peace and Conflict: Journal of Peace Psychology, 27*(4), 554–567. https://doi.org/10.1037/pac0000460

Berbrier, M. (1998). White supremacists and the (pan-)ethnic imperative: On "European-Americans" and "White student unions." *Sociological Inquiry, 68*(4), 498–516. https://doi.org/10.1111/j.1475-682X.1998.tb00482.x

Berlet, C., & Vysotsky, S. (2006). Overview of US white supremacist groups. *Journal of Political & Military Sociology, 34*(1), 11–48. www.jstor.org/stable/45294185

Blazak, R. (2001). White boys to terrorist men. *American Behavioral Scientist, 44*(6), 982–1000. https://doi.org/10.1177/00027640121956629

Blee, K. M. (1996). Becoming a racist: Women in contemporary Ku Klux Klan and neo-Nazi groups. *Gender & Society, 10*(6), 680–702. https://doi.org/10.1177/089124396010006002

Bond, S. (2023, April 25). How Tucker Carlson took fringe conspiracy theories to a mass audience. NPR Morning Edition. www.npr.org/2023/04/25/1171800317/how-tucker-carlsons-extremist-narratives-shaped-fox-news-and-conservative-politi

Brehm, J. W. (1966). *A theory of psychological reactance.* Academic Press.

Brewer, M. B. (1999). The psychology of prejudice: Ingroup love and outgroup hate? *Journal of Social Issues, 55*(3), 429–444. https://doi.org/10.1111/0022-4537.00126

Brewer, M. B. (2003). Optimal distinctiveness, social identity, and the self. In M. R. Leary & J. P. Tangney (Eds.), *Handbook of self and identity* (pp. 480–491). Guilford Press.

Brewer, M. B., & Gardner, W. (1996). Who is this "we"? Levels of collective identity and self representations. *Journal of Personality & Social Psychology, 71*(1), 83–93.

Brewer, M. B., & Pierce, K. P. (2005). Social identity complexity and outgroup tolerance. *Personality and Social Psychology Bulletin, 31*(3), 428–437. https://doi.org/10.1177/0146167204271710

Castle, T., Kristiansen, L., & Shifflett, L. (2020). White racial activism and paper terrorism: a case study in far-right propaganda. *Deviant Behavior, 41*(2), 252–267. https://doi.org/10.1080/01639625.2018.1557380

Chou, E. Y., Parmar, B. L., & Galinsky, A. D. (2016). Economic insecurity increases physical pain. *Psychological Science, 27*(4), 443–454. https://doi.org/10.1177/0956797615625640

Cialdini, R. B., Trost, M. R., & Newsom, J. T. (1995). Preference for consistency: The development of a valid measure and the discovery of surprising behavioral implications. *Journal of Personality and Social Psychology, 69*(2), 318–328. https://doi.org/10.1037/0022-3514.69.2.318

Craig, M. A., & Richeson, J. A. (2014). On the precipice of a "majority-minority" America: Perceived status threat from the racial demographic shift affects White Americans' political ideology. *Psychological Science, 25*(6), 1189–1197. https://doi.org/10.1177/0956797614527113

Cross, Jr., W. E., & Vandiver, B. J. (2001). Nigrescence theory and measurement: Introducing the Cross Racial Identity Scale (CRIS). In J. G. Ponterotto, J. M. Casas, L. A. Suzuki, & C. M. Alexander (Eds.), *Handbook of multicultural counseling* (2nd ed.; pp. 371–393). Sage.

Davey, J., & Ebner, J. (2019). "The great replacement": The violent consequences of mainstreamed extremism. *Institute for Strategic Dialogue, 7,* 1–36.

Dean, K. K., Wentworth, G., & LeCompte, N. (2019). Social exclusion and perceived vulnerability to physical harm. *Self & Identity, 18*(1), 87–102. https://doi.org/10.1080/15298868.2017.1370389

Dixon, T. L., & Maddox, K. B. (2005). Skin tone, crime news, and social reality judgments: Priming the stereotype of the dark and dangerous black criminal. *Journal of Applied Social Psychology, 35*(8), 1555–1570. https://doi.org/10.1111/j.1559-1816.2005.tb02184.x

Dobratz, B. A. (2001). The role of religion in the collective identity of the white racialist movement. *Journal for the Scientific Study of Religion, 40*(2), 287–301. https://doi.org/10.1111/0021-8294.00056

Dobratz, B. A., & Shanks-Meile, S. L. (2000). *The white separatist movement in the United States: "White power, white pride!"* Johns Hopkins University Press.

Donders, N. C., Correll, J., & Wittenbrink, B. (2008). Danger stereotypes predict racially biased attentional allocation. *Journal of Experimental Social Psychology, 44*(5), 1328–1333. https://doi.org/10.1016/j.jesp.2008.04.002

Doosje, B., Loseman, A., & Van Den Bos, K. (2013). Determinants of radicalization of Islamic youth in the Netherlands: Personal uncertainty, perceived injustice, and perceived group threat. *Journal of Social Issues, 69*(3), 586–604.

Doosje, B., Moghaddam, F.M., Kruglanski, A.W., et al. (2016). Terrorism, radicalization and de-radicalization. *Current Opinion in Psychology, 11,* 79–84. https://doi.org/10.1016/j.copsyc.2016.06.008

Ekman, M. (2022). The great replacement: Strategic mainstreaming of far-right conspiracy claims. *Convergence, 28*(4), 1127–1143. https://doi.org/10.1177/13548565221091983

Farrington, B. (2022, January 18). Florida could shield whites from "discomfort" of racist past. Associated Press. https://apnews.com/article/business-florida-law suits-ron-desantis-racial-injustice-3ec10492b7421543315acf4491813c1b

Ferber, A. L. (2012). The culture of privilege: Color-blindness, postfeminism, and christonormativity. *Journal of Social Issues, 68*(1), 63–77. https://doi.org/10.1111/j.1540-4560.2011.01736.x

Festinger, L. (1957). *A theory of cognitive dissonance.* Stanford University Press.

Ford, B. Q., Green, D. J., & Gross, J. J. (2022). White fragility: An emotion regulation perspective. *American Psychologist, 77*(4), 510–524. https://doi.org/10.1037/amp0000968

Forgas, J. P., & Williams, K. D. (2002). The social self: Introduction and overview. In J. P. Forgas & K. D. Williams (Eds.), *The social self: Cognitive, interpersonal, and intergroup perspectives* (pp. 1–18). Psychology Press.

Germer, C. K., & Neff, K. D. (2013). Self-compassion in clinical practice. *Journal of Clinical Psychology, 69*(8), 856–867. https://doi.org/10.1002/jclp.22021

Graupmann, V. (2018). Show me what threatens you, and I can tell who you are: Perception of threat and the self. *Self & Identity, 17*(4), 407–417. https://doi.org/10.1080/15298868.2017.1412346

Graupmann, V., Frey, D., & Streicher, B. (2013). The self-fortress: motivational responses to threats to the self. In B. O. Hunter & T. J. Romero (Eds.), *Psychology of threat* (pp. 1–29). Nova Science Publishers.

Graupmann, V., Vazquez, K., Vazquez, M., & Dulaney, E. (2023). *Comfort with the uncomfortable: Using an anti-racist framework to mitigate threat to the self.* Unpublished manuscript.

Greenberg, J., Schimel, J., Martens, A., Solomon, S., & Pyszczynski, T. (2001). Sympathy for the devil: Evidence that reminding Whites of their mortality promotes more favorable reactions to White racists. *Motivation & Emotion, 25*(2), 113–133. https://doi.org/10.1023/A:1010613909207

Hales, A. H., & Williams, K. D. (2018) Marginalized individuals and extremism: The role of ostracism in openness to extreme groups. *Journal of Social Issues, 74* (1), 75–92. https://doi.org/10.1111/josi.12257

Hales, A. H., & Williams, K. D. (2020) Extremism leads to ostracism. *Social Psychology, 51*(3), 149–156. https://doi.org/10.1027/1864-9335/a000406

Hardiman, R., & Keehn, M. (2011). White identity development revisited: Listening to White students. In C. Wijeyesinghe & B. W. Jackson (Eds.), *New perspectives on racial identity development: Integrating emerging frameworks* (2nd ed.; pp. 121–137). New York University Press.

Harvey, J. (2022, July 19). *Tucker Carlson all out embraces "great replacement" theory.* Huffington Post. www.huffpost.com/entry/tucker-carlson-great-replacement_n_62d76c96e4b081f3a8f87d45

Heckhausen, J., & Schulz, R. (1995). A life-span theory of control. *Psychological Review, 102*(2), 284–304. https://doi.org/10.1037/0033-295X.102.2.284

Helms, J. E. (1997). Toward a model of white racial identity development. In K. Arnold & I. C. King (Eds.), *College student development and academic life: Psychological, intellectual, social, and moral issues* (pp. 207–224). Garland Publishing.

Hoffman, B. (1995). "Holy terror": The implications of terrorism motivated by a religious imperative. *Studies in Conflict & Terrorism, 18*(4), 271–284. https://doi.org/10.1080/10576109508435985

Hogg, M. A. (2014). From Uncertainty to Extremism: Social Categorization and Identity Processes. *Current Directions in Psychological Science, 23*(5), 338–342. https://doi.org/10.1177/0963721414540168

Hughes, R. T. (2018). *Myths America lives by: White supremacy and the stories that give us meaning* (2nd ed.). University of Illinois Press.

Ipsos (2023, June 15). *Majority of Americans believe racism adds barriers to people of color's success.* www.ipsos.com/en-us/majority-americans-believe-racism-adds-barriers-people-colors-success

Iyer, A. (2022). Understanding advantaged groups' opposition to diversity, equity, and inclusion (DEI) policies: The role of perceived threat. *Social and Personality Psychology Compass, 16*(5), e12666. https://doi.org/10.1111/spc3.12666

Jaffe, A., & Siemaszko, C. (2016, June 23). *Outrage as Trump inspired candidate wants to "Make America White Again."* NBC News. www.nbcnews.com/news/us-news/outrage-trump-inspired-congressional-candidate-wants-make-amer ica-white-again-n597916

Jasko, K., LaFree, G., & Kruglanski, A. (2017). Quest for significance and violent extremism: The case of domestic radicalization. *Political Psychology, 38*(5), 815–831.

Kachanoff, F. J., Kteily, N., & Gray, K. (2022). Equating silence with violence: When white Americans feel threatened by anti-racist messages. *Journal of Experimental Social Psychology, 102*, 104348. https://doi.org/10.1016/j.jesp.2022.104348

Katersky, A., & Hutchinson, B. (2022, October 18). *Buffalo mass shooting suspect 'radicalized' by fringe social media: NY attorney general.* ABC News. https://abcnews.go.com/US/buffalo-mass-shooting-suspect-radicalized-fringe-social-media/story?id=91670651

Kay, A. C., & Eibach, R. P. (2013). Compensatory control and its implications for ideological extremism. *Journal of Social Issues, 69*(3), 564–585. https://doi.org/10.1111/josi.12029

Kendi, I. X. (2019). *How to be an antiracist.* One World.

King's College London. (2023, June 13). *"Great replacement theory" and conspiracies about 15-minute cities, cost of living and digital currencies said to be definitely or probably true by one in three in UK.* King's College London News Centre. www.kcl.ac.uk/news/great-replacement-theory-and-conspiracies-about-15-minute-cities-cost-of-living-and-digital-currencies-said-to-be-defin itely-or-probably-true-by-one-in-three-in-uk

Kruglanski, A. W., Chen, X., Dechesne, M., Fishman, S., & Orehek, E. (2009). Fully committed: Suicide bombers' motivation and the quest for personal significance. *Political Psychology, 30*(3), 331–357.

Kumashiro, M., Rusbult, C. E., & Finkel, E. J. (2008). Navigating personal and relational concerns: The quest for equilibrium. *Journal of Personality & Social Psychology, 95*(1), 94–110. https://doi.org/10.1037/0022-3514.95.1.94

Leary, M. R. (1999). Making sense of self-esteem. *Current Directions in Psychological Science, 8*(1), 32–35. https://doi.org/10.1111/1467-8721.00008

Long, S. (2023). White identity, Donald Trump, and the mobilization of extremism. *Politics, Groups, & Identities, 11*(3), 638–666. https://doi.org/10.1080/21565503.2022.2025868

MacBeth, A., & Gumley, A. (2012). Exploring compassion: A meta-analysis of the association between self-compassion and psychopathology. *Clinical Psychology Review, 32*(6), 545–552. https://doi.org/10.1016/j.cpr.2012.06.003

Markus, H. R., & Kitayama, S. (2010). Cultures and selves: A cycle of mutual constitution. *Perspectives on Psychological Science, 5*(4), 420–430. https://doi.org/10.1177/1745691610375557

Michel, C. (2021, April 12). Fox News star Tucker Carlson's "great replacement" segment used a new frame for an old fear. NBC News. www.nbcnews.com/think/opinion/tucker-carlson-s-great-replacement-fox-news-segment-uses-newer-ncna1263880

Neff, K. D. (2011). Self-compassion, self-esteem, and well-being. *Social & Personality Psychology Compass, 5*(1), 1–12. https://doi.org/10.1111/j.1751-9004.2010.00330.x

Neidig, H., & Beitsch, R. (2021, May 12). *Biden officials testify that white supremacists are greatest domestic security threat.* The Hill. https://thehill.com/policy/national-security/553161-biden-officials-testify-that-white-supremacists-are-greatest/

Neville, H. A., Awad, G. H., Brooks, J. E., Flores, M. P., & Bluemel, J. (2013). Color-blind racial ideology: Theory, training, and measurement implications in psychology. *American Psychologist, 68*(6), 455–466. https://doi.org/10.1037/a0033282

New York Times (2022, April 20). *Inside the apocalyptic worldview of 'Tucker Carlson Tonight'.* www.nytimes.com/interactive/2022/04/30/us/tucker-carlson-tonight.html

NPR 1A (2023, April 26). *Tucker Carlson is out at Fox. What happened?* www.npr.org/2023/04/25/1171951112/tucker-carlson-is-out-at-fox-what-happened

Obaidi, M., Bergh, R., Akrami, N., & Anjum, G. (2019). Group-based relative deprivation explains endorsement of extremism among Western-born Muslims. *Psychological Science, 30*(4), 596–605. https://doi.org/10.1177/0956797619834879

Obaidi, M., Kunst, J., Ozer, S., & Kimel, S. Y. (2022). The "great replacement" conspiracy: How the perceived ousting of whites can evoke violent extremism and Islamophobia. *Group Processes & Intergroup Relations, 25*(7), 1675–1695. https://doi.org/10.1177/13684302211028293

Ornstein, M. (director/producer), & Ornstein, N. (producer). (2016). *Accidental courtesy: Daryl Davis, race, and America.* First Run Features.

Pfundmair, M. (2019). Ostracism promotes a terroristic mindset. *Behavioral Sciences of Terrorism & Political Aggression, 11*(2), 134–148. https://doi.org/10.1080/19434472.2018.1443965

Pfundmair, M., Aßmann, E., Kiver, E., et al. (2022) Pathways toward Jihadism in Western Europe: an empirical exploration of a comprehensive model of terrorist radicalization. *Terrorism & Political Violence, 34*(1), 48–70. https://doi.org/10.1080/09546553.2019.1663828

Pfundmair, M., & Mahr, L. A. (2022a). Regaining power: How feelings of exclusion during COVID-19 are associated with radicalism among critics of containment policies. *Frontiers in Psychology*, *13*, 952760.

Pfundmair, M., & Mahr, L. A. (2022b). How group processes push excluded people into a radical mindset: An experimental investigation. *Group Processes & Intergroup Relations*. https://doi.org/10.1177/13684302221107782

Phinney, J. S. (1996). When we talk about American ethnic groups, what do we mean? *American Psychologist*, *51*(9), 918–927. https://doi.org/10.1037/0003-066X.51.9.918

Picciolini, C. (2017a). *White American youth: My descent into America's most violent hate movement – and how I got out*. Hachette Book.

Picciolini, C. (2017b, November). *My descent into America's neo-Nazi movement*. TEDxMileHigh. www.ted.com/talks/christian_picciolini_my_descent_into_a merica_s_neo_nazi_movement_and_how_i_got_out

Reid, S. A., & Hogg, M. A. (2005). Uncertainty reduction, self-enhancement, and ingroup identification. *Personality and Social Psychology Bulletin*, *31*(6), 804–817. https://doi.org/10.1177/0146167204271708

Reyna, C., Bellovary, A., & Harris, K. (2022). The psychology of white nationalism: Ambivalence towards a changing America. *Social Issues & Policy Review*, *16*(1), 79–124.

Riva, P., Wirth, J. H., & Williams, K. D. (2011). The consequences of pain: The social and physical pain overlap on psychological responses. *European Journal of Social Psychology*, *41*(6), 681–687. https://doi.org/10.1002/ejsp.837

Roccas, S., & Brewer, M. B. (2002). Social identity complexity. *Personality and Social Psychology Review*, *6*(2), 88–106. https://doi.org/10.1207/S15327957PSPR0602_01

Rockwell, G. L. (1972). *White power*. Ragnarok Press.

Romero, A. J., Edwards, L. M., Fryberg, S. A., & Orduña, M. (2014). Resilience to discrimination stress across ethnic identity stages of development. *Journal of Applied Social Psychology*, *44*(1), 1–11. https://doi.org/10.1111/jasp.12192

Rose, S. (2022). A deadly ideology: How the "great replacement theory" went mainstream. *The Guardian*. www.theguardian.com/world/2022/jun/08/a-deadly-ideology-how-the-great-replacement-theory-went-mainstream

Rothbaum, F., Weisz, J. R., & Snyder, S. S. (1982). Changing the world and changing the self: A two-process model of perceived control. *Journal of Personality & Social Psychology*, *42*(1), 5–37. https://doi.org/10.1037/0022-3514.42.1.5

Rowe, W., Bennett, S. K., & Atkinson, D. R. (1994). White racial identity models: A critique and alternative proposal. *The Counseling Psychologist*, *22*(1), 129–146. https://doi.org/10.1177/0011000094221009

Ruiz, A. S. (1990). Ethnic identity: Crisis and resolution. *Journal of Multicultural Counseling & Development*, *18*(1), 29–40. https://doi.org/10.1002/j.2161-1912.1990.tb00434.x

Sabnani, H. B., Ponterotto, J. G., & Borodovsky, L. G. (1991). White racial identity development and cross-cultural counselor training: A stage model. *The Counseling Psychologist*, *19*(1), 76–102. https://doi.org/10.1177/0011000091191007

Schafer, J. A., Mullins, C. W., & Box, S. (2014). Awakenings: The emergence of white supremacist ideologies. *Deviant Behavior*, *35*(3), 173–196. https://doi.org/10.1080/01639625.2013.834755

Schwarzbaum, S. E., & Thomas, A. J. (2013). *Dimensions of multicultural counseling: A life story approach*. Sage.

Scott, D. A., & Robinson, T. L. (2001). White male identity development: The key model. *Journal of Counseling & Development*, *79*(4), 415–421. https://doi.org/10.1002/j.1556-6676.2001.tb01988.x

Scully, R. (2022, January 20). *Bill to ban lessons making white students feel "discomfort" advances in Florida Senate*. The Hill. https://thehill.com/homenews/state-watch/590554-bill-to-ban-lessons-making-white-students-feel-discomfort-advances-in/

Sedikides, C., & Brewer, M. B. (2001). Individual self, relational self, and collective self: Partners, opponents, or strangers? In C. Sedikides & M. B. Brewer (Eds.), *Individual self, relational self, cognitive self* (pp. 1–4). Psychology Press.

Sellers, R. M., Smith, M. A., Shelton, J. N., Rowley, S. A., & Chavous, T. M. (1998). Multidimensional model of racial identity: A reconceptualization of African American racial identity. *Personality & Social Psychology Review*, *2*(1), 18–39. https://doi.org/10.1207/s15327957pspr0201_2

Smedley, A., & Smedley, B. D. (2005). Race as biology is fiction, racism as a social problem is real: Anthropological and historical perspectives on the social construction of race. *American Psychologist*, *60*(1), 16–26. https://doi.org/10.1037/0003-066X.60.1.16

Solomon, S., Greenberg, J., & Pyszczynski, T. (1991). A terror management theory of social behavior: The psychological functions of self-esteem and cultural worldviews. In M. P. Zanna (Ed.), *Advances in experimental social psychology* (Vol. 24, pp. 93–159). Academic Press. https://doi.org/10.1016/S0065-2601(08)60328-7

Spoor, J., & Williams, K. D. (2007). The evolution of an ostracism detection system. In J. P. Forgas, M. Haselton, & W. von Hippel (Eds.), *The evolution of the social mind: Evolutionary psychology and social cognition* (pp. 279–292). Psychology Press.

SS Action Group (n. d.). *Who we are and what we are all about*. Aryans Awake!

Steele, C. M. (1988). The psychology of self-affirmation: Sustaining the integrity of the self. In L. Berkowitz (Ed.), *Advances in experimental social psychology* (Vol. 21, pp. 261–302). Academic Press. https://doi.org/10.1016/S0065-2601(08)60229-4

Sullivan, E., & Benner, K. (2021, May 12). Top law enforcement officials say the biggest domestic terror threat comes from white supremacists. *New York Times*. www.nytimes.com/2021/05/12/us/politics/domestic-terror-white-supremacists.html

Swim, J. K., Aikin, K. J., Hall, W. S., & Hunter, B. A. (1995). Sexism and racism: Old-fashioned and modern prejudices. *Journal of Personality & Social Psychology*, *68*(2), 199–214. https://doi.org/10.1037/0022-3514.68.2.199

Tajfel, H. (Ed.). (1978). *Differentiation between social groups: Studies in the social psychology of intergroup relations*. Academic Press.

Taylor, S. E., & Brown, J. D. (1988). Illusion and well-being: a social psychological perspective on mental health. *Psychological Bulletin, 103*(2), 193–210. https://doi.org/10.1037/0033-2909.103.2.193

The cause continues in the name of Ian Stuart. (1994). *Blood and Honor, 16*. No page numbers.

Tourish, D., & Wohlforth, T. (2000). Prophets of the apocalypse: White supremacy and the theology of Christian identity. *Cultic Studies Journal, 17*(1), 15–41. www.culteducation.com/group/871-christian-identity/3692-prophets-of-the-apocalypse-white-supremacy-and-the-theology-of-christian-identity.html

Tucker Carlson [@TuckerCarlson] (2022a, July 19). *The Immigration and Nationality Act of 1965 turned out to be one of the most significant pieces of legislation ever* ... [Video attached] [Tweet]. Twitter. https://twitter.com/TuckerCarlson/status/1549576493189283846

Tucker Carlson [@TuckerCarlson] (2022b, July 19). *This is too much change. Throw in millions of new people who have no connection to America– who broke our* ... [Video attached] [Tweet]. Twitter. https://twitter.com/TuckerCarlson/status/1549576493189283846

US Department of Justice (2021, August). *2020 Hate Crime Statistics*. www.justice.gov/crs/highlights/2020-hate-crimes-statistics

US Department of Justice (2023, July 19). *2021 Hate Crime Statistics*. www.justice.gov/hatecrimes/hate-crime-statistics

Vysotsky, S., & McCarthy, A. L. (2017). Normalizing cyberracism: A neutralization theory analysis. *Journal of Crime and Justice, 40*(4), 446–461. https://doi.org/10.1080/0735648X.2015.1133314

Walters, J., & Chang, A. (2021, September 8). Far-right terror poses bigger threat to US than Islamist extremism post-9/11. *The Guardian*. www.theguardian.com/us-news/2021/sep/08/post-911-domestic-terror

Wesselmann, E. D., Nairne, J. S., & Williams, K. D. (2012). An evolutionary social psychological approach to studying the effects of ostracism. *Journal of Social, Evolutionary, & Cultural Psychology, 6*, 308–327. http://doi.org/10.1037/h0099249

Wilkins, V. M., & Wenger, J. B. (2014). Belief in a just world and attitudes toward affirmative action. *Policy Studies Journal, 42*(3), 325–343. https://doi.org/10.1111/psj.12063

Williams, K. D. (2009). Ostracism: Effects of being excluded and ignored. In M. P. Zanna (Ed.), *Advances in Experimental Social Psychology* (Vol. 41, pp. 275–314). Academic Press.

Wilson, J. (2020, March 18). White nationalist hate groups have grown 55% in Trump era, report finds. *The Guardian*. www.theguardian.com/world/2020/mar/18/white-nationalist-hate-groups-southern-poverty-law-center

Yousef, O. (2022, May 17). *The "great replacement" conspiracy theory isn't fringe anymore, it's mainstream*. NPR.

Buying the Blackpill

Perceived Exclusion and the Psychology of Incels

GREGORY J. ROUSIS AND WILLIAM B. SWANN, JR.

5.1 Introduction

Incels – short for "involuntary celibates" – have two grievances against women. First, women reject them. Second, it is women's shallow preoccupation with physical appearance that prompts this rejection. Incensed by what they perceive as a wrongful exclusion from the dating market, incels withdraw to an online world where sympathetic ears offer support for their frustration and loneliness. Occasionally, incels are spurred to lash out against their perceived oppressors, with the most egregious instances including mass murder. Our goal in this chapter is to illuminate the mechanisms that underlie the psychology of incels. After reviewing empirical research designed to explore the role of several potential contributors to the incel phenomenon, we explore strategies for extricating incels from the toxic online environments in which they immerse themselves. We begin with a brief history of the incel movement.

5.1.1 The Blackpill and the Injunction to "Lie Down and Rot"

Incels are part of the "manosphere," a loose typology of misogynistic groups united by feelings of exclusion and disempowerment (Ging, 2019). Most manosphere groups, such as Men's Rights Activists and Men Going Their Own Way, subscribe to the *redpill* ideology – a broadly antifeminist worldview that posits that men are disadvantaged in society. The incel worldview, known as the *blackpill* (Glace et al., 2021), takes this a step further by embracing nihilism befitting Nietzsche. The blackpill holds that women, and particularly feminists, have usurped men's dominant position in the gender hierarchy. Due to their unjust control over status, power, and resources, women can be highly selective when it comes to romantic partners. Shamefully, women purportedly focus almost exclusively on attractiveness while eschewing personality, occupation, and socioeconomic status. This bias gives rise to the "80–20 rule" wherein 20 percent of the men ("Chads" or good-looking men) have 80 percent of the sex (Moonshot, 2020).

Incels' lack of success within the realm of romantic and sexual relationships can poison their other relationships as well. For example, one online forum user complained that "people in the social groups I've chosen to join have bullied me for the way I fail at getting lady's [sic]." He went on to describe several instances of bullying by people he thought were friends and ends with imagining shooting one of them with a gun (incels.is, 2023). But the problem is not limited to sexual relationships, for the larger society is "lookist": biased against unattractive people, particularly unattractive men (Speckhard & Ellenberg, 2022). Combined with their lack of romantic success, their mediocre looks make unattractive men less popular with peers, friends, and even family members. Some incels even assert that their incel status compromises their careers, as witnessed by evidence that many incels are NEET (not in education, employment, or training; Costello et al., 2022). Convinced that their plight is due to the lack of a relatively immutable characteristic – physical attractiveness – incels conclude that their lot in life is hopeless and that the only logical reaction is to "lie down and rot" (LDAR).

The mandate to LDAR has predictable consequences. Most incels report feeling loathed by the broader society (Daly & Reed, 2022) and high levels of depression and anxiety (Moskalenko et al., 2022). In this sea of hopelessness, fellow incels provide islands of shared despair. Given this, it is understandable that they respond harshly when fellow incels attempt to improve their life situation: online incel discussion forums are rife with ridicule for men who go to the gym ("gym maxxing") or attempt to obtain a highly lucrative job ("wealth maxxing"). Moreover, some forums are specifically devoted to incels who lack employment prospects, have concerns regarding body image, or are contemplating suicide (CCDH Quant Lab, 2022; Twohey & Dance, 2021). Such incel forums often promote anger and hopelessness, with only 5.8 percent of discussion threads being positive in nature (CCDH Quant Lab, 2022). Rather than offering conventional forms of support, members provide each other with tips regarding optimal strategies for dying by suicide. Researchers have confirmed that incels have taken their own lives at least forty-five times but believe that the actual number is substantially higher (Twohey & Dance, 2021).

The reported self-loathing of incels cannot be uncoupled from the virulent misogyny and dehumanizing rhetoric of their worldview. Overweight women are "landwhales." All women are "foids" (short for "female androids"), at best indifferent to, and at worst active participants in, depriving incels of a fulfilling life (Gothard et al., 2021). Attractive, yet unobtainable women are "Stacys," and their male counterparts are "Chads" (Cottee, 2020). Both Chads and Stacys are demonized for their presumed successful romantic and sexual lives. Men who are in romantic relationships but are not Chads are referred to as "Cucks" because their partners will inevitably cheat on them with a (better-looking) Chad if given the opportunity. A staggering percentage of discussions include some positive mention of sexual assault, with a recent report estimating that 89 percent of forum users have posted approvingly of rape (CCDH Quant Lab, 2022). Some forum members have gone so far as to propose chattel slavery for women so incels no longer suffer the indignity of sexless lives (incels.is, 2018).

The sexism of incels may be attributable, in part, to inappropriately negative self-views. In a study examining the roots of "curvilinear sexism," Bosson et al. (2022) found that blatant misogynists possessed low *subjective* mate value (i.e., self-ratings of one's value as a romantic partner) but not low *objective* mate value (i.e., number of short- and long-term relationships, number of sexual partners). That is, only men who *perceived* themselves as low in the romantic hierarchy evinced high levels of hostile sexism without the mollifying chivalry and paternalism characteristic of benevolent sexism (Glick & Fiske, 1996). Unfortunately, incels' perception of themselves as unlovable misanthropes appears to be a major contributor to their misogyny.

Another disturbing theme on incel forums is the veneration of incels who have committed violent acts (O'Donnell & Shor, 2022). Elliot Rodger is the prototypic incel hero. In 2014 Rodger murdered six people in Isla Vista, California, after posting a manifesto decrying his exclusion from a happy romantic life. Today, incel forums refer to Rodger as "Saint ER" (in reference to his initials). Forum members goad each other to "go ER" by committing mass murder. There have been takers. Toronto resident Alek Minassian explicitly referenced Elliot Rodger before going on his 2018 rampage, in which he murdered eleven people. When forum users first identified Nikolas Cruz, the Marjorie Stoneman Douglas High School shooter, they argued among themselves as to whether he was an incel and if they should "claim" him. More recently, in 2021 an active incel forum member was arrested in Ohio in possession of a modified AR-15 rifle and a plan to "slaughter" women at a nearby university (CCDH Quant Lab, 2022).

Although the misogyny of incels is obviously unwarranted and indefensible, the movement may represent, at least partially, a response to cultural shifts in the economic and interpersonal spheres. Incels correctly diagnose a cultural trend of alienating economic inequality (Piketty, 2014, 2020). As noted earlier, the injunction to LDAR often extends to the workplace, wherein incels decry "wage-slavery" as meek acquiescence to inherently unfair social structures. The wealthy accrue capital and political power while the underclass is left holding the bag. Consider, for example, the recent debt ceiling negotiations in the United States. Just as Congress added onerous work requirements for welfare benefits, it left the ballooning military budget intact. Rather than participate in what they perceive to be a rigged system, incels purportedly remain aloof by being NEET, refusing to engage in the labor market.

Furthermore, to a degree the incel movement may represent a reaction to real cultural shifts in mate preferences (Eagly & Wood, 1999; but see Walter et al., 2020). In the West, more egalitarian gender roles have diminished the extent to which women are financially dependent on men. Their newfound independence has freed women to shift from a heavy emphasis on traditional markers of male attractiveness (e.g., financial security) to physical attractiveness (although women still value financial security in their romantic partners more than men do; Walter et al., 2020). From this vantage point, incels may be bristling against an emerging trend for women to embrace one of the shallow priorities that men have championed for centuries.

To be sure, there may be a basis for some of incels' beliefs. Nevertheless, many of their convictions are groundless and ill conceived. Consider their penchant for singling out women for valuing physical attractiveness and men as their unwitting victims. In reality, both men and women are stereotyped according to the "what is beautiful is good" heuristic (Dion et al., 1972), wherein attractive people are ascribed more positive traits than less attractive people. Moreover, attractive people – men and women alike – are favored in nearly every type of interaction throughout the lifespan (for a meta-analytic review, see Langlois et al., 2000). Even schoolteachers expect physically attractive children to outperform less attractive ones (Dusek & Joseph, 1983). Clearly, women are not the only connoisseurs of physical attractiveness nor are unattractive men the only victims of attractiveness-based discrimination.

Whatever the sources of incels' grievances may be, the foregoing discussion fails to explore the question of why some men become incels while others do not. To address this issue, we turn to two social-psychological formulations, self-verification and identity fusion.

5.1.2 Compensating for Social Exclusion: Incels, Self-Verification, and Identity Fusion

Humans have a fundamental need for social connectedness and belonging (Baumeister & Leary, 1995). When this need is frustrated, negative effects abound, from the physical (e.g., higher levels of stress, heart disease) to the psychological (e.g., lower well-being). Social exclusion also engenders compensatory mechanisms, including a desire to seek self-esteem and belongingness from other sources. Experiencing consistent social exclusion can encourage openness to radicalism that would otherwise be absent (Pfundmair et al., 2022). Thus, for incels, exclusion from meaningful relationships in the offline world may cause them to seek solace from a group of like-minded individuals who purportedly understand them.

Another key priority that people experience is a desire to be known and understood or "self-verified" (Swann, 1983, 2012). Dozens of studies indicate that people prefer and seek evaluations that confirm both negative and positive self-views (Bosson & Swann, 1999; Swann et al., 1990). Moreover, people desire verification of their global characteristics ("I am a worthwhile person") as well as their specific characteristics ("I am athletic"; Swann et al., 1989; for reviews see Kwang & Swann, 2010; Swann, 2012). Furthermore, people are not only more committed to, and productive within, work groups and settings in which they receive self-verification (Swann et al., 2000, 2003; Wiesenfeld et al., 2007) but also more inclined to remain in relationships in which partners verify their self-views (De La Ronde & Swann, 1998; Neff & Karney, 2005; Swann et al., 1992).

Potential incels may be especially interested in self-verification from incel communities. As noted previously, self-identified incels typically feel excluded from and loathed by the wider society (Daly & Reed, 2022) – feelings that are decidedly non-verifying for most people. Starved for self-verification and suffused with anxiety and depression (Moskalenko et al., 2022), incels may eagerly align themselves with any group that shows signs of understanding them. Groups that embrace the blackpill ideology will be alluring because such groups offer a face-saving explanation for the perceived plight of incels. That is, by buying the blackpill, incels can convince themselves that they are the unfortunate victims of the shallow mate preferences of women. Budding incels may therefore seek and find verification from online incel communities.

Once potential incels ally themselves with an incel group, the self-verification they receive will likely encourage them to develop strong, family-like ties to other group members. Over time, these ties may morph into a powerful form of alignment with the incel group called identity fusion (e.g., Swann et al., 2009). When identity fusion occurs, the boundaries between the individual's personal and group identities become porous. These porous boundaries allow the individual to maintain a sense of personal agency while simultaneously experiencing a deep, familial connection to the group. A sense of oneness with other group members – *and* the defining beliefs and values of the group –will result.

Fusion with the group can have important consequences. Strongly fused individuals will evince an intense sense of group-based agency that motivates them to enact behaviors compatible with the group's goals and values (Swann et al., 2009; Swann et al., 2012; Whitehouse et al., 2014). This may even include violence and retribution against outgroup members (Fredman et al., 2017; Swann et al., 2014). In fact, identity fusion is an exceptionally strong predictor of violent pro-group behavior, consistently out-predicting rival variables such as group identification (for reviews, see Gómez et al., 2020; Swann & Buhrmester, 2015; Varmann et al., 2023; Wolfowicz et al., 2021), sacred values, and moral convictions (Martel et al., 2021). This suggests that fusion with an incel group may motivate acceptance of the blackpill ideology and the violent misogyny that it supports.

To test the foregoing ideas, we (Rousis et al., 2023) conducted several studies. In all studies, participants were considered incels only if they (1) self-identified as incels and (2) were knowledgeable regarding key beliefs of incels (e.g., the meaning of LDAR). We began with a preliminary study in which we asked if active members of incel communities exhibited stronger identity fusion than active members of other male-dominated online communities, including other gender-based groups (Men's Rights Activist [MRA] communities; Hodapp, 2017) and an apolitical control group comprising only male members (New England Patriots fans). We found that incels did in fact report significantly higher identity fusion than members of other male-centric groups, even when controlling for variables such as exposure to, and agreement with, the group's worldviews. This is important as it demonstrates that, even relative to an adjoining group in the manosphere, incels attain a unique sense of alignment with the group that cannot be explained by more frequent website visitation and exposure to the group's worldview.

The remaining studies tested three related hypotheses. First, members of incel communities would seek self-verification that adherents of the blackpill ideology are uniquely able to provide. Second, once embedded in incel groups, the self-verification that participants received should encourage them to fuse to the group. Third, identity fusion would, in turn, predict endorsement of violence against, and actual online harassment of, women.

To test these hypotheses we focused on global, rather than specific, self-verification. Global self-verification is a broad, felt sense of being understood by others. Whereas specific self-verification focuses on a series of traits (e.g., social skills, athleticism), global self-verification assesses the degree to which respondents believe that others see them as they see themselves. Our data indicated that global self-verification was indeed related to identity fusion with the group. For incels, then, it appears that receiving verification from other incels contributed to their relatively higher levels of identity fusion.

We then asked whether the self-verification to identity fusion link would help explain endorsement of group-based violence against women. To do so, we focused on support for past and future incel-inspired violence. To assess support for past violence, we briefly described Eliot Rodger's shooting spree and manifesto and then asked a series of questions to determine support for his actions (e.g., "Elliot Rodger did the right thing." "If there were more people like Elliot Rodger, the world would be a better place."). To assess support for future violence against women, we asked incels whether they supported various statements about incel-inspired violence against women (e.g., "Incels can only take so much abuse from women – then it is psychologically impossible not to retaliate." "The only way for incels to regain our pride is to avenge the injustices we have suffered from women.").

Across two independent samples with 396 self-identified incels, incels who felt globally verified by other incels were more fused to the group, and fusion, in turn, predicted support for past and future violence. In our final study, we extended this to include an outcome of online harassment of women (e.g., "In the last month, how often have you shared, liked, upvoted, or retweeted a post that promoted aggression toward a woman (or toward women in general)?"

"In the last month, how often have you sent provocative messages to a woman online with the intention of making her uncomfortable?"). We found the same pattern: Global self-verification predicted identity fusion, which in turn predicted online harassment of women.

Together, these results point to two conclusions. First, the global verification that incels receive from other group members seems to be a crucial aspect of becoming a fused incel. Second, among incels, identity fusion translates to endorsement of extreme acts and real-world harassing behavior that can have dire consequences for the women they target. These conclusions are bolstered by the results of a series of eight studies by Gómez et al. (in press).

The goal of this research was to replicate the correlational connection between self-verification and identity fusion described earlier and to establish a causal link between the two. Three correlational studies replicated Rousis et al.'s (2023) finding that increased self-verification was associated with higher identity fusion and willingness to engage in extreme acts for a group. Two experiments, one cross-sectional and one longitudinal, demonstrated that manipulating perceived verification increased participants' fusion with the group, which in turn predicted their willingness to fight and die on its behalf. Finally, in interviews with incarcerated Spanish gang members, Gómez et al. (in press) found that feelings of being known and understood by other gang members predicted their fusion with the gang, which in turn predicted their willingness to engage in costly sacrifices for the gang (also see Chinchilla & Gómez, this volume).

The results of the Gómez et al., (in press) studies offer strong support for Rousis et al.'s (2023) contention that self-verification leads to extreme behavior through identity fusion. Nevertheless, Rousis et al. (2023) report one additional finding that took us by surprise: the link between self-verification and support for violence against women was especially strong among narcissistic incels – that is, incels who possess exalted but fragile self-views (Morf & Rhodewalt, 2001). But it was not just that some incels scored high on our index of narcissism. In two studies, Rousis et al. asked participants to rate their self-views on ten different traits, including physical attractiveness and social skills. Self-identified incels rated themselves between the 68th and 79th percentiles, in keeping with the "better-than-average" effect (Zell et al., 2020). Even more surprising were our relationship and sexual history findings. Only 18 percent of our participants reported never having had sex and only 11 percent reported never having had a casual dating or serious romantic relationship partner. Instead, 75 percent reported having had sex ten or more times and 76 percent reported having had ten or more casual or serious romantic relationship partners. In our second study, we also asked participants to report their current relationship status. To our surprise, only 27 percent of our self-identified incels reported being single, whereas nearly half (47 percent) reported being married or in a civil union.

Additional findings emerged that contradict incels' self-descriptions. In our samples, we found that fully 87 percent of incels indicated having completed a college education (other researchers reported that 64 percent (Costello et al., 2022) and 37 percent (Moskalenko et al., 2022) of their incel samples finished college). Belying incels' self-descriptions as mainly NEET, our studies found that only 6 percent reported not being in education, employment, or training. Independently, other researchers found that only 17 percent were NEET (Costello et al., 2022).

Clearly, the most counterintuitive finding was the high rates of involvement in relationships and sexual activity reported by our participants relative to those recruited from incel forums (e.g., Costello et al., 2022; Moskalenko et al., 2022; Speckhard et al., 2022). This discrepancy could reflect a tendency for incels on forums to exaggerate their lack of sexual and romantic success to come across as "good," that is, prototypical (Hogg & Williams, 2000; Turner et al., 1987) group members. Note that in contrast to most groups, which revel in believing that their members possess socially valued qualities (Crocker & Luhtanen, 1990; Tajfel & Turner, 1979), incels do just the opposite. To be a card-carrying incel, men must profess that they are unattractive, romantically unsuccessful, and preferably socially awkward. Whereas these qualities would be ignored or criticized in most groups, among incels they are celebrated. Like a funhouse mirror, incels' supposedly negative attributes are reflected back to them as desirable and necessary for group membership.

A second potential explanation for the discrepant findings is that there was a fundamental difference between our MTurk participants and the visitors to incel forums (Costello et al., 2022; Moskalenko et al., 2022). Consider, for example, that MTurk participants were noticeably older (M_{age} = 33, SD = 7.55) than forum participants (M_{age} = 25.94, SD = 6.95). This raises the disturbing possibility that at least some incels "grow up" and get married but still cling to the dangerously toxic views of the blackpill. In this scenario, the incel identity may be quite sticky, persisting long after believers no longer meet the group's membership criteria. Such "resilient identities" are characteristic of identity fusion (Swann et al., 2012).

A third explanation is that older incels may feel doubly alienated from society at large and from other incels because of their age. As a result, they may use compensatory mechanisms to protect their self-worth. Relative to younger men, men in their thirties may feel that society is less tolerant of both their inability to attract a romantic partner and the extreme beliefs they harbor. Furthermore, their age may alienate them from other incels: as people in their age cohort who previously identified as incels have shorn their incel identity, these men are left as the elder statesmen among a much larger pool of perpetual twenty-somethings. They may accordingly resort to motivated reasoning (Kunda, 1990) to protect their feelings of self-worth. For such individuals, the act of asserting that they have many sexual partners may say less about their actual experiences and more about what they *want* to believe about themselves. From this vantage point, the positive self-views of incels in the MTurk studies may reflect a motivated ideal self – a statement of who they want to be rather than who they truly believe they are.

Although it is premature to select one of these explanations as the most appropriate (we suspect that they all have merit), each of them suggests the need to ask some very basic questions regarding the nature of incels. We begin with the most basic question of all.

5.1.3   Who Are Incels Anyway?

In young adulthood, Abe (who would later become an incel) developed a crush on his female best friend. When he finally got the nerve to ask her out, she said yes, and they dated for a month. But during that time, she cheated on Abe with her ex and eventually got engaged to him ... It was a crushing blow, and Abe turned to the internet for support. He found incel communities on Reddit, ones that helped reaffirm his belief that his looks were responsible for his terrible dating experience.

(Beauchamp, 2019)

Although lovers have been having experiences like Abe's for centuries, his ability to turn to the blackpill is a relatively recent development. The incel movement as we know it today began in the early 2000s. Most of the early incel user base came from 4chan and 8chan (Beauchamp, 2019), image boards notorious for a laissez-faire approach to racism, sexism, and anti-Semitism (Rieger et al., 2021). The pipeline was rather straightforward: internet-savvy, romantically frustrated young men flocked to online spaces rife with shocking content. There, they found common cause with others who shared their interests, experiences, and worldviews. Their interactions in these spaces alerted them to incel-specific forums on Reddit or independent websites dedicated to men's sexual and romantic frustration.

To the best of our knowledge, most, if not all, interactions between incels occur online. For this reason, the reputed characteristics of group members are drawn almost entirely from online discussion forums. This introduces a degree of uncertainty to claims made on forums, as assertions made there are notoriously susceptible to misrepresentation (Donath, 2002; Huang & Yang, 2013). This uncertainty is manifest even among incel forum members, where internecine arguments about who is and who is not a "true incel" are commonplace. Some forum members are derided as "volcel" or voluntarily celibate: men who are "too attractive" to be incels, but who are nonetheless sexually and romantically unsuccessful (or at least, represent themselves as such online). Incels accused of being "volcels" by other incels may feel ostracized, which is a particularly worrying proposition if their identities are deeply aligned with the group: ostracized individuals who are deeply aligned with a group are likely to endorse extreme acts to prove themselves worthy group members (Gómez et al., 2011).

Given that incels themselves disagree about the criterial attributes of incels, it is not surprising that outsiders are similarly confused. From a cultural and scientific standpoint, knee-jerk assumptions of incels as self-hating, sexless, right-wing Americans (ADL, 2023; Cottee, 2020) may not reflect the true nature of people who identify as incels. Consider that in the research we reviewed in preparing this chapter there was considerable heterogeneity in incels' self-views and their sexual and relationship experiences (e.g., they were politically left-leaning and sexually active).

As diverse as the psychological profile of incels may be, one theme emerges consistently: All incels embrace extremely negative attitudes toward women. At first blush, it may seem counterintuitive that a group that embraces such toxic attitudes toward half of the planet's population might attract so much loyalty from its followers. This loyalty becomes even more puzzling when one recognizes that the incel movement lacks a coherent leadership structure and cogent political ideology. That is, although some researchers have argued that incels see themselves as part of a political movement (e.g., O'Donnell & Shor, 2022), there is no "head incel" who directs other incels' activities in a strategic manner. In contrast, men's rights groups do have influential figures who guide their members' instrumental behavior (Mountford, 2018; O'Donnell, 2019). Despite this, Rousis et al. (2023) discovered that the rates of fusion were much higher in incel groups than men's rights groups. Why?

We suggest that incels enjoy high levels of fusion due to a combination of offline exclusion and online verification. Rebuffed by women in their daily lives, incels retreat to online worlds, seeking to share their pain with a group of like-minded others. Online, they discover kindred spirits who encourage them to blame others for their perceived romantic and sexual failures and reassure them that they deserve more romantic success than they currently enjoy. Furthermore, just as conspiracy theories satisfy the need for uniqueness (Imhoff, this volume; Imhoff & Lamberty, 2017; Snyder & Fromkin, 1977) and provide adherents with a sense of meaning (Schöpfer et al., 2023), the blackpill might boost incels' self-views as the privileged holders of unique, esoteric knowledge. Only incels, the argument goes, see the world for what it truly is: a harsh landscape of biological determinism that offers little hope to unattractive men. Having these views verified by other incels may boost their wavering sense of self-worth. As they move between their offline and online worlds, the resulting emotional ups and downs fuel volatility that has been shown to promote fusion to the group (Newson et al., 2021; Whitehouse et al., 2017). Consistent with this reasoning, incels who received verification from other group members were more fused to the group, and fusion, in turn, predicted endorsement of past and future violence on incels' behalf (Rousis et al., 2023). Moreover, incels whose current level of sexual or romantic involvement fell short of what their narcissistic self-views led them to expect were especially inclined to support incel-inspired violence. Insofar as they frequent websites that marinate them in narratives that promise meaning through violence (Ellenberg & Kruglanski, this volume; Kruglanski et al., 2009; Webber & Kruglanski, 2017), they may be tempted to translate their concerns into violence.

Of course, it is important to acknowledge that the base rate of violence is exceedingly low among extremists in general (Sageman, 2021). This generalization surely applies to incels. The vast majority of incels will not attack others, no matter how abhorrent their beliefs about women and society in general. Instead, a more common response may be to direct their anger and frustration inwards. Incels report significantly higher rates of depression and anxiety than demographically similar non-incels (Costello et al., 2022) and online posts about considering or attempting suicide are common (CCDH, 2022). Sadly, these mental health struggles may be compounded by other conditions as well, including autism spectrum disorder and posttraumatic stress disorder, both of which are more common in incel samples than the general population (Speckhard & Ellenberg, 2022). For incels committed to LDAR, the presence of comorbid mental health issues is worrying. This lifestyle opposes the very things that make life worth living: social relationships, pleasurable activities, and meaningful work. By depriving themselves of what humans most value, incels, and particularly those with preexisting mental health concerns, may enter a spiral of self-imposed isolation and meaninglessness.

5.1.4 Solving the Incel Problem: Understanding and Disrupting the Radicalization Process

The conclusion emerging from the foregoing remarks is clear: Incels are miserable and at least some of them are poised to bring misery to the people around them. Unfortunately, the movement itself is gaining momentum. Originally confined largely to the United States and Canada, incel forums have now spread to Europe and India. For example, one recent report (Speckhard et al., 2021) indicated that only 30.9 percent of their sample of incels resided in North America, whereas 32.4 percent resided in Western Europe. These findings suggest that the blackpill is now a cross-cultural phenomenon that appeals even to men who are not its traditional targets. Given this, it is important to take a close look at the process through which incels are radicalized in the hope of identifying ways of disrupting that process. The first step involves finding the group.

5.1.4.1 Finding the Group

How do disaffected young men find the blackpill in the first place? Research on the manosphere has often treated these groups as silos, failing to address the extent to which cross-pollination occurs between, for example, Men's Rights

Activists and incels (Ging & Murphy, 2021). This raises multiple questions: Is there a straightforward path from antifeminist groups to incels? Are lonely, sexually frustrated Men's Right Activists primed to become incels or do incels represent a unique population within the manosphere?

Recent research may offer tentative answers to the foregoing questions. A social network analysis of YouTube videos discovered a potential radicaliza-tion pathway for incel-related content. In particular, incel-adjacent videos with many views are often connected to more extreme content. This could lead viewers down a rabbit hole of radicalization (Champion, 2021). Other forms of internet-based research, such as the "scroll-back" method (Ging & Murphy, 2021; Robards & Lincoln, 2017), show promise in illuminating the journey that ends with incel membership. Nonetheless, a broad, internet-literate approach is needed to track the pathways that lead men down the road to membership in incel groups.

When soon-to-be incels become acquainted with an incel group, they will evaluate the degree to which its properties fit with their own characteristics, sentiments, and goals. If there is a good match, they will experience affinity for the group. If contact with the group fulfills expectation, they will form collect-ive ties to that group – that is, an allegiance based on the similarity between their own characteristics and the groups' characteristics. Some will also develop relational ties – that is, an allegiance based on interpersonal liking for individual group members. The presence of strong collective and relational ties will foster fusion with the group (Gómez et al., in press). With fusion will come a modicum of group-related agency and a conviction that they can, and should, enact behaviors befitting an incel.

5.1.4.2   Joining the Group

Offline, incels feel misunderstood and lament putative rejection both in romance and more generally. Convinced that the levers of power in society are aligned against them, they are drawn to a group of like-minded others. Once they become members of an incel group, they are rewarded with a cogent worldview – the blackpill – that supplies a rationale for their feelings of frustration and victimization. Most important, the blackpill encourages them to make an external attribution for their own shortcomings: the negative events in men's lives are simply the result of large, external power structures that govern society. This is a compelling idea. Perhaps the only surprise here is that the blackpill has not won over an even larger audience of disaffected young men.

According to the blackpill, the physical appearance of incels is so appalling that others have absolutely no desire to interact with them. Incels who endorse the blackpill may consequentially be sensitized to possible exclusion, a state version of the rejection sensitivity trait (Downey et al., 1994; Feldman & Downey, 1994). Rejection-sensitive people expect rejection in intimate relationships, misinterpret insensitivity for intentional rejection, and overreact to any slight, real or imagined (Downey & Feldman, 1996). Such concerns lead to less successful and fulfilling intimate relationships. Thus, for incels, a vicious cycle of self-fulfilling prophecies may be at play. Internalizing the tenets of the blackpill causes them to expect rejection. This expectation fosters overreactions to any perceived slight, which will, in turn, jeopardize the relationship. And when a social relationship ends, incels can refer to the blackpill and assign blame to a "lookist" society that overvalues attractiveness.

Of course, our findings suggest that not all incels hold negative self-views. In fact, some hold quite positive self-views and enjoy long-term intimate relationships. For these incels, stigma consciousness (Pinel, 1999) rather than rejection sensitivity may be key. Consider that the majority of incels' offline relationships are likely with non-incels. Whether or not their incel status is known, incels likely feel acutely aware of being a member of a small and, in their eyes, unfairly stigmatized group. So convinced, the stigma consciousness formulation suggests that they will attribute negative social interactions to their group membership. This could serve as an ego-defense mechanism that enables them to preserve their positive self-views and attribute difficult social interactions to their status as an incel (e.g., Crocker et al., 1991).

Although the precise nature of the psychological benefits associated with identity fusion have not yet been documented, our findings point to several potential rewards. Being a member of a self-verifying group not only aligns incels with a group of like-minded others (thereby verifying a group identity), it also provides verification of a host of personal self-views (e.g., unattractiveness, social ineptitude, and unjust victimization). By simultaneously validating both personal and collective self-views (Gómez et al., 2009), membership in an incel group may provide men who otherwise feel excluded with a sense of being known and understood. This double whammy of verification of group and personal identity should make fusion with the group enormously attractive.

5.1.4.3 Abandoning the Group and the Unfortunate Sentiments It May Inspire

As attractive as membership in an incel group may be in the short term, the long-term consequences of membership are dire: Whereas some incels lash out in violence, others sink into depression and despair. Given this, researchers should engineer strategies designed to extricate incels from the pernicious online worlds in which they sometimes embed themselves.

Research by Gómez et al. (in press) outlines a general scheme for inducing incels to break away from the group and cease pro-group behavior. Their findings point to a series of four steps that induce people to join groups and enact pro-group behaviors. That is, people find that group membership is self-verifying; perceived self-verification fosters relational ties; relational ties, in turn, foment fusion; and fusion, in turn, encourages group-related agency and behavior. Given that each step in this chain of events foments the next step, it should be possible to break the chain by disrupting any of the four processes: self-verification; relational ties; fusion with the group; and pro-group-related agency. We consider each of these processes in turn.

5.1.4.3.1 Self-verification Interrupting the verification incels receive from other incels and pointing them to alternative, healthier sources of verification could be an effective strategy for redirecting the self-verification strivings of incels. Although there are surely many avenues for self-verification redirec-tion, one promising route is targeting the veracity of other incels' online identities. Most incels are likely savvy internet users familiar with all manner of identity misrepresentation and online trolling. However, they appear to hold earnest beliefs about other incels. It is here that verification redirection can take place. Presenting incels with evidence that other incels have generally positive self-views and are likely more sexually active than they admit on incel forums could undermine the credibility of these other incels. This may make incels more open to alternative sources of self-verification and weaken their relational and collective ties to the group.

Another possibility, informed by militant *jihadist* deradicalization efforts (Ashour, 2010), might be to use the insights of previous members into why they left the group to counteract the faith incels have in the group. A former incel is a reliable messenger, one who has been through similar experiences and may produce more "buy-in" from current incels (Hart & Huber, 2023). Using the narratives of loneliness, mental health issues, and substance use issues that undergirded their incel identity (Hintz & Baker, 2021) may sap some of the appeal of the verification incels receive from the group.

For effective verification redirection, change agents should examine the content of verification that incels receive from other incels. Rousis et al. (2023) focused on verification of general self-views, looks, and personality, but there could be other dimensions of self-concept that are important to incels. Some research has suggested that incels represent a "hybrid masculinity" wherein their romantic failures place them squarely in stereotypically non-masculine territory, but their attitudes toward male hegemony and male–female sexual relations are stereotypically masculine (Ging, 2019). Thus, for incels, the appeal of the group may be rooted in verifying specific negative and positive self-views key to the incel identity. Delineating these self-views will be crucial to steering incels to healthier sources of verification that can replace verification from fellow incels.

Finally, although self-verification redirection could take many forms, one of the most effective may be to simply encourage incels to try new things. Indeed, previous qualitative work suggests that some incels leave the group because they had new experiences, such as going to college or moving to a new city

(Hintz & Baker, 2021). These incels were able to replace their relational and collective ties to incels with healthier sources of psychological support.

5.1.4.3.2 Relational Ties   In a series of six experiments, Gómez et al. (2019) found that experimentally degrading relational ties resulted in a significant reduction of state (vs. trait) fusion to nations and gender groups. Lowered fusion, in turn, predicted less willingness to fight and die for the group. To target relational ties, participants thought of two actions a fellow group member (e.g., a Spaniard) undertook that made them question their commitment to the group. These are powerful findings because the manipulation consisted of a one-shot, rather perfunctory set of instructions. Although the intervention developed by Gómez et al. (2019) was not powerful enough to lower trait fusion, administering similar instructions repeatedly might accomplish that goal.

For example, the change agent could encourage incels to consider negative interpersonal and group-based interactions. These could include difficulties they are encountering with fellow incels or recounting episodes that made their support for the group waver. Rather than seeing the group as consisting of close-knit family members, this may lead incels to see discord and rancor among the group members. The result may be weakened alignment with the group. Through repetition, incels may slowly begin to question their deep commitment to other incels and the group. For fused incels, repeated interventions would likely be necessary to decouple their personal identity from the group identity.

5.1.4.3.3 Fusion   There is compelling evidence that degrading collective ties reduces state fusion. Gómez et al. (2019) targeted collective ties by simply asking participants to consider two actions their group (e.g., the nation) engaged in that made them question their commitment to it. This strategy could be applied to incels. A qualitative analysis of former incels' testimonials found that many left the group after Elliot Rodger's acts of violence (Hintz & Baker, 2021). These former incels could not countenance being tied to a group associated with such abhorrent acts. Although discussions on their forums suggest incels sometimes venerate acts that most other people would find deplorable, it is conceivable that emphasizing the negative consequences of such acts (e.g., the devastation experienced by relatives of victims) could undermine sympathy for the perpetrators and, in the process, the incel movement itself. This may lead to deradicalization for some (or most) incels, whereas others may be energized by these events and increase their commitment to the group. Known as "condensation" (McCauley & Moskalenko, 2008), this process weeds out members who cannot stomach extreme acts, while increasing the radicalism of those who remain. Thus, although individual members may leave the group, those who remain may become increasingly radicalized.

Note also that Gómez et al. (2019) used participant-driven (rather than researcher-driven) narratives. Rather than telling participants what actions they *should* feel bad about, they allowed participants to generate these scenarios. Such an intervention among incels may encourage a degree of introspection and thoughtful reflection that is simply not possible on incel message boards. As with relational ties, for this sort of intervention to be effective, repeated administrations would likely be necessary.

5.1.4.3.4 Group-Related Agency   If one is concerned with the potential that incels might engage in extreme acts, targeting group-based agency may be the most appropriate target of interventions. The good news is that because the "incel movement" is amorphous and leaderless, being an incel may be less about achieving instrumental goals, such as political change, and more about finding a support network. Insofar as incels join the group primarily for companionship, interventions designed to thwart group-based agency may be unnecessary. Nonetheless, as demonstrated by the cases of Elliot Rodger and Alek Minassian, some incels do lash out at perceived oppressors.

Because group-related agency theoretically grows out of fusion, the extent to which an individual is fused determines, at least in part, the strength of their belief that they can and should act on behalf of the group. This means that an intervention designed to address the lack of agency for individual incels to effect change in the group may weaken the willingness of fused individuals to commit extreme acts. Indeed, simply telling participants that they had little ability to exercise control over their group was enough to weaken the association between fusion and willingness to engage in extreme acts (Gómez et al., 2019; Study 5). Such interventions designed to reduce group-related agency could be complemented by interventions designed to reduce personal agency. There is evidence, for example, that personal agency (feelings of self-confidence and competence) is related to identity fusion (Besta et. al., 2016). Conceivably, diminishing incels' feelings of personal and group-related agency could reduce both identity fusion and pro-group behavior.

5.2 Conclusion

From a cultural perspective, incels' feelings of exclusion from "normie" society may be symptomatic of yet another yawning divide between the "haves" and "have-nots." To be sure, incels' main focus is on the shallow, insensitive "Stacys" who putatively deprive them of sex and the facile, indifferent "Chads" who unfairly monopolize the pool of eligible female partners. Although these antagonists inhabit center stage in the dilemmas that incels face, the true villains may be off stage in the political and economic power structures that deprive them of a decent shot at achieving financial viability. The federal minimum wage plateaued in 2009 and salaries for college graduates remain too low to repay the loans they took out to earn the credentials needed to land decent jobs. Failing banks are bailed out by the government, while SNAP benefits for individuals are slashed; the military budget balloons, while housing subsidies wither. At some level, then, the frustration of incels may be based on a realistic despair stemming from the precarity of their situation. Of course, their frustration should not be displaced onto women and embracing the hopelessness of their situation by LDAR is not a solution to their problem.

To be sure, addressing the root causes of the incel phenomena would require sweeping societal changes that are unlikely to occur. Instead, we propose more modest goals that focus on directly altering the psychology of incels. Specifically, we suggest that future research on incels should take a multifaceted approach. For example, one might use internet-based methods to track migration to incel websites, the sources and content of verification provided by the incel group, and the factors that motivate withdrawal from the group. By gaining a clearer understanding of the psychology of incels, researchers will hopefully triangulate ways to extricate incels from their pernicious online worlds.

References

ADL (2023). *Murder and extremism in the United States in 2022.* American Defamation League Center on Extremism. www.adl.org/sites/default/files/pdfs/2023-02/Murder-and-Extremism-in-the-United-States-in-2022.pdf

Ashour, O. (2010). Online de-radicalization? Countering violent extremist narratives. *Perspectives on Terrorism, 4*(6), 15–19.

Back, M. D., Küfner, A. C. P., Dufner, M., et al. (2013). Narcissistic admiration and rivalry: Disentangling the bright and dark sides of narcissism. *Journal of Personality and Social Psychology, 105*(6), 1013–1037. https://doi.org/10.1037/a0034431

Baumeister, R. F., & Leary, M. R. (1995). The need to belong: Desire for interpersonal attachments as a fundamental human motive. *Psychological Bulletin, 117* (3), 497–529.

Beauchamp, Z. (2019, April 16). *The rise of incels: How a support group for the dateless became a violent internet subculture.* Vox. www.vox.com/the-highlight/2019/4/16/18287446/incel-definition-reddit

Beck, A. T. (Ed.). (1979). *Cognitive therapy of depression* (13. Print). Guilford Press.

Besta, T., Mattingly, B., & Błażek, M. (2016). When membership gives strength to act: Inclusion of the group into the self and feeling of personal agency. *The Journal of Social Psychology, 156*(1), 56–73. https://doi.org/10.1080/00224545.2015.1053838

Bosson, J. K., Rousis, G. J., & Felig, R. N. (2022). Curvilinear sexism and its links to men's perceived mate value. *Personality and Social Psychology Bulletin, 48*(4), 516–533. https://doi.org/10.1177/01461672211009726

Bosson, J. K., & Swann, W. B., Jr. (1999). Self-liking, self-competence, and the quest for self-verification. *Personality and Social Psychology Bulletin, 25*(10), 1230–1241. https://doi.org/10.1177/0146167299258005

Broyd, J., Boniface, L., Parsons, D., Murphy, D., & Hafferty, J. D. (2022). Incels, violence and mental disorder: A narrative review with recommendations for best practice in risk assessment and clinical intervention. *BJPsych Advances, 26* (9), 254–264. https://doi.org/10.1192/bja.2022.15

CCDH Quant Lab (2022). *The Incelosphere: Exposing pathways into incel communities and the harms they pose to women and children* (pp. 1–48). Center for Countering Digital Hate. https://counterhate.com/wp-content/uploads/2022/09/CCDH-The-Incelosphere.pdf

Champion, A. R. (2021). Exploring the radicalization pipeline on YouTube. *The Journal of Intelligence, Conflict, and Warfare, 4*(2), 122–126. https://doi.org/10.21810/jicw.v4i2.3754

Costello, W., Rolon, V., Thomas, A. G., & Schmitt, D. (2022). Levels of well-being among men who are incel (involuntarily celibate). *Evolutionary Psychological Science, 8*(4), 375–390. https://doi.org/10.1007/s40806-022-00336-x

Cottee, S. (2020). Incel Imotives: Resentment, shame and revenge. *Studies in Conflict & Terrorism, 44*(2), 93–114. https://doi.org/10.1080/1057610X.2020.1822589

Crocker, J., & Luhtanen, R. (1990). Collective self-esteem and ingroup bias. *Journal of Personality and Social Psychology, 58*(1), 60–67. https://doi.org/10.1037/0022-3514.58.1.60

Crocker, J., Voelkl, K., Testa, M., & Major, B. (1991). Social stigma: The affective consequences of attributional ambiguity. *Journal of Personality and Social Psychology, 60*(2), 218–228. https://doi.org/10.1037/0022-3514.60.2.218

Daly, S. E., & Reed, S. M. (2022). "I think most of society hates us": A qualitative thematic analysis of interviews with incels. *Sex Roles, 86*(1–2), 14–33. https://doi.org/10.1007/s11199-021-01250-5

De La Ronde, C., & Swann, W. B. (1998). Partner verification: Restoring shattered images of our intimates. *Journal of Personality and Social Psychology, 75*(2), 374–382. https://doi.org/10.1037/0022-3514.75.2.374

Dion, K., Berscheid, E., & Walster, E. (1972). What is beautiful is good. *Journal of Personality and Social Psychology, 24*(3), 285–290. https://doi.org/10.1037/h0033731

Donath, J. S. (2002). Identity and deception in the virtual community. In P. Kollock & M. Smith (Eds.), *Communities in cyberspace* (pp. 37–68). Routledge.

Downey, G., & Feldman, S. I. (1996). Implications of rejection sensitivity for intimate relationships. *Journal of Personality and Social Psychology, 70*(6), 1327–1343. https://doi.org/10.1037/0022-3514.70.6.1327

Downey, G., Feldman, S., Khuri, J., & Friedman, S. (1994). Maltreatment and childhood depression. In W. M. Reynolds & H. F. Johnston (Eds.), *Handbook of depression in children and adolescents* (pp. 481–508). Springer US. https://doi.org/10.1007/978-1-4899-1510-8_22

Dusek, J. B., & Joseph, G. (1983). The bases of teacher expectancies: A meta-analysis. *Journal of Educational Psychology*, *75*(3), 327–346. https://doi .org/10.1037/0022-0663.75.3.327

Eagly, A. H., & Wood, W. (1999). The origins of sex differences in human behavior: Evolved dispositions versus social roles. *American Psychologist*, *54*(6), 408–423. https://doi.org/10.1037/0003-066X.54.6.408

Feldman, S., & Downey, G. (1994). Rejection sensitivity as a mediator of the impact of childhood exposure to family violence on adult attachment behavior. *Development and Psychopathology*, *6*(1), 231–247. https://doi.org/10.1017/ S0954579400005976

Fredman, L. A., Bastian, B., & Swann, W. B. (2017). God or country? Fusion with Judaism predicts desire for retaliation following Palestinian stabbing intifada. *Social Psychological and Personality Science*, *8*(8), 882–887. https://doi.org/ 10.1177/1948550617693059

Fredman, L. A., Buhrmester, M. D., Gomez, A., et al. (2015). Identity fusion, extreme pro-group behavior, and the path to defusion: Identity fusion and extreme behavior. *Social and Personality Psychology Compass*, *9*(9), 468–480. https://doi.org/10.1111/spc3.12193

Ging, D. (2019). Alphas, betas, and incels: Theorizing the masculinities of the manosphere. *Men and Masculinities*, *22*(4), 638–657. https://doi.org/10.1177/ 1097184X17706401

Ging, D., & Murphy, S. (2021, September 15). Tracking the pilling pipeline: Limitations, challenges and a call for new methodological frameworks in incel and manosphere research. AoIR Selected Papers of Internet Research. The 22nd Annual Conference of the Association of Internet Researchers. https://doi.org/ 10.5210/spir.v2021i0.12174

Glace, A. M., Dover, T. L., & Zatkin, J. G. (2021). Taking the black pill: An empirical analysis of the "incel." *Psychology of Men & Masculinities*, *22*(2), 288–297. https://doi.org/10.1037/men0000328

Glick, P., & Fiske, S. T. (1996). The ambivalent sexism inventory: Differentiating hostile and benevolent sexism. *Journal of Personality and Social Psychology*, *70* (3), 491–512. https://doi.org/10.1037/0022-3514.70.3.491

Gómez, Á., Chinchilla, J., Vázquez, A., et al. (2020). Recent advances, misconceptions, untested assumptions, and future research agenda for identity fusion theory. *Social and Personality Psychology Compass*, *14*(6), 1–15. https://doi.org/ 10.1111/spc3.12531

Gómez, Á., Morales, J. F., Hart, S., Vázquez, A., & Swann, W. B. (2011). Rejected and excluded forevermore, but even more devoted: Irrevocable ostracism intensifies loyalty to the group among identity-fused persons. *Personality and Social Psychology Bulletin*, *37*(12), 1574–1586. https://doi.org/10.1177/ 0146167211424580

Gómez, Á., Seyle, D. C., Huici, C., & Swann, W. B. (2009). Can self-verification strivings fully transcend the self–other barrier? Seeking verification of ingroup identities. *Journal of Personality and Social Psychology, 97*(6), 1021–1044. https://doi.org/10.1037/a0016358

Gómez, Á., Vázquez, A., & Swann, W. B. (in press). Feeling understood fosters identity fusion. *Journal of Personality and Social Psychology.*

Gómez, Á., Vázquez, A., López-Rodríguez, L., et al. (2019). Why people abandon groups: Degrading relational vs collective ties uniquely impacts identity fusion and identification. *Journal of Experimental Social Psychology, 85,* 103853. https://doi.org/10.1016/j.jesp.2019.103853

Gothard, K., Dewhurst, D. R., Minot, J. R., et al. (2021). *The incel lexicon: Deciphering the emergent cryptolect of a global misogynistic community* (arXiv:2105.12006). arXiv. http://arxiv.org/abs/2105.12006

Hart, G., & Huber, A. R. (2023). Five things we need to learn about incel extremism: Issues, challenges and avenues for fresh research. *Studies in Conflict & Terrorism,* 1–17. https://doi.org/10.1080/1057610X.2023.2195067

Hintz, E. A., & Baker, J. T. (2021). A performative face theory analysis of online facework by the formerly involuntarily celibate. *International Journal of Communication, 15,* 3047–3066.

Hodapp, C. (2017). *Men's rights, gender, and social media.* Lexington Books.

Hogg, M. A., & Williams, K. D. (2000). From I to we: Social identity and the collective self. *Group Dynamics: Theory, Research, and Practice, 4*(1), 81–97. https://doi.org/10.1037/1089-2699.4.1.81

Huang, C. L., & Yang, S. C. (2013). A study of online misrepresentation, self-disclosure, cyber-relationship motives, and loneliness among teenagers in Taiwan. *Journal of Educational Computing Research, 48*(1), 1–18. https://doi.org/10.2190/EC.48.1.a

Imhoff, R., & Lamberty, P. K. (2017). Too special to be duped: Need for uniqueness motivates conspiracy beliefs: Need for uniqueness and conspiracies. *European Journal of Social Psychology, 47*(6), 724–734. https://doi.org/10.1002/ejsp.2265

incels.is (2018). *Which status would you prefer women to have in society?* Incels.Is – Involuntary Celibate. https://incels.is/threads/which-status-would-you-prefer-women-to-have-in-society

incels.is (2023, March 9). *I've been bullied for failing to get a lady.* Incels.Is – Involuntary Celibate. https://incels.is/threads/ive-been-bullied-for-failing-to-get-a-lady.467004/

Kruglanski, A. W., Chen, X., Dechesne, M., Fishman, S., & Orehek, E. (2009). Fully committed: Suicide bombers' motivation and the quest for personal significance. *Political Psychology, 30*(3), 331–357.

Kunda, Z. (1990). The case for motivated reasoning. *Psychological Bulletin, 108*(3), 480–498. https://doi.org/10.1037/0033-2909.108.3.480

Kwang, T., & Swann, W. B. (2010). Do people embrace praise even when they feel unworthy? A review of critical tests of self-enhancement versus self-verification. *Personality and Social Psychology Review, 14*(3), 263–280. https://doi.org/10.1177/1088868310365876

Langlois, J. H., Kalakanis, L., Rubenstein, A. J., et al. (2000). Maxims or myths of beauty? A meta-analytic and theoretical review. *Psychological Bulletin, 126*(3), 390–423. https://doi.org/10.1037/0033-2909.126.3.390

Martel, F. A., Buhrmester, M., Gómez, A., Vázquez, A., & Swann, W. B. (2021). Why true believers make the ultimate sacrifice: Sacred values, moral convictions, or identity fusion? *Frontiers in Psychology, 12*(779120), 1–12. https://doi.org/10.3389/fpsyg.2021.779120

Maxwell, D., Robinson, S. R., Williams, J. R., & Keaton, C. (2020). "A short story of a lonely guy": A qualitative thematic analysis of involuntary celibacy using reddit. *Sexuality & Culture, 24*(6), 1852–1874. https://doi.org/10.1007/s12119-020-09724-6

Moonshot (2020). *Incels: A guide to symbols and terminology* (p. 19). https://moonshotteam.com/resource/incels-a-guide-to-symbols-and-terminology/

Morf, C. C., & Rhodewalt, F. (2001). Unraveling the paradoxes of narcissism: A dynamic self-regulatory processing model. *Psychological Inquiry, 12*(4), 177–196. https://doi.org/10.1207/S15327965PLI1204_1

Moskalenko, S., González, J. F.-G., Kates, N., & Morton, J. (2022). Incel ideology, radicalization and mental health: A survey study. *The Journal of Intelligence, Conflict, and Warfare, 4*(3), 1–29. https://doi.org/10.21810/jicw.v4i3.3817

Mountford, J. (2018). Topic modeling the red pill. *Social Sciences, 7*(42), 1–16. https://doi.org/10.3390/socsci7030042

Neff, L. A., & Karney, B. R. (2005). To know you is to love you: The implications of global adoration and specific accuracy for marital relationships. *Journal of Personality and Social Psychology, 88*(3), 480–497. https://doi.org/10.1037/0022-3514.88.3.480

Newson, M., Khurana, R., Cazorla, F., & Van Mulukom, V. (2021). "I get high with a little help from my friends": How raves can invoke identity fusion and lasting co-operation via transformative experiences. *Frontiers in Psychology, 12* (719596), 1–18. https://doi.org/10.3389/fpsyg.2021.719596

O'Donnell, C., & Shor, E. (2022). "This is a political movement, friend": Why "incels" support violence. *The British Journal of Sociology, 73*(2), 336–351. https://doi.org/10.1111/1468-4446.12923

O'Donnell, J. (2019). Militant meninism: The militaristic discourse of Gamergate and Men's Rights Activism. *Media, Culture & Society, 42*(5), 654–674. https://doi.org/10.1177/0163443719876624

Pfundmair, M., Wood, N. R., Hales, A., & Wesselmann, E. D. (2022). How social exclusion makes radicalism flourish: A review of empirical evidence. *Journal of Social Issues.* Advance online publication. https://doi.org/10.1111/josi.12520

Piketty, T. (2014). *Capital in the twenty-first century* (A. Goldhammer, Trans.). Belknap Press.

Piketty, T. (2020). *Capital and ideology* (A. Goldhammer, Trans.). Harvard University Press.

Pinel, E. C. (1999). Stigma consciousness: The psychological legacy of social stereotypes. *Journal of Personality and Social Psychology, 76*(1), 114–128. https://doi.org/10.1037/0022-3514.76.1.114

Rieger, D., Kümpel, A. S., Wich, M., Kiening, T., & Groh, G. (2021). Assessing the extent and types of hate speech in fringe communities: A case study of alt-right communities on 8chan, 4chan, and Reddit. *Social Media + Society*, *7*(4), 1–14. https://doi.org/10.1177/20563051211052906

Robards, B., & Lincoln, S. (2017). Uncovering longitudinal life narratives: Scrolling back on Facebook. *Qualitative Research*, *17*(6), 715–730. https://doi.org/10.1177/1468794117700707

Rousis, G. J., Martel, F. A., Bosson, J. K., & Swann, W. B. (2023). Behind the blackpill: Self-verification and identity fusion predict endorsement of violence against women among self-identified incels. *Personality and Social Psychology Bulletin*. https://doi.org/10.1177/01461672231166481

Sageman, M. (2021). The implication of terrorism's extremely low base rate. *Terrorism and Political Violence*, *33*(2), 302–311. https://doi.org/10.1080/09546553.2021.1880226

Schöpfer, C., Abatista, A. G. F., Fuhrer, J., & Cova, F. (2023). "Where there are villains, there will be heroes": Belief in conspiracy theories as an existential tool to fulfill need for meaning. *Personality and Individual Differences*, *200*, 111900. https://doi.org/10.1016/j.paid.2022.111900

Snyder, C. R., & Fromkin, H. L. (1977). Abnormality as a positive characteristic: The development and validation of a scale measuring need for uniqueness. *Journal of Abnormal Psychology*, *86*(5), 518–527. https://doi.org/10.1037/0021-843X.86.5.518

Speckhard, A., & Ellenberg, M. (2022). Self-reported psychiatric disorder and perceived psychological symptom rates among involuntary celibates (incels) and their perceptions of mental health treatment. *Behavioral Sciences of Terrorism and Political Aggression*, 1–18. https://doi.org/10.1080/19434472.2022.2029933

Speckhard, A., Ellenberg, M., Morton, J., & Ash, A. (2021). Involuntary celibates' experiences of and grievance over sexual exclusion and the potential threat of violence among those active in an online incel forum. *Journal of Strategic Security*, *14*(2), 89–121. https://doi.org/10.5038/1944-0472.14.2.1910

Swann, W. B., Jr. (1983). Self-verification: Bringing social reality into harmony with the self. In J. Suls & A. G. Greenwald (Eds.), *Social psychological perspectives on the self* (2nd ed., pp. 33–66). Erlbaum.

Swann, W. B., Jr. (2012). Self-verification theory. In P. Van Lange, A. Kruglanski, & E. Higgins, *Handbook of theories of social psychology* (pp. 23–42). SAGE Publications. https://doi.org/10.4135/9781446249222.n27

Swann, W. B., Jr., & Buhrmester, M. D. (2015). Identity fusion. *Current Directions in Psychological Science*, *24*(1), 52–57. https://doi.org/10.1177/0963721414551363

Swann, W. B., Jr., Buhrmester, M. D., Gómez, A., et al. (2014). What makes a group worth dying for? Identity fusion fosters perception of familial ties, promoting self-sacrifice. *Journal of Personality and Social Psychology*, *106*(6), 912–926. https://doi.org/10.1037/a0036089

Swann, W. B., Jr., Gómez, Á., Seyle, D. C., Morales, J. F., & Huici, C. (2009). Identity fusion: The interplay of personal and social identities in extreme group behavior. *Journal of Personality and Social Psychology, 96*(5), 995–1011. https://doi.org/10.1037/a0013668

Swann, W. B., Jr., Hixon, J. G., & De La Ronde, C. (1992). Embracing the bitter "truth": Negative self-concepts and marital commitment. *Psychological Science, 3*(2), 118–121. https://doi.org/10.1111/j.1467-9280.1992.tb00010.x

Swann, W. B., Jr., Hixon, J. G., Stein-Seroussi, A., & Gilbert, D. T. (1990). The fleeting gleam of praise: Cognitive processes underlying behavioral reactions to self-relevant feedback. *Journal of Personality and Social Psychology, 59*(1), 17–26. https://doi.org/10.1037/0022-3514.59.1.17

Swann, W. B., Jr., Jetten, J., Gómez, Á., Whitehouse, H., & Bastian, B. (2012). When group membership gets personal: A theory of identity fusion. *Psychological Review, 119*(3), 441–456. https://doi.org/10.1037/a0028589

Swann, W. B., Jr., Kwan, V. S. Y., Polzer, J. T., & Milton, L. P. (2003). Fostering group identification and creativity in diverse groups: The role of individuation and self-verification. *Personality and Social Psychology Bulletin, 29*(11), 1396–1406. https://doi.org/10.1177/0146167203256868

Swann, W. B., Jr., Milton, L. P., & Polzer, J. T. (2000). Should we create a niche or fall in line? Identity negotiation and small group effectiveness. *Journal of Personality and Social Psychology, 79*(2), 238–250. https://doi.org/10.1037/0022-3514.79.2.238

Swann, W. B., Jr., Pelham, B. W., & Krull, D. S. (1989). Agreeable fancy or disagreeable truth? Reconciling self-enhancement and self-verification. *Journal of Personality and Social Psychology, 57*(5), 782–791.

Tajfel, H., & Turner, J. (1979). An integrative theory of intergroup conflict. In W. G. Austin & S. Worchel (Eds.), *The social psychology of intergroup relations* (pp. 33–47). Brooks-Cole. http://ark143.org/wordpress2/wp-content/uploads/2013/05/Tajfel-Turner-1979-An-Integrative-Theory-of-Intergroup-Conflict.pdf

Turner, J. C., Hogg, M. A., Oakes, P. J., Reicher, S. D., & Wetherell, M. S. (1987). *Rediscovering the social group: A self-categorization theory.* Basil Blackwell.

Twohey, M., & Dance, G. J. X. (2021, December 9). Where the despairing log on, and learn ways to die. *New York Times.* www.nytimes.com/interactive/2021/12/09/us/where-the-despairing-log-on.html

Varmann, A. H., Kruse, L., Bierwiaczonek, K., et al. (2023). How identity fusion predicts extreme pro-group orientations: A meta-analysis. *European Review of Social Psychology,* 1–36. https://doi.org/10.1080/10463283.2023.2190267

Walter, K. V., Conroy-Beam, D., Buss, D. M., et al. (2020). Sex differences in mate preferences across 45 countries: A large-scale replication. *Psychological Science, 31*(4), 408–423. https://doi.org/10.1177/0956797620904154

Webber, D., & Kruglanski, A. W. (2017). Psychological factors in radicalization: A "3 N" approach. In G. LaFree & J. D. Freilich (Eds.), *The handbook of the criminology of terrorism* (pp. 33–46). John Wiley & Sons. https://doi.org/10.1002/9781118923986.ch2

Whitehouse, H., Jong, J., Buhrmester, M. D., et al. (2017). The evolution of extreme cooperation via shared dysphoric experiences. *Scientific Reports, 7*(1), 44292. https://doi.org/10.1038/srep44292

Whitehouse, H., McQuinn, B., Buhrmester, M., & Swann Jr., W. B. (2014).Brothers in arms: Libyan revolutionaries bond like family. *Proceedings of the National Academy of Sciences, 111*(50), 17783–17785.

Wiesenfeld, B. M., Swann, W. B., Brockner, J., & Bartel, C. A. (2007). Is more fairness always preferred? Self-esteem moderates reactions to procedural justice. *Academy of Management Journal, 50*(5), 1235–1253. https://doi.org/10.5465/amj.2007.20159922

Wolfowicz, M., Litmanovitz, Y., Weisburd, D., & Hasisi, B. (2021). Cognitive and behavioral radicalization: A systematic review of the putative risk and protective factors. *Campbell Systematic Reviews, 17*(3). https://doi.org/10.1002/cl2.1174

Zell, E., Strickhouser, J. E., Sedikides, C., & Alicke, M. D. (2020). The better-than-average effect in comparative self-evaluation: A comprehensive review and meta-analysis. *Psychological Bulletin, 146*(2), 118–149.

PART II

Drivers of the Exclusion–Extremism Link

Extremism and Exclusion

The Role of the Quest for Significance

MOLLY ELLENBERG AND ARIE W. KRUGLANSKI

6.1 Introduction

How far would you go to lose weight? To get a rush of adrenaline? To feel like you belong? Would you sacrifice your health, your physical safety, your moral opposition to violent action? The motivational imbalance model of extremism posited by Kruglanski and colleagues (2021) holds that extreme dieters, extreme athletes, and violent extremists, though seemingly quite different from one another in their behavior, are tied together through an experience of motivational imbalance. The model explains that for most people, different needs are attended to equitably: When one is hungry, one eats; when one is thirsty, one drinks; and when one is lonely, one seeks the company of friends. Each need is fulfilled when it is activated, and no singular need becomes dominant over all others. In the case of extremism, no matter the type, one need becomes so dominant that all other needs are suppressed and ignored. One becomes willing to go to greater and greater lengths in order to meet the dominant need, relaxing previously held behavioral constraints. Consider an individual experiencing a state of extreme hunger. They are unable to focus on anything other than relieving their hunger, and they are willing to eat things they might not have eaten in a less extreme state of hunger. As they become hungrier, they are willing to eat normally despised foods. Even hungrier, they are willing to eat grass or rodents if nothing else is available. At the most extreme state of hunger, they may even resort to cannibalism. One who feels their stomach lightly growl after skipping lunch would never dream of such behavior – their need for nourishment is not dominant over all else.

6.2 The Quest for Significance

One particularly important need whose dominance can result in extreme behavior is the need for significance and mattering (Kruglanski et al., 2022). The need for significance and mattering is the universal and fundamental human need to feel accepted, respected, and socially worthy. The quest for significance is activated in instances of significance loss, threatened significance loss, and opportunity for significance gain (Kruglanski et al., 2013). When the need for significance is activated, information as to how to meet the need is provided by a narrative, a culturally specific set of norms and values that prescribes actions that should be taken in order to gain significance. The narrative is perpetuated and validated by a network, one's respected in-group, which rewards with significance those who adhere to the narrative and serve its values (Kruglanski et al., 2019). Often, the need for significance is met without sacrificing other needs; significance can be gained through achieving success in one's chosen career field, through winning an athletic competition, or even through falling in love! All of these can be achieved without neglecting one's needs for food, water, safety, security, or anything else.

But for some, the need for significance is so dominant, and its magnitude so great, that it can be met only through extreme behavior that disregards, or even impedes, one's other needs. In these cases, an adherent to a militant jihadist ideology, for example, might sacrifice their needs for safety and security and leave their home country to travel to help build what they believe to be a true Islamic Caliphate and to protect innocent civilians suffering under a brutal regime, even if doing so will include committing acts of violence (Speckhard & Ellenberg, 2022). A Palestinian young adult experiencing a profound sense of hopelessness and oppression may come to believe that their only path to dignity is by committing a suicide attack, suppressing their most basic need for survival, in pursuit of becoming a martyr and a hero to their community, as well as receiving divine rewards after death (Kruglanski et al., 2009; Speckhard, 2012). Among adherents to White supremacist ideologies, the quest for sig-nificance may be so great that one suppresses their need to be accepted by the broader society and may even engage in behavior that permanently precludes future acceptance (Graupmann & Wesselmann, this volume). Such a person may proudly display racist symbols as tattoos, willing to be rejected by one's biological family or coworkers for the sake of being viewed by their valued network of White supremacists as being completely committed to their cause (Speckhard, Ellenberg, & Garret, 2022b). In still other cases, a world leader may experience a quest for significance so great that he is willing to become a global pariah and sacrifice the lives of thousands of his countrymen for the sake of restoring his country to its former glory and conquering land he views as his (Kruglanski, 2022).

6.3   Exclusion as Loss of Significance

Hence, extremism of all types can be seen as arising from a motivational imbalance wherein one need becomes dominant over all other needs, which are subsequently suppressed until the focal need is met (Kruglanski et al., 2021). The quest for significance is one such need that can become dominant, resulting in deviant if not outright violent behavior in order to meet that need in accordance with a narrative upheld by a network (Kruglanski et al., 2022; Kruglanski et al., 2019). As mentioned previously, the quest for significance is activated by loss of significance, threatened loss of significance, or opportunity for significance gain (Kruglanski et al., 2013). These categories are rather broad and can range from rejection or humiliation on an individual level, to oppression of one's community, to the opportunity to become famous or powerful. The present chapter focuses on one specific type of significance loss that can lead to the quest for significance becoming dominant and the subsequent incidence of extreme behavior: exclusion.

Exclusion is often conceptualized as the thwarted need to belong and thus a threat to the many evolutionary benefits of living in groups (Bernstein, 2016). Yet, research on social exclusion highlights the myriad consequences of being ostracized from one's group, beyond those threats often highlighted by evolutionary psychologists such as physical protection from interlopers or division of labor. The psychological literature on exclusion begins with William James (1890), who equated exclusion with being treated as though one does not exist (the ultimate loss of significance!), and has proliferated ever since. In the workplace, social exclusion is associated with lower satisfaction and poorer mental health, particularly among men (Hitlan et al., 2006). Research in clinical psychology has demonstrated that emotional exclusion, "perceiving oneself to be a less valuable member of a relationship or group," even in the absence of physical exclusion, can contribute to the onset and severity of psychological disorders including social anxiety disorder, obsessive compulsive disorder, posttraumatic stress disorder, depression, schizophrenia, and borderline personality disorder, among others (Fung et al., 2016, p. 157). Those who are socially excluded are also more likely to engage in self-defeating behavior (Twenge et al., 2002), aggressive behavior (Twenge et al., 2001), and unethical behavior (Kouchaki & Wareham, 2015; Thau et al., 2015). Social exclusion has also been found to reduce intelligence, particularly as it applies to complex logic (Baumeister et al., 2002). It is also associated with increased religiosity (Aydin et al., 2010).

Such consequences of exclusion are varied and may seem counterintuitive (DeWall & Richman, 2011). If one is feeling rejected, why would they act in an antisocial manner that is unlikely to earn them the acceptance they crave? This type of behavior may be explained by understanding the need to belong, which Baumeister and Leary (1995) categorized as "a powerful, fundamental, and extremely pervasive motivation," as a facet of the broader need for significance (p. 497). Indeed, research exploring the link between exclusion and aggression has highlighted the role of hostile attribution bias, suggesting that it is the perception of disrespect or insult, and thus loss of significance, that leads excluded individuals to act aggressively (DeWall et al., 2009). Further evidence of the critical role of significance in the need to belong is found in research showing that being rejected by members of one's in-group – their network – leads to increased essentialist beliefs about in-groups and out-groups, that is, beliefs that group membership is innate and that differences between groups are naturally occurring, rather than socially constructed (Bernstein et al., 2010). In other words, membership in the in-group becomes even more valuable when one has been excluded from it, and gaining acceptance by that group becomes key to maintaining one's self-concept and significance. In this case, one would need to behave in ways that are consistent with the relevant narrative in order to return to the network's good graces, thus engaging in affiliative behavior (Ren et al., 2017). For prosocial groups, acting aggressively might not serve this purpose and would be counterproductive. Some groups, however, reward aggression on behalf of its goals; thus, acting in an antisocial manner would serve the purpose of gaining significance.

In still other cases, however, one might come to believe that they will never be accepted by their former group. In the workplace, this might result in extreme antisocial behaviors against that group, ranging from low-level work-place deviance (Hollinger, 1986) to mass shootings (Lankford, 2013; Kowalski & Leary, this volume). If someone believes that they will never be accepted by a group that has ostracized them, they are also likely to seek out a new group that will accept them and grant their need for significance, even, and some-times especially, if this group has an extreme ideology and promotes antisocial behavior (Gonsalkorale & Williams, 2007; Hales & Williams, 2018). Whether an individual (1) engages in extreme behavior to ingratiate themselves with a valued group that has excluded them, (2) aggresses against that group, or (3) joins an extreme group when inclusion in an old group is no longer an option, each of these cases is emblematic of the effect that exclusion can have when it activates the need for significance.

6.4   Exclusion and Extremism

Before examining each of these exclusion situations in turn, it is worth considering that in addition to the exclusion itself preceding extremism, the reason for the exclusion has also been found to play a role in this relationship. Notably, some research has suggested that being unfairly excluded results in more anger and more antisocial behavior than being excluded for a fair, or even simply a clear, reason (Chow et al., 2008; Sommer et al., 2001). This is consistent with the conceptualization of aggression as arising from signifi-cance-reducing frustration (Kruglanski et al., 2023), with "arbitrary" or unfair frustrations resulting in more significance loss than nonarbitrary or reasonable frustrations (Pastore, 1952). Thus, we may posit that exclusion leads to extreme, antisocial behavior to the extent that the exclusion engenders a loss of significance.

Let us turn first to the issue of regaining social acceptance and inclusion by engaging in violent extremism. Some female suicide attackers, for example, have been found to have experienced exclusion and isolation from their communities (Pedahzur, 2005). Particularly in highly collectivist societies in which family and community honor are prioritized (Oyserman, 2017), these women's need for significance, to restore themselves and their families to positions of dignity, leads them to suppress their need for survival and to volunteer to sacrifice their lives in service of a greater cause (Pedahzur, 2005). Similarly, letters from Japanese kamikaze pilots during World War II reveal that these men feared that if they did not execute their fatal task, they would bring dishonor, and thus ostracism, on themselves and their families (Kruglanski et al., 2014; Ohnuki-Tierney, 2007). At a less lethal level, Goldman and Hogg (2016) found that peripheral, as opposed to central, members of fraternities and sororities, particularly those who identified highly with their groups, were most likely to engage in aggressive behavior against rival groups. These individuals on the periphery of their valued group are more likely to have an activated quest for significance than more central members, who are already respected and valued. Thus, peripheral members, when their need for significance is dominant, are willing to take extreme actions, suppressing their need to adhere to broader societal norms of behavior, if they believe that doing so will earn them significance through acceptance and esteem from the group. These examples illustrate the idea of "sacred values," as explained by Atran and Ginges (2012): When one seeks to be granted acceptance and significance by their group and to strengthen their group identity, the clearest way to do so is often by acting in defense of a divine being or a cause important to the group. For example, among supporters of both pro-life and pro-choice movements in the United States, social exclusion was predictive of support for extreme actions on behalf of their goal. This effect was explained, in part, by increased group identification, emblematic of excluded individuals' dominant need to be accepted and respected by members of their in-group (Knapton et al., 2022; Renström & Bäck, this volume).

When considering extremism, there has perhaps been more interest in the applicability of the research on the interface between exclusion and extremism in the cases where social exclusion feels permanent and reacceptance impossible. It is in these cases that DeWall and Richman (2011) highlight the shift from prosocial behavior for the sake of ingratiating oneself with their group (although such prosocial behavior may also be conceived of as pro-group behavior that is otherwise unethical or aggressive) to antisocial behavior, including aggression against one's former group (Twenge et al., 2001).

Significance-reducing exclusion, as defined previously, particularly when reacceptance to the mainstream group is unlikely, has been highly researched with regard to violent extremism but referred to by different terms, such as ostracism, alienation, and marginalization. As Williams and Nida (2011) make clear, ostracism threatens more than just belonging; it is a form of "social death" that thwarts the needs for "self-esteem, sense of control, and sense of meaningful existence" (p. 72). Similarly, alienation tends to be used in the terrorism literature to describe the securitization of Muslim communities in Western countries that may be targeted for recruitment by militant jihadist groups (Shanaah, 2022; Taylor, 2020). At its core, alienation is a form of significance-reducing exclusion in which individuals feel as though they are not accepted as true members of their countries or communities and that they are perceived as unworthy of trust or protection. In one study, Lobato and colleagues (2023) found that, among Spanish adults, social alienation predicted support for political violence when obsessive passion was high. Given that obsessive passion has been linked to extremism of many types (Resta et al., 2022), this study demonstrates the role of motivational imbalance in which the quest for significance becomes dominant in linking exclusion to violent or deviant behavior. Finally, marginalization has been defined as a feeling of "cultural homelessness" in which one feels that they do not belong in the majority culture of their society nor in the minority culture of their home country or family's home country, resulting in a loss of self-worth (Lyons-Padilla et al., 2015, pp. 2–3). Thus, ostracism, alienation, and marginalization can each be understood as forms of significance-reducing exclusion, with the latter two implying irreparable exclusion from mainstream society.

The experience of such significance-reducing exclusion is often accompanied by a sense of self-uncertainty (Wagoner & Hogg, this volume). Ostracism, marginalization, and alienation all result in uncertainty as to where someone belongs and who they are. When self-uncertainty occurs, people seek to identify with new groups that are highly entitative – groups that have "clear boundaries, internal homogeneity, social interaction, clear internal structure, common goals, and common fate" (Hogg et al., 2007, p. 136). By definition, then, highly entitative groups tend to be more extreme in their ideological positions and in their group-related behaviors than less entitative groups. It is these very qualities that make extreme groups attractive to people experiencing significance loss after being socially excluded. In the forthcoming sections, we describe three cases that illustrate significance-reducing exclusion resulting in extremism.

6.4.1   Discrimination and Militant Jihadism

The powerful effect of marginalization and alienation on the radicalization of young Muslim men and women living in Western countries has long been the subject of discussion in academic literature and mainstream media. Particularly, the effect of increased securitization and surveillance of Muslim communities in the wake of the September 11th attacks in the United States, the July 7th attacks in the United Kingdom, the 2004 Madrid train bombings, and subsequent unprecedented migration of foreign fighters to join ISIS has been of great interest. It is important to note, of course, that terrorism and radicalization in general have a low base rate – very few Muslims radicalize to militant jihadist violent extremism, just as very few White Christians radicalize to White supremacism.

Yet, a common thread among the small proportion of Western Muslims who radicalize to militant jihadism appears to be an experience of discrimination, marginalization, and alienation (Hafez & Mullins, 2015; Pfundmair, this volume). For example, between 1970 and 2006, countries in which minority groups faced economic discrimination, and thus exclusion from opportunities for mainstream success, were more likely to face acts of terrorism than countries that did not have such discrimination or had taken remedial steps to reduce such discrimination. Notably, poverty in and of itself was not a predictor of terrorist incidents, implying that it is the exclusion from economic advancement, and not a widespread lack of opportunity, that plays a role in radicalization to violent extremism (Piazza, 2011). Similarly, perceived discrimination, in addition to younger age, predicted justification of and support for suicide bombings among Muslim diaspora populations in the United Kingdom, France, Germany, Spain, and the United States (Victoroff et al., 2012). An analysis of Twitter in France, the United Kingdom, Germany, and Belgium found that increased Islamophobic tweets (emblematic of anti-Muslim exclusion) were significantly correlated with increased ISIS-related tweets in the same local geographic areas (Mitts, 2019). In the Netherlands, Muslim Dutch youth of Moroccan and Turkish descent were more likely to support violent defense of their religious group if they felt disconnected from mainstream society (via exclusion) and if they felt that they lacked the same economic opportunities as people of European descent in the Netherlands (van Bergen et al., 2015). In France, the national ban on headscarves both increased feelings of discrimination and decreased educational attainment among Muslim women, both of which contribute to a sense of exclusion from mainstream society (Abdelgadir & Fouka, 2020). In 2020, militant jihadists worked to recruit supporters online by highlighting that while surgical face coverings were required in France due to the COVID-19 pandemic, religious face and head coverings remained banned (Kruglanski et al., 2020; McAuley, 2020). And, indeed, European countries with bans on Islamic modesty dress such as *niqabs* and *burqas* have experienced greater numbers of and more lethal terrorist attacks than European countries without such bans (Saiya & Manchanda, 2020). Among American Muslims, more experiences of discrimination strengthened the positive relationship between feelings of marginalization and feelings of significance loss, which subsequently predicted support for extremist interpretations of Islam and attraction to groups that promoted such interpretations (Lyons-Padilla et al., 2015). Additionally, perceived religious discrimination, but not religiosity, was found to predict support for suicide attacks among Muslim Americans (Beller & Kröger, 2021).

It is noteworthy that marginalization of Muslim communities often arises from counterterrorism efforts that create and target entire "suspect communities" (Taylor, 2020; Bull & Rane, 2019). In the United Kingdom, scholars have noted that this phenomenon is not new. During "The Troubles" of the 1970s–1990s, Irish communities in the United Kingdom felt alienated by counterterrorism and surveillance measures, which served to justify and support violence against the British by militant groups such as the Irish Republican Army and the Provisional IRA (Duffy, 2009; Hickman et al., 2011). In China, extreme securitization and ostracism of the Muslim Uyghur population in Xinjiang, including indefinite detainment in brutal conditions, have been found to have increased radicalization and subsequent violence among Uyghur separatists (Trédaniel & Lee, 2018). Similar radicalizing effects have been found among Palestinians subjected to home demolitions and checkpoint closures in acts of "indiscriminate counterterrorism" (Freedman & Klor, 2023, p. 1592).

6.4.2   Sexual Exclusion and Incels

Another pertinent example of the link between exclusion and extremism is the involuntary celibate (incel) movement (Rousis & Swann, this volume). Although in existence online for nearly three decades, the incel community has recently come under the media spotlight following a number of high-profile violent attacks by self-proclaimed incels (Hoffman & Ware, 2020). The incel ideology, the "blackpill," holds that feminism and gender equality in Western society have resulted in the complete exclusion of low-status men from dating and sexual relationships since they cannot compete with "Chads" – the handsome, wealthy, ultra-masculine men whom they believe women prefer (Speckhard et al., 2021). Although some have argued that incels as a community should not all be labeled as violent extremists, it is clear that a significant minority (i.e., 21 percent in a sample of 257) of self-described incels do support violence, especially toward women, as a way of demonstrating their power and causing harm to those whom they believe have condemned them to a life of loneliness and rejection (Ellenberg et al., 2023). Recent research has found that male self-described incels were more depressed, anxious, and lonely and had a lower life satisfaction than non-incel males of the same age. Notably, the largest difference between incels and non-incels was in loneliness (Cohen's $d = 0.97$; Costello et al., 2022). Another study found that loneliness was higher among incels than non-incels, and that loneliness was significantly and positively correlated with scores on the Incel Traits Scale, which includes two factors, "defeated" and "hateful" (Scaptura & Boyle, 2020; Sparks et al., 2023).

In addition to rejection from potential romantic and sexual partners, a survey of 272 active members on an online incel forum found that these men experienced exclusion and ostracism throughout their lives, dating back to grade school (Speckhard et al., 2021). Such exclusion, combined with bullying that focused on their perceived lack of masculinity, over many years, which may be conceived of as a chronic experience of significance loss, was found to predict violent ideations, especially among those who had read the manifesto of mass murderer and incel "saint" Elliot Rodger (Kruglanski et al., 2023; Witt, 2020). Moreover, being bullied was positively and significantly associated with radical intentions among incels (Moskalenko et al., 2022). Additionally, a survey of heterosexual American men found that feelings of lack of acceptance were positively associated with violent fantasies, but that this relationship was statistically significant only for participants who scored high on the "defeated" and "hateful" incel traits (Scaptura & Boyle, 2020).

6.4.3   Veteran Radicalization

Yet another example of extremism, albeit one with a perhaps less obvious link to exclusion, that has garnered increased attention in recent years is that of far-right violent extremist radicalization among military service members and veterans (Jensen et al., 2022; Milton & Mines, 2021; Torchinsky, 2022). Researchers have highlighted the need for significance among recently separated members of the military who seek camaraderie and a noble purpose among militias and White supremacist violent extremist groups that paint themselves as defenders of their respective countries (Speckhard & Ellenberg, 2023; Speckhard, Ellenberg, & Garret, 2022a). Evidence for exclusion as a precursor to this significance loss can be found in theories of veteran mental health challenges more generally, which point to negative transition experiences from military to civilian life as an antecedent to poor physical and psychological outcomes (Castro & Kintzle, 2018).

Military transition theory highlights a number of significance loss-related factors in contributing to risk among veterans, including loss of a military identity (Simi et al., 2013), and one important such factor is a feeling of exclusion from mainstream society following separation. As explained by Keeling and colleagues (2019) of the struggles of post-discharge employment, "both veterans and employers may struggle to translate military experience to comparable civilian credentials ... [and] mismatch in communication and being misunderstood can lead to feelings of invalidation" (Keeling et al., 2019, p. 699). The same research found that veterans in a number of focus groups "reported having to 'start over' in civilian life such as taking entry-level and low-paying jobs, returning to education, and gaining civilian certifications in things they were trained to do in the military" (Keeling et al., 2019, p. 699). In addition to unemployment or underemployment, veterans may feel that their combat experiences or different expectations regarding workplace culture create psychological distance from their coworkers, creating a sense of exclusion (Shepherd et al., 2021).

Such exclusion from well-paying and psychologically rewarding jobs can make the draw of violent extremist groups difficult to resist, as these groups explicitly recruit veterans for their military skills and experience, as well as their ability to impart weapons and tactical training to other group members (Speckhard, Ellenberg, & Garret, 2022a). Similarly, White supremacist and far-right violent extremist groups may validate some veterans' worldviews, particularly, in the twenty-first century, the Islamophobia and dehumanization "that soldiers are trained to embrace as a battlefield tactic" (Miller-Idriss, 2021, p. 62). In German far-right violent extremist groups, this effect is amplified dramatically in narratives that venerate the Nazis as heroic warriors, first allowing veterans and then their descendants to feel accepted in and respected for the same actions that led to their banishment from mainstream society following World War II (Hurd & Werther, 2016). These violent extremist groups thus convey their acceptance of and respect for veterans in ways that may seem more empathetic than coworkers and supervisors in mainstream workplaces, thus boosting veterans' sense of significance and ameliorating the pain of exclusion (MacDonald & Leary, 2005).

6.5   The Quest for Significance Explains the Relationship between Exclusion and Extremism

The link between exclusion and extremism is clear from examples of militant jihadists, incels, and radicalized military veterans, along with many other violent extremist groups. This link can be explained by the quest for significance, which is activated by the experience of exclusion. This relationship was demonstrated in the work of Knapton et al., (2022), who found that the link between social exclusion and endorsement of radical pro-choice or pro-life action was serially mediated by an activated need for significance and increased in-group identity. In another study, Bélanger (2013) found that participants who recalled an experience of social exclusion were more ready to sacrifice themselves for an important cause than participants who recalled an experience of physical pain. In another academic realm, social exclusion was found to increase financial risk-taking (which could reach extreme levels), and this relationship was explained by activating a need for popularity (i.e., significance) (Duclos et al., 2013).

According to Williams's (2009) temporal need-threat model of social ostracism, ostracism threatens needs for, in addition to belonging, self-esteem, control, and meaningful existence. Indeed, significance quest theory subsumes these needs (Kruglanski et al., 2022) and loss of social identity (i.e., loss of significance) has been found to decrease satisfaction of all four of these needs (Greenaway et al., 2016). Further, manipulation checks from numerous studies that use exclusion as a proxy for loss of significance demonstrate that exclusion can indeed result in extremism by activating the quest for significance. For example, the well-known exclusion "Cyberball" paradigm (Williams & Jarvis, 2006) produced threats to significance needs and was subsequently predictive of support for and willingness to engage in extreme behavior (Pfundmair & Wetherell, 2019). Alas, other studies that have used exclusion manipulations to predict extremism simply state outright that exclusion is a prime example of significance loss, thus rendering such a manipulation check irrelevant (Bäck et al., 2018; Renström et al., 2020).

6.6 Conclusion

Exclusion, whether described as ostracism, alienation, discrimination, or marginalization, produces social pain. It threatens one's goals to belong, to have self-esteem, to have autonomy and control, and to live a meaningful life (Hales et al., this volume; Williams, 2009). It can even provide a taste of social death and nonexistence (Greenberg et al., 1990; Williams, 2007). At its core, exclusion is the prototypical experience of significance loss. Just as a need for food can result in extreme eating behavior when dominant and a need for a thrill can result in extreme sports when dominant, the need for significance (when accompanied by a supportive narrative and network) can result in violent extremism when dominant. The quest for significance, when activated, including by social exclusion, motivates an individual to do whatever they can to restore their degraded need. As exemplified in this chapter, extremism can be used to restore one's sense of significance by joining highly entitative groups that clearly demarcate group norms, demonstrating deep commitment to cultural values, and by enacting violence both on behalf of those norms and values and against the excluding group, which is painted as the culprit behind one's loss of significance.

Still, it is important to note that the link between exclusion and extremism via loss of significance is not unidirectional. Openness to extremism and membership in extreme groups has been found, perhaps unsurprisingly, to increase ostracism by people who do not adhere to such ideologies or support such actions (Hales & Williams, 2019). Ergo, a cycle of ostracism, significance loss, and extremism emerges: In order to regain significance following social exclusion, one joins an extreme group. They are then further isolated from their previous, nonextreme group and deal with that continued rejection and significance by demonstrating even more stalwart commitment to their newfound extreme group and its ideology. This cycle is important to remember for those working to bring people out of extreme groups, as exclusion and isolation, while potentially warranted given some extremists' abhorrent beliefs, can reinforce the idea that the excluded person's best and only way of gaining significance is through extremism. Indeed, welcoming individuals back into the mainstream and promoting reintegration, difficult as it can be, may be a more successful way to promote deradicalization than by shunning or shaming.

References

Abdelgadir, A., & Fouka, V. (2020). Political secularism and Muslim integration in the West: Assessing the effects of the French headscarf ban. *American Political Science Review*, *114*(3), 707–723.

Atran, S., & Ginges, J. (2012). Religious and sacred imperatives in human conflict. *Science*, *336*(6083), 855–857.

Aydin, N., Fischer, P., & Frey, D. (2010). Turning to God in the face of ostracism: Effects of social exclusion on religiousness. *Personality and Social Psychology Bulletin*, *36*(6), 742–753.

Bäck, E. A., Bäck, H., Altermark, N., & Knapton, H. (2018). The quest for significance: Attitude adaption to a radical group following social exclusion. *International Journal of Developmental Science*, *12*(1–2), 25–36.

Baumeister, R. F., & Leary, M. R. (1995). The need to belong: Desire for interpersonal attachments as a fundamental human motivation. *Psychological Bulletin*, *117*(3), 497–529.

Baumeister, R. F., Twenge, J. M., & Nuss, C. K. (2002). Effects of social exclusion on cognitive processes: anticipated aloneness reduces intelligent thought. *Journal of personality and social psychology*, *83*(4), 817–827.

Bélanger, J. J. (2013). The psychology of martyrdom [Unpublished doctoral dissertation]. University of Maryland–College Park.

Beller, J., & Kröger, C. (2021). Religiosity and perceived religious discrimination as predictors of support for suicide attacks among Muslim Americans. *Peace and Conflict: Journal of Peace Psychology*, *27*(4), 554–567.

Bernstein, M. J. (2016). Research in social psychology: Consequences of short- and long-term social exclusion. In P. Riva & J. Eck (Eds.), *Social exclusion: Psychological approaches to understanding and reducing its impact* (pp. 51–72). Springer.

Bernstein, M. J., Sacco, D. F., Young, S. G., Hugenberg, K., & Cook, E. (2010). Being "in" with the in-crowd: The effects of social exclusion and inclusion are enhanced by the perceived essentialism of ingroups and outgroups. *Personality and Social Psychology Bulletin*, *36*(8), 999–1009.

Bull, M., & Rane, H. (2019). Beyond faith: social marginalisation and the prevention of radicalisation among young Muslim Australians. *Critical Studies on Terrorism*, *12*(2), 273–297. https://doi.org/10.1080/17539153.2018.1496781

Castro, C. A., & Kintzle, S. (2018). *Military transition theory*. Springer.

Chow, R. M., Tiedens, L. Z., & Govan, C. L. (2008). Excluded emotions: The role of anger in antisocial responses to ostracism. *Journal of Experimental Social Psychology*, *44*(3), 896–903.

Costello, W., Rolon, V., Thomas, A. G., & Schmitt, D. (2022). Levels of well-being among men who are incel (involuntarily celibate). *Evolutionary Psychological Science*, *8*(4), 375–390.

DeWall, C. N., & Richman, S. B. (2011). Social exclusion and the desire to reconnect. *Social and Personality Psychology Compass*, *5*(11), 919–932.

DeWall, C. N., Twenge, J. M., Gitter, S. A., & Baumeister, R. F. (2009). It's the thought that counts: The role of hostile cognition in shaping aggressive responses to social exclusion. *Journal of Personality and Social Psychology, 96* (1), 45–59.

Duclos, R., Wan, E. W., & Jiang, Y. (2013). Show me the honey! Effects of social exclusion on financial risk-taking. *Journal of Consumer Research, 40*(1), 12–135.

Duffy, D. (2009). Alienated radicals and detached deviants: what do the lessons of the 1970 Falls Curfew and the alienation–radicalisation hypothesis mean for current British approaches to counter-terrorism? *Policy Studies, 30*(2), 127–142.

Ellenberg, M., Speckhard, A., & Kruglanski, A. W. (2023). Beyond violent extremism: A 3 N perspective of inceldom. *Psychology of Men & Masculinities.* Advance online publication. https://psycnet.apa.org/doi/10.1037/men0000439

Freedman, M., & Klor, E. F. (2023). When deterrence backfires: House demolitions, Palestinian radicalization, and Israeli fatalities. *Journal of Conflict Resolution, 67*(7–8), 1592–1617.

Fung, K., Xu, C., Glazier, B. L., Parsons, C. A., & Alden, L. E. (2016). Research in clinical psychology: Social exclusion and psychological disorders. In P. Riva & J. Eck (Eds.), *Social exclusion: Psychological approaches to understanding and reducing its impact* (pp. 157–176). Springer.

Goldman, L., & Hogg, M. A. (2016). Going to extremes for one's group: The role of prototypicality and group acceptance. *Journal of Applied Social Psychology, 46* (9), 544–553.

Gonsalkorale, K., & Williams, K. D. (2007). The KKK won't let me play: Ostracism even by a despised outgroup hurts. *European Journal of Social Psychology, 37*(6), 1176–1186.

Greenaway, K. H., Cruwys, T., Haslam, S. A., & Jetten, J. (2016). Social identities promote well-being because they satisfy global psychological needs. *European Journal of Social Psychology, 46*(3), 294–307.

Greenberg, J., Pyszczynski, T., & Solomon, S. (1990). Anxiety concerning social exclusion: Innate response or one consequence of the need for terror management? *Journal of Social and Clinical Psychology, 9*(2), 202–213.

Hafez, M., & Mullins, C. (2015). The radicalization puzzle: A theoretical synthesis of empirical approaches to homegrown extremism. *Studies in Conflict & Terrorism, 38*(11), 958–975.

Hales, A. H., & Williams, K. D. (2018). Marginalized individuals and extremism: The role of ostracism in openness to extreme groups. *Journal of Social Issues, 74* (1), 75–92.

Hales, A. H., & Williams, K. D. (2019). Extremism leads to ostracism. *Social Psychology, 51*(3), 149–156. https://doi.org/10.1027/1864-9335/a000406

Hickman, M., Thomas, L., Silvestri, S., & Nickels, H. (2011). *"Suspect communities?" Counter-terrorism policy, the press, and the impact on Irish and Muslim communities in Britain.* London Metropolitan University.

Hitlan, R. T., Cliffton, R. J., & DeSoto, M. C. (2006). Perceived exclusion in the workplace: The moderating effects of gender on work-related attitudes and psychological health. *North American Journal of Psychology*, 8(2), 217–236.

Hoffman, B., & Ware, J. (2020). *Incels: America's newest domestic terrorism threat.* Lawfare blog. www.lawfareblog.com/incels-americas-newest-domestic-terrorism-threat

Hogg, M. A., Sherman, D. K., Dierselhuis, J., Maitner, A. T., & Moffitt, G. (2007). Uncertainty, entitativity, and group identification. *Journal of Experimental Social Psychology*, 43(1), 135–142.

Hollinger, R. C. (1986). Acts against the workplace: Social bonding and employee deviance. *Deviant Behavior*, 7(1), 53–75.

Hurd, M., & Werther, S. (2016). Retelling the past, inspiring the future: Waffen-SS commemorations and the creation of a "European" far-right counter-narrative. *Patterns of Prejudice*, 50(4–5), 420–444.

James, W. (1890). *The principles of psychology.* Macmillan.

Jensen, M., Yates, E., & Kane, S. (2022). *Radicalization in the ranks: An assessment of the scope and nature of criminal extremism in the United States military.* START. www.start.umd.edu/sites/default/files/publications/local_attachments/Radicalization%20in%20the%20Ranks_April%202022.pdf

Keeling, M. E., Ozuna, S. M., Kintzle, S., & Castro, C. A. (2019). Veterans' civilian employment experiences: Lessons learnt from focus groups. *Journal of Career Development*, 46(6), 692–705.

Knapton, H., Renström, E., & Lindén, M. (2022). The abortion divide: Exploring the role of exclusion, loss of significance and identity in the radicalization process. *Frontiers in Psychology*, 13, 1–14.

Kouchaki, M., & Wareham, J. (2015). Excluded and behaving unethically: social exclusion, physiological responses, and unethical behavior. *Journal of Applied Psychology*, 100(2), 547–556.

Kruglanski, A. W. (2022, March 1). *Putin is on a quest for historical significance by invading Ukraine and gambling on his own and Russia's glory.* The Conversation. https://theconversation.com/putin-is-on-a-quest-for-historical-significance-by-invading-ukraine-and-gambling-on-his-own-and-russias-glory-177887.

Kruglanski, A. W., Bélanger, J. J., Gelfand, M., et al. (2013). Terrorism – A (self) love story: Redirecting the significance quest can end violence. *American Psychologist*, 68(7), 559–575.

Kruglanski, A. W., Bélanger, J. J., & Gunaratna, R. (2019). *The three pillars of radicalization: Needs, narratives, and networks.* Oxford University Press.

Kruglanski, A. W., Chen, X., Dechesne, M., Fishman, S., & Orehek, E. (2009). Fully committed: Suicide bombers' motivation and the quest for personal significance. *Political Psychology*, 30(3), 331–357.

Kruglanski, A. W., Ellenberg, M., Szumowska, E., et al. (2023). Frustration-aggression hypothesis reconsidered: The role of significance quest. *Aggressive Behavior*, 49(5), 445–468. https://doi.org/10.1002/ab.22092

Kruglanski, A. W., Gelfand, M. J., Bélanger, J. J., et al. (2014). The psychology of radicalization and deradicalization: How significance quest impacts violent extremism. *Political Psychology, 35*, 69–93.

Kruglanski, A. W., Gunaratna, R., Ellenberg, M., & Speckhard, A. (2020). Terrorism in time of the pandemic: Exploiting mayhem. *Global Security: Health, Science and Policy, 5*(1), 121–132.

Kruglanski, A. W., Molinario, E., Jasko, K., et al. (2022). Significance-quest theory. *Perspectives on Psychological Science, 17*(4), 1050–1071.

Kruglanski, A. W., Szumowska, E., Kopetz, C. H., Vallerand, R. J., & Pierro, A. (2021). On the psychology of extremism: How motivational imbalance breeds intemperance. *Psychological Review, 128*(2), 264–289.

Lankford, A. (2013). A comparative analysis of suicide terrorists and rampage, workplace, and school shooters in the United States from 1990 to 2010. *Homicide Studies, 17*(3), 255–274.

Lobato, R. M., García-Coll, J., & Moyano, M. (2023). Disconnected out of passion: relationship between social alienation and obsessive passion. *Journal of interpersonal violence, 38*(1–2), 1950–1969.

Lyons-Padilla, S., Gelfand, M. J., Mirahmadi, H., Farooq, M., & Van Egmond, M. (2015). Belonging nowhere: Marginalization & radicalization risk among Muslim immigrants. *Behavioral Science & Policy, 1*(2), 1–12.

MacDonald, G., & Leary, M. R. (2005). Why does social exclusion hurt? The relationship between social and physical pain. *Psychological Bulletin, 131*(2), 202–223.

McAuley, J. (2020). France mandates masks to control the coronavirus. Burqas remain banned. *Washington Post.* www.washingtonpost.com/world/europe/france-face-masks-coronavirus/2020/05/09/6fbd50fc-8ae6-11ea-80df-d24b35a568ae_story.html

Miller-Idriss, C. (2021). From 9/11 to 1/6: The War on Terror supercharged the far right. *Foreign Affairs.* www.foreignaffairs.com/articles/united-states/2021-08-24/war-on-terror-911-jan6

Milton, D., & Mines, A. (2021). *"This is war": Examining military experience among the Capitol Hill siege participants.* Program on Extremism. https://extremism.gwu.edu/sites/g/files/zaxdzs5746/files/This_is_War.pdf

Mitts, T. (2019). From isolation to radicalization: Anti-Muslim hostility and support for ISIS in the West. *American Political Science Review, 113*(1), 173–194.

Moskalenko, S., González, J. F. G., Kates, N., & Morton, J. (2022). Incel ideology, radicalization and mental health: A survey study. *The Journal of Intelligence, Conflict, and Warfare, 4*(3), 1–29.

Ohnuki-Tierney, E. (2007). *Kamikaze diaries: Reflections of Japanese student soldiers.* University of Chicago Press.

Oyserman, D. (2017). Culture three ways: Culture and subcultures within countries. *Annual Review of Psychology, 68*, 435–463.

Pastore, N. (1952). The role of arbitrariness in the frustration-aggression hypothesis. *The Journal of Abnormal and Social Psychology, 47*(3), 728–731.

Pedahzur, A. (2005). *Suicide terrorism.* Polity.

Pfundmair, M., Hales, A., & Williams, K. D. (Eds.). (2024). *Exclusion and extremism: A psychological perspective.* Cambridge University Press.

Pfundmair, M., & Wetherell, G. (2019). Ostracism drives group moralization and extreme group behavior. *The Journal of Social Psychology, 159*(5), 518–530.

Piazza, J. A. (2011). Poverty, minority economic discrimination, and domestic terrorism. *Journal of Peace Research, 48*(3), 339–353.

Ren, D., Hales, A. H., & Williams, K. D. (2017). Ostracism: Being ignored and excluded. In K. D. Williams & S. A. Nida (Eds.), *Ostracism, exclusion, and rejection* (pp. 20–38). Routledge.

Renström, E. A., Bäck, H., & Knapton, H. M. (2020). Exploring a pathway to radicalization: The effects of social exclusion and rejection sensitivity. *Group Processes & Intergroup Relations, 23*(8), 1204–1229.

Resta, E., Ellenberg, M., Kruglanski, A. W., & Pierro, A. (2022). Marie Curie vs. Serena Williams: Ambition leads to extremism through obsessive (but not harmonious) passion. *Motivation and Emotion, 46*(3), 382–393.

Saiya, N., & Manchanda, S. (2020). Do burqa bans make us safer? Veil prohibitions and terrorism in Europe. *Journal of European Public Policy, 27*(12), 1781–1800.

Scaptura, M. N., & Boyle, K. M. (2020). Masculinity threat, "incel" traits, and violent fantasies among heterosexual men in the United States. *Feminist Criminology, 15*(3), 278–298.

Shanaah, S. (2022). Alienation or cooperation? British Muslims' Attitudes to and engagement in counter-terrorism and counter-extremism. *Terrorism and Political Violence, 34*(1), 71–92.

Shepherd, S., Sherman, D. K., MacLean, A., & Kay, A. C. (2021). The challenges of military veterans in their transition to the workplace: A call for integrating basic and applied psychological science. *Perspectives on Psychological Science, 16*(3), 590–613.

Simi, P., Bubolz, B. F., & Hardman, A. (2013). Military experience, identity discrepancies, and far right terrorism: An exploratory analysis. *Studies in Conflict & Terrorism, 36*(8), 654–671.

Sommer, K. L., Williams, K. D., Ciarocco, N. J., & Baumeister, R. F. (2001). When silence speaks louder than words: Explorations into the intrapsychic and interpersonal consequences of social ostracism. *Basic and Applied Social Psychology, 23*(4), 225–243.

Sparks, B., Zidenberg, A. M., & Olver, M. E. (2023). One is the loneliest number: Involuntary celibacy (incel), mental health, and loneliness. *Current Psychology,* 1–15.

Speckhard, A. (2012). *Talking to terrorists: Understanding the psycho-social motivations of militant jihadi terrorists, mass hostage takers, suicide bombers & "martyrs".* Advances Press.

Speckhard, A., & Ellenberg, M. (2022). The effects of Assad's atrocities and the call to foreign fighters to come to Syria on the rise and fall of the ISIS Caliphate. *Behavioral Sciences of Terrorism and Political Aggression, 14*(2), 169–185.

Speckhard, A., & Ellenberg, M. (2023). An analysis of active-duty and veteran military members involved in white supremacist and violent anti-government militias and groups: 2017–2022. *International Center for the Study of Violent Extremism.*

Speckhard, A., Ellenberg, M., & Garret, T. M. (2022a). The challenge of extremism in the military is not going away without a new perspective. *International Center for the Study of Violent Extremism.*

Speckhard, A., Ellenberg, M., & Garret, T. M. (2022b). White supremacists speak: Recruitment, radicalization & experiences of engaging and disengaging from hate groups. *International Center for the Study of Violent Extremism.*

Speckhard, A., Ellenberg, M., Morton, J., & Ash, A. (2021). Involuntary celibates' experiences of and grievance over sexual exclusion and the potential threat of violence among those active in an online incel forum. *Journal of Strategic Security, 14*(2), 89–121.

Taylor, J. D. (2020). "Suspect categories," alienation and counterterrorism: Critically assessing PREVENT in the UK. *Terrorism and Political Violence, 32* (4), 851–873.

Thau, S., Derfler-Rozin, R., Pitesa, M., Mitchell, M. S., & Pillutla, M. M. (2015). Unethical for the sake of the group: risk of social exclusion and pro-group unethical behavior. *Journal of Applied Psychology, 100*(1), 98–113.

Torchinsky, R. (2022, February 9). *1 in 5 Patriot Front applicants say they have ties to the military.* NPR. www.npr.org/2022/02/09/1079700404/1-in-5-patriot-front-applicants-say-they-have-ties-to-the-military

Trédaniel, M., & Lee, P. K. (2018). Explaining the Chinese framing of the "terrorist" violence in Xinjiang: insights from securitization theory. *Nationalities Papers, 46*(1), 177–195.

Twenge, J. M., Baumeister, R. F., Tice, D. M., & Stucke, T. S. (2001). If you can't join them, beat them: effects of social exclusion on aggressive behavior. *Journal of Personality and Social Psychology, 81*(6), 1058–1069.

Twenge, J. M., Catanese, K. R., & Baumeister, R. F. (2002). Social exclusion causes self defeating behavior. *Journal of Personality and Social Psychology, 83*(3), 606–615.

Van Bergen, D. D., Feddes, A. F., Doosje, B., & Pels, T. V. (2015). Collective identity factors and the attitude toward violence in defense of ethnicity or religion among Muslim youth of Turkish and Moroccan Descent. *International Journal of Intercultural Relations, 47*, 89–100.

Victoroff, J., Adelman, J. R., & Matthews, M. (2012). Psychological factors associated with support for suicide bombing in the Muslim diaspora. *Political Psychology, 33*(6), 791–809.

Williams, K. D. (2007). Ostracism: The kiss of social death. *Social and Personality Psychology Compass, 1*(1), 236–247.

Williams, K. D. (2009). Ostracism: A temporal need-threat model. *Advances in Experimental Social Psychology, 41*, 275–314.

Williams, K. D., & Jarvis, B. (2006). Cyberball: A program for use in research on interpersonal ostracism and acceptance. *Behavior Research Methods, 38*, 174–180.

Williams, K. D., & Nida, S. A. (2011). Ostracism: Consequences and coping. *Current Directions in Psychological Science, 20*(2), 71–75.

Witt, T. (2020). "If i cannot have it, i will do everything i can to destroy it": the canonization of Elliot Rodger: "Incel" masculinities, secular sainthood, and justifications of ideological violence. *Social Identities, 26*(5), 675–689.

Divided Groups, Polarized Identities, and Extremist Behavior

The Role of Exclusion-Contingent Self and Identity Uncertainty

JOSEPH A. WAGONER AND MICHAEL A. HOGG

7.1 Introduction

An integral part of human life is coping with the uncertainties we encounter. For instance, people can experience uncertainty when deciding where to live, where to work, whom to spend the rest of their life with, and how they fit into society. Beyond these self-induced uncertainties, numerous aspects of the world can make people feel uncertain. Whether a society is experiencing an economic recession, national disaster, global pandemic, or threat to its democratic institutions, events can make people uncertain about society, its cultural values, and its future. Thus, humans encounter infinite uncertainties when navigating their social lives.

Communities and groups have historically brought people together and helped them cope with their life uncertainties. Different factions have been able to unite to counter external threats and reduce the uncertainties affecting them all. However, many societies are now defined by partisanship, conflict, and hostility toward out-group members. Within these divided societies, different factions no longer come together to cope with externally induced uncertainties. Instead, when people turn to groups or communities of individuals, they turn to identity silos that are characterized by ideological zealotry, intolerance of others, and extremist tactics to promote their view of society. People who feel excluded from society can also become attracted to orthodox belief systems and radical social movements to reduce uncertainty about their place in society, provide an explanation for societal events, and clarify how to address them. Thus, because divided societies are ineffective at reducing uncertainties, people seek out segregated identity silos that encourage extremist behaviors and belief systems that are very effective at reducing self- and identity-related uncertainty.

In this chapter, we use uncertainty-identity theory as a framework for understanding how feelings of uncertainty about oneself and one's identity can steer people toward ideological rigidity and extremist behavior. At the heart of the theory is the proposition that people are averse to feelings of uncertainty and are motivated to reduce them, and that identification with groups, particularly groups that have a clearly defined identity and associated set of norms, very effectively reduces uncertainty. However, because some groups are defined by norms of intolerance and worldviews that promote violence, the possibility exists that people's desire to reduce uncertainty can, ultimately, result in different forms of extremism. Overall, this chapter outlines how uncertainty can attract people to extreme groups and ideologies and discusses how feelings of exclusion and ostracism can elicit this uncertainty-extremism link.

7.2   Uncertainty-Identity Theory: Overview, Core Propositions, and Evidence

Uncertainty-identity theory (UIT) outlines how feelings of self-related uncertainty can be resolved through social identity processes (Hogg, 2007, 2021a, 2021b). A core proposition of UIT is that feelings of uncertainty are averse, and that people are motivated to reduce its presence. People view some uncertainties as pleasant, including sporadic vacations, receiving unexpected gifts, or watching a new film (e.g., Wilson et al., 2005). However, uncertainties related to ourselves, our place in the world, or the meaning of our lives can be associated with feelings of anxiety, sadness, or anger (Arkin et al., 2010). Feeling uncertain about how to interact with others can also make it difficult to plan and execute social behavior and can violate needs of belonging and esteem.

When people feel uncertain, they allocate cognitive resources to reducing its presence and seek out greater certainty. As noted by Pollock (2003), people allocate such resources to "sufficiently" reduce uncertainty to the point that allows them to dedicate their attention to other domains of life. Similarly, the philosopher John Dewey noted that "in the absence of actual certainty in the midst of a precarious and hazardous world, men cultivate all sorts of things that would give them a feeling of certainty" (Dewey, 1929/2005, p. 33). From this perspective, people are motivated to reduce feelings of uncertainty, even if it does not provide them with chronic, long-term certainty.

Because uncertainty reduction is cognitively demanding, people allocate energy to reducing only those uncertainties that impact them most, and among these are uncertainties about or reflecting on who they are – their self and identity. Whether people are making decisions that reflect on their abilities, contemplating their core values, or trying to understand their place in society, the types of uncertainties that make people question who they are as a person and their ultimate purpose are the types of uncertainties that people seek to resolve. Furthermore, people can experience uncertainty as a challenge that they have the resources to resolve or as a threat that they feel they do not have the resources to resolve (Blascovich & Tomaka, 1996). Feelings of uncertainty that are appraised to represent a threat typically result in defensive and maladaptive intergroup responses (e.g., Frings et al., 2012; Scheepers, 2009).

UIT proposes that identifying with and becoming psychologically attached to a group (i.e., group identification) can effectively resolve self-uncertainty by providing people with a consensually validated prototype to internalize and follow. A core argument of social identity theory (SIT; Tajfel & Turner, 1986) is that people define part of their self-concept through their social groups. People who identify with groups engage in a process of *depersonalization*, in which they shift from their personal identity to a salient social identity. This shift results in a process of self-categorization where people view their own and other people's behavior through this group-based lens (Turner et al., 1987).

People who depersonalize also shift to a *prototype*, which is a set of attributes, values, and behaviors that defines being a normative group member. Prototypes not only provide people with a set of attitudes to internalize and norms to follow but also allow them to distinguish in-group and out-group members. For instance, US partisans likely agree about the values, attitudes, and behaviors that define their political party compared to opposing political parties. Moreover, people often accentuate within-group similarities and between-group differences to highlight the distinctiveness and clarity of their prototype. Overall, UIT is framed by a social identity approach, which notes the importance of group identification but extends it by showing how group identification can resolve epistemic motives of uncertainty.

The core propositions of UIT have over twenty years of evidence to support them (see Choi & Hogg, 2020; Hogg, 2021a, 2021b). Some of the original studies (e.g., Grieve & Hogg, 1999; Hogg & Grieve, 1999; Mullin & Hogg; 1998) showed that (1) experimentally inducing uncertainty strengthened identification with novel groups and (2) strengthening identification reduced feelings of uncertainty. A meta-analysis of thirty-five relevant studies ($N = 4,657$) showed that experimentally inducing uncertainty, either directly or indirectly, strengthens identification (see Choi & Hogg, 2020). This meta-analysis also showed that the relationship between self-uncertainty and group identification was negative in nonexperimental designs, suggesting that people's internalization of a prototype relates to lower self-uncertainty.

Recent evidence by Brown et al. (2021) provided direct evidence for the uncertainty-reducing properties of group identification. Specifically, they found that stronger identification related to lower autonomic nervous system activity (e.g., lower skin conductance and heart rate) for people experimentally induced to experience high (vs. low) self-uncertainty. Because activation of the autonomic nervous system is often an indicator of uncertainty and threat (Arkin et al., 2010), it suggests that stronger identification can reduce uncertainty across multiple contexts and measures.

7.2.1   Moderators of the Uncertainty–Identification Relationship

Although feelings of self-uncertainty make people more prone to identify with and join groups, not all groups are equally effective at reducing such uncertainty. A core claim of UIT is that groups can reduce self-related uncertainty by prescribing a consensually validated and clearly defined identity to their members. Such identities can effectively reduce uncertainty because they clarify who one is, how one should act and think in various situations, and how one should interact with others. From this perspective, groups with clear and distinct identities and associated prototypes are desirable under uncertainty.

One feature of a group that enhances the clarity of its identity is *entitativity*, which is the degree that a group is perceived to be a distinct, cohesive entity of like-minded individuals with common backgrounds and fates (Campbell, 1958; Hamilton & Sherman, 1996; Lickel et al., 2000). High entitativity groups have prototypes that are clear, distinct, and unambiguous, have boundaries that are difficult to penetrate, and possess members who frequently interact with each other, have similar attributes, and have common backgrounds and fates. Comparatively, low entitativity groups have loosely defined prototypes that are ambiguous and hard to distinguish from other groups. Low entitativity groups also possess members with different traits, goals, and backgrounds who have infrequent interaction. Finally, low entitativity groups are easy to join and leave. People often identify more strongly with highly entitative groups (Castano et al., 2003; Lickel et al., 2000) and perceive entitative groups as having greater collective efficacy (Wagoner et al., 2017). Furthermore, entitative groups enhance a group's ability to fulfill various psychological functions related to belonging, achievement, and esteem (Crawford & Salaman, 2012; Johnson et al., 2006).

In line with the theorizing that entitative groups are appealing under uncertainty, Hogg and colleagues (2007) found that people identified more strongly with highly entitative groups under high (vs. low) uncertainty. Sherman et al. (2009) also found that people perceived their group as more entitative under high (vs. low) uncertainty, suggesting that people will enhance a group's entitativity to reduce uncertainty and provide a sense of epistemic certainty. Finally, people's physiological responses to uncertainty are reduced most sharply after identifying with highly entitative groups (Brown et al., 2021). Overall, there is ample evidence to show that entitativity moderates the uncertainty–identification relationship.

In addition to entitativity, the perceived traits and characteristics of a group and its members can influence the uncertainty–identification relationship. Various social-psychological frameworks have noted that people evaluate people and groups on their warmth (e.g., sociability, friendliness, acceptance) and competence (e.g., responsibility, intelligence, efficacy). Although people typically ascribe warmth and competence to their in-groups (Fiske et al., 2002), Wagoner and Hogg (2016a) investigated how experimentally manipulating warmth and competence affected the uncertainty–identification relationship. They found weakened identification with high competence but low warmth groups under high (vs. low) uncertainty.

Other researchers have similarly shown that a group's status (which significantly relates to perceived competence, $r = .77$; Cuddy et al., 2007) becomes less important under uncertainty. Reid and Hogg (2005) randomly assigned people to high or low-status groups before experimentally manipulating uncertainty. Under low uncertainty, people preferred high (vs. low) status groups, indicating a self-enhancement motive. However, under high uncertainty, the preference for status disappeared. These findings suggest that self-enhancement becomes less important under uncertainty, and acceptance by a group with a clear prototype becomes essential.

Finally, people's own prototypicality can affect the uncertainty–identification relationship. Some people view themselves as prototypical of their group's identity and representative of what it means to be a group member; others view themselves as peripheral members who are on the fringes of the group and are unrepresentative of what the group stands for. Researchers have shown that people are more prone to exhibit in-group bias and out-group derogation when they view themselves as relatively unprototypical members (Jetten et al., 2002).

From a UIT perspective, feeling relatively unprototypical of a group one strives to belong to (i.e., being a fringe member) creates membership uncertainty that can motivate in-group bias and strengthen group identification to resolve the uncertainty. Hohman and colleagues (2017) directly investigated whether such peripheral group status relates to uncertainty and, consequently, greater susceptibility to group identification and in-group bias. Both propositions were supported – peripheral (vs. prototypical) members reported stronger feelings of uncertainty, and peripheral (vs. prototypical) members identified more strongly under high than low uncertainty. Strengthening group identification further predicted in-group bias – peripheral group members were willing to defend their in-group to resolve the self-related uncertainty created by their marginal status.

7.2.2   Domains of Uncertainty

Feelings of uncertainty must relate to the self to motivate identification processes. These uncertainties can be short-lived and unique to a person (e.g., change in occupation, loss of a friend) or chronic and experienced by all people in society (e.g., global pandemics, economic recessions). Regardless of how it is caused, self-uncertainty motivates a group identification dynamic. However, the self is multifaceted. People can define themselves in terms of idiosyncratic attributes (personal self), relationships with individual others (relational self), and attributes shared among a group (collective self) (Brewer & Gardner, 1996; Sedikides et al., 2013). Feelings of self-uncertainty (and thus reduction of self-uncertainty) originating in one domain can spread to others (Hogg & Mahajan, 2018).

The notion of collective (i.e., social identity-related) uncertainty is particularly relevant. Just as people can feel uncertain about various aspects of their self-concept, they can feel uncertain about different aspects of their group. For instance, they can feel uncertain about the attributes and prototype of their group (*identity uncertainty*; Wagoner et al., 2017) or fitting into their group and being viewed as a prototypical group member (*membership uncertainty*; Goldman & Hogg, 2016; Wagoner et al., 2017). People can also feel uncertain about their subgroup fitting into a superordinate collective (which we can refer to as *subgroup-membership uncertainty*; Wagoner & Hogg, 2016b; Wagoner et al., 2018).

Where self-uncertainty originates in uncertainty about one's group's identity, people can directly focus on clarifying the group's identity (e.g., making the group more distinctive and clearly defined, rejecting dissenting voices – e.g., Hogg, 2021b). Or they can (1) focus their uncertainty-reduction behaviors onto (2) more clearly defined subgroups (which can lead to schisms at the superordinate group level), or (3) other aspects of their lives and sense of self (an individual "exit" strategy) – their personal relations or their individual self (Hogg & Mahajan, 2018). However, relevant research is still in its early days (but see Wagoner & Chur, 2024).

7.2.3   Uncertainty and Intergroup Relations

SIT proposes that people are motivated to protect and secure a social identity that is both distinctive and, perhaps primarily, favorable (Abrams & Hogg, 1988; for more on SIT, see the chapter by Doosje and colleagues in this volume). UIT focuses on distinctiveness rather than valence – a group's valence is less important than its ability to provide a clear and distinct prototype and identity that clarifies intergroup boundaries. One method for clearly differentiating between in-group and out-groups is *intergroup discrimination*, where people engage in differential treatment and allocation of resources based on category membership. Because intergroup discrimination can clarify a group's prototype, it is an effective way to reduce self-uncertainty. Stronger group identification is often associated with greater out-group prejudice and discrimination (e.g., Castano et al., 2002; Cowling et al., 2019; Rios et al., 2018). If stronger group identification relates to intergroup discrimination, and uncertainty strengthens group identification, then it follows that uncertainty can strengthen intergroup discrimination and prejudice through group identification.

Earl research on UIT found that group identification mediated the relationship between uncertainty and in-group bias (e.g., Grieve & Hogg, 1999; Hogg & Grieve, 1999). Recent research by Mastandrea et al. (2021) examined how US and Italian residents evaluated two types of art (representational, abstract) by artists of either US or Italian nationality. Representational art is a type of art that clearly and coherently depicts objects in the world, whereas abstract art does not attempt to represent external reality and uses shapes, colors, and textures to convey its meaning. Audiences are much more likely to prefer representational art over abstract art due to its clarity and ability to comprehend. However, the authors predicted that if a group's identity was associated with abstract art, it would enhance its preferability. The results mostly confirmed the hypotheses. People preferred representational over abstract art; however, people liked the set of abstract artworks more when it came from an in-group member than an out-group member. These findings show that people use their group's identity as an evaluative heuristic for uncertain judgments during intergroup contexts.

Beyond in-group bias, uncertainty can strengthen out-group prejudice. Mullin and Hogg (1998) initially showed that stronger identification mediated the relationship between task-related uncertainty and intergroup discrimination. Niedbala and Hohman (2019) examined whether intergroup conflict created feelings of self-uncertainty and how uncertainty affected intergroup retaliation. They had university students focus on a rival university (Study 1) or US residents focus on ISIS (Study 2) as potential threats while measuring (or manipulating) self-uncertainty. In support of UIT, feelings of uncertainty played a pivotal role in intergroup retaliations. Uncertainty mediated the relationship between threat and retaliation. Moreover, uncertainty produced intergroup retaliation irrespective of threat, fitting past research that shows uncertainty and threat are related but distinct processes (e.g., Hass & Cunningham, 2014).

7.3 Exclusion and Uncertainty

Just as people can experience uncertainty for various reasons, they can also experience exclusion for various reasons. For instance, people can be excluded based on their musical tastes, hairstyle, clothing, shoes, speech, performance on a task, or various other trivial or mundane reasons. People can also be (or feel) excluded because of their race, gender, sexual orientation, nationality, or religious orientation. Irrespective of whether they are excluded for personal or identity-based reasons, people are likely to experience uncertainty about who they are, what they value, and their future in the group. Research has confirmed that people who feel marginalized in groups are more likely to experience uncertainty (Hohman et al., 2017). Research on the needs-based model of ostracism also confirms that people's feeling of certainty and meaning is violated if they are ostracized (see Hales et al., this volume).

It follows that people may respond to exclusion- or marginalization-invoked self-uncertainty in very similar ways as they respond to self-uncertainty invoked in other ways. If a group is an available and effective resource, people will engage in behaviors to reduce their uncertainty and achieve belonging in a group that can address uncertainty in the future. Goldman and Hogg (2016) investigated whether peripheral (or prototypical) members of groups were more likely to engage in aggressive behaviors toward out-group members when it increased their likelihood of acceptance. Because prototypical members already felt accepted in the group, there was no need to engage in aggression to signal one's loyalty to the group. However, peripheral members *were* more likely to engage in aggressive behaviors, especially when primed to believe that their behavior would (vs. would not) increase their acceptance. Because uncertainty is elicited for people on the periphery (Hohman et al., 2017), these findings suggest that people will engage in group-centric and potentially violent behavior when they believe it will reduce their status-based uncertainty and create a sense of acceptance and inclusion.

In addition to individuals feeling excluded by a group, subgroups can feel excluded or marginalized by a superordinate group. People typically identify with a nested subgroup and its overarching superordinate group to differing degrees (Hornsey & Hogg, 2000). For instance, people can differ in their identification with their state in a nation (e.g., California in the US); their religious sect in its overarching category (e.g., Sunni within Islam); and their nation in a supranational entity (e.g., Italy in the EU). Within superordinate groups, people's subgroups can have a majority, dominant status or a minority, non-dominant status. People in the majority often project their subgroup's values, identity, and norms onto the superordinate group, especially when they identify with both the superordinate and subgroup (Wenzel et al., 2016).

However, people in the minority project their subgroup's values and identity onto the superordinate group less frequently, typically due to the historical relations they have with the superordinate group and with other subgroups. Minority subgroups, whether based on race, gender, sexuality, or religious orientation, often experience discrimination at an interpersonal and institutional level. Feeling marginalization and discrimination against them not only affects people's well-being (Wenzel et al., 2016) but also creates uncertainty about their relations with the superordinate group and other subgroups, and about their subgroup's distinctiveness and future. When people feel uncertain about their superordinate group or their subgroup's position, they will support actions or policies that preserve or promote their subgroup's distinctive identity and enhance its autonomy.

Numerous studies have supported the proposition that people more strongly support subgroup autonomy and independence when they feel uncertain about their superordinate group (or their subgroup's position in it), including studies in Sardinia in Italy ($N = 174$; Wagoner et al., 2018), Texas in the US ($N = 254$; Wagoner & Hogg, 2016b), and Scotland in the UK (Jung et al., 2018). Similarly, South Koreans have been found to reject Korean reunification when they feel uncertainty about their ethnic Korean (superordinate) identity ($N = 148$; Jung et al., 2016). Thus, people's uncertainty about their self and identity often stems from feelings of ostracism from the group or perceptions that one's subgroup has been marginalized in society.

7.4 Uncertainty in Divided Societies: The Allure of Extremism

People can reduce feelings of uncertainty through quick decision-making or emotion regulation processes (e.g., reappraisal, suppression). However, extreme and chronic uncertainties, and possibly uncertainties that are experienced in all three domains of self (personal, relational, collective), may not be so effectively mitigated in this way. When people are experiencing an unavoidable uncertainty that cannot be reduced through available means, they will very likely look to external groups and belief systems to reduce their uncertainty.

The term "extremism" is used in various ways. For this chapter, we broadly refer to *extremist groups* as groups with dogmatic and ethnocentric worldviews, intolerance of in-group dissent, authoritarian leaders, hostility toward outsiders, or norms promoting radical collective action. Because extremist groups often have rigid norms, an intolerance for in-group deviance, clearly structured hierarchies, and belief systems promoting an "us vs. them" mentality, they are perceived as highly entitative. Thus, people could be attracted to extremist groups as a means to an end to reducing their uncertainty. We outline various lines of research that support these propositions next.

7.4.1 Radicalism

Research has shown that group members support collective action to strengthen their group's identity and overcome social identity threats and other injustices (e.g., van Zomeren et al., 2018). Most people engage in societally approved and normative forms of collective action (e.g., activism, peaceful and nondisruptive protests); however, some engage in nonnormative collective actions that society can disapprove of (e.g., public disruption, property damage, violence toward others; Becker & Tausch, 2015). Although non-in-group members typically view nonnormative collective action as immoral (Feinberg et al., 2020), in-group members see things differently. They view such action as legitimate ways to combat identity threat. Thus, even though people often view radicalism as immoral, uncertainty changes people's views of this tactic.

Initial evidence to support the uncertainty–extremism link came from Australian college students protesting tuition increases and structural university changes (Hogg et al., 2010). Participants were assigned to watch one of two videos from ostensibly campus groups that were protesting the changes. The moderate group was described as having an informal structure with less hierarchical leadership and an open membership criterion. The video emphasized that the moderate group had an open atmosphere and would adopt normative actions (e.g., letters to newspapers, meetings). The radical group was described as being clearly and hierarchically structured and having a strict membership criterion. They noted that this group had no tolerance for disagreement and that people needed to commit to its vision. This group further promoted different forms of nonnormative action (e.g., public disruption, road blockages). After watching one of two videos, participants were primed about how certain (or uncertain) they felt about their future education. In general, people preferred the moderate group more than the extremist group. However, in support of UIT, there was a significant shift in people's preference for the radical group under high rather than low uncertainty. These findings were the first to show that self-relevant uncertainty can elicit attraction to extremist groups.

Subsequent research has supported the proposition that uncertainty can make extremism attractive. For example, Adelman et al. (2012) examined how uncertainty interacted with people's national identities to affect support for radicalism among Jewish Israelis and Muslim Palestinians. Among Jewish Israelis, strong Israeli identification predicted support for military strikes (an available resource) against Palestine under high, not low, uncertainty. Among Muslim Palestinians, strong Palestinian identification predicted justification of suicide bombings (an available resource for Palestinians) against Israel, again under high, not low, uncertainty. Similarly, other research, on Pakistani youth, has found that stronger self- and collective uncertainty predicted endorsement of political violence and display of religious intolerance (Hassan et al., 2021). These findings show that people's support and justification of violence can be exacerbated as an uncertainty-reduction method.

Researchers have also recently examined whether personality traits predispose people to radical and extremist intentions. It has long been known that certain Big-5 personality traits, particularly openness, predict prejudice. People with low openness are often opposed to new ideas and experiences and instead prefer conventional ideas and ways of thinking. Low openness relates to prejudice toward numerous groups, including ethnic minorities, the LGBTQ+ community, and immigrants (Sibley & Duckitt, 2008). Building on the proposition that low openness reflects a preference for tradition and convention, Gøtzsche-Astrup (2021b) conducted two studies in the United States, one correlational and one experimental ($N_{Total} = 4,806$), that examined whether low openness moderated the relationship between uncertainty and radicalism. As predicted, people high in openness, who are comfortable with change and novelty, were not drawn to radicalism under uncertainty, whereas people low in openness were, showing that radicalism is a potential uncertainty-reduction method for some people.

However, researchers have noted that some people are naturally attracted to extremist ideas and violence toward others, which the Big-5 taxonomy cannot fully explain. The *dark triad traits* have been proposed as an alternative personality taxonomy to understand people's proclivity toward interpersonal aggression and violence. The dark triad comprises three traits: *Machiavellianism* (reflecting cynicism and interpersonal manipulation of others), *narcissism* (reflecting dominance, grandiosity, and entitlement), and *psychopathy* (reflecting high impulsivity and lack of empathy). Gøtzsche-Astrup (2021a) conducted three studies (N_{Total} = 3,797) that examined whether dark triad traits predicted partisans' radical intentions beyond mere partisanship and Big-5 traits. He found that dark triad traits, independent of Big-5 traits and political party identification, predicted radicalism.

Gøtzsche-Astrup (2019) further examined whether the dark triad traits moderate the uncertainty-identity relationship or whether dark triad traits and uncertainty are separate predictors of radicalism. From the perspective that personality moderates the impact of uncertainty on radicalism, one might reason that possession of traits related to lack of empathy, manipulation and domination of others, and high impulsivity would predispose people who feel uncertain about their place in the world to reduce uncertainty by callous means. However, the pathways would be separate if the dark triad were more about interpersonal manipulation and dominance than fulfilling epistemic needs. The results of two studies, one in the United States and one in Denmark (N_{Total} = 2,889), showed that high, not low, uncertainty strengthened intentions to engage in political violence, irrespective of dark triad traits. Moreover, dark triad traits predicted radicalism under low uncertainty but not high uncertainty. These findings show that uncertainty and dark triad traits are separate paths to radicalism and suggest that uncertainty attracts people to radicalism as an uncertainty-reduction process.

Finally, some researchers have applied UIT to understand people's attraction to militant groups. In one study, Mutallimzada and Steiner (2022) interviewed nine fighters from the Right Sector's Volunteer Ukraine Corps (RS VUC), created in response to Russia's annexation of Crimea in 2014. These fighters reported that RS VUC had a clear ideology that promoted an "us vs. them" mentality, along with family-like bonds between members, a clear leadership structure, and clear and rigid normative prescriptions for behavior. These fighters also reported distrusting society and its institutions, thus providing a breeding ground for uncertainty and for attraction to uncertainty-reducing extremist factions.

7.4.2   Leadership

Self-categorization generates stronger group identification and, consequently, a willingness to internalize the identity-defining norms and values prescribed by the group. While people often learn about the group's identity through observing and interacting with in-group members, they can also learn directly from formal or informal group leaders. According to the social identity theory of leadership (Hogg, 2001; Hogg et al., 2012), people prefer leaders who embody their group's prototype and promote their group's interests. Two separate meta-analyses have confirmed that people support and trust leaders more when they are prototypical of the group, and that this is stronger among those who identify strongly with the group (Barreto & Hogg, 2017; Steffens et al., 2017).

Under uncertainty this preference can be accentuated as a consequence of uncertainty reduction inducing stronger identification. But, in situations where prototypical leader options are sparse or nonexistent, the preference can disappear – people will prefer and support any leader who can reduce uncertainty and provide a clear and distinctive identity for their group. Researchers have confirmed that uncertainty under these conditions can strengthen support for non-prototypical leaders (Rast et al., 2012). Moreover, non-prototypical leaders are then in a position to attract support that allows them to act as entrepreneurs of the group's identity and thus reconstruct the group's identity and promote change (Abrams et al., 2013; Abrams et al., 2018).

Furthermore, under uncertainty, people become more attracted to authoritarian leaders, who typically promote a rigid and ethnocentric identity for the group. For example, Hogg et al. (2010) conducted an experiment that presented Australian university students with controlled video interviews of a campus protest group that described itself in extremist (radical – including authoritarian leadership) or nonextremist (moderate, and including nonauthoritarian leadership) terms, and then primed the participants to feel self-uncertain or not. As predicted, the students preferred the moderate/nonauthoritarian group, but this preference was significantly reduced or erased under high uncertainty. Focusing more specifically on leadership, Rast and colleagues (2013) found similar results in organizational settings – that is, people trusted and saw moderate (vs. authoritarian) leaders as more prototypical of their group under low uncertainty. However, under high uncertainty, people trusted authoritarian (vs. moderate) leaders more and saw them as more prototypical of their group's identity. Finally, Guillén et al. (2024) found that leaders with dark triad traits are more likely to seek leadership positions under uncertainty, which can further set the group down a path of authoritarianism and hostility.

7.4.3 Conspiracy Beliefs

Conspiracy beliefs have become more common in society, and a significant focus in social psychology (Douglas & Sutton, 2018; Douglas et al., 2017; Imhoff, this volume). For instance, some people believe that NASA faked the moon landing, that political elites run sex-trafficking organizations, or that their government exaggerated a health pandemic to restrict freedoms. People believe in conspiracy theories when they hold an "explanation for important events and circumstances that involve secret plots by groups with malevolent agendas" (Hornsey et al., 2023, p. 86). People with low cognitive ability, low self-esteem, and a combination of high paranoia and high schizotypy are predisposed to harbor conspiracy theory beliefs (Hornsey et al., 2023).

Beyond these individual difference factors, a body of literature shows that uncertainty-reduction motives are related to belief in conspiracy theories. Studies have shown that experimentally inducing high (vs. low) uncertainty resulted in people subscribing more strongly to conspiracy theories (van Prooijen, 2016; van Prooijen & Jostmann, 2013). Two separate meta-analyses (Biddlestone et al., 2022, N_{Total} = 48,697; Bowes et al., 2023, N_{Total} = 113,638) also confirm that epistemic motives (e.g., high need for closure, low cognitive ability) related to a stronger belief in conspiracy theories. Because conspiracy theories fulfill many of the same psychological functions as extremist ideologies, they should certainly become stronger and more attractive under uncertainty (Hogg 2021b; Hogg & Gøtzsche-Astrup, 2021).

7.4.4 Populism

In addition to conspiracy beliefs, another domain that has gained global attention is the notion of populism. Unlike other ideologies, *populism* is viewed as a "loose ideology" that extends to both the political right and left. Populism often consists of an anti-elitism mentality that is accompanied by a people-centric focus that paints an "us" (the citizens) against "them" (the elites). Populism is also associated with a Manichean outlook that paints the world as a cosmic, moral battle between good-and-evil forces (Forgas & Crano, 2021). Stronger populism relates to a distrust of national institutions and belief in conspiracy theories across cultures (Erisen et al., 2021) and predicts hostility and antagonism toward out-groups (Kende & Krekó, 2020).

Populism has become an especially attractive rhetoric style among political candidates and leaders to paint national institutions and political elites as untrustworthy and morally corrupt. Populist leaders use rhetoric that emphasizes collective victimization to engender third-party support (Belavadi & Hogg, 2018) and frame their political discontent as an existential threat to citizens' survival (Belavadi et al., 2020). Populism also relates to collective narcissism and a feeling of deprivation (Marchlewska et al., 2018), further driving their perception of collective victimization. These factors used in political rhetoric can elicit collective uncertainty and draw people to a populist ideology to reduce self-related uncertainty (Hogg & Gøtzsche-Astrup, 2021).

A recent set of studies (N = 5,882 US participants), two secondary data analyses (using American National Election Survey (ANES) 2012 and 2016 data) and an experiment, found that increasing uncertainty (measured or manipulated) predicted increasing support for right-wing populist ideologies, political parties (in this case the American Tea Party), and leaders (in this case former US president Donald Trump) who promoted such populist ideologies (Gøtzsche-Astrup & Hogg, 2023). Only those individuals who scored most highly on authoritarianism were unaffected by uncertainty – they resolutely endorsed right-wing populism significantly more strongly than moderates and nonauthoritarians.

7.5   Mitigating the Impact of Exclusion and Uncertainty on Extremism

Although the literature discussed so far paints a grim picture of how humans cope with feelings of uncertainty, it begs the question: Can anything be done to reduce the uncertainty-induced appeal of extremism? We propose four approaches to harnessing social identity and uncertainty-reduction mechanisms to reduce the appeal of extremism behavior.

The first possibility relates to the underlying mechanism of self-uncertainty. As already noted, people turn to groups to cope with uncertainty they feel about their life, purpose, and future. If people had the opportunity to clarify their self-concept before encountering a group, they would, theoretically, be less likely to engage in defensive, group-centric reactions to mitigate their uncertainty. A large body of literature on self-affirmation theory shows that people who affirm their self-integrity are less likely to react to self-threats in a defensive manner (Cohen & Sherman, 2014). Building on this logic, Wichmann (2010) conducted two studies (N = 120) that randomly assigned people to high (or low) uncertainty primes before randomly providing the opportunity to affirm values that were important (or unimportant). People made to feel uncertain showed a typical reactive, group-centric response without affirmations of important values. However, self-affirmations of important values weakened people's group-centric responses under uncertainty.

Han and Kim (2020) also provide evidence for self-affirmations' effectiveness in reducing uncertainty's impact. They conducted a large-scale experiment in South Korea (N = 840) that exposed participants to polarizing information that elicited defensiveness. However, in addition to reading through this information, some participants were provided the opportunity to self-affirm their values or write about aspects of their lives that made them feel *certain*. From a UIT perspective, because self-affirmations clarify one's self-concept and highlight one's personal values, they reduce uncertainty by giving people a feeling of self-clarity. Results showed that sound self-affirmations provided people with a feeling of certainty about their life and surroundings, which elicited cognitive reappraisal across various topics.

A second possibility for reducing people's shift toward extremism under uncertainty is to reappraise the uncertainty itself. We have primarily focused on how people feel self-related uncertainties about their life and future, or about groups that are central to their identity. Although self-related uncertainties ubiquitously affect people's group identification, not all types of uncertainties elicit this defensive, group-centric response. For instance, McGregor et al. (2013, Study 4) distinguished between personal (self) uncertainty and *informational uncertainty*, which is related to people feeling uncertain about their decisions for others. This research found that although stronger self-uncertainty was related to reactive extremism concerning lifestyle choices, stronger informational uncertainty was related to *lower* reactive extremism.

Similarly, Kappes et al. (2018) focused on two types of uncertainty associated with decision-making: specifically, people's uncertainty about (1) the outcomes they will get from a situation (*outcome uncertainty*) and (2) the impacts their behaviors will have on other people (*impact uncertainty*). In the context of infectious diseases, they found that people experiencing impact uncertainty engaged in more prosocial behavior in a Prisoner's Dilemma context compared to outcome uncertainty. These studies suggest that when people's source of uncertainty is other-focused, whether focusing on understanding the environment or how their behavior impacts others, it can result in prosocial behavior aimed at reducing uncertainty about how others will be negatively affected by one's behavior. It is thus possible that if people appraise (or reappraise) events in such a way that they refocus their attention on the uncertainty surrounding other people (rather than themselves), it could result in less defensive responses and more prosocial responses.

The third possibility relates to the group's prescriptive identity-defining norms. Most extremist groups have an all-encompassing ideology that strictly prescribes behavior that promotes their interests and goals, along with norms of hostility toward outsiders and intolerance of in-group dissent. However, if people were allowed to identify or affirm a group encompassing different subgroups into an overarching collective identity, then the uncertainty might promote tolerance of out-groups and weaken the appeal of subgroup factionalism.

One way that norms and identity are constructed is by a group's leader. As noted earlier, group leaders are uniquely positioned to effectively define and promote a group's identity (Hogg, 2001). They can also frame group norms to prescribe collective action, which is especially effective among highly identified followers (e.g., Khumalo et al., 2022; Wagoner et al., 2021). Because leaders can construct what the group stands for and elicit action on behalf of the group, they are in an especially unique position to counteract the uncertainty elicited by external threats and provide a more cooperative, tolerant path forward. It all then depends on whether leaders choose to do this, or choose to fan the flames of uncertainty to secure their authoritarian leadership of a cult-like group.

Research on social identity framing (Seyranian, 2014) shows that leaders who emphasize collective identity are more effective at eliciting collective action. Some studies also suggest that people are more willing to display self-sacrificial and prosocial behavior when their in-group leader displays similar sacrificial and prosocial behavior (e.g., Ruggieri et al., 2023). Moreover, people's tendency to model their leader's self-sacrificial behavior is enhanced under uncertainty because it strengthens people's identification with their team and organization (Zhou et al., 2016). These findings suggest that leaders are pivotal in constructing an identity that can reduce uncertainty for their followers and shape the identity to promote prosocial norms. However, this latter perspective of leadership takes a singular focus on group identity and does not account for people's subgroup identity nor the relations between a subgroup and its superordinate group and to opposing subgroups.

Thus, a final possibility to reduce uncertainty-induced extremism rests on recognition that extremist identities and partisan intergroup relations are typically nested within a superordinate identity, and that leadership operates at both subgroup and superordinate group levels. This characterization of social structure is a premise of *intergroup leadership theory* (Hogg & Rast, 2022), which assigns to leaders an important role in combating conflict and extremism. Leadership strategies, particularly at the superordinate leadership level, that erode the social identity distinctiveness of subgroups pose a subgroup identity threat and create a great deal of identity- and self-uncertainty. To combat this, leaders should promote an intergroup relational identity, which is an identity that is defined by the cooperative intergroup relations between the subgroups and promotes the unique value and distinctiveness of each group. To be most effective at pulling this off, intergroup leaders should be viewed as nonpartisan, for example by boundary spanning. A growing body of research supports these key propositions from intergroup leadership theory (Kershaw et al., 2021a; Kershaw et al., 2021b; Rast et al., 2018; Rast et al., 2020; van der Stoep et al., 2020).

Intergroup relational identities differ from the common in-group identity model (Gaertner & Dovidio, 2000), which promotes a singular, superordinate group while ignoring subgroup identity distinctiveness, and the dual-identification approach (Dovidio et al., 2008), which acknowledges different subgroups in a superordinate group but does not highlight each of their contributions to defining the overarching identity. Thus, an intergroup relational perspective can ensure subgroups do not feel marginalized or excluded from the superordinate identity.

7.6 Conclusion

People will always encounter uncertainties in their life, whether self- or externally induced. Uncertainty-identity theory outlines the social identity processes that can reduce people's feelings of uncertainty by prescribing members a consensually validated prototype to follow and internalize. As noted earlier, a common reason that people feel uncertain about their self and identity is that they feel ostracized by a group or that they feel unrepresentative of the group's identity and prototype. Moreover, people can feel uncertain about their subgroup's identity and its status when they perceive it to be marginalized by their larger society. Because people yearn to reduce their uncertainties, authoritarian leaders and extremist groups can become appealing because they can effectively prescribe their members with an all-consuming ideology and belief system to follow in numerous situations. People are more prone to join extremist groups to obtain a sense of certainty about their place in the world or support factionalism and other forms of autonomy-motivated separatism to maintain a cohesive and clear identity. Thus, while extremist groups and all-encompassing ideologies can reduce people's uncertainty that stems from their perceived exclusion, they will prescribe a set of identity dynamics that can result in aggression, violence, and threats to democratic institutions. Overall, uncertainty-identity theory accounts for psychological motivations and social identity processes when explaining people's self-related uncertainties and how they cope with them.

References

Abrams, D., & Hogg, M. A. (1988). Comments on the motivational status of self-esteem in social identity and intergroup discrimination. *European Journal of Social Psychology, 18,* 317–334. https://doi.org/10.1002/ejsp.2420180403

Abrams, D., Randsley de Moura, G., & Travaglino, G. A. (2013). A double standard when group members behave badly: Transgression credit to ingroup leaders. *Journal of Personality and Social Psychology, 105,* 799–815. https://doi.org/10.1037/a0033600

Abrams, D., Travaglino, G. A., Marques, J. M., Pinto, I., & Levine, J. M. (2018). Deviance credit: Tolerance of deviant ingroup leaders is mediated by their accrual of prototypicality and conferral of their right to be supported. *Journal of Social Issues, 74,* 36–55. https://doi.org/10.1111/josi.12255

Adelman, J. R., Hogg, M. A., & Levin, S. (2012). *Uncertainty and extremism in the Middle East: The role of Israeli and Palestinian social identity dynamics.* [Manuscript submitted for publication]. Claremont Graduate University.

Arkin, R. M., Oleson, K. C., & Carroll, P. J. (Eds.). (2010). *Handbook of the uncertain self.* Psychology Press.

Barreto, N. B., & Hogg, M. A. (2017). Evaluation of and support for group prototypical leaders: A meta-analysis of twenty years of empirical research. *Social Influence*, *12*, 41–55. https://doi.org/10.1080/15534510.2017.1316771

Becker, J. C., & Tausch, N. (2015). A dynamic model of engagement in normative and non-normative collective action: Psychological antecedents, consequences, and barriers. *European Review of Social Psychology*, *26*, 43–92. https://doi.org/10.1080/10463283.2015.1094265

Belavadi, S., & Hogg, M. A. (2018). We are victims! How observers evaluate a group's claim of collective victimhood. *Journal of Applied Social Psychology*, *48*, 651–660. https://doi.org/10.1111/jasp.12555

Belavadi, S., Rinella, M. J., & Hogg, M. A. (2020). When social identity-defining groups become violent: Collective responses to identity uncertainty, status erosion, and resource threat. In C. A. Ireland, M. Lewis, A. C., Lopez, & J. L. Ireland (Eds.), *The Handbook of Collective Violence* (pp. 17–30). Routledge.

Biddlestone, M., Green, R., Cichocka, A., Douglas, K., & Sutton, R. (2022). A systematic review and meta-analytic synthesis of the motives associated with conspiracy beliefs. *PsyArXiv Preprint*. https://doi.org/10.31234/osf.io/rxjqc

Blascovich, J., & Tomaka, J. (1996). The biopsychosocial model of arousal regulation. *Advances in Experimental Social Psychology*, *28*, 1–51. https://doi.org/S0065-2601(08)60235-X

Bowes, S. M., Costello, T. H., & Tasimi, A. (2023). The conspiratorial mind: A meta-analytic review of motivational and personological correlates. *Psychological Bulletin*, *149*, 259–293. https://doi.org/10.1037/bul0000392

Brewer, M. B., & Gardner, W. (1996). Who is this "we"? Levels of collective identity and self representations. *Journal of Personality and Social Psychology*, *71*, 83–93. https://doi.org/10.1037/0022-3514.71.1.83

Brown, J. K., Hohman, Z. P., Niedbala, E. M., & Stinnett, A. J. (2021). Sweating the big stuff: Arousal and stress as functions of self-uncertainty and identification. *Psychophysiology*, *58*, e13836. https://doi.org/10.1111/psyp.13836

Campbell, D. T. (1958). Common fate, similarity, and other indices of the status of aggregates of persons as social entities. *Behavioral Science*, *3*, 14–26. https://doi.org/10.1002/bs.3830030103

Castano, E., Yzerbyt, V., & Bourguignon, D. (2003). We are one and I like it: The impact of ingroup entitativity on ingroup identification. *European Journal of Social Psychology*, *33*, 735–754. https://doi.org/10.1002/ejsp.175

Castano, E., Yzerbyt, V., Bourguignon, D., & Seron, E. (2002). Who may enter? The impact of in-group identification on in-group/out-group categorization. *Journal of Experimental Social Psychology*, *38*, 315–322. https://doi.org/10.1006/jesp.2001.1512

Choi, E. U., & Hogg, M. A. (2020). Self-uncertainty and group identification: A meta-analysis. *Group Processes & Intergroup Relations*, *23*, 483–501. https://doi.org/10.1177/1368430219846990

Cohen, G. L., & Sherman, D. K. (2014). The psychology of change: Self-affirmation and social psychological intervention. *Annual Review of Psychology, 65*, 333–371. https://doi.org/10.1146/annurev-psych-010213-115137

Cowling, M. M., Anderson, J. R., & Ferguson, R. (2019). Prejudice-relevant correlates of attitudes towards refugees: A meta-analysis. *Journal of Refugee Studies, 32*, 502–524. https://doi.org/10.1093/jrs/fey062

Crawford, M. T., & Salaman, L. (2012). Entitativity, identity, and the fulfilment of psychological needs. *Journal of Experimental Social Psychology, 48*, 726–730. https://doi.org/10.1016/j.jesp.2011.12.015

Cuddy, A. J., Fiske, S. T., & Glick, P. (2007). Warmth and competence as universal dimensions of social perception: The stereotype content model and the BIAS map. *Advances in Experimental Social Psychology, 40*, 61–149. https://doi.org/10.1016/S0065-2601(07)00002-0

Dewey, J. (1929/2005). *The quest for certainty: A study of the relation of knowledge and action.* Kessinger Publishing.

Douglas, K. M., & Sutton, R. M. (2018). Why conspiracy theories matter: A social psychological analysis. *European Review of Social Psychology, 29*, 256–298. https://doi.org/10.1080/10463283.2018.1537428

Douglas, K. M., Sutton, R. M., & Cichoka, A. (2017). The psychology of conspiracy theories. *Current Directions in Psychological Science, 26*, 538–542. https://doi.org/10.1177/0963721417718261

Dovidio, J. F., Gaertner, S. L., & Saguy, T. (2008). Another view of "we": Majority and minority group perspectives on a common ingroup identity. *European Review of Social Psychology, 18*, 296–330. https://doi.org/10.1080/10463280701726132

Erisen, C., Guidi, M., Martini, S., et al. (2021). Psychological correlates of populist attitudes. *Political Psychology, 42*, 149–171. https://doi.org/10.1111/pops.12768

Feinberg, M., Willer, R., & Kovacheff, C. (2020). The activist's dilemma: Extreme protest actions reduce popular support for social movements. *Journal of Personality and Social Psychology, 119*, 1086–1111. https://doi.org/10.1037/pspi0000230

Fiske, S. T., Cuddy, A. J., Glick, P., & Xu, J. (2002). A model of (often mixed) stereotype content: competence and warmth respectively follow from perceived status and competition. *Journal of Personality and Social Psychology, 82*, 878–902. https://doi.org/10.1037/0022-3514.82.6.878

Forgas, J. P., & Crano, W. D. (2021). The psychology of populism: The tribal challenge to liberal democracy. In J. P. Forgas, W. D. Crano, & K. Fielder (Eds.), *The psychology of populism* (pp. 1–19). Routledge.

Frings, D., Hurst, J., Cleveland, C., Blascovich, J., & Abrams, D. (2012). Challenge, threat, and subjective group dynamics: Reactions to normative and deviant group members. *Group Dynamics: Theory, Research, and Practice, 16*, 105–121. https://doi.org/10.1037/a0027504

Gaertner, S. L., & Dovidio, J. F. (2000). *Reducing intergroup bias: The common ingroup identity model.* Psychology Press.

Goldman, L., & Hogg, M. A. (2016). Going to extremes for one's group: The role of prototypicality and group acceptance. *Journal of Applied Social Psychology, 46*, 544–553. https://doi.org/10.1111/jasp.12382

Gøtzsche-Astrup, O. (2019). Personality moderates the relationship between uncertainty and political violence: Evidence from two large US samples. *Personality and Individual Differences, 139*, 102–109. https://doi.org/j.paid.2018.11.006

Gøtzsche-Astrup, O. (2021a). Dark triad, partisanship and violent intentions in the United States. *Personality and Individual Differences, 173*, 110633. https://doi.org/j.paid.2021.110633

Gøtzsche-Astrup, O. (2021b). Pathways to violence: Do uncertainty and dark world perceptions increase intentions to engage in political violence? *Behavioral Sciences of Terrorism and Political Aggression, 13*, 142–159. https://doi.org/10.1080/19434472.2020.1714693

Gøtzsche-Astrup, O., & Hogg, M. A. (2023). Let the people's will prevail: Self-uncertainty and authoritarianism predict support for populism. *Group Processes & Intergroup Relations*. https://doi.org/10.1177/13684302231211291

Grieve, P. G., & Hogg, M. A. (1999). Subjective uncertainty and intergroup discrimination in the minimal group situation. *Personality and Social Psychology Bulletin, 25*, 926–940. https://doi.org/10.1177/01461672992511002

Guillén, L., Jacquart, P., & Hogg, M. A. (2023). To lead, or to follow? How self-uncertainty and the dark triad of personality influence leadership motivation. *Personality and Social Psychology Bulletin, 49*, 1043–1057. https://doi.org/01461672221086771

Haas, I. J., & Cunningham, W. A. (2014). The uncertainty paradox: Perceived threat moderates the effect of uncertainty on political tolerance. *Political Psychology, 35*, 291–302. https://doi.org/10.1111/pops.12035

Hamilton, D. L., & Sherman, S. J. (1996). Perceiving persons and groups. *Psychological Review, 103*, 336–355. https://doi.org/10.1037/0033-295X.103.2.336

Han, J., & Kim, Y. (2020). Defeating merchants of doubt: Subjective certainty and self-affirmation ameliorate attitude polarization via partisan motivated reasoning. *Public Understanding of Science, 29*, 729–744. https://doi.org/10.1177/0963662520939315

Hassan, B., Khattak, A. Z., Qureshi, M. S., & Iqbal, N. (2021). Development and validation of extremism and violence risk identification scale. *Pakistan Journal of Psychological Research, 36*, 51–70. https://doi.org/10.33824/PJPR.2021.36.1.04

Hogg, M. A. (2001). A social identity theory of leadership. *Personality and Social Psychology Review, 5*, 184–200. https://doi.org/10.1207/S15327957PSPR0503_1

Hogg, M. A. (2007). Uncertainty-identity theory. *Advances in Experimental Social Psychology, 39*, 69–126. https://doi.org/10.1016/s0065-2601(06)39002-8

Hogg, M. A. (2021a). Self-uncertainty and group identification: Consequences for social identity, group behavior, intergroup relations, and society. *Advances in Experimental Social Psychology, 64*, 263–316. https://doi.org/10.1016/bs.aesp.2021.04.004

Hogg, M. A. (2021b). Uncertain self in a changing world: A foundation for radicalisation, populism, and autocratic leadership. *European Review of Social Psychology*, *32*, 235–268. https://doi.org/10.1080/10463283.2020.1827628

Hogg, M. A., & Gøtzsche-Astrup, O. (2021). Self-uncertainty and populism: Why we endorse populist ideologies, identify with populist groups, and support populist leaders. In J. P. Forgas, W. D. Crano, & K. Fiedler (Eds.), *The psychology of populism: The tribal challenge to liberal democracy* (pp. 197–218). Routledge.

Hogg, M. A., & Grieve, P. (1999). Social identity theory and the crisis of confidence in social psychology: A commentary, and some research on uncertainty reduction. *Asian Journal of Social Psychology*, *2*, 79–93. https://doi.org/10.1111/1467-839X.00027

Hogg, M. A., & Mahajan, N. (2018). Domains of self-uncertainty and their relationship to group identification. *Journal of Theoretical Social Psychology*, *2*, 67–75. https://doi.org/10.1002/jts5.20

Hogg, M. A., Meehan, C., & Farquharson, J. (2010). The solace of radicalism: Self-uncertainty and group identification in the face of threat. *Journal of Experimental Social Psychology*, *46*, 1061–1066. https://doi.org/10.1016/j.jesp.2010.05.005

Hogg, M. A., & Rast III, D. E. (2022). Intergroup leadership: The challenge of successfully leading fractured groups and societies. *Current Directions in Psychological Science*, *31*, 564–571. https://doi.org/10.1177/0963721422 1121598

Hogg, M. A., Sherman, D. K., Dierselhuis, J., Maitner, A. T., & Moffitt, G. (2007). Uncertainty, entitativity, and group identification. *Journal of Experimental Social Psychology*, *43*, 135-142. https://doi.org/10.1016/j.jesp.2005.12.008

Hogg, M. A., van Knippenberg, D., & Rast III, D. E. (2012). The social identity theory of leadership: Theoretical origins, research findings, and conceptual developments. *European Review of Social Psychology*, *23*, 258–304. https://doi.org/10.1080/10463283.2012.741134

Hohman, Z. P., Gaffney, A. M., & Hogg, M. A. (2017). Who am I if I am not like my group? Self-uncertainty and feeling peripheral in a group. *Journal of Experimental Social Psychology*, *72*, 125–132. https://doi.org/10.1016/j.jesp/2017.05.002

Hornsey, M. J., Bierwiaczonek, K., Sassenberg, K., & Douglas, K. M. (2023). Individual, intergroup and nation-level influences on belief in conspiracy theories. *Nature Reviews Psychology*, *2*, 85–97. https://doi.org/10.1038/s44159-022-00133-0

Hornsey, M. J., & Hogg, M. A. (2000). Assimilation and diversity: An integrative model of subgroup relations. *Personality and Social Psychology Review*, *4*, 143–156. https://doi.org/10.1207/S15327957PSPR0402_03

Jetten, J., Branscombe, N. R., & Spears, R. (2002). On being peripheral: Effects of identity insecurity on personal and collective self-esteem. *European Journal of Social Psychology*, *32*, 105–123. https://doi.org/10.1002/ejsp.64

Johnson, A. L., Crawford, M. T., Sherman, S. J., et al. (2006). A functional perspective on group memberships: Differential need fulfillment in a group typology. *Journal of Experimental Social Psychology*, *42*, 707–719. https://doi.org/10.1016/j.jesp.2005.08.002

Jung, J., Hogg, M. A., & Choi, H. S. (2016). Reaching across the DMZ: Identity uncertainty and reunification on the Korean peninsula. *Political Psychology*, *37*, 341–350. https://doi.org/10.1111/pops.12252

Jung, J., Hogg, M. A., & Lewis, G. J. (2018). Identity uncertainty and UK–Scottish relations: Different dynamics depending on relative identity centrality. *Group Processes & Intergroup Relations*, *21*, 861–873. https://doi.org/10.1177/1368430216678329

Kappes, A., Nussberger, A. M., Faber, N. S., et al. (2018). Uncertainty about the impact of social decisions increases prosocial behaviour. *Nature Human Behaviour*, *2*, 573–580. https://doi.org/10.1038/s41562-018-0372-x

Kende, A., & Krekó, P. (2020). Xenophobia, prejudice, and right-wing populism in East-Central Europe. *Current Opinion in Behavioral Sciences*, *34*, 29–33. https://doi.org/10.1016/j.cobeha.2019.11.011

Kershaw, C., Rast III, D. E., Hogg, M. A., & van Knippenberg, D. (2021a). Divided groups need leadership: A study of the effectiveness of collective identity, dual identity, and intergroup relational identity rhetoric. *Journal of Applied Social Psychology*, *51*, 53–62. https://doi.org/10.1111/jasp.12715

Kershaw, C., Rast III, D. E., Hogg, M. A., & van Knippenberg, D. (2021b). Battling ingroup bias with effective intergroup leadership. *British Journal of Social Psychology*, *60*, 765–785. https://doi.org/10.1111/bjso.12445

Khumalo, N., Dumont, K. B., & Waldzus, S. (2022). Leaders' influence on collective action: An identity leadership perspective. *The Leadership Quarterly*, *33*, 101609. https://doi.org/10.1016/j.leaqua.2022.101609

Lickel, B., Hamilton, D. L., Wieczorkowska, G., et al. (2000). Varieties of groups and the perception of group entitativity. *Journal of Personality and Social Psychology*, *78*, 223–246. https://doi.org/10.1037/0022-3514.78.2.223

Marchlewska, M., Cichocka, A., Panayiotou, O., Castellanos, K., & Batayneh, J. (2018). Populism as identity politics: Perceived in-group disadvantage, collective narcissism, and support for populism. *Social Psychological and Personality Science*, *9*, 151–162. https://doi.org/10.1177/1948550617732393

Mastandrea, S., Wagoner, J. A., & Hogg, M. A. (2021). Liking for abstract and representational art: National identity as an art appreciation heuristic. *Psychology of Aesthetics, Creativity, and the Arts*, *15*, 241–249. https://doi.org/10.1037/aca0000272

McGregor, I., Prentice, M., & Nash, K. (2013). Anxious uncertainty and reactive approach motivation (RAM) for religious, idealistic, and lifestyle extremes. *Journal of Social Issues*, *69*, 537–563. https://doi.org/10.1111/josi.12028

Mullin, B. A., & Hogg, M. A. (1998). Dimensions of subjective uncertainty in social identification and minimal intergroup discrimination. *British Journal of Social Psychology*, *37*, 345–365. https://doi.org/10.1111/j.2044-8309.1998.tb01176.x

Mutallimzada, K., & Steiner, K. (2023). Fighters' motivations for joining extremist groups: Investigating the attractiveness of the Right Sector's Volunteer Ukrainian Corps. *European Journal of International Security*, *8*, 47–69. https://doi.org/10.1017/eis.2022.11

Niedbala, E. M., & Hohman, Z. P. (2019). Retaliation against the outgroup: The role of self-uncertainty. *Group Processes & Intergroup Relations*, *22*, 708–723. https://doi.org/10.1177/1368430218767027

Pollack, H. N. (2003). *Uncertain science . . . uncertain world*. Cambridge University Press.

Rast III, D. E., Gaffney, A. M., Hogg, M. A., & Crisp, R. J. (2012). Leadership under uncertainty: When leaders who are non-prototypical group members can gain support. *Journal of Experimental Social Psychology*, *48*, 646–653. https://doi.org/10.1016/j.jesp.2011.12.013

Rast III, D. E., Hogg, M. A., & Giessner, S. R. (2013). Self-uncertainty and support for autocratic leadership. *Self and Identity*, *12*, 635–649. https://doi.org/10.1080/15298868.2012.718864

Rast III, D. E., Hogg, M. A., & van Knippenberg, D. (2018). Intergroup leadership across distinct subgroups and identities. *Personality and Social Psychology Bulletin*, *44*, 1090–1103. https://doi.org/10.1177/0146167218757466

Rast III, D. E., van Knippenberg, D., & Hogg, M. A. (2020). Intergroup relational identity: Development and validation of a scale and construct. *Group Processes & Intergroup Relations*, *23*, 943–966. https://doi.org/10.1177/1368430219883350

Reid, S. A., & Hogg, M. A. (2005). Uncertainty reduction, self-enhancement, and ingroup identification. *Personality and Social Psychology Bulletin*, *31*, 804–817. https://doi.org/10.1177/0146167204271708

Rios, K., Sosa, N., & Osborn, H. (2018). An experimental approach to intergroup threat theory: Manipulations, moderators, and consequences of realistic vs. symbolic threat. *European Review of Social Psychology*, *29*, 212–255. https://doi.org/10.1080/10463283.2018.1537049

Ruggieri, S., Gagliano, M., Servidio, R., Pace, U., & Passanisi, A. (2023). The effects of leader self-sacrifice in virtual teams on prosocial behavior: The mediational role of team identification and self-efficacy. *Sustainability*, *15*, 6098. https://doi.org/10.3390/su15076098

Scheepers, D. (2009). Turning social identity threat into challenge: Status stability and cardiovascular reactivity during inter-group competition. *Journal of Experimental Social Psychology*, *45*, 228–233. https://doi.org/10.1016/j.jesp.2008.09.011

Sedikides, C., Gaertner, L., Luke, M. A., O'Mara, E. M., & Gebauer, J. E. (2013). A three-tier hierarchy of self-potency: Individual self, relational self, collective self. *Advances in Experimental Social Psychology*, *48*, 235–295. https://doi.org/10.1016/B978-0-12-407188-9.00005-3

Seyranian, V. (2014). Social identity framing communication strategies for mobilizing social change. *The Leadership Quarterly*, *25*, 468–486. https://doi.org/10.1016/j.leaqua.2013.10.013

Sherman, D. K., Hogg, M. A., & Maitner, A. T. (2009). Perceived polarization: Reconciling ingroup and intergroup perceptions under uncertainty. *Group Processes & Intergroup Relations, 12*, 95–109. https://doi.org/10.1177/1368430208098779

Sibley, C. G., & Duckitt, J. (2008). Personality and prejudice: A meta-analysis and theoretical review. *Personality and Social Psychology Review, 12*, 248–279. https://doi.org/10.1177/1088868308319226

Steffens, N. K., Munt, K. A., van Knippenberg, D., Platow, M. J., & Haslam, S. A. (2017). Advancing the social identity theory of leadership: A meta-analytic review of leader group prototypicality. *Organizational Psychology Review, 11*, 35–72. https://doi.org/10.1177/2041386620962569

Tajfel, H., & Turner, J. C. (1986). The social identity theory of intergroup behaviour. In S. Worchel & W. G. Austin (Eds.), *Psychology of intergroup relations* (2nd ed., pp. 7–24). Nelson-Hall.

Turner, J. C., Hogg, M. A., Oakes, P. J., Reicher, S. D., & Wetherell, M. S. (1987). *Rediscovering the social group: A self-categorization theory.* Blackwell.

van der Stoep, J., Sleebos, E., van Knippenberg, D., & van de Bunt, G. (2020). The empowering potential of intergroup leadership: How intergroup leadership predicts psychological empowerment through intergroup relational identification and resources. *Journal of Applied Social Psychology, 50*, 709–719. https://doi.org/10.1111/jasp.12707

van Prooijen, J. W. (2016). Sometimes inclusion breeds suspicion: Self-uncertainty and belongingness predict belief in conspiracy theories. *European Journal of Social Psychology, 46*, 267–279. https://doi.org/10.1002/ejsp.2157

van Prooijen, J. W., & Jostmann, N. B. (2013). Belief in conspiracy theories: The influence of uncertainty and perceived morality. *European Journal of Social Psychology, 43*, 109–115. https://doi.org/10.1002/ejsp.1922

van Zomeren, M., Kutlaca, M., & Turner-Zwinkels, F. (2018). Integrating who "we" are with what "we" (will not) stand for: A further extension of the social identity model of collective action. *European Review of Social Psychology, 29*, 122–160. https://doi.org/10.1080/10463283.2018.1479347

Wagoner, J. A., Antonini, M., Hogg, M. A., Barbieri, B., & Talamo, A. (2018). Identity-centrality, dimensions of uncertainty, and pursuit of subgroup autonomy: The case of Sardinia within Italy. *Journal of Applied Social Psychology, 48*, 582–589. https://doi.org/10.1111/jasp.12549

Wagoner, J. A., Belavadi, S., & Jung, J. (2017). Social identity uncertainty: Conceptualization, measurement, and construct validity. *Self and Identity, 16*, 505–530. https://doi.org/10.1080/15298868.2016.1275762

Wagoner, J. A., & Chur, M. (2024). Domains of uncertainty, identification processes, and exit intentions. *Group Processes & Intergroup Relations.* https://doi.org/10.1177/13684302231215043

Wagoner, J. A., & Hogg, M. A. (2016a). Uncertainty and group identification: Moderation by warmth and competence as cues to inclusion and identity validation. *Self and Identity, 15*, 525–535. https://doi.org/10.1080/15298868.2016.1163284

Wagoner, J. A., & Hogg, M. A. (2016b). Normative dissensus, identity-uncertainty, and subgroup autonomy. *Group Dynamics: Theory, Research, and Practice, 20*, 310–322. https://doi.org/10.1037/gdn0000057

Wagoner, J. A., Rinella, M. J., & Barreto, N. B. (2021). "It was rigged": Different types of identification predict activism and radicalism in the US 2020 election. *Analyses of Social Issues and Public Policy, 21*, 189–209. https://doi.org/10.1111/asap.12270

Wenzel, M., Waldzus, S., & Steffens, M. C. (2016). Ingroup projection as a challenge of diversity: Consensus about and complexity of superordinate categories. In C. G. Sibley & F. K. Barlow (Eds.), *The Cambridge Handbook of the Psychology of Prejudice* (pp. 65–89). Cambridge University Press. https://doi.org/10.1017/9781316161579.004

Wichman, A. L. (2010). Uncertainty and religious reactivity: Uncertainty compensation, repair, and inoculation. *European Journal of Social Psychology, 40*, 35–42. https://doi.org/10.1002/ejsp.712

Wilson, T. D., Centerbar, D. B., Kermer, D. A., & Gilbert, D. T. (2005). The pleasures of uncertainty: Prolonging positive moods in ways people do not anticipate. *Journal of Personality and Social Psychology, 88*, 5–21. https://doi.org/10.1037/0022-3514.88.1.5

Zhou, R., Long, L., & Hao, P. (2016). Positive affect, environmental uncertainty, and self-sacrificial leadership influence followers' self-sacrificial behavior. *Social Behavior and Personality: An International Journal, 44*, 1515–1524. https://doi.org/10.2224/sbp.2016.44.9.1515.

8

It's the Group, Not Just the Individual

Social Identity and Its Link to Exclusion and Extremism

BERTJAN DOOSJE, ALLARD R. FEDDES, AND LIESBETH MANN

Example 8.1 Violent attacks by a group based on a group's ideology: 9/11/2001 – attacks on the United States: These attacks on the Pentagon in Washington and the Twin Towers in New York were executed by several small groups. These attacks were inspired by their larger group's ideology.

Example 8.2 Violent attacks by an individual based on a group's ideology: Anders Breivik's attacks in Norway (July 2011) on a governmental building in Oslo and on a holiday island where left-wing youngsters were staying. These attacks were executed by an individual, but based on an extreme right-wing group's ideology of the superiority of the White race.

Example 8.3 Violent attack by an individual (or dyad) not based on a group's ideology: The Columbine high school shootings (April 1999) involved two young male high school students who shot several teachers and fellow students. This attack was carried out by a dyad (but often times such shootings involve a sole individual) who was not inspired by a larger group's ideology.

8.1 Introduction

If one wants to understand extremism, one must understand group membership. In this chapter, we focus on the role of group membership in explaining extremism. In the three examples provided at the start of this chapter, we have highlighted the role of the group. This is most obvious in the first example, in which small groups carried out violent attacks based on a larger group's ideology. However, as indicated in the second example, even when a violent attack is carried out by an individual, a group's ideology can still inspire individuals to display such acts. Only in the third example is the role of a larger group's ideology less obvious.

In this chapter, we argue that there are two routes of group membership to extremism: (1) by feeling and being included in a violent in-group, people are more likely to display extremism than when they are alone, and (2) by experiencing exclusion and rejection from the mainstream (majority) group, people are more likely to display extremism than when they feel included.

We start by describing what we mean with group membership and social identity (section 8.2). Subsequently, we outline how membership of an in-group is related to extremism by providing evidence of the importance of social identity in extremism (section 8.3). In section 8.4, we describe how the experience of social exclusion from the mainstream group is associated with various forms of extreme behavior. Finally, we draw conclusions from the present analysis of extremism in terms of social identity (section 8.5).

8.2   What Is Group Membership and Social Identity?

Groups are powerful. As humans, we have organized a great deal of our activities in such a manner that we interact with other people. Already from birth, babies strongly attend to other humans and learn to be social and have fun in spending time with others, be it with other babies or caregivers. When we die, there are often ceremonies where people come together in a group to commemorate our lives. And in between, we do a great number of things together with other people: we often work together (on this chapter, for example), play sports together (e.g., soccer, basketball, cricket, baseball, rowing in an "eight") or against another individual (e.g., solo tennis, chess), make art together (music in bands or an orchestra, plays in theater groups, a film or documentary with a team of filmmakers) or enjoy art together (e.g., in a pop avenue, a theater, or a museum), and we often eat with others. Why do we do so many things together with other people?

One basic reason why we seek out group memberships is to survive. Simply stated, we are more likely to survive in harsh natural circumstances (e.g., experiencing hurricanes or floods) or harsh city surroundings (e.g., living in poor and violent neighborhoods) when we are with others than when we are alone. Given the fact that we have an innate survival instinct, group membership is strongly pursued because it can provide physical security.

In a less extreme manner, the second reason why we aim to be and do things with other people is that, in groups, we are less at risk of adverse experiences (e.g., being harassed on the street or being bullied) than when we are alone. As such, groups can provide a form of mental security and are an important source of physical and social support.

A third reason why we seek out and value group membership is because it can strengthen our social identity. We want to feel good about ourselves, and we derive part of our self-esteem via group memberships (social identity theory – Tajfel & Turner, 1986). Indeed, we feel good about ourselves if we belong to various groups (e.g., Jetten et al., 2015).

Interestingly, this is all the more true when we face adversity or experience problems. As the saying goes, "A problem shared is a problem halved," which indicates that if we tell another person about our problem, it makes it easier to cope with that problem. In line with this reasoning, a recent systematic review shows that social support was one of the most important sources of resilience during hard times (Fadhlia et al., under review).

This is related to the fourth reason why we value group membership: It can be fun, and it feels good to do things together. This can be in playing sports together, making music together, dancing together, eating together, and so on. This can even feel better when we do things in synchrony with other in-group members (Mogan et al., 2017).

A fifth reason why people consider group membership important is that groups can reduce our uncertainty and provide meaning to our world (Hogg & Mullin, 1999; see Wagoner & Hogg, this volume). We can feel uncertain about our attitudes, our emotions, and/or our behavior. For example, in terms of global warming, we can ask ourselves: "Is global warming really happening or it is exaggerated?," which exemplifies attitudinal uncertainty. Similarly, we might wonder: "Is it okay to display anxiety about global warming to others?," which is a form of emotional uncertainty. Finally, we can experience behavioral uncertainty: "Should I stop flying due to global warming?"

Importantly for our discussion, when we feel uncertain about our attitudes, our emotions, or our behavior, we are likely to seek similar others to find out what they are thinking (attitudes), what they are feeling (emotions), and/or what they are doing (behavior; Festinger, 1954). Who are these similar others? Often, they are fellow in-group members. Finding out what others like us think, feel, and/or do can make us feel more certain about roles and norms. They provide us with information as to which ideas, which emotions, and which behaviors are accepted and perceived as normal in our group.

Finally, the sixth reason we value groups is that we can achieve larger goals with(in) a group than is possible for us on our own. For example, many caretakers would agree with the saying: "it takes a village to raise a child" (the exact roots of which are unclear). It also takes a large group of humans to create pyramids or to fly to the moon. This is why, as humans, we often work together on bigger projects, such as construction of roads or housing. These bigger housing projects, for example, involve multiple skills from various people, including planners (e.g., architects), dealing with legal aspects (e.g., lawyers), building the housing complex (e.g., building companies), and selling the houses (e.g., real estate agents). Only a cluster of groups interacting with each other can make such a big project possible.

So far, we have argued that groups play an important role in our society. People value groups for various reasons. We care about groups in order to survive physically and mentally, to strengthen our social identity, to reduce uncertainty about ourselves, to give meaning to our world, and to be able to achieve large goals. But how is group membership connected to extremism? We explain that in the next section.

8.3 The Role of Group Membership in Extremism

We now know that group memberships and social identities are powerful for various reasons. They can guide us in our attitudes, emotions, and behavior. But are they also important when it comes to explaining extremism? In this section, we present eight arguments why we think they do.

(1) Argument 1: Terrorist attacks are mainly perpetrated by individuals in groups, rarely by individuals on their own.

Do we have empirical evidence to support our argument that group membership is important when explaining terrorism? If it is true, as we argue in this chapter, that groups are more important than an individual when explaining terrorism, we should be able to find empirical evidence in support of that claim. In particular, it seems important to empirically demonstrate that more attacks have been carried out by groups than by individuals (the "lone actors").

Luckily, we have excellent data at our disposal. The Global Terrorism Database (GTD) from the University of Maryland is one of the most elaborate data sets describing terrorists' attacks that have happened in the world from 1970 through 2021 (www.start.umd.edu/gtd/). It contains statistics and descriptions of 209,707 terrorist attacks (as of February 23, 2023).

Importantly for the current focus, in the GTD, terrorist attacks are coded in terms of "number of perpetrators." In line with our argument, the overwhelmingly majority (99.6 percent) of the attacks have been undertaken by groups of two or more individuals – while lone actors account for a mere 0.4 percent of the attacks. This is a strong argument in favor of a focus on (individuals in) groups rather than lone actors when explaining terrorism.

We argue that it is easier to display violence in groups than alone (see Argument 6). It is not a coincidence that most other forms of violence (e.g., robbery or assaults) are often done by criminals in groups rather than individuals. Similarly, a standard army typically chooses to create small and cohesive groups of soldiers to carry out missions.

Thus, the first argument is that empirical evidence shows that an overwhelming majority of terrorist attacks are committed by individuals in groups rather than by individuals on their own.

(2) Argument 2: Most terrorists do not suffer from mental illness.

News media often argue that certain terrorists suffer from mental illness (for a critical look at the media themselves, see Betus et al., 2019, in the

Washington Post). This can create a focus on the individual: It was a sole disturbed person who committed the terrorist attack. To some extent, this can be a comforting idea: "Only mentally ill people do such horrible things." But is that true? What does research tell us?

This is an ongoing debate. Initially, there has been a focus on potential mental illness of terrorists. For example, Cooper (1978, p. 254) states that terrorists "might more accurately be described as psychopathic or sociopathic personalities for whom political terrorism provides a vehicle for impulses that would otherwise find another outlet."

Subsequent work has provided a more nuanced picture. For example, Corner and colleagues (2016; see also Gill et al., 2021) provide evidence for different percentages of terrorists suffering from mental illness as a function of the type of terrorism. Specifically, they find that in their sample, lone-actor terrorists are much more likely to have a history of mental disorders (i.e., 40 percent) than solo-terrorists (i.e., terrorists that received support from a group but who executed an attack on their own: 20 percent). For dyads this figure was even lower (5 percent), and it was lowest among group terrorists (less than 3 percent). Corner and colleagues indicate that only the lone actors are significantly more likely to have a history of mental disorders than the general population (22 percent).

Thus, these figures indicate that lone actors more often have a history of mental disorders than the general population, but that this is not the case for other types of actors, in particular not for group-based actors. Remember the numbers presented in Argument 1: Only 0.4 percent of terrorists' attacks are carried out by lone actors, and 99.6 percent by group-based actors (including dyads). In combination, these figures lead us to conclude that examining the mental disorders of individuals does not help us much if we want to understand terrorism.

In addition, even if a terrorist does suffer from a mental disorder, this only indicates a *correlation*. Importantly, it cannot provide us with information about *causation*. The mental disorder is not the cause of terrorism. Rather, the potential correlation between displaying violent acts and suffering from mental disorders may very well have been caused by a shared third variable, for example a history of being bullied at secondary school (e.g., a threat to one's significance; see Kruglanski, et al., 2022; see Ellenberg & Kruglanski, this volume).

Thus, we conclude that a focus on individual characteristics (such as mental disorders) of individual terrorists might not provide a strong (causal) framework to study terrorism. We agree with the statement of political scientist Martha Crenshaw, who in 1981 already concluded that "the outstanding common characteristic of terrorists is their normality" (p. 390). We therefore argue that it is more fruitful to examine elements of the social context in which most acts of violence are displayed by mentally healthy group members.

(3) Argument 3: It's a group's grievance, not an individual grievance.

A central element of a social identity approach to terrorism is that it's a group's grievance, not an individual grievance, that is triggering the intention to use violence in people (e.g., Doosje et al., 2016). Indeed, (empirical) studies show a strong focus on group processes associated with terrorism and radicalization (e.g., Feddes et al., 2020). These group processes include us-versus-them thinking, perceived in-group superiority, and a sense of intergroup threat. Such processes consist of four elements: (1) the idea that in current society one's in-group is not treated with respect, (2) the idea that there is an external threat to the in-group, (3) the idea that current politics do not address this perceived mistreatment and perceived external threat; and (4) the idea that the use of violence is a legitimate means to regain respect from one's in-group and address the perceived external threat.

For example, right-wing extremists in Germany hold the idea that their in-group (White Germans) is not treated with the societal respect it deserves (in their eyes). In addition, they might see current incoming refugees (for example, from Syria) as a threat to their in-group (e.g., Caniglia et al., 2020). When they also believe that the current politicians do not address their concerns (i.e., the perceived external threat to their group's identity), they are more open to the use of violence to achieve their goals. As we will discuss at a later point in this chapter, perceived group efficacy (the perception that you or your group can instigate change on behalf of your group) plays an important role in the decision to turn toward extremism. This might include violent attacks to install fear in a larger population with the aim of changing the political landscape.

Interestingly, while people might experience rejection, disrespect, and discrimination at both the individual level and the group level, people report that experience at the *group* level more often than at the individual level. This robust effect has been labeled the personal/group discrimination discrepancy (e.g., Taylor et al., 1990). In addition, in general, these group-based forms of perceived discrimination or relative deprivation are at least equally but often more strongly linked to radical attitudes or violent intentions (e.g., Doosje et al., 2013; Obaidi et al., 2019; Van Bergen et al., 2015).

(4) Argument 4: They come in groups, rarely as individuals.

In Argument 1, we have already indicated that most violent attacks, including politically motivated attacks, are carried out by individuals in groups rather than by individuals on their own. This fourth argument is that, in most cases, when people must travel to new places to join a terrorist group, they do so in groups, rarely as individuals. For example, when ISIS proclaimed the Caliphate in Syria and Iraq in 2014, this attracted thousands of (mostly young) people from close by, such as Iraq and Syria, but also from far away, including Europe and the United States. In a report by the UN (2015), it was estimated that there were 25,000 foreign terrorist fighters in the Caliphate, who had traveled from more than 100 UN-Member States. Did these 25,000 foreign fighters all travel from their home countries to the Caliphate by themselves as individuals? No! They came in groups. In most cases, small groups of people from one city (or one part of a city) traveled together.

For example, in Vilvoorde, a small town in Belgium of 42,400 inhabitants in 2015, thirty-two young people left for ISIL territory. Similarly, of the 450 Belgian people who left for the Caliphate, 207 people were from Brussels (from a western district named Molenbeek) and another 115 people from Antwerp. In other countries, it was also possible to find such "hubs" of people leaving for ISIS territory. Thus, people not only are more likely to execute violent attacks in groups but also often join such groups with like-minded others rather than continuing alone. This was also observed among the Red Army Faction in Germany (McCauley & Moskalenko, 2008). So, it seems that group processes have already started to develop *before* people (physically) join an extremist group.

(5) Argument 5: Basic and powerful group processes take place in extremist groups.

One basic and powerful group process that takes place in extremist groups involves us-versus-them thinking. Importantly, most extremist groups have developed a clear radical world view (e.g., Doosje et al., 2013) in which there is an important role for the threat that stems from a well-defined out-group to which the in-group can be contrasted in a process of "mutual radicalization" (Moghaddam, 2018). One way this can occur is by interpreting actions of in- and out-groups in a biased manner. For example, a violent attack by an individual out-group member is perceived as being supported by a large section of that out-group (Doosje et al., 2007). This may (further) motivate the idea of revenge on the whole out-group. When this same mechanism takes place in both groups, the result is a process of mutual radicalization, supporting the notion that group membership plays an important role when explaining extremism (De Graaf & Van den Bos, 2021).

The second basic and important group process that often takes place is a need for strong leadership. Extremist groups call for extremist actions due to perceived group threat and these are best advocated by strong and autocratic leaders (e.g., Hogg, 2021). Conversely, to the extent that violent attacks can cause turmoil and distrust in populations (an idea that is *not* strongly supported by data; see Doosje et al., 2018), this population may support tough leaders, with a clear vision of where to go from here and how best to respond to violent attacks. Interestingly, these strong leaders might call for strong actions ("We will hunt them down and bring them to court"), but they may also call for restraint and calmness, to "show them that we will not allow our open and free society to be influenced by their violence."

Thus, our fifth argument in favor of a focus on social identity is that basic and powerful group processes take place in extremist groups, such as us-versus-them-thinking and support for a strong leader in times perceived as threatening.

(6) Argument 6: The group facilitates the final steps to violent attacks.

While in Argument 1 we presented data to show that most violent attacks are executed by groups rather than individuals, Argument 6 addresses why this is the case. While we argue that this can be partly explained in terms of practicality (it is easier to organize a large-scale attack if you have many people), there are other and more important roles for the group when it comes to the use of violence. First, there is diffusion of responsibility (Bandura, 2016), such that people feel less personally responsible for actions when many others are involved in the action and each person only executes a part of the action. Second, the group often provides legitimacy (i.e., the norms) for the violent attacks. In most cases, groups prepare their members for violence by dehumanizing the enemy, for example, portraying them as an animal, ideally an insect (cockroaches) or vermin (rats) that should be "cleaned up" (Haslam & Loughnan, 2014). Similarly, the leaders of the group often sketch a threatening picture: It is either us or them who will survive the battle between good and evil. In addition, leaders of a group often describe a rosy vision about what will happen if you were to die. This can include some sort of heaven for yourself, but the group also may provide means to your family, with the promise that your name will be honored forever as a martyr who has died for a good cause. Another strategy that extremist groups (and military groups, for that matter) often employ is to create small subgroups that will execute an attack. This has the advantage of creating compact, cohesive units with "pals" that will support each other in their joint mission that includes displaying violence.

Thus, several techniques provided by the group make it easier for individuals in groups to respond to the call for action and display violence against others, in order to create a "better world," than for individuals on their own.

(7) Argument 7: It takes groups to get out of extremists' groups.

Our seventh and final argument in favor of a focus on the group in the case of extremism/terrorism involves the way in which individuals might leave an extremist group. Often, this occurs via the help of individuals from (other) groups, for example, a former right-wing extremist who helps a youngster to leave the scene. EXIT, for instance, is a program that helps individuals leave extremist groups by providing hands-on and practical help, such as finding a new house in a new place (which makes it easier to break the contact with the old group) or trying to find a new way to spend the day, in terms of either their career (e.g., a new education or a new job) or of a new hobby that will broaden their horizon (e.g., playing soccer in a club in the new place; Hardy, 2019). Thus, it can take a group to get individuals leave an extremist group.

In Argument 1 through Argument 7, we have presented seven arguments regarding why we think it is important to focus on a meso or group level when explaining violent attacks by individuals in extremist groups. In section 8.4, we will illustrate how, via an experimental manipulation, cumulative experiences of group-based rejection and exclusion can prepare group members to slowly move into a more radical direction, in which the display of violence might be perceived as a slightly more attractive course of action to consider.

8.4   The Role of Social Exclusion in Extremism: The Bovenland Paradigm

8.4.1   Introduction

Imagine you are from a poor southern region of a country and move to the wealthier northern region aiming for a better life. One day, you go to the bakery to buy bread. In the bakery, the baker refuses to sell you bread because he "does not sell bread to southerners." What would you do?

An increasing number of studies systematically investigate the role of social exclusion in extremism in the laboratory. For example, Pfundmair and Wetherell (2019) make use of the Cyberball paradigm, in which participants are systematically ostracized during a computer-simulated ball game (see Williams & Jarvis, 2006, for a detailed discussion of this paradigm). They showed that being ostracized was correlated with more support for extreme actions on behalf of a social group, which was measured by scales including statements such as "I would fight someone threatening the beliefs of [my group]" (Renström & Bäck, this volume).

Collective action research, however, teaches us that group members often have multiple options in their repertoire to deal with injustice. Wright and colleagues (1990) define collective action as any time a group member acts as a representative of the group and the action of the group member is directed at improving the condition of the entire group. The group member has multiple options to deal with injustice. First, doing nothing, or inaction. In this strategy the group member accepts the situation as it is. Second, a group member can engage in normative collective action. Such behavior is in line with the norms in the social system in which the person resides, for example, organizing a demonstration or a petition. Third, the action may go beyond the norms of acceptable behavior, which is called nonnormative behavior, such as vandalism. Importantly, Wright and colleagues consider collective nonnormative action to be the most socially disruptive. So, when actual change is needed, nonnormative action has the strongest implications. In a later study, Tausch and colleagues (2011) added another, fourth behavioral option, namely extreme nonnormative action. Whereas nonnormative action goes beyond the norms of the social system, extreme nonnormative action entails the use of violence to instigate social change.

8.4.2 The Bovenland Paradigm

Making use of this fine-grained analysis of collective action, we created a research paradigm in which participants are asked to imagine they live in a fictitious country named "Bovenland." They then repeatedly experience social exclusion.[1] At the start of the paradigm, all participants learn that they are from the southern part of Bovenland. They are informed that this is a poor region, and that many southerners move toward the North in hope of a better life. However, in the north, they are repeatedly discriminated against in different social situations, such as the bakery example at the start of this section. The hypothesis to be tested with this paradigm is straightforward: the more often people are excluded because of their group membership, the more they move away from "doing nothing" and "normative collective action" and opt for "nonnormative" and perhaps even "extreme nonnormative" collective action.

To make clear to participants the distinction between "normative," "nonnormative," and "extreme nonnormative" collective action, the constitution of Bovenland is presented at the start of the paradigm, and the participants are asked to read the laws carefully. The constitution, including eleven articles, is depicted in Figure 8.1. As can be seen, the different behaviors, and which of these are and are not allowed in Bovenland, are outlined and described. Regarding nonnormative action, Article 6 states that "All those in Bovenland will not cause damage to public property." Extreme nonnormative violence is considered as someone threatening to use or actually using violence (Articles 5 and 6). Note that it is allowed to organize protests in Bovenland (Article 3), which refers to normative action.

When reading the different social situations from which they were excluded or in which they were discriminated against, the constitution always appeared at the top of the screen so participants were reminded of what is and what is not allowed in Bovenland.

Shukla (2019) and Holt (2019) worked further with this paradigm and created ten different social situations of exclusion (ten "rounds").[2] The first two situations (round 1 and round 2) set the stage of social exclusion. Participants are rejected two times in bakeries by a baker who refuses to sell

---

[1] The Bovenland paradigm was developed in cooperation with Dr. Bastiaan Rutjens and Richtsje Kurpershoek.

[2] The materials and data reported here were part of the master's thesis projects of Nilam Shukla and Lorenzo Holt, supervised by Allard Feddes.

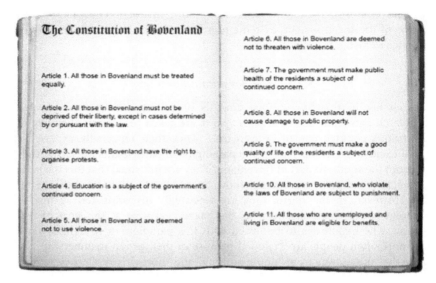

Figure 8.1 The constitution of Bovenland includes eleven articles that are used to distinguish between normative, nonnormative, and extreme nonnormative collective action behaviors.

them bread because they are southerners. In round 3, participants are refused medicine by a pharmacist. Now the participant is offered three response options: the choice to do nothing (*inaction*), initiate a discussion with the pharmacist (*individual normative action*), or throw a rock through the pharmacist's window (*individual nonnormative action*). In round 4, participants apply for financial social support. The application is rejected, and it is made clear that this is because they are southerners. Participants have similar options to respond to this injustice as used in round 3.

After this, the participant is given information about two local protest groups. One is called SLOVE (South LOVE) – this is a group conducting normative action in response to the social exclusion and discrimination that southerners in the north are facing. The second group is called RFS (Rights for Southerners) – this is a group that conducts *non*normative action. Participants learn that the aim of both groups is to respond to the social exclusion southerners are facing in the north of Bovenland; it is the nature of the actions they conduct that differs (normative vs. nonnormative).

In rounds 5, 6, and 7, participants are again excluded because they are southerners. In these rounds, however, they have the option for not only (besides inaction) individual normative and nonnormative action, but they now also have the option for *collective normative action* (joining SLOVE) or *collective nonnormative action* (joining RFS). Importantly, once the participant decides to join SLOVE, individual option choices are not shown in the next rounds. They have the choice to leave SLOVE and do nothing, conduct the normative action that SLOVE is suggesting, or join the group RFS and conduct nonnormative action.

Importantly, when participants joined RFS (at any point), the paradigm ended, as they had decided to join the radical nonnormative group (the most extreme behavioral option). If the participant decided to join the group SLOVE, further rounds of social exclusion were presented to them, to see if they at one point would join the more radical group RFS. At no point could participants join both groups. Participants could, however, join SLOVE, and in later rounds RFS. But not vice versa, as the paradigm ended when participants opted for the nonnormative collective action.

In rounds 8 to 10, the individual collective action choice options disappeared for all participants, so also for the participants who consistently chose individual actions. In these last three rounds, participants could only choose among the options inaction, joining (or conducting actions for) SLOVE (normative collective action), or joining RFS (nonnormative collective action).

8.4.3   Does Bovenland Work?

A total of 254 participants (179 females, 72 males; mean age was 23.13, SD was 7.98) participated in the study (Holt, 2019; Shukla, 2019). The participants were recruited through convenience sampling, social media (Facebook), and the Psychology of Amsterdam Student Participant Pool. The study was approved beforehand by the Ethical Board of the Psychology Department of the University of Amsterdam.

To examine whether the repeated experience of social exclusion was effective, participants were asked after completion of the paradigm to indicate to what extent they felt *included* in the northern community of Bovenland. This measure was based on previous work to capture one's sense of connectedness to others (Aron, Aron, & Smollan, 1992) and other groups (Schubert & Otten, 2002). Answers could be given on a scale of 1 (indicating a *low level of social inclusion*) to 6 (indicating a *high level of social inclusion*). See Figure 8.2.

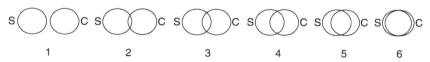

Figure 8.2 Measure of social inclusion ("S" = Self and "C" = Community of the North of Bovenland); higher scores indicate a higher level of social inclusion.

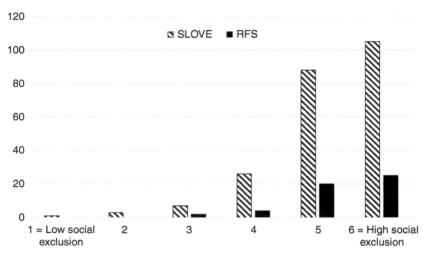

Figure 8.3 Number of participants (vertical axis) opting for the normative group SLOVE or the nonnormative group RFS based on the reported level of social exclusion (horizontal axis).

The answers were recoded such that *a higher score indicated people felt more excluded.* The results clearly showed that the Bovenland paradigm succeeded in making people feel excluded; the mean value on the recoded six-point scale (with 6 being highest levels of feeling excluded) was 5.26 ($SD = .89$).

So how did the repeated experience of social exclusion affect participants' choice for the protest groups? The results showed that a total of 211 participants (83 percent) joined the group SLOVE at least at one point throughout the paradigm. Importantly, of these participants who joined SLOVE at least at one point, 201 (95 percent) reported a high exclusion score (6 on the scale of 1–6). A considerable number of participants, fifty-two (20 percent) joined the radical, nonnormative RFS group at least at one point in the paradigm. Of these "radicals," forty-nine (96 percent) reported a high exclusion score.

As can be seen in Figure 8.3, when participants experienced higher levels of social exclusion based on their group membership, they were more likely to join the normative action group SLOVE. Participants were also more likely to join the nonnormative RFS group when they experienced social exclusion.

Table 8.1 shows the number of participants who joined the normative group SLOVE or the nonnormative group RFS in each round. It is important to note that from round 8 onwards, the individual normative and nonnormative action options were no longer given. Participants only had the option to do nothing (inaction), take normative action (joining SLOVE), or take nonnormative action (joining RFS).

Table 8.1 *Overview of the number of participants (and percentage of the total number of participants, N = 254) joining (or active) in the normative group SLOVE or joining the nonnormative group RFS in the different rounds*

Behavior	Joined in round 5 N (%)	Active/ joined in round 6 N (%)	Active/ joined in round 7 N (%)	Active/ joined in round 8 N (%)	Active/ joined in round 9 N (%)	Active/ joined in round 10 N (%)
Inaction	9 (4%)	2 (1%)	12 (4%)	5 (2%)	4 (2%)	10 (4%)
Individual normative	38 (15%)	30 (12%)	6 (2%)	–	–	–
Normative group SLOVE	183 (72%)	198 (77%)	211 (83%)	193 (76%)	183 (72%)	165 (65%)
Nonnormative group RFS	24 (9%)	0 (0%)	1 (1%)	13 (5%)	6 (2%)	8 (3%)

Notes. From round 8 onwards, individual normative and nonnormative options were not given, and participants could only choose inaction, joining SLOVE (normative action), or joining RFS (nonnormative action). Furthermore, when participants opted for RFS, the paradigm ended.

A first observation is that when the group was presented as an option to engage in collective action from round 5 onwards, participants in great numbers preferred the group over inaction and individual action. Furthermore, the majority of participants opted for normative group action when they had the opportunity. From round 9 onwards, participants had the option to leave SLOVE and join RFS, or do nothing. As can be seen, from round 8 to round 10 the number of participants active in SLOVE decreased from 193 to 165 (out of the total of 254).

In sum, the results of the research paradigm indicate that the higher the level of reported social exclusion, the more participants opt for normative collective action (by joining SLOVE) or nonnormative collective action (by joining RFS). Importantly, these results show that most of the participants chose normative options to counter injustice instead of nonnormative options. This is in line with the notion from the collective action literature: When individuals perceive normative action as effective in countering injustice, they prefer this over nonnormative behavior. For example, Tausch and colleagues (2011) found that when the perceived efficacy of group behavior is high, participants opted for nonviolent collective action instead of extreme violent collective action.

Another important observation is that when groups are presented, participants preferred collective action in a group context, rather than inaction, or engaging in individual forms of action. Overall, these results show that groups become more attractive options for countering injustice when individuals experience higher levels of social exclusion.

8.5   Conclusions

In this chapter, we have highlighted the role of group membership and social identity in explaining extremism. We have presented seven arguments as to why we consider social identity to be key in predicting who is most likely to feel attracted to radical groups and to display violent attacks and when this is the case. In addition, we have presented our attempt to manipulate the rejection of one's social identity in an artificially created context called "Bovenland."

This does not mean we want to argue that being rejected as an individual (rather than as a group member) is not important. When people feel rejected as an individual, for example, in a classroom setting at school, they might feel attracted to radical groups because these can fulfill deprived needs. In addition, when people feel excluded as an individual, they are more susceptible to persuasive attempts by radical groups to join their group. For example, in the third example that we presented at the start of this chapter, the Columbine high school shooting, it seemed that the two individuals who displayed the violence felt rejected *as individuals* and not so much rejection based on a particular group membership. Indeed, interpersonal rejection (such as bullying) has been empirically linked with shootings (e.g., Leary et al., 2003; see Kowalski & Leary, this volume) and aggressive behavior (Quarmley et al., 2022).

However, the most important point we want to make in this chapter is that exclusion as a group member can be a powerful force that makes people vulnerable to radical ideas and groups. From this analysis, we draw two central conclusions. The first is that an in-group can provide a strong sense of identity, purpose, and meaning to people. To the extent that people identify with that group, they are more likely to follow the group norms. These norms can inform group members how to perceive the social world, how to feel group-based emotions, and how to behave in line with the concerns of the group.

The second conclusion is that, when people as group members feel rejected, they want to reclaim their group's sense of respect and worth to reaffirm their group's identity. This can involve the use of nonnormative actions such as violence when people feel the current society (e.g., politicians) is not addressing their concerns properly.

Thus, when rejected as a group member, one's social identity can be triggered and become important in explaining violence. Clearly grievances at the group level are very strong triggers for actions aimed at restoring the respect, worth, and honor of the group, whether these actions are normative or nonnormative. Within a group, people are not only more able to achieve something "big" with which to attract the attention of others but they also experience and share strong group-based emotions that motivate such actions. Therefore, if one wants to understand the link between exclusion and extremism, it is essential to go beyond the individual to consider the group.

References

Aron, A., Aron, E. N., & Smollan, D. (1992). Inclusion of other in the self scale and the structure of interpersonal closeness. *Journal of Personality and Social Psychology, 63*(4), 596–612. https://doi.org/10.1037/0022-3514.63.4.596

Bandura, A. (2016). *Moral disengagement: How people do harm and live with themselves.* Worth.

Betus, A., Kearns, E. M., & Lemieux, A. (2019). Who's a terrorist and who's mentally ill? We looked at 10 years of news coverage to find out. *Washington Post.* www.washingtonpost.com/politics/2019/08/08/whos-terrorist-whos-mentally-ill-we-looked-years-news-coverage-find-out/

Caniglia, M., Winkler, L., & Métais, S. (2020). The rise of the right-wing violent extremism threat in Germany and its transnational character. European Strategic Intelligence and Security Center. www.esisc.org/publications/analyses/the-rise-of-the-right-wing-violent-extremism-threat-in-germany-and-its-transnational-character

Cooper, H. H. A. (1978). Psychopath as terrorist: A psychological perspective. *Legal Medical Quarterly, 2,* 253–262. https://heinonline.org/HOL/P?h=hein.journals/medquar2&i=253

Corner, E., Gill, P., & Mason, O. J. (2016). Mental health disorders and the terrorist: A research note probing selection effects and disorder prevalence. *Studies in Conflict & Terrorism, 39,* 560–568. https://doi.org/10.1080/1057610X.2015.1120099

Crenshaw, M. (1981). The causes of terrorism. *Comparative Politics, 13*(4), 379–399. https://doi.org/10.2307/421717

De Graaf, B., & Van den Bos, K. (2021). Religious radicalization: Social appraisals and finding redemption in extreme beliefs. *Current Opinions in Psychology, 40,* 56–60. https://doi.org/10.1016/j.copsyc.2020.08.028

Doosje, B., Loseman, A., & Bos, K. (2013). Determinants of radicalization of Islamic youth in the Netherlands: Personal uncertainty, perceived injustice, and perceived group threat. *Journal of Social Issues, 69,* 586–604. https://doi.org/10.1111/josi.12030

Doosje, B., Moghaddam, F. M., Kruglanski, A. W., et al. (2016). Terrorism, radicalization and de-radicalization. *Current Opinion in Psychology, 11,* 79–84. https://doi.org/10.1016/j.copsyc.2016.06.008

Doosje, B., Van Der Veen, J., & Klaver, L. (2018). Can societies experience post-traumatic growth after a terror attack? The influence of terror attacks on political, institutional, and social trust in European countries. *International Journal of Conflict and Violence*, *12*, 1–19. https://doi.org/10.4119/UNIBI/ ijcv.645

Doosje, B., Zebel, S., Scheermeier, M., & Mathyi, P. (2007). Attributions of responsibility for terrorist attacks: The role of group membership and identification. *International Journal of Conflict and Violence*, *1*, 127–141. https://doi.org/ 10.4119/ijcv-2749

Fadhlia, T. N., Sauter, D. A., & Doosje, B. (under review). A systematic review of the socio-ecological factors affecting resilience in refugees. University of Amsterdam.

Feddes, A. R., Nickolson, L., Mann, L., & Doosje, B. (2020). *Psychological perspectives on radicalization*. Routledge.

Festinger, L. (1954). A theory of social comparison processes. *Human Relations*, *7*, 117–140.

Gill, P., Clemmow, C., Hetzel, F., et al. (2021). Systematic review of mental health problems and violent extremism. *Journal of Forensic Psychiatry and Psychology*, *32*(1), 51–78. https://doi.org/10.1080/14789949.2020.1820067

Global Terrorism Database (n.d.). University of Maryland. www.start.umd.edu/gtd/

Hardy, K. (2019). Countering right-wing extremism: Lessons from Germany and Norway. *Journal of Policing, Intelligence and Counter Terrorism*, *14*(3), 262–279. https://doi.org/10.1080/18335330.2019.1662076

Haslam, N., & Loughnan, S. (2014). Dehumanization and infrahumanization. *Annual Review of Psychology*, *65*, 399–423. https://doi.org/10.1146/annurev-psych-010213-115045

Hogg, M. A. (2021). Uncertain self in a changing world: A foundation for radicalisation, populism, and autocratic leadership. *European Review of Social Psychology*, *32*(2), 235–268. https://doi.org/10.1080/10463283.2020.1827628

Hogg, M. A., & Mullin, B. A. (1999). Joining groups to reduce uncertainty: Subjective uncertainty reduction and group identification. In D. Abrams & M. A. Hogg (Eds.), *Social identity and social cognition* (pp. 249–279). Blackwell.

Holt, L. (2019). Radicalisation in the laboratory: The role of injustice, need for justice and contempt. [Unpublished master's thesis]. University of Amsterdam.

Jetten, J., Branscombe, N. R., Haslam, S. A., et al. (2015). Having a lot of a good thing: Multiple important group memberships as a source of self-esteem. *PLoS ONE*, *10*(5), e0124609.

Kruglanski, A. W., Molinario, E., Jasko, K., et al. (2022). Significance-quest theory. *Perspectives on Psychological Science*, *17*(4), 1050–1071. https://doi.org/10.1177/ 17456916211034825

Leary M. R., Kowalski R. M., Smith L., & Phillips S. (2003). Teasing, rejection, and violence: Case studies of the school shootings. *Aggressive Behavior*, *29*, 202–214. https://doi.org/10.1002/ab.10061

McCauley, C., & Moskalenko, S. (2008). Mechanisms of political radicalization: Pathways toward terrorism. *Terrorism and Political Violence*, *20*(3), 415–433. https://doi.org/10.1080/09546550802073367

Mogan, R., Fischer, R., & Bulbulia, J. A. (2017). To be in synchrony or not? A meta-analysis of synchrony's effects on behavior, perception, cognition and affect. *Journal of Experimental Social Psychology, 72*, 13–20. https://doi.org/10.1016/j.jesp.2017.03.009

Moghaddam, F. M. (2018). *Mutual radicalization: How groups and nations drive each other to extremes.* American Psychological Association. https://doi.org/10.1037/0000089-000

Obaidi, M., Bergh, R., Akrami, N., & Anjum, G. (2019). Group-based relative deprivation explains endorsement of extremism among Western-born Muslims. *Psychological Science, 30*(4), 596-605. https://doi.org/10.1177/0956797619834879

Quarmley, M., Feldman, J., Grossman, H., et al. (2022). Testing effects of social rejection on aggressive and prosocial behavior: A meta-analysis. *Aggressive Behavior, 48*, 529–545. https://doi.org/10.1002/ab.22026

Schubert, T. W., & Otten, S. (2002). Overlap of self, ingroup, and outgroup: Pictorial measures of self-categorization. *Self and Identity, 1*(4), 353–376. https://doi.org/1529-8868/2002

Shukla, N. (2019). Escalation to joining a radical group: The role of social exclusion. [Unpublished master's thesis]. University of Amsterdam.

Tajfel, H., & Turner, J. C. (1986). The social identity theory of intergroup behavior. In S. Worchel & W. G. Austin (Eds.), *Psychology of intergroup relations* (pp. 7–24). Nelson-Hall.

Tausch, N., Becker, J. C., Spears, R., et al. (2011). Explaining radical group behavior: Developing emotion and efficacy routes to normative and nonnormative collective action. *Journal of Personality and Social Psychology, 101*(1), 129–148. https://doi.org/10.1037/a0022728

Taylor, D. M., Wright, S. C., Moghaddam, F. M., & Lalonde, R. N. (1990). The personal/group discrimination discrepancy: Perceiving my group, but not myself, to be a target for discrimination. *Personality and Social Psychology Bulletin, 16*(2), 254–262. https://doi.org/10.1177/0146167290162006

UN (2015). Analysis and recommendations with regard to the global threat from foreign terrorist fighters. www.securitycouncilreport.org/atf/cf/%7B65BFCF9B-6D27-4E9C-8CD3-CF6E4FF96FF9%7D/s_2015_358.pdf

Van Bergen, D. D., Feddes, A. F., Doosje, B., & Pels, T. V. M. (2015). Collective identity factors and the attitude toward violence in defense of ethnicity or religion among Muslim youth of Turkish and Moroccan descent. *International Journal of Intercultural Relations, 47*, 89–100. https://doi.org/10.1016/j.ijintrel.2015.03.026

Wright, S. C., Taylor, D. M., & Moghaddam, F. M. (1990). Responding to membership in a disadvantaged group: From acceptance to collective protest. *Journal of Personality and Social Psychology, 58*(6), 994–1003. https://doi.org/10.1037/0022-3514.58.6.994

"Who Do They Think We Are?!"

How Status Indignity and Exclusion Can Motivate Radicalization

J. N. RASMUS MÖRING AND FELICIA PRATTO

9.1 Introduction

In the past century, the world has seen two contradictory sociopolitical changes: (1) the spread of democracy and liberal ideals such as civil rights, human rights, freedom, due process, and social equality, and (2) the resurrection of authoritarian constraints and prejudices with the rejection of civil liberties and democratic processes. We situate our theoretical analysis of radicalization (defined as adopting, in ideology or in action, violence as a means to achieve political ends) in the interplay of these political movements. From this intergroup/political perspective, we consider the psychology of exclusion and radicalization in group status comparisons and ideological aspirations. Specifically, we outline how people's ideals for intergroup relations as being egalitarian or hierarchical influence how they assess their own status. We also consider the contents of sociopolitical ideologies that can legitimize violence to achieve political goals. These considerations lead us to discuss the psychological differences between people attracted to progressive political movements versus regressive political movements and the circumstances, beliefs, and psychological predilections that might provoke either side to radicalization.

As such, we begin by considering people's political and social-structural context.

9.2 Setting the Stage: Group Hierarchies and Power Contests

9.2.1 Status, Power, and Group Hierarchies

Social dominance theory notes that nearly all stable contemporary societies can be considered group-based dominance hierarchies in which at least one socially defined category or group, such as a particular race, nationality, religion or religious sect, ethnicity, caste, or class enjoys superior power and normatively higher status than at least one other complementary group (Sidanius & Pratto, 1999). For example, the Türkiye government persecutes ethnic Kurds and certain religious sects, and throughout both hemispheres, European colonizers subjected Indigenous peoples and those of African descent to systematic subjugation and exploitation. In social dominance theory, such social categories that are associated with differential power are called "arbitrary set groups."

In addition, social dominance theory observes that group-based dominance societies also have two other intersecting kinds of group-based dominance hierarchies: those based on gender inequality, with men and gender stereotypical people having more power and privilege than women and non–gender stereotypical people, and a third intersecting group hierarchy with at least some adults having more power than children. Aspects of social dominance theory also pertain to cross-national relationships (e.g., Pratto et al., 2014).

9.2.2   Institutional Discrimination and Violence

Social dominance theory further states that group-based inequality is maintained by systematic, often institutionalized discrimination that benefits dominant groups (Sidanius & Pratto, 1999). For example, since its inception, the United States has used laws concerning education, employment, marriage, ownership, and the like to very effectively subordinate Native Americans and African Americans (e.g., Dunbar-Ortiz, 2014; Sidanius & Pratto, 1999; Turner et al., 1984). Importantly, institutional and other kinds of systematic discrimination can include violence that is systematically targeted against subordinate groups and their allies, by legal/official, semiofficial, and extralegal means. For example, the wars the United States waged against Native American tribes, their forced removal (e.g., Dunbar-Ortiz, 2014), and the way the legal system harasses, imprisons, and kills African Americans and lets individual Whites get away with doing the same (e.g., Turner et al., 1984) is violent institutionalized discrimination (Sidanius & Pratto, 1999). The operation of "death squads," which perform violence like murder and torture in the service of certain elites with the cooperation of government agents, is "semiofficial" institutional violence (e.g., Campbell, 2000). Torture, imprisonment, and murder by mobs in the heyday of US lynching (1860–1930) was nearly always illegal and mainly targeted racial and ethnic subordinates (e.g., Pfeifer, 2004). These and many other examples show that violence as a means of achieving a political goal (or radicalization) is not the sole purview of nongovernmental actors, nor is it necessarily extralegal. Therefore, we reject the assumption that radicalization is always against the government by those outside the government.

9.2.3   Legitimizing Ideologies

Social dominance theory further states that shared cultural ideologies help to coordinate and legitimize the action patterns that influence how unequal societies are, both internally and externally. For example, stereotypes about gender roles influence what jobs boys and girls aspire to, and, in some countries, gender stereotypes justify making certain jobs illegal for men or women. The operation of institutionalized discrimination and consensual legitimizing ideologies help to maintain the stability of group inequality, even if the degree of it and methods by which it is enacted change in time. Shared cultural legitimizing ideologies prescribe how institutions should operate, and they can lead to public approval for policies or practices. If societies have widely accepted means of arbitrating this fundamental political contest, they can maintain stability and cohesion even as they undergo internal change.

Social dominance theory also posits that when legitimizing ideologies are more consensual, dominant groups use violence less frequently and more selectively to maintain dominance. In other words, social dominance theory has posited an ideology–violence trade-off for dominant groups. But there is a boundary condition: If enough people view certain types of violence or a large quantity of violence as illegitimate, this may curb dominants' use of violence against subordinates, and/or lead violent actors to hide their use of violence. For example, US President Reagan's operatives illegally and secretly provided aid to the Contras, right-wing rebels in Nicaragua, in violation of US law (Walsh, 1996).

9.2.3.1   Ideology and Violence Are Not Mutually Exclusive Mechanisms of Control

A critical question concerning social change is what happens when there is no longer consensus about legitimizing ideologies in a society. When people doubt or reject ideologies that bolstered institutional policies and normative practices, and when people reject certain institutions, they may stop following prohibitions on using violence. They may also try to promote a new legitimizing ideology. Different from social dominance theory's original statement, we propose that ideological persuasion and violence are not alternative methods: Individuals and groups can try to undermine the current legitimized system by using violent means as well as by promoting new ideologies. For example, White racism was seldom accepted by Native Americans, Africans, and African Americans as a legitimizing ideology for colonization. Rather, many Native Americans and African Americans tried to delegitimize White racism and its practices, for example by expounding on its contradiction to other cultural ideals like liberty and Christianity (e.g., Foner, 1999; Young, 1879). Further, speakers propounded alternative ideologies concerning, for example, justice. Others engaged in hidden or violent resistance to racist practices to try to eliminate oppression (e.g., Aptheker, 1943; Dunbar-Ortiz, 2014; Feagin, 2013).

To prevent violent action, it therefore makes sense to have a consensual ideology to prescribe and proscribe violence. To develop a *consensual* ideology rather than feigned agreement, relevant parties need to have a voice and be heard. Excluding or silencing some of the parties may prevent deliberation as the means of developing consensus and cooperation. Likewise, to arbitrate policies through any legal system, the relevant parties must be recognized as having legal standing and must at least appear to accept the legitimacy of the legal system in question. Limiting discursive or deliberative processes leaves violence as an alternative option of effecting desired political goals.

9.3 Normal Politics: Contests between Hierarchy-Enhancing and Hierarchy-Attenuating Forces

In addition, social dominance theory holds that societies maintain their stable form when forces (i.e., ideologies, movements, individual action, and institutions) that would attenuate group-based dominance are roughly balanced in strength with forces that would maintain or even enhance group-based dominance. That means that the normal social politics of societies is the struggle between hierarchy-enhancing and hierarchy-attenuating forces. This political-structural dynamic is the context in which to understand how status indignity and a sense of exclusion may lead to radicalization. To approach those particular social-psychological processes, we now consider hierarchy-attenuating and hierarchy-enhancing political movements in the past century or so.

9.3.1 Progressive Movements

Despite many instances of genocide, wars, dictatorships, and repressive violence, the twentieth century witnessed many political movements that were successful in expanding rights and self-determination. Movements for national liberation from colonization that had been ongoing since the 1700s were finally successful, with more and more countries declaring themselves democratic (Bundeszentrale für Politische Bildung, 2017), thereby granting marginalized groups more rights.

Women's rights and empowerment expanded substantially in the twentieth century. The colony of New Zealand allowed women to vote in 1886, followed by many others (World Population Review, 2023), and girls' access to primary education increased substantially, reducing girls' illiteracy rates faster than boys' (UNESCO, 2017). Other arenas in which women and their allies are still working for equality are freedom from violence, child marriage, and coercion but also in higher education, parental leave and job security, or the gender pay gap. Gender equality and female empowerment are one of the UN's development goals (e.g., United Nations, n.d.). Hence, the last century saw substantial, if uneven and incomplete, advancement of women's status, empowerment, and rights.

The normative expansion of concepts of human rights and dignity also extended, albeit incompletely, to marginalized religious sects, ethnic or racial groups, and Indigenous peoples in the twentieth and twenty-first centuries.

The United Nations Charter in 1945 changed the hierarchical traditional norms of many societies by declaring that all persons are born free and equal in their rights and dignity. The political advocacy of subordinated people, for example, workers and disabled people, changed laws and government programs substantially on several continents. Subordinated groups and their allies are also challenging the legitimizing myths that glorify past subordination and nation-formation by detailing historical wrongs and their link to contemporary methods of subordination. For example, in 2021 the government of New Zealand acknowledged wrongdoing against the Indigenous Moriori people of Rēkohu, and in 2008 the Canadian government formed a commission to investigate crimes committed against children of Indigenous communities. This commission led to the recognition of these crimes as cultural genocide, and to apologies and reconciliation programs of the Canadian government, even though there is criticism that these measures are not extensive enough (Monkman, 2020). Acknowledging the wrongs of colonization and instantiating justice is an ongoing project.

Furthermore, after decades of discrimination and violence against queer people, their fight for recognition and equal rights began to bear fruit late in the last century: The decriminalization of homosexuality in many Western states and later the de-pathologizing of homosexuality in the DSM-III-R in 1987 and the ICD-10 in 1991 are examples of this. The number of countries that allow same-sex marriage also increased in recent decades, through, for example, the US Supreme Court Decision *Obergefell* v. *Hodges* in 2015 or through legislative action in 2016 in Germany. There is also movement in some countries to recognize transgender and intersex people: Malta, Denmark, and Norway all have legislation that grant citizens self-determination about their gender recognition, and Canada, India, and New Zealand allow a third gender identity option aside from "male" and "female." Although there is a long way to go to achieve recognition and equality, these changes are all steps toward more security and equality for queer people.

Summing up, it often takes decades of protest and lobbying, as well as changes in normative ideologies, to enact equal rights, and even more work to reduce or reverse institutional discrimination (e.g., Sidanius & Pratto, 1999), let alone to enact affirmative, reparative programs. But hierarchy-attenuating or, more commonly, progressive change has reduced the degree of group-based inequality and expanded the set of people with social recognition, rights, and access to resources.

9.3.2 Regressive Countermovements

Progressive movements are often not only resisted but can also be met with backlash to undo progressive change, sometimes creating a more oppressive climate than existed prior (e.g., Faludi, 1991; Norris & Inglehart, 2019). We call political movements that increase or maintain the gap between the status or empowerment of different groups not merely conservative or resistant, but *regressive*. Regressive changes can include any means of curtailing rights, access to resources, or social legitimacy, whether done through enforcing laws, failing to enforce laws, defunding progressive institutions, voter intimidation, gerrymandering, or other methods.

For example, in 2022 the US Supreme Court rejected its 1973 ruling that all pregnant individuals have a right to choose an abortion (*Dobbs* v. *Jackson*). The new ruling denies pregnant people autonomy over their family relationships and bodies. Similarly, the government of Poland banned abortions in almost every case and executes severe punishments for those helping people to find safe ways of ending a pregnancy (Amnesty International, 2023). Poland and Hungary suspended funding for women's rights organizations and portray a narrative of women as only housekeepers and mothers (Peto & Grzebalska, 2016). Prime Minister Victor Orban of Hungary banned gender studies in his nation in 2018. Even more draconian, the Taliban-led government of Afghanistan has restricted girls' education and barred women from paid employment, judicial positions, travel, and even their presence in public (Türk, 2023).

Like the regressive movements against reproductive rights and gender equality, there are regressive movements to strip only recently won rights and social recognition from queer people. For example, a flurry of legislation in the United States tries to prohibit books, films, and discussion about the existence of LGBTQIA+ people and their presence in public. Governor Ron DeSantis of Florida signed House Bill 1557 into law, which prohibits "classroom discussion [and instruction] about sexual orientation and gender identity" (Florida Senate, 2022, p. 1). Currently, 491 anti-LGBTQIA+ laws are being considered in US state legislatures (ACLU, 2023), 45 states have considered legislation restricting the rights of transgender children and adults (Track Trans Legislation, 2023), and the list goes on: In Poland, some towns declare themselves to be "LGBT Ideology Free," trying to exclude queer people from their society (Amnesty International, 2022). Uganda has again joined eleven other nations in making homosexuality punishable by death (DPIC, 2023). In addition to the impact these measures have on their own, changing norms through hateful rhetoric or legislation can encourage individuals to perpetrate violence against subordinated group members (e.g., Ruisch & Ferguson, 2023).

In addition to gender-related regressive movements, a number of countries have begun new oppressions against other subordinated groups and detoured around democratic procedures. After having a constitutional democracy for some decades, the Philippines elected President Rodrigo Duterte (2016–2022), who made it a national policy to persecute drug dealers and drug users outside the law, such as by extrajudicial killings by the police (e.g., Timberman, 2019).

Indian President Narendra Modi's Hindu nationalist government has overseen brutality against Muslims (Freedom House, 2021). Although an important leader in transitioning Myanmar from military rule to partial democracy, as State Counsellor, Aung San Suu Kyi refused to prevent or even speak out against several of her country's genocidal and "ethnic cleansing" campaigns (Kennedy, 2019). Indeed, Freedom House reports that more nations have increased their practice of authoritarianism than have increased liberal democratic practices in every year for the past sixteen years (Repucci & Slipowitz, 2022).

9.4   Radicalization

As we have seen, there are a number of ways that people can seek to change their societies, including ideological dissemination and change in normative practices and institutional policies. McCauley and Moskalenko (2017) note that radicalization can occur with respect to both ideology and behavior in that they distinguish between radicalized opinion – that is, justifying and agreeing with violence to support one's own political or a societal goal – and radicalized action – that is, using violence to achieve one's own political or a societal goal. Using this definition, then, radicalization is not a feature only of either progressive or regressive political movements. Racists and anti-Semites murdering worshippers are radical regressive actions, whereas the ANC bombing South African government offices to pressure the government to end apartheid was a radical progressive action (e.g., Landau, 2012). Drawing on our discussion of institutional discrimination and violence earlier, we note that the process of ideological radicalization may include inculcating ideologies that: prescribe the sociopolitical goals, prescribe who are legitimate targets of violence (and who are not), prescribe what methods of violence are legitimate (and which are not), and/or prescribe particular methods of violence (see, e.g., Braithwaite, 2014, for a detailed discussion).

Moskalenko (2021) argues that usually, people adhere to societal norms and values that inhibit them from violent actions. Therefore, the radicalization process entails "unfreezing," deviating from violence-prohibiting norms. Importantly, she also notes that certain roles and institutions normalize use of violence, such as the police, military, and paramilitary, roles and institutions that are categorized as hierarchy-enhancing in social dominance theory (e.g., Sidanius & Pratto, 1999).

Moskalenko (2021) further argues that entire groups can be "unfrozen," leading their members to become radicalized. In fact, many violent radical actors who appear to have acted alone nonetheless have been influenced by others in a number of ways critical to radicalization, including adopting and elaborating shared legitimizing myths, emulating violent "heroes," and commemorating significant historical events. Berntzen and Sandberg (2014), for example, showed the importance of social processes on the case of Anders Breivik, an often-cited example of a "lone wolf" terrorist. Schuurman and colleagues (2019) suggest eliminating the "lone wolf" classification, since the term seems to ignore all the social processes that are part of a radicalization process. Nearly all radicals who act alone have group-relevant goals, nearly always goals adopted from intergroup-relevant symbols and ideologies of other people (Doosje et al., this volume). Hence, we expect our intergroup-based analysis pertains to most radical actors even if they act alone.

9.5 Social-Psychological Drivers of Politicization and Radicalization

Let us then delve into the way people relate to social groups in order to understand how these regressive and progressive politics might foment or prevent radicalization. We consider first people's need to belong with others, and then how they understand and manage their identities vis-à-vis intergroup relations.

9.5.1 Belonging and Exclusion

Humans are such a social species that they are strongly motivated to be accepted in a community (Baumeister & Leary, 1995). As such, people are highly sensitive to cues about their status in others' eyes, to stigma, and to social exclusion. Interpersonal social exclusion can be defined as "being kept apart from others" (Pfundmair et al., 2022, p. 1), but can take two different forms: rejection, in which a person's existence is acknowledged but an ongoing interaction with them is declined, like an explicit "No, I don't want to marry you," and ostracism, which entails non-acknowledgment of another's existence, such as ignoring the presence or speech of another person. Considerable research has shown that being excluded, even temporarily when interacting in a game with unseen strangers, causes substantial pain, including resignation and depression (Eisenberger et al., 2003; see for a review Williams, 2009). Being excluded can even lead to suicidal thoughts (Chen et al., 2020). We can expect the pain of exclusion to be highly motivating to change this state of exclusion, at least in some stages (Williams, 2009).

Although the need-threat model (Williams, 2009) focuses on interpersonal exclusion, there is reason to think that some of the psychological processes involved can pertain to person–group relationships as well. In fact, in intergroup relations, social exclusion can take the form of group segregation: Rejection can take the form of legal exclusions (e.g., denying members of certain groups the right to legal standing, to ownership, to autonomy), and ostracism can take the form of group-linked stigma and lack of representation of certain groups in cultural histories, in mass media, and so on. Research has shown that political campaigning can induce the feeling of ostracism: for example, an anti-immigrant campaign of the right-wing–populist parties in Europe induced social exclusion among migrants (Schnepf, 2020). To the extent that individuals view part of their identities to be linked to their social categories (e.g., Tajfel & Turner, 1979), people often respond emotionally on behalf of their group (e.g., Smith et al., 2007). Therefore, we are convinced that the phenomenon of social exclusion pertains to individual–group and inter-group relations.

9.5.2   Exclusion in Political Movements

Although few studies have investigated the relationship between the sense of social exclusion and political leanings, we can conjecture that a variety of political movements are inspired by the sense of social exclusion or from the accusation of being excluded. Both political conservatives and liberals have accused their political opponents of caring only about "special interests," as if normative people are excluded from consideration. Populism sometimes comes in right-wing and sometimes comes in left-wing flavors or can be difficult to classify as left or right. However, populism speaks deeply of exclusion because populist rhetoric movements advocate for "the people," a broad, often vague but only *apparently* inclusive term, because populist movements define "the people's" interests and virtues in contrast to those of some enemy "others" who may or may not be specified (e.g., elites, foreigners, politicians, industrialists, atheists; Berman, 2021; Deiwiks, 2009). Hence, populism invokes the injustice that "the people" have been excluded by politicians or representatives of other movements or parties who ignore "the people." Ironically, populism does so by being exclusionary itself about who constitutes "the people."

Progressive movements strive against the exclusion of marginalized and subordinated groups from public consideration and from access to resources by making marginalized and subordinated groups visible and demanding respect for them. Their aim may be stated as making such groups into "first-class" rather than "second-class" citizens.

Among people sympathetic to the status quo, progressive change, too, can evoke a sense of exclusion, exclusion among members of regressive groups, given that progressive movements adopt new norms of inclusion. For example, if people who make sexist jokes are no longer invited to social events, they are excluded. If these new progressive norms are broken by individuals who are opposed to this progressive change, individuals might be excluded from groups where progressive norms are adhered to (Rudert, et al., 2023).

It seems, then, that groups with a range of political ideologies can rally the motivation of having been socially excluded.

9.5.3   Status and Belonging

Individuals derive a substantial amount of their ascribed status from the status of social categories to which they belong (Sidanius & Pratto, 1999; Tajfel, 1974; Turner et al., 1979). There are two politically and psychologically distinct signs that people might rely on to know whether they are accepted in a community. One positive sign of belonging is that one is included and given ordinary dignity by one's community (Pratto et al., 2011). Communities can be inclusive by addressing the needs of everyone in the community and enabling each person to be respected. Note that this model of social relationships is fundamentally inclusive and egalitarian. A different sign one might use to infer that one belongs is having high social status (Pratto et al., 2011). In many societies and in their elite organizations, having high status is the entry ticket to belonging. But given that, by definition, not everyone can have high status, status ranking also implies that some people "belong" more than others do. Hence, people who rely on superior status to belong establish social relationships in which others must be excluded. The distinction we draw here between these two signals of belonging is between a social-psychological orientation in which everyone matters, and an orientation that is zero-sum such that only some can win. This speaks directly to the goals of progressive versus regressive political movements, respectively.

Another very central signal of belonging, and one that also relates fundamentally to the nature of intra- and intergroup relations, is self-esteem. In fact, Leary (e.g., 2005) posits that the purpose of people's fluctuating sense of their own esteem is to signal how much they are accepted by others. A social situation that questions or lowers one's self-esteem therefore also is painful and motivates action to repair that pain.

The reputation and status of groups to which one belongs are an important source of, or threat to, one's self-esteem (e.g., Tajfel, 1974). Given the common drive to maintain positive self-esteem, people in low-status groups are motivated to improve their group's status, or to disidentify from the group, whereas people in high-status groups are motivated to maintain their group's superior status. Akin to the sense of exclusion, we posit that the sense that one is not being accorded the status that one believes one deserves evokes a self-defensive kind of pain we call *status indignity*.

9.5.4   Status Indignity

It has been observed since the 1940s that people can feel resentful if they sense that their own lot (or that of their group) relative to a comparable other group, or their own lot compared to their own past, has worsened (for theoretical discussions of relative deprivation, deservingness, and entitlement, see Feather, 2015; Pettigrew, 2015). A critical theoretical aspect of relative deprivation is that the sense of relative deprivation is not an automatic result of having objective low or comparatively lower resources. Rather, the sense of relative deprivation results from a cognitive comparison to a relevant reference group (also known as "social comparison") or to a relevant standard.

Broadening relative deprivation theory to include the importance of social identities (i.e., aspects of identity concerning one's belonging to certain groups or categories), and recalling that desire for positive self-esteem is also a basic human psychological motive (e.g., Baumeister & Leary, 1995; Tajfel & Turner, 1979), we posit that relative deprivation linked to social identity will be seen as not only unjust but also an assault on one's social worth, because it damages the esteem originating from being a member of this group. *Status indignity* is the resentment stemming from perceiving one's individual or group status to be lower than one assumes is deserved or entitled.

Extending relative deprivation to the more modern acknowledgment of emotions that derive from intergroup relations, we can also draw upon Petersen's (2011) analysis of how emotions matter in conflict. He proposes that when group members have "cognition that one's group is located in an unwarranted subordinate position on a status hierarchy" (p. 40), they feel "resentment." Petersen (2011) analyzes such resentment as a reaction to "status reversal." Status reversal is experienced when specific markers of group status, like the day-to-day language of the government or symbols like street names, change from one (former dominant) group to another (former subordinate) group. For example, when colonial forces change a government's official language, native language speakers may feel resentment.

Our conception of status indignity differs slightly from Petersen's (2011) conception of status reversal and resentment in the nature of the cognitions held. In our understanding, status reversal suggests that there had to be an objective inversion of status relationships between groups. However, in line with relative deprivation theory, we hold that indignity and resentment can come from perceiving less status compared to a subjective criterion, including one's group's imagined past, one's group relative to another group, an ideal, or to an objective group criterion such as equality. Further, status indignity can occur also for long-term subordinated groups: The experience of feeling unfairness about occupying a low-status position doesn't require the prior experience of having been in a superior position. For example, feminists have been motivated by feeling that patriarchal practices did not accord women enough respect and autonomy, despite the fact that women have seldom had superior positions over men. Our conception of status indignity also allows that it can occur for dominant groups when they perceive that subordinate groups may close the status difference between them, because status as a relative concept keeps its worth by being superior to others.

Status indignity, then, is a reason to engage in political action: the combination of moral outrage and injustice associated with social identity has been shown to motivate collective political action in numerous relatively open societies (e.g., van Zomeren et al., 2018).

Note, then, that people supporting progressive and regressive political movements both might experience status indignity, but that the comparisons and evaluations that form the basis of status indignity and their end goals will depend on the type of movement. For people who hold group equality to be the ideal, status indignity and relative deprivation motivate support for progressive political action (e.g., Stewart et al., 2016). For example, advocating that an adult has the right to marry another consenting adult regardless of either's gender extends principles of liberty and equality to nonheterosexual couples. It is not demanding *superior* treatment for nonheterosexual couples, but rather demanding equal legal protections and recognition, for nonheterosexual couples, resulting in equal legal status. This is progressive movement.

In contrast, members of high-status groups may feel entitled to privileges and status due to the endowment effect (e.g., Knetsch, 1989), to socialization to one's higher group position (e.g., Blumer, 1958; Major, 1994), and/or to endorsement of hierarchy-enhancing legitimizing myths (e.g., Pratto et al., 2000). As such, members of high-status groups might experience status indignity because of progressive change, or even because of anticipated progressive change. For example, arguing against the possibility of marriage equality in 2008, US politician Rick Santorum declared, "same-sex marriage is . . . taking away a privilege that is given to two people, a man and a woman who are married," reflecting a desire for heterosexuals to maintain a higher status than other people (Masci, 2008).

Status indignity that is anticipated, or what we could call *Abstiegsangst* after the German word for fear of derogation, may also inspire opposition to progressive political movements and support for regressive ones. For example, Craig and Richeson (2014) found that White US Americans who were reminded that Whites will become a racial minority in the next decades increased their alignment with conservatism. In short, progressive status indignity stems from the desire for equality and inclusion, and regressive status indignity stems from the desire for superiority.

9.5.5 Exclusion and Status Indignity

Social exclusion appears to happen more often to people who have low status. There is evidence that poor families, with a low socioeconomic status, are excluded more often due to their economic situation (Mitchell & Campbell, 2011), and low socioeconomic status is a risk factor of being excluded for students in school (Wahl et al., 2022). The reverse process, that being excluded leads to having lower status, may also occur. For example, being dismissed from school or getting fired are two forms of exclusion that can contribute to reducing one's socioeconomic status afterwards. When low status is interpreted as undeserved, then exclusion and status indignity are connected.

More generally speaking, exclusion can produce status indignity, for example in the political discourse: The feeling of not being seen by politicians while marginalized people, like refugees, minorities, disabled people, women, and so on, are getting more attention than they did previously, as we discussed leading to the feeling of exclusion, might invoke feelings of status indignity as well. Hence, the sense of exclusion provoking status indignity appears possible for both progressive and regressive movements (see also Noor et al., 2012, concerning how more and less powerful groups can claim victimhood as a political tool). Exclusion is in this case one, but not the only possible, predecessor of status indignity: Anything that induces the feeling of having an undeserved inferior status might evoke status indignity, such as public derogation of one's group or the ideal of equality for subordinated groups.

9.5.6   Status Indignity and Radicalization

The thesis this discussion has been leading to is that status indignity is a risk factor for radicalization, because status indignity motivates action toward righting the perceived wrong of not being accorded as much status as one feels one deserves. Other theoretical approaches identify other motivational risk factors, such as compensating for personal social issues (e.g., uncertainty, Wagoner & Hogg, this volume) or searching for a greater meaning in life (Reiter et al., 2021) or for personal significance (Ellenberg & Kruglanski, this volume), and we do not think our thesis subsumes all other motivations.

However, some prior research can be interpreted as supporting the thesis that status indignity is a motivator for radicalization. In fact, the motivation of improving one's status has been identified as a risk factor for radicalization (Reiter et al., 2021). Similar to status indignity, the condition of having low status coupled with feelings of oppression was associated with more radicalization (Lobato et al., 2020). In a critical review, Taspinar (2009) showed that status-striving in the face of deprivation, a proxy for status indignity, was an important motivator of known violent radicals. Further, it was shown that *Abstiegsangst* is a driver of radicalization of the far-right party AfD in Germany (Isemann & Walther, 2019). Therefore, it can be assumed that anticipatory status indignity is also connected to radicalization. The connection Roger Petersen proposed for status reversal and resentment, which can lead – under specific circumstances – to intergroup conflict and violence, is also evidence for the relation of status indignity and political violence (Petersen, 2011). Having a poor employment situation or history, and being rejected by others, was associated with radicalization rather than nonviolent crimes supporting ideologies (Jasko et al., 2016). Hence, there is some evidence that status indignity and *Abstiegsangst* promote radicalization.

Notice that social exclusion and status indignity can occur simultaneously and lead to each other. Hence, they may both contribute to radicalization and they may also amplify the effects of the other on radicalization (see also Kruglanski et al., 2022). This can be true not only for individuals but also in a group context: a group is excluded and feels entitled to a higher status, which leads to the groups' radicalization. A qualitative study showed that unemployed men in Kenya experienced unemployment as threatening their need to belong and unfairly demeaning their status (status indignity), resulting in higher rates of connecting to Al-Shabab (Hernandez, 2020). This can be interpreted as a link between exclusion (threatened need to belong), status indignity (being in an unfair position), and the radicalization process (membership in the militia Al-Shabab).

Important models of radicalization, including McCauley and Moskalenko (2017) and Moghaddam (2005), delineate how psychological frames of understanding, such as relative deprivation, group identification, or status indignity, must also contain a component of how people come to accept or advocate for violence. In the next section, we consider two different but related factors that may contribute to the process of adopting violence: psychological orientations toward groups, and legitimizing ideologies and roles.

9.6 Psychological Characteristics that Attract People to Progressive or Regressive Political Movements and Radicalization

To this point, we have identified hierarchy-enhancing (regressive) and hierarchy-attenuating (progressive) political movements as having opposing societal goals, mentioned that ideological adoption of tolerance of or support for violence is part of the process of political radicalization, and explained how wanting to belong and to have self-esteem can motivate political action, especially when one experiences exclusion and status indignity. As noted previously, status indignity occurs due to somewhat different psychological goals and ideologies for progressive and regressive movements. In order to understand whether radicalization might be more or less likely to occur in each type of movement, we now turn to research on the psychological processes or orientations that would lead people in progressive and regressive movements to endorse violence differentially.

9.6.1   Personality Variables

9.6.1.1   Social Dominance Orientation

At the beginning of the chapter, we introduced coordinated individual action and institutional discrimination as the most proximate causes of how the social order of group-based dominance is maintained. We further considered whether consensual legitimizing ideologies might bolster support for and engagement in hierarchy-enhancing or hierarchy-attenuating behaviors. The coordination of individual behavior and institutional behavior are often aspects of the societal level, whereas more immediate contexts, such as one's friendship network or one's occupational industry, are at a more person–group level of organization. Individuals can also become socialized to their group's status position, adopting the particular legitimizing ideology of not only their culture but also those that explain or bolster their group's situation. The generalized orientation adults have toward group-based hierarchy or group equality and inclusion is called social dominance orientation (SDO; Pratto et al., 1994).

SDO is typically measured with its own scale with items pertaining to whether groups in general should be hierarchical or equal (see also Ho et al., 2017; Pratto et al., 2013). People who are defined to be relatively "high" on SDO are comfortable with particular kinds of group-based inequality found in their own societies, such as racism, nationalism, sexism, heterosexism, and even speciesism, whereas people relatively "low" on SDO prefer group inclusion and equality and progressive ideologies such as anti-colonialism, antiracism, and feminism. Such findings have been found in numerous countries (see for a meta-analysis: Lee et al., 2011). Likewise, hierarchy-enhancing practices and policies appeal more to those high on SDO whereas hierarchy-attenuating practices and policies appeal more to those low on SDO. As such, we expect people higher on SDO to support regressive political movements and people lower on SDO to support progressive political movements.

In fact, studies in several countries have found people higher on SDO to support conservative or right-wing political parties and politicians more than people lower on SDO, with the reverse finding for support of liberal or left-wing political parties and politicians (e.g., Aichholzer & Zandonella, 2016; Assche et al., 2019; Franco & Pound, 2022; Grünhage & Reuter, 2020). More to the point, SDO correlates negatively with support for women's rights, rights for gays and lesbians, and care of poor people and positively with support for nationalism, religious prejudice, transprejudice, and various kinds of racism (e.g., Bondü et al., 2021; Makwana et al., 2018; Naik & Kamble, 2015; Pratto et al., 1994, 2013). And, even more related to support for using violence for political ends, higher SDO has been found to be associated with support for the death penalty in the United States, mediated by anti-Black racism (e.g., Pratto et al., 1998), with prospectively predicting support among US Americans for the 1991 and 2003 wars against Iraq (Pratto et al., 1998; Pratto et al., 2006) and negatively with support for further intergroup violence among both US and Lebanese students following the September 11th, 2001, attacks (Pratto et al., 2003). Whereas attitudinal support for anti-terrorism and military action among dominant countries is more typical of people high on SDO, attitudinal support for violent militias and attacks on the US military are more typical of people low on SDO in more subordinate countries (e.g., Henry et al., 2005; Vorsina et al., 2019).

There are few studies concerning SDO and participation in political violence. But there are reasons to argue that people high on SDO are more prone to becoming radicalized. Research shows that people high on SDO fail to see much wrong with many instances of violence, including spanking a child with various objects (Hess et al., 2012), civilian casualties of wars of dominance (Pratto et al., 2003), sexual abuse of minors (Alcantara et al., 2019), and sexual abuse of women (e.g., Vincheckar, 2019). It was also shown in a student sample that SDO is associated with acceptance of violence (Besta et al., 2015). Further, in several large national samples, Bartusevičius and colleagues (2020) find that preferences for autocratic versus democratic governance and desire for dominance, in some studies assessed with SDO, are associated with participation in political violence. Hence, there is considerable evidence that high SDO is associated with acceptance of violence.

9.6.1.2 Right-Wing Authoritarianism

The concept of authoritarianism as an orientation related to regressive and antidemocratic sociopolitical attitudes dates to the early twentieth century. For most of the history of authoritarianism, the hypothesis that left-wingers could be dogmatic was theorized, but studies repeatedly failed to find authoritarianism among left-wingers (see Stone, 1980, for a review). Even dogmatism was more characteristic of right-wing than left-wing people (see Eckhardt, 1991, for a review). Although there are recent left-wing authoritarian scales (e.g., Costello et al., 2022) and alternative authoritarian scales (Dunwoody & Funke 2016; Zhirkov et al., 2023), the great majority of research on authoritarianism has used versions of Altemeyer's (1988) Right-Wing Authoritarianism (RWA) scale.

According to Engelhardt and colleagues (2021, p. 4), RWA is "a personality adaptation that values social cohesion and conformity to in-group norms over personal freedom and individual autonomy." The underlying worldview of RWA is that the world is dangerous and that individuals have to comply to social norms to combat the dangers ahead (Duckitt et al., 2002). The three subfacets of RWA are conservatism or traditionalism, authority adherence, and punitiveness. When connecting RWA and regressive politics, we see that maintaining status hierarchies fits the need for security and also aligns with conservatism. Authority adherence also aligns with having hierarchies in place in order to maintain social structure and security. This connects having a high score on RWA to supporting regressive movements. One might also assume that people high on RWA would oppose radicalism against their governments, since this would threaten the security authorities provide. Further, authoritarians often endorse following norms, so if authorities tell them not to use violence, we expect they would obey. However, if high RWA people view their government's support for progressive policies as threatening their security, or if authorities call people to violence, especially to uphold some "moral" norm, then people high on RWA also should radicalize.

In fact, individuals high on RWA support regressive policies (Chirumbolo et al., 2016; Harnish et al., 2018) and support leaders who stand for regressive politics (Choma & Hanoch, 2017; Grünhage & Reuter, 2020; Oosterhoff et al., 2022). Even further, RWA is positively connected to the acceptance of political violence, or radicalization (Besta et al., 2015), and the support for radical right-wing parties (Aichholzer & Zandonella, 2016). Having a high score on RWA is also associated with facets of radicalization, like the belief in a divine power (religious extremism; Vukčević Marković et al., 2021). Although, again, further research directly on radicalization and RWA is warranted, evidence to date suggests a link between RWA and radicalization.

9.6.1.3   Collective Narcissism

Conceptually, an important aspect of status deprivation is entitlement. Entitlement is also part of the concept of collective narcissism: Collective narcissism (CN) is an "ingroup identification tied to an emotional investment in an unrealistic belief about the unparalleled greatness of an ingroup" (de Zavala et al., 2009, p. 1074). This narcissistic belief also comes with a sense of special entitlement, which means that the group deserves more than others, perceived superiority, which says that the group has a higher status generally, and lack of recognition, which means that superiority and entitlement are not given to the group as much as deserved. (The remaining facets of CN are special significance and self-absorption.) This again meets the conceptualization of hierarchy-enhancing status indignity.

Empirically, it was shown that CN is a root of regressive political attitudes and support for leaders who execute regressive politics (Federico & de Zavala, 2018; Lantos & Forgas, 2021). And not only this: It was also shown that CN is connected to support for political violence and joining radical groups (Bélanger et al., 2019).

9.6.2   Legitimizing Myths and Radicalization

As we alluded to in the introduction, the contents of legitimizing ideologies may facilitate radicalization (see also Doosje et al., 2016). This is because some ideologies prescribe who is "legitimately" allowed to use certain types of violence, and in which particular circumstances (e.g., to restore honor; Levin et al., 2015), and who is forbidden from using certain types of violence. Further, some ideologies prescribe who is an appropriate target of violence (e.g., sinners, infidels, combatants). Some ideologies help dehumanize or demonize other people, which psychologically facilitates unfreezing the prohibition against harming or killing other people (Kteily & Bruneau, 2017).

Some ideologies promise glory or other rewards for engaging in violence (e.g., warrior cultures). When people claim to use violence on behalf of a god, they sanctify their violence. Many ideologies posit that certain groups cannot be influenced in any way other than violence (e.g., groups who can't/won't listen to reason, who are too primitive to negotiate with, who do not feel pain). Other ideologies prescribe that the way to bring about some valued end is by using violence (e.g., "we have to defend our way of life"), especially the idea of self-defense. Many ideologies tout that violence is necessary to realize some greater good (e.g., protecting the "innocent"). Some ideologies even tout the use of violence to reduce the use of violence (e.g., violence as deterrence, the US public excuse for using the atom bomb to end World War II). Many of the legitimizing ideologies that justify violence are more associated with regressive rather than progressive movements.

9.6.3   Summary: Personality, Legitimizing Myths, and Radicalization

Our review found some evidence that SDO and RWA and CN are associated with radicalization. In addition, SDO, RWA, and CN all make the ideologies and policy prescriptions of regressive movements more palatable. These findings suggest that regressive movements are more prone to radicalization than progressive movements are. Similarly, most of the forms of violence-legitimizing myths we recalled are more typical of regressive movements than of progressive movements. This is not to say that progressive movements cannot become radicalized: research on SDO, empathy, and support for violence suggests that violence also can originate in a deeply egalitarian, counter-dominance motive (e.g., Henry et al., 2005; Pratto et al., 2023). But overall, the evidence suggests that regressive movements are more likely to radicalize than progressive movements. And this is reflected empirically, for example in the report of the German domestic intelligence services (Bundesamt für Verfassungsschutz, 2023), which clearly shows that the most political violent crimes were committed by right-wing extremists, representing regressive movements. Likewise, expert US Congressional testimony by Byman (2023) attests that right-wing extremists are more dangerous than left-wing extremists in the United States. Most definitively, studies across decades on both the United States and the Global Terrorism Database show that after Islamicist violence, far more violence was committed by adherents to right-wing rather than to left-wing ideologies, with concomitant effects on fatalities (Jasko et al., 2022).

9.7   Conclusion and Implications

The goal of this chapter was to provide a framework for understanding the relationship between intergroup status, exclusion, and radicalization. In order to do this, we first provided an overview about how status and dominance work in societies through the lens of social dominance theory. Most people live in societies with status hierarchies in place that are preserved through various mechanisms, legitimizing ideologies being one of the most important. In those societies, progressive forces (which want to minimize status differences between groups) and regressive forces (which want to maintain or enhance status differences between groups) are constantly in battle with each other. When the other group seems more advantaged than one likes, one may experience social exclusion and status indignity, which are connected and can amplify each other. Status indignity, which we define as the resentment stemming from perceiving one's individual or group status being lower than one assumes is deserved, can motivate radicalization. But not everyone and every group has the same risk of radicalization: We found that individuals high on SDO, RWA, and CN, as well as groups with ideologies facilitating violence, are more likely to become radicalized. We saw that regressive movements are more prone to becoming radicalized than progressive movements.

Our framework can explain recent radicalized movements and actions: The rise of radicalized regressive forces in the United States, canalized at the January Sixth Insurrection at Capitol Hill in 2021, can be interpreted as a form of status indignity and exclusion that was felt by former US President Trump and his allies. The Incel Movement, which is responsible for violent acts like the murder of two women in Florida in 2018 (Trotta, 2022), fits our frame, considering that part of their ideology is that they deserve the same status as men who have intercourse with women ("Chads") have. Incels' starting point is that being rejected by women is a form of unfair status derogation, and that some incels believe women should be forced into sexual relationships with men (also see Rousis & Swann, this volume).

Our frame can also be used to understand why movements do not radicalize. Ideologies that eschew violence can prevent radicalization, regardless of the movement's agenda. Also, preventing status indignity by for example communicating respectfully and not derogating social groups with other political leanings or giving everybody a voice to raise their concerns in a democratic way would contribute to less radicalization. We hope that our framework might increase understanding of the underlying mechanisms of different radicalized or non-radicalized movements and help to develop preventive or deradicalization strategies.

References

ACLU (2023, July 21). Mapping attacks on LGBTQ rights in U.S. state legislatures. American Civil Liberties Union. www.aclu.org/legislative-attacks-on-lgbtq-rights

Aichholzer, J., & Zandonella, M. (2016). Psychological bases of support for radical right parties. *Personality and Individual Differences*, *96*, 185–190. https://doi .org/10.1016/j.paid.2016.02.072

Alcantara, R., Shortway, K. M., & Prempeh, B. A. (2019). The relationship between social dominance orientation and child sexual abuse credibility assessment. *Journal of Child Sexual Abuse, 28*(4), 400–416. https://doi.org/10.1080/10538712.2019.1592271

Altemeyer, B. (1988). *Enemies of freedom: Understanding right-wing authoritarianism.* Jossey-Bass.

Amnesty International (2022, July 22). *Poland: Authorities must stop hateful rhetoric against LGBTI people and act to protect them from violence and discrimination.* www.amnesty.org/en/latest/news/2022/07/poland-authorities-must-stop-hateful-rhetoric-against-lgbti-people-and-act-to-protect-them-from-violence-and-discrimination/

Amnesty International (2023, March 20). Conviction of Polish abortion activist "chilling." www.amnesty.org/en/latest/news/2023/03/poland-conviction-of-activist-prosecuted-for-aiding-an-abortion-offers-chilling-snapshot-of-future/

Aptheker, H. (1943). *American Negro slave revolts.* Columbia University Press.

Assche, van, J., Dhont, K., & Pettigrew, T. F. (2019). The social-psychological bases of far-right support in Europe and the United States. *Journal of Community and Applied Social Psychology, 29*, 385–401. https://doi.org/10.1002/casp.2407

Bartusevičius, H., van Leeuwen, F., & Petersen, M. B. (2020). Dominance-driven autocratic political orientations predict political violence in Western, educated, industrialized, rich, and democratic (WEIRD) and non-WEIRD samples. *Psychological Science, 31*(12), 1511–1530. https://doi.org/10.1177/0956797620922476

Baumeister, R. F., & Leary, M. R. (1995). The need to belong: Desire for interpersonal attachments as a fundamental human motivation. *Psychological Bulletin, 117*(3), 497–529. https://doi.org/10.1037/0033-2909.117.3.497

Bélanger, J. J., Moyano, M., Muhammad, H., et al. (2019). Radicalization leading to violence: A test of the 3 N model. *Frontiers in Psychiatry, 10.* https://doi.org/10.3389/fpsyt.2019.00042

Berman, S. (2021). The causes of populism in the West. *Annual Review of Political Science, 24*(1), 71–88. https://doi.org/10.1146/annurev-polisci-041719-102503

Berntzen, L. E., & Sandberg, S. (2014). The collective nature of lone wolf terrorism: Anders Behring Breivik and the anti-Islamic social movement. *Terrorism and Political Violence, 26*(5), 759–779. https://doi.org/10.1080/09546553.2013.767245

Besta, T., Szulc, M., & Jaśkiewicz, M. (2015). Political extremism, group membership and personality traits: Who accepts violence? / Extremismo político, pertenencia al grupo y rasgos de personalidad: ¿Quién acepta la violencia? *Revista de Psicologia Social, 30*(3), 563–585. https://doi.org/10.1080/02134748.2015.1065085

Blumer, H. (1958). Race prejudice as a sense of group position. *The Pacific Sociological Review, 1*(1), 3–7. https://doi.org/10.2307/1388607

Bondü, R., Schwemmer, F., & Pfetsch, J. (2021). Justice sensitivity is positively and negatively related to prejudice and discrimination. *International Journal of Conflict and Violence (IJCV), 15.* https://doi.org/10.11576/IJCV-4463

Braithwaite, J. (2014). Limits on violence; limits on responsive regulatory theory. *Law & Policy*, 36(4), 432–456. https://doi.org/10.1111/lapo.12026

Bundesamt für Verfassungsschutz. (2023). Verfassungsschutzbericht 2022. Bundesministerium des Inneren und für Heimat.

Bundeszentrale für Politische Bildung. (2017). Verbreitung demokratischer Staaten. www.bpb.de/kurz-knapp/zahlen-und-fakten/globalisierung/52838/ver breitung-demokratischer-staaten/

Byman, D. L. (2023, May 16). Countering organized violence in the United States. Testimony provided to the US House of Representatives Committee on Homeland Security's Subcommittee on Oversight, Investigations, and Accountability. www.brookings.edu/articles/countering-organized-violence-in-the-united-states/

Campbell, B. B. (2000). Death squads: Definition, problems, and historical context. In B. B. Campbell, & A. D. Brenner (Eds.), *Death squads in global perspective: Murder with deniability* (pp. 1–26). Palgrave Macmillan US. https://doi.org/10.1057/9780230108141_1

Chen, Z., Poon, K.-T., DeWall, C. N., & Jiang, T. (2020). Life lacks meaning without acceptance: Ostracism triggers suicidal thoughts. *Journal of Personality and Social Psychology*, 119(6), 1423–1443. https://doi.org/10.1037/pspi0000238

Chirumbolo, A., Leone, L., & Desimoni, M. (2016). The interpersonal roots of politics: Social value orientation, socio-political attitudes and prejudice. *Personality and Individual Differences*, 91, 144–153. https://doi.org/10.1016/j.paid.2015.12.001

Choma, B. L., & Hanoch, Y. (2017). Cognitive ability and authoritarianism: Understanding support for Trump and Clinton. *Personality and Individual Differences*, 106, 287–291. https://doi.org/10.1016/j.paid.2016.10.054

Costello, T. H., Bowes, S. M., Stevens, S. T., et al. (2022). Clarifying the structure and nature of left-wing authoritarianism. *Journal of Personality and Social Psychology*, 122(1), 135–170. https://doi.org/10.1037/pspp0000341

Craig, M. A., & Richeson, J. A. (2014). On the precipice of a "majority-minority" America. *Psychological Science*, 25(6), 1189–1197. https://doi.org/10.1177/0956797614527113

de Zavala, A. G., Cichocka, A., Eidelson, R., & Jayawickreme, N. (2009). Collective narcissism and its social consequences. *Journal of Personality and Social Psychology*, 97(6), 1074–1096. https://doi.org/10.1037/a0016904

Deiwiks, C. (2009). Populism. *Living Reviews in Democracy*, 1, 1–9.

Doosje, B., Moghaddam, F. M., Kruglanski, A. W., et al. (2016). Terrorism, radicalization and de-radicalization. *Current Opinion in Psychology*, 11, 79–84. https://doi.org/10.1016/j.copsyc.2016.06.008

DPIC. (2023, June 1). *Uganda's controversial "anti-homosexuality act" includes possibility of death sentence*. Death Penalty Information Center. https://death penaltyinfo.org/news/ugandas-controversial-anti-homosexuality-act-includes-possibility-of-death-sentence

Duckitt, J., Wagner, C., du Plessis, I., & Birum, I. (2002). The psychological bases of ideology and prejudice: Testing a dual process model. *Journal of Personality and Social Psychology, 83*(1), 75–93. https://doi.org/10.1037/0022-3514.83.1.75

Dunbar-Ortiz, R. (2014). *An Indigenous peoples' history of the United States*. Beacon Press. https://books.google.de/books?id=btpmDwAAQBAJ

Dunwoody, P. T., & Funke, F. (2016). The aggression-submission-conventionalism scale: Testing a new three factor measure of authoritarianism. *Journal of Social and Political Psychology, 4*(2), 571–600. https://doi.org/10.5964/jspp.v4i2.168

Eckhardt, W. (1991). Authoritarianism. *Political Psychology, 12*, 97–124.

Eisenberger, N. I., Lieberman, M. D., & Williams, K. D. (2003). Does rejection hurt? An fMRI study of social exclusion. *Science, 302*(5643), 290–292. https://doi.org/10.1126/science.1089134

Engelhardt, A. M., Feldman, S., & Hetherington, M. J. (2021). Advancing the measurement of authoritarianism. *Political Behavior, 45*, 537–560. https://doi.org/10.1007/s11109-021-09718-6

Faludi, S. (1991). *Backlash: The undeclared war against women*. Chatto & Windus.

Feagin, J. R. (2013). *The white racial frame: Centuries of racial framing and counter-framing* (2nd ed.). Routledge.

Feather, N. T. (2015). Analyzing relative deprivation in relation to deservingness, entitlement and resentment. *Social Justice Research, 28*(1), 7–26. https://doi.org/10.1007/s11211-015-0235-9

Federico, C. M., & de Zavala, A. G. (2018). Collective narcissism and the 2016 US presidential vote. *Public Opinion Quarterly, 82*(1), 110–121. https://doi.org/10.1093/poq/nfx048

Florida Senate. (2022). *Parental rights in education*. CS/ CS/ HB 1557 Florida Statute § 1001.42,8 c. www.flsenate.gov/Session/Bill/2022/1557/BillText/er/PDF

Foner, P. S. (Ed.). (1999). The Meaning of July Fourth for the Negro: A speech given at Rochester, New York, July 5, 1852. In *Frederick Douglass: Selected Speeches and Writings* (pp. 188–205). Lawrence Hill Books.

Franco, A. B., & Pound, N. (2022). The foundations of Bonsonaro's support: Exploring the psychological underpinnings of political polarization in Brazil. *Journal of Community and Applied Social Psychology, 32*, 846–859. https://doi.org/10.1002/casp.2599

Freedom House (2021). *India*. https://freedomhouse.org/country/india/freedom-world/2021

Grünhage, T., & Reuter, M. (2020). Personality's influence on political orientation extends to concrete stances of political controversy in Germany – Cross-Nationally and Consistently. *Journal of Social and Political Psychology, 8*, 686–707. https://doi.org/10.5964/jspp.v8i2.1133

Harnish, R. J., Bridges, K. R., & Gump, J. T. (2018). Predicting economic, social, and foreign policy conservatism: The role of right-wing authoritarianism, social dominance orientation, moral foundations orientation, and religious fundamentalism. *Current Psychology, 37*(3), 668–679. https://doi.org/10.1007/s12144-016-9552-x

Henry, P. J., Sidanius, J., Levin, S., & Pratto, F. (2005). Social dominance orientation, authoritarianism, and support for intergroup violence between the Middle
East and America. *Political Psychology, 26*, 569–584. https://doi-org.ezproxy.lib
.uconn.edu/10.1111/j.1467-9221.2005.00432.x

Hernandez, M. (2020). *Impact of unemployment and lack of education in Kenya on
Al- Shabab recruitment.* Walden University.

Hess, C. A., Gray, J. M., & Nunez, N. L. (2012). The effect of social dominance
orientation on perceptions of corporal punishment. *Journal of Interpersonal
Violence, 27*(13), 2728–2739. https://doi.org/10.1177/0886260512436392

Ho, A. K., Kteily, N. S., & Chen, J. M. (2017). "You're one of us": Black Americans'
use of hypodescent and its association with egalitarianism. *Journal of
Personality and Social Psychology, 113*(5), 753–768. https://doi.org/10.1037/
pspi0000107

Isemann, S. D., & Walther, E. (2019, June). Die AfD – psychologisch betrachtet. In
E. Walther, & S. D. Isemann (Eds.), *Die AfD – psychologisch betrachtet.* Springer
Fachmedien Wiesbaden. https://doi.org/10.1007/978-3-658-25579-4

Jasko, K., LaFree, G., & Kruglanski, A. (2016). Quest for significance and violent
extremism: The case of domestic radicalization. *Political Psychology, 38*,
815–831. https://doi.org/10.1111/pops.12376

Jasko, K., LaFree, G., Piazza, J., & Becker, M. H. (2022). A comparison of political
violence by left-wing, right-wing, and Islamist extremists in the United States
and the world. *Proceedings of the National Academy of Sciences, 119*, 1–9. www
.pnas.org/doi/10.1073/pnas.2122593119

Kennedy, E. J. (2019, August 26). A hero has fallen. World Without Genocide.
http://worldwithoutgenocide.org/a-hero-has-fallen

Knetsch, J. L. (1989). The endowment effect and evidence of nonreversible indif-
ference curves. *The American Economic Review, 79*, 1277–1284.

Kteily, N. S., & Bruneau, E. (2017). Darker demons of our nature: The need to (re)
focus attention on blatant forms of dehumanization. *Current Directions in
Psychological Science, 26*(6), 487–494. https://doi.org/10.1177/0963721417
708230

Landau, P. S. (2012). The ANC, MK, and "the turn to violence" (1960–1962). *South
African History Journal, 3*, 538–563. https://doi.org/10.1080/02582473.2012
.660785

Lantos, D., & Forgas, J. P. (2021). The role of collective narcissism in populist
attitudes and the collapse of democracy in Hungary. *Journal of Theoretical
Social Psychology, 5*(2), 65–78. https://doi.org/10.1002/jts5.80

Leary, M. R. (2005). Sociometer theory and the pursuit of relational value: Getting
to the root of self-esteem. *European Review of Social Psychology, 16*(1), 75–111.
https://doi.org/10.1080/10463280540000007

Lee, I.-C., Pratto, F., & Johnson, B. T. (2011). Intergroup consensus/disagreement
in support of group-based hierarchy: An examination of socio-structural and
psycho-cultural factors. *Psychological Bulletin, 137*(6), 1029–1064. https://doi
.org/10.1037/a0025410

Levin, S., Roccas, S., Sidanius, J., & Pratto, F. (2015). Personal values and intergroup outcomes of concern for group honor. *Personality and Individual Differences, 86*, 374–384. https://doi.org/10.1016/j.paid.2015.06.047

Lobato, R. M., Moya, M., & Trujillo, H. M. (2020). Minority- versus majority-status group intentions to transgress the law when oppression is perceived. *Analyses of Social Issues and Public Policy, 20*(1), 397–416. https://doi.org/10.1111/asap.12207

Major, B. (1994). From social inequality to personal entitlement: The role of social comparisons, legitimacy appraisals, and group membership. *Advances in Experimental Social Psychology, 26*, 293–355. https://doi.org/10.1016/S0065-2601(08)60156-2

Makwana, A. P., Dhont, K., De keersmaecker, J., et al. (2018). The motivated cognitive basis of transphobia: The roles of right-wing ideologies and gender role beliefs. *Sex Roles, 79*(3–4), 206–217. https://doi.org/10.1007/s11199-017-0860-x

Masci, D. (2008, April 24). *An argument against same-sex marriage: An interview with Rick Santorum.* Pew Research Center. www.pewresearch.org/religion/2008/04/24/an-argument-against-same-sex-marriage-an-interview-with-rick-santorum/

McCauley, C., & Moskalenko, S. (2017). Understanding political radicalization: The two-pyramids model. *American Psychologist, 72*(3), 205–216. https://doi.org/10.1037/amp0000062

Mitchell, G., & Campbell, L. (2011). The social economy of excluded families. *Child & Family Social Work, 16*(4), 422–433. https://doi.org/10.1111/j.1365-2206.2011.00757.x

Moghaddam, F. M. (2005). The staircase to terrorism: A psychological exploration. *American Psychologist, 60*(2), 161–169. https://doi.org/10.1037/0003-066X.60.2.161

Monkman, L. (2020, December 15). *5 years after report, Truth and Reconciliation commissioners say progress is "moving too slow."* CBC. www.cbc.ca/news/indigenous/trc-5-years-final-report-1.5841428

Moskalenko, S. (2021). Zip-tie guys: Military-grade radicalization among Capitol Hill insurrectionists. *Dynamics of Asymmetric Conflict: Pathways toward Terrorism and Genocide, 14*(2), 179–191. https://doi.org/10.1080/17467586.2021.1912374

Naik, D. B. A., & Kamble, D. V. S. (2015). Social dominance orientation among different social groups leads to caste discrimination attitude and communal violence in India. *International Journal of Education and Psychological Research, 4*, 77–80.

Noor, M., Shnabel, N., Halabi, S., & Nadler, A. (2012). When suffering begets suffering: The psychology of competitive victimhood between adversarial groups in violent conflicts. *Personality and Social Psychology Review, 16*(4), 351–374.

Norris, P., & Inglehart, R. (2019). *Cultural backlash: Trump, Brexit, and authoritarian populism.* Cambridge University Press.

Oosterhoff, B., Poppler, A., & Palmer, C. A. (2022). Early adolescents demonstrate peer-network homophily in political attitudes and values. *Psychological Science*, *33*(6), 874–888. https://doi.org/10.1177/09567976211063912

Petersen, R. D. (2011). *Western intervention in the Balkans*. Cambridge University Press. https://doi.org/10.1017/CBO9780511862564

Peto, A., & Grzebalska, W. (2016). *How Hungary and Poland have silenced women and stifled human rights*. The Conversation. https://theconversation.com/how-hungary-and-poland-have-silenced-women-and-stifled-human-rights–66743

Pettigrew, T. F. (2015). Samuel Stouffer and relative deprivation. *Social Psychology Quarterly*, *78*(1), 7–24. https://doi.org/10.1177/0190272514566793

Pfeifer, M. J. (2004). *Rough justice: Lynching and American society, 1874–1947*. University of Illinois Press. https://books.google.de/books?id=zAGwb3G6soMC

Pfundmair, M., Wood, N. R., Hales, A., & Wesselmann, E. D. (2022, June). How social exclusion makes radicalism flourish: A review of empirical evidence. *Journal of Social Issues*. https://doi.org/10.1111/josi.12520

Pratto, F., Çidam, A., Stewart, A. L., et al. (2013). Social dominance in context and in individuals. *Social Psychological and Personality Science*, *4*(5), 587–599. https://doi.org/10.1177/1948550612473663

Pratto, F., Glasford, D. E., & Hegarty, P. J. (2006). Weighing the prospects of war. *Group Processes and Intergroup Relations*, *9*, 219–233. http://doi.org/10.1177/1368430206062078

Pratto, F., Lee, I., Tan, J., & Pitpitan, E. (2011). Power basis theory: A psycho-ecological approach to power. In D. Dunning (Ed.), *Social motivation* (pp. 191–222). Psychology Press.

Pratto, F., Lemieux, A. F., Glasford, D. E., & Henry, P. J. (2003). American and Lebanese college students' responses to the events of September 11, 2001: The relation of hopes and fears to the psychology of group positions. *Psicología Política*, *27*, 13–35.

Pratto, F., Levin S., & Ruscowicz, A. (2023). When empathy predicts greater support for intergroup violence counter-dominance against the U.S. in Syria and Lebanon [Unpublished manuscript]. University of Connecticut.

Pratto, F., Liu, J. H., Levin, S., et al. (2000). Social dominance orientation and the legitimization of inequality across cultures. *Journal of Cross-Cultural Psychology*, *31*(3), 369–409. https://doi.org/10.1177/0022022100031003005

Pratto, F., Sidanius, J., Bou Zeineddine, F., Kteily, N., & Levin, S. (2014). When domestic politics and international relations intermesh: Subordinated publics' factional support within layered power structures. *Foreign Policy Analysis, 10* (2), 127–148. https://doi.org/10.1111/fpa.12023

Pratto, F., Sidanius, J., Stallworth, L. M., & Malle, B. F. (1994). Social dominance orientation: A personality variable predicting social and political attitudes. *Journal of Personality and Social Psychology*, *67*(4), 741–763. https://doi.org/10.1037/0022-3514.67.4.741

Pratto, F., Stallworth, L. M., & Conway-Lanz, S. (1998). Social dominance orientation and the ideological legitimization of social policy. *Journal of Applied Social*

Psychology, 28(20), 1853–1875. https://doi.org/10.1111/j.1559-1816.1998.tb01349.x

Reiter, J., Doosje, B., & Feddes, A. R. (2021). Radicalization and deradicalization: A qualitative analysis of parallels in relevant risk factors and trigger factors. *Peace and Conflict: Journal of Peace Psychology*, 27(2), 268–283. https://doi.org/10.1037/pac0000493

Repucci, S., & Slipowitz, A. (2022). *The global expansion of authoritarian rule*. Freedom House. https://freedomhouse.org/sites/default/files/2022-03/FITW_World_2022_digital_abridged_FINAL.pdf

Rudert, S. C., Möring, J. N. R., Kenntemich, C., & Büttner, C. M. (2023). When and why we ostracize others: Motivated social exclusion in group contexts. *Journal of Personality and Social Psychology*, 125(4), 803–826. https://doi.org/10.1037/pspi0000423

Ruisch, B. C., & Ferguson, M. J. (2023). Did Donald Trump's presidency reshape Americans' prejudices? *Trends in Cognitive Sciences*, 27(3), 207–209. https://doi.org/10.1016/j.tics.2022.12.013

Schnepf, J. (2020). "Heimatliebe statt Marokkaner-Diebe!": Rechtspopulistische Rhetorik und ihre Effekte auf In- und Out-Group-Ebene. *Conflict & Communication Online*, 19(1), 1–9.

Schuurman, B., Lindekilde, L., Malthaner, S., et al. (2019). End of the lone wolf: The typology that should not have been. *Studies in Conflict and Terrorism*, 42(8), 771–778. https://doi.org/10.1080/1057610X.2017.1419554

Sidanius, J., Liu, J., Pratto, F., & Shaw, J. (1994). Social dominance orientation, hierarchy-attenuators and hierarchy-enhancers: Social dominance theory and the criminal justice system. *Journal of Applied Social Psychology*, 24, 338–366.

Sidanius, J., & Pratto, F. (1999). *Social dominance: An intergroup theory of social hierarchy and oppression*. Cambridge University Press.

Smith, E. R., Seger, C. R., & Mackie, D. M. (2007). Can emotions be truly group level? Evidence regarding four conceptual criteria. *Journal of Personality and Social Psychology*, 93(3), 431–446. https://doi.org/10.1037/0022-3514.93.3.431

Stewart, A. L., Pratto, F., Bou Zeineddine, F., et al. (2016). International support for the Arab uprisings: Understanding sympathetic collective action using theories of social dominance and social identity. *Group Processes & Intergroup Relations*, 19(1), 6–26. https://doi.org/10.1177/1368430214558310

Stone, W. F. (1980). The myth of left-wing authoritarianism. *Political Psychology*, 2, 3–19.

Tajfel, H. (1974). Social identity and intergroup behaviour. *Social Science Information*, 13(2), 65–93.

Tajfel, H., Turner, J. C., Austin, W. G., & Worchel, S. (1979). An integrative theory of intergroup conflict. In W. G. Austin, & S. Worchel (Eds.), *The social psychology of intergroup relations* (pp. 33–47). Brooks/Cole.

Taspinar, Ö. (2009). Fighting radicalism, not "terrorism": Root causes of an international actor redefined. *SAIS Review of International Affairs*, 29, 75–86.

Timberman, D. G. (2019). *Philippine politics under Duterte: A midterm assessment.* Carnegie Endowment for International Peace. https://carnegieendowment.org/2019/01/10/philippine-politics-under-duterte-midterm-assessment-pub-78091

Track Trans Legislation. (2023). *2023 anti-trans bills.* www.tracktranslegislation.com/

Trotta, D. (2022, March 15). *U.S. report identifies misogynist "incels" as violence threat.* Reuters. www.reuters.com/world/us/us-report-identifies-misogynist-incels-violence-threat-2022-03-15/

Türk, V. (2023, April 5). Comment by UN High Commissioner for Human Rights Volker Türk on Afghanistan. OHCHR. www.ohchr.org/en/statements/2023/04/comment-un-high-commissioner-human-rights-volker-turk-afghanistan

Turner, J. C., Brown, R. J., & Tajfel, H. (1979). Social comparison and group interest in ingroup favouritism. *European Journal of Social Psychology, 9*(2), 187–204. https://doi.org/10.1002/ejsp.2420090207

Turner, J. H., Singleton, R., & Musick, D. (1984). *Oppression: A socio-history of Black–white relations in America.* Wadsworth Publishing Company.

UNESCO (2017). *Literacy rates continue to rise from one generation to the next.* UNESDOC (FS/2017/LIT/45). https://unesdoc.unesco.org/ark:/48223/pf0000258942

United Nations (n.d.). *The 17 goals.* Department of Economic and Social Affairs Sustainable Development. https://sdgs.un.org/goals

van Zomeren, M., Kutlaca, M., & Turner-Zwinkels, F. (2018). Integrating who "we" are with what "we" (will not) stand for: A further extension of the social identity model of collective action. *European Review of Social Psychology, 29*(1), 122–160. https://doi.org/10.1080/10463283.2018.1479347

Vincheckar, M. (2019). Social dominance orientation and sexual violence against Dalit women in India. *Think India, 22*, 5–12.

Vorsina, M., Manning, M., Sheppard, J., & Fleming, C. M. (2019). Social dominance orientation, fear of terrorism and support for counter-terrorism policies. *Australian Journal of Political Science, 54*(1), 99–113. https://doi.org/10.1080/10361146.2018.1552920

Vukčević Marković, M., Nicović, A., & Živanović, M. (2021). Contextual and psychological predictors of militant extremist mindset in youth. *Frontiers in Psychology, 12.* https://doi.org/10.3389/fpsyg.2021.622571

Wahl, S., Trauntschnig, M., Hoffmann, L., & Schwab, S. (2022). Peer acceptance and peer status in relation to students' special educational needs, migration biography, gender and socio-economic status. *Journal of Research in Special Educational Needs, 22*(3), 243–253. https://doi.org/10.1111/1471-3802.12562

Walsh, L. E. (1996). *Iran-Contra: The final report.* Random House.

Williams, K. D. (2009). Ostracism: A temporal need-threat model. In M. P. Zanner (Ed.), *Advances in Experimental Social Psychology* (Vol. 41, pp. 275–314). Elsevier. https://doi.org/10.1016/S0065-2601(08)00406-1

World Population Review. (2023). *Countries where women cannot vote 2023.* https://worldpopulationreview.com/country-rankings/countries-where-women-cant-vote

Young, J. R. (1879). *Around the world with General Grant: A narrative of the visit of General US Grant, ex-president of the United States, to various countries in Europe, Asia, and Africa, in 1877, 1878, 1879: To which are added certain conversations with General Grant on questions connected with American politics and history* (Vol. 2). American News Company.

Zhirkov, K., Ponarin, E., & Rivera, S. W. (2023). The child-rearing scale as a measure of authoritarianism in a non-Western context: Evidence from mass and elite surveys in Russia, *International Journal of Public Opinion Research, 35,* 1–7.

10

The Exclusion–Extremism Link in Non-WEIRD Populations

JUANA CHINCHILLA AND ÁNGEL GÓMEZ

10.1 Introduction

In 1984 Audre Lorde observed "It is not our differences that divide us. It is our inability to recognize, accept, and celebrate those differences" (Lorde, 1984). Then and now, violent radicalization is one of the biggest global threats of the present era. Terrorist attacks kill thousands of civilians each year, leading to social instability and disorder and breaking apart people from different communities (IEP, 2023). Although several of the most shocking terrorist incidents of the last decades, such as the 9/11 attacks, the Madrid train bombings, or the Christchurch mosque shootings, have taken place in WEIRD – i.e., Western, educated, industrialized, rich, and democratic – countries, the majority of them occur in countries that are not WEIRD, as in countries from the Sahel region, the Middle East, and Asia; and most attacks are perpetrated by groups claiming to fight for Islam and the Muslim community, such as the Islamic State or Al-Shabab, or for ethnic minorities, such as the Balochistan Liberation Army or the Kurdistan Workers' Party (IEP, 2023).

People from WEIRD and non-WEIRD countries inhabit different cultural universes and are finely tuned to their culture through social learning and direct experience (Atran & Medin, 2008). Because of that, we cannot be sure that the psychosocial processes and mechanisms relevant to understanding human behavior in one cultural context are also important in other contexts without conducting cross-cultural research (Henrich, 2021). The scientific study of the link between social exclusion and violent extremism is relatively new; and there are still many aspects of this relationship that we do not understand well (e.g., Pfundmair & Mahr, 2022). However, there are enough studies with individuals from WEIRD and non-WEIRD populations to conclude that social exclusion might be a universal driver of violent extremism and one of the factors responsible for the rise of jihadist terrorism and other types of politically, religiously, or ideologically inspired violence (e.g., Gómez, Atran et al., 2022; Gómez, Chiclana et al., 2022; Gómez, Martínez et al., 2021; Pretus et al., 2019). In the present chapter, we provide a contextualized overview of this research.

We begin with a summary of research on the distinction between WEIRD and non-WEIRD populations and the link between social exclusion and extremism. After that, we review the role of social exclusion in several models of radicalization, deradicalization, and disengagement and pay particular attention to a theoretical model co-originated by the second author of this chapter together with Professor William B. Swann Jr.: *identity fusion* (see also Rousis & Swann, this volume). Lastly, we discuss some applications for countering terrorism, talk about some of the main barriers for the study of violent extremism, and point out strategies that can be used to overcome them.

10.2   The Distinction between WEIRD and Non-WEIRD Populations

Humans are cultural creatures. People are born with a basic set of mental capacities that are easily molded by the elements that dominate the cultural landscape of their development (e.g., Atran & Medin, 2008). They learn from others to adapt their hearts and minds to the beliefs, norms, values, and practices they encounter, which gives rise to important psychological variations between them (e.g., Heine, 2010; Henrich et al., 2010). Differences between human populations have been identified in many fundamental psychological processes, setting apart people from WEIRD and non-WEIRD cultures (e.g., Henrich, 2021; Henrich et al., 2010). Among other things, they differ in their self-concepts, motivations, moral views, and approaches to regulating social relationships.

First, WEIRD and non-WEIRD people prioritize *different things to build their view of themselves and have disparate self-concepts*. Self-construal processes are influenced by a host of sociocultural factors, such as socioeconomic development, religious heritage, or endorsement of honor, which drive cultural groups to emphasize different ways of being independent and interdependent and generate different models of selfhood in diverse countries (e.g., Markus & Kitayama, 1991; Uskul et al., 2023; Vignoles et al., 2016). In general, people with an independent self-concept envision themselves as self-contained entities that can be described by reference to a series of immutable attributes, like dispositional traits, that invariably influence behavior (Markus & Kitayama, 1991). Contrarily to that, people with an interdependent self-concept derive their identity from their social relationships; their behavior is contingent upon their roles within each social context and influenced by the perceived thoughts, feelings, and behaviors of others (Markus & Kitayama, 1991). Consequently, individuals with an independent self-concept behave more consistently than people with an interdependent self-concept across different kinds of relationships – for example, with friends, parents, or strangers (Efron et al., 2018; English & Chen, 2011). Also, people with an independent self-concept are more focused on the impact of events on themselves and less focused on their impact on others (Mesquita, 2001) and give more weight to their own perspective and less weight to the imagined perspective of others (e.g., Cohen & Gunz, 2002; Wong & Tsai, 2007). People with an independent self-concept see the self as less malleable and capable of improving than people with an interdependent self-concept as well (e.g., Heine et al., 2001).

Second, *there are several key motivations that appear differently* in WEIRD and non-WEIRD populations. For example, WEIRD people tend to be more interested in cultivating a positive view of their personal self (e.g., Heine & Hamamura, 2007); have a higher desire of making personal choices (e.g., Iyengar & Lepper, 2002); and are less inclined to defend their honor or reputation through aggression than non-WEIRD people (e.g., Nisbett & Cohen, 1996; Uskul et al., 2019). Honor cultures tend to emerge in contexts in which resources are scarce, law enforcement is weak or absent, and people's possessions are easily appropriated by others, such as the countries around the Mediterranean, the Middle East, and Latin America, and are also typical of the South of the United States, which was settled by Celtic herders of the Scottish, Irish, and Welsh borderlands who brought with them honor-based norms, values, beliefs, and practices (Nisbett & Cohen, 1996). Because they emerge in lawless environments, honor cultures create a strong norm of reciprocity, which push individuals to return gifts and favors – to develop a reputation as trustworthy partners – as well as to retaliate for insulting or harming actions – to develop a reputation for strong response to injustices (Uskul et al., 2019).

Third, WEIRD and non-WEIRD people have *unmatched morals*. Whereas WEIRD people tend to focus exclusively on issues related to harm and injustice to assess the morality of different behaviors, non-WEIRD people are inclined to focus as well on issues related to lack of loyalty, disrespect to authorities, and contamination or lack of purity (Haidt, 2012; Shweder et al., 1997). Because of that, WEIRD people value less the virtue of conformity and have a higher need to be unique (Heejung & Markus, 1999; Kim & Marcus, 1999); are less prone to diffuse responsibility and shame across groups lines (Henrich, 2021); and judge more negatively the acts of cronyism and nepotism than non-WEIRD people (Trompenaars & Hampden-Turner, 1998).

Fourth, WEIRD people also diverge from non-WEIRD people in the *strategies that they use to regulate their relationships with others*. According to relational models theory (Fiske, 1992), there are four elementary models to regulate social relations: (1) communal sharing – unity, oneness, and solidarity; (2) authority ranking – mutual acceptance of a power differential; (3) equality matching – reciprocity, equality, and balance; and (4) market pricing – proportionality and transaction. These models are universal, but there are different cultural rules to choose which relational model to use, how to use it, with whom, and when (Fiske, 1992). Given that people generally follow the rules provided by their own culture, this can lead to misunderstandings or conflicts of values between people from different cultures (Fiske, 1992; Fiske & Rai, 2015). For instance, market pricing relationships are more predominant in WEIRD cultures, which has led to emergence of noncompatible views of fairness. WEIRD people are more inclined to distribute resources following a proportionality norm – that is, the ratio between incomes and outcomes is held constant – and less inclined to distribute them following norms based on need and equality than non-WEIRD people (e.g., Berman et al., 1985; Kashima et al., 1988). Furthermore, the expansion of market pricing relationships in the West also has driven WEIRD people to trust more in strangers (Algan & Cahuc, 2013; Fehr et al., 2002) and to cooperate more with unknown individuals and social institutions, such as the police or government (Henrich, 2021; Schultz et al., 2019)

WEIRD and non-WEIRD people differ in so many ways that we cannot assume that the psychological processes and mechanisms that matter among WEIRD populations are universal (e.g., Henrich et al., 2010, Heine, 2010). We need to conduct cross-cultural studies to know the processes that generalize and differ across cultures (e.g., Brady et al., 2018). On top of that, the scope of cultural differences goes beyond the dichotomy of WEIRD and non-WEIRD populations. Cultural differences also manifest within these categories and within cultures – for example, between members of different social groups or subcultures – creating a rich tapestry of beliefs, norms, and practices that vary significantly from one community to another (Heine, 2010; Henrich et al., 2010). Fortunately, the research on the link between social exclusion and extremism has focused on a wide number of WEIRD and non-WEIRD populations, and we can reasonably argue that social exclusion can spark the psychological machinery that drives individuals toward violent extremism across cultures. We focus on this research next.

10.3   Social Exclusion and Extremism

Social exclusion has been broadly defined as being kept apart from others emotionally or physically (e.g., Wesselmann et al., 2022), and it is a complex phenomenon that encompasses experiences of rejection and ostracism (e.g., Riva & Eck, 2016). When people are rejected, they receive negative attention from others, indicating that they are not positively valued or wanted, whereas when they are ostracized, they receive no attention and are ignored (Riva & Eck, 2016). People can feel excluded at a personal level (i.e., when they are excluded for their personal characteristics or their group membership) or at a group level (i.e., when the group to which they belong is excluded); and the experience of social exclusion can result from a myriad of events. For example, negative stereotypes and meta-stereotypes (Gómez, 2002; Kamans et al., 2009), dehumanizing language (Haslam, 2006), stigmatization and discrimination (Smart Richman & Leary, 2009), relative deprivation (Koomen & van der

Plight, 2016; Smith et al., 2012), threats to the security or the values of the group (Stephan & Stephan, 2000), or negative contact with members of other groups (Barlow et al., 2012; Crisp & Abrams, 2008) can cause feelings of social rejection. Feelings of ostracism can occur when people are denied access to relevant information (Jones et al., 2009), are not given the possibility to voice their opinions (van den Boss, 2018), are forgotten (King & Geise, 2011), or are ghosted (Williams, 2009), among others.

Social exclusion leads to hurt feelings, depression, loneliness, and anxiety (e.g., Kowalski & Leary, this volume; Smart Richman & Leary, 2009) and augments the risk of cardiovascular ailments and chronic diseases (Jin & Josephs; 2016; van Bergen et al., 2018). It threatens several basic needs, such as the need to belong, self-esteem, control, meaning, and self-certainty, motivating individuals to engage in compensatory actions to ensure need satisfaction (Gerber & Wheeler, 2009; Williams, 2009). Of particular interest for this chapter, although single episodes of exclusion can be highly aversive, its effects are particularly nefarious in the case of marginalized populations (Williams, 2009), such as Muslims, who are pervasively exposed to experiences of rejection and ostracism.

Muslims are often portrayed as "radicals" and "terrorists" and treated with fear and contempt by others; face restrictions on manifestations of religion or belief; have problems in the areas of schooling, health, and housing; and are frequently exposed to hate-directed violence (Saheed, 2021). Such experiences have contributed to the emergence of worldwide feelings of injustice, humiliation, and marginalization among Muslims communities (Saheed, 2021), which might have driven a substantial amount of individuals to increase their distance from the people or groups envisioned as responsible (e.g., Jasinskaja-Lahti et al., 2009), augment their commitment to their own group (e.g., Branscombe et al., 1999), join a radical network (e.g., Wesselmann et al. 2022), or engage in extreme actions (e.g., Gómez, Morales et al., 2011).

The research on the link between exclusion and extremism is still in its infancy (Pfundmair & Mahr, 2022), but there is strong evidence supporting that social exclusion has played an important role in the spread of violent jihad since the beginning of the present century and contributed to the unfolding of other types of extremist violence in WEIRD and non-WEIRD contexts. For instance, many correlational studies have revealed that several events related to social exclusion are associated with violent extremism across countries. In this regard, it has been found that: (1) perceived injustice of Western military and foreign policy motivates behavioral intentions to commit acts of violence among Muslims living in Western and non-Western countries (Obaidi, Kunst, et al., 2018), and that this effect is mediated by anger (Obaidi et al., 2020); (2) feelings of lack of respect and humiliation are related to behavioral extremism among Palestinians living in the West Bank and Gaza and Liberation Tigers of Tamil Eelam living in Sri Lanka (Ginges & Atran, 2008; Webber et al., 2018); (3) the desire to protect fellow Muslims from oppression augments group identification and adherence to radical ideological tenets among Islamist terrorists imprisoned in Indonesia (Milla et al., 2022); (4) threats to the values that are central to the group diminish the will to negotiate and reach compromises with others in Palestine, Iran, Indonesia, and India (Ginges & Atran, 2013); (5) insecure life attachment is associated with extremism endorsement in India and among Muslims living in the United Kingdom (Ozer et al., 2020); (6) exclusion from the political arena increases the likelihood that groups that differ from the majority in religion will opt for violence and terrorism globally (Santana et al., 2013); (7) perceived group deprivation predicts support for violence among Muslims living in the Netherlands (Doosje et al., 2013; van Bergen et al., 2015); (8) perceived exploitation by the United States is related to endorsement of violent action among Christians and Muslims in Syria and Lebanon (Sidanius et al., 2016); and (9) perceptions that the majority have negative stereotypes about the in-group – that is, meta-stereotypes – augments support for Islamist extremism among Dutch Moroccan teenagers (Kamans et al., 2009).

Although most experiments revealing a relationship between exclusion and extremism have included WEIRD samples (e.g., Hales and Williams, 2018; Pfundmair, 2019; Pfundmair & Wetherell, 2019), there are some with non-WEIRD people showing convergent results. For instance, Obaidi, Thomsen, and collaborators (2018) conducted two experiments with Muslims living in Denmark and Sweden showing that depicting the dominant group as envisioning Muslim culture as inferior and incompatible with their own culture increased endorsement of extremist violence against the West. Obaidi et al. (2023) also found that cultural threats – that is, to values, worldviews, and symbols – drove Muslims from Western and non-Western countries to violent extremism, increasing their need for certain and unambiguous answers. Moreover, several systematic reviews highlight that relative deprivation, injustice, marginalization, victimization, and discrimination are among the risk factors of violent radicalization more frequently studied and mentioned (Vergani et al., 2018; Wolfowicz et al., 2020); a recent meta-analysis has shown that experiences related to social exclusion might be key to understanding the causal roots of violent extremism (Wolfowicz et al., 2021). Given this, it is not strange that the role played by social exclusion is also emphasized by the most widely accepted theories of radicalization leading to violence, deradicalization, and disengagement. We review some of these theories next.

10.4 The Role of the Exclusion–Extremism Link for Approaches to Explaining Radicalization Leading to Violence, Deradicalization, and Disengagement

Violent radicalization is a complex process that involves a gradual compromise with the use of violence (e.g., Horgan, 2008; Molinario et al., 2021). Many contemporary models of radicalization leading to violence, such as the *staircase model* (Moghaddam, 2005), the *model of the three-levels of political radicalization* (McCauley & Moskalenko, 2008; Moskalenko & McCauley, 2020), the *model of the determinants of radicalization* (Doosje et al., 2013; Feddes et al., 2020), the *sacred values model* (Atran et al., 2007; Ginges et al., 2007), the *devoted actors model* (Gómez et al., 2017; Sheikh et al., 2016), *uncertainty-identity theory* (Hogg, 2021; Hogg et al., 2010; Wagoner & Hogg, this volume), and the *3-N model of radicalization* (Ellenberg & Kruglanski, this volume; Kruglanski et al., 2014, 2019), picture social exclusion as key to understanding this process.

The *staircase model* depicts radicalization using the metaphor of a narrowing staircase that has a ground floor and five higher floors, and posits that individuals move to the first floor when they are victims of material injustices and to the second floor when they do not see a possibility to improve their situation through social mobility or participation in peaceful politics. The *model of the three-levels of political radicalization* identifies several risk factors linked to social exclusion that operate at the level of the individual – personal victimization and political grievances; the group – external threats, social isolation, and state repression; and the masses – external attacks and prolonged violence. And the *model of the determinants of radicalization* pinpoints several triggering factors related to exclusion that act at the level of the person – for example, discrimination, racism, social rejection, unjust confrontations with authorities; the group – for example, isolation; and the society – for example, attacks on the group, such as cartoons in the media, military actions, arrests, or repressive measures of the government seen as out of proportion. The *sacred values model* posits that acts of disrespect or threats to values that people envision as sacred – immune to material and nonmaterial trade-offs – galvanizes individuals to engage in extreme behaviors to protect these values. And the *devoted actors model* asserts that people are particularly willing to get involved in extreme actions for their sacred values when they are viscerally committed or fused to a group that shares these values. *Uncertainty-identity theory* postulates that experiences of rejection and injustice cause feelings of self-uncertainty that might motivate individuals to join extremist groups because they provide descriptive and prescriptive identities that are extraordinarily clear and consensual. And the *3-N model of radicalization* argues that direct or anticipated experiences of personal or group exclusion activate the quest for personal significance – that is, the need to matter, to be respected, and to have a meaningful existence – and that this quest can turn into the dominant motivational force, pushing individuals toward behavioral extremism.

In addition to that, most researchers studying deradicalization – the process by which ideological commitment to violent extremism diminishes to a point in which there is no longer risk of engagement in terrorist actions – and disengagement – a change of role or function that involves not using violence – have come to the conclusion that fighting social exclusion is essential to helping violent extremists offenders to leave terrorism behind. For instance, the *staircase model* considers that the first step to solving the problem of terrorism is the eradication of social injustice (Moghaddam, 2005). The *3-N model* argues that individuals can disengage from terrorism when they are provided social opportunities to establish positive relationships outside the extremist network and achieve significance through peaceful means (Bélanger, 2017; Kruglanski et al., 2019). The *model of the trajectory of disengagement* (Rabasa et al., 2010) conceives of disengagement as a process that culminates when individuals are fully integrated into mainstream society. The *phoenix model of deradicalization and disengagement* (Silke et al., 2021) considers that the catalysts that facilitate the processes of deradicalization and disengagement only are effective in a climate based on trust, security, and perceived opportunity, which requires a genuine interest in the social reintegration of violent extremist offenders. And the *pro-integration model* (Barrele, 2015) posits that people who abandon terrorism typically go through a gradual process that entails a radical transformation of their identity and the development of a sustained positive engagement with society: a process involving changes in several fundamental areas of life – for example, social relations, coping, identity – that only are possible when people feel socially accepted and included.

When they do not remain silent about the issue, the models reviewed tend to assume that personal and group exclusion are threats that lead to extremist behavior through two motivational routes that can be dissociated: (1) the desire to promote self-interest, and (2) the desire to promote the interest of an entity different from the self, like a leader, a group, or a set of ideological convictions. For instance, *identity-uncertainty theory* (e.g., Hogg, 2021) and the *3-N model* (Kruglanski et al., 2019) argue that social exclusion threatens the needs of self-certainty and personal significance, respectively; and that the motivation to satisfy these needs – that is, self-interest – can make a unique contribution to the radicalization process. The *sacred values model* (e.g., Ginges & Atran, 2013) emphasizes that the desire to defend sacred values invigorates extremist behavior. And the *model of the determinants of radicalization* (Doosje et al., 2013) posits that the motivation to protect the group drives some individuals to engage in extremist actions.

In the following section, we introduce a theory that has a peculiar view of the motivational processes that explain the link between social exclusion and extremism, and that has provided enough insights to be applied to WEIRD and non-WEIRD populations: *identity fusion*. Strongly fused individuals are particularly willing to engage in extreme self-sacrifices for their group, leader, or values because the motivation to protect and defend them turns into a personal issue (e.g., Gómez et al., 2020, 2023), and their will to self-sacrifice is encouraged when they are excluded and rejected (Gómez, Morales et al., 2011).

10.5   A Particular Type of Link between Exclusion and Extremism in WEIRD and Non-WEIRD Populations: Identity Fusion

Identity fusion is a visceral feeling of oneness with a group, person, value, or ideological conviction that motivates individuals to engage in extreme actions on its behalf (e.g., Gómez et al., 2020; Swann et al., 2009, 2012), and that occurs in different countries across five continents (Swann, Buhrmester et al., 2014). When people are strongly fused, they see themselves and the target of fusion as inextricably linked to each other, which leads them to believe that what happens to the target of fusion has a direct impact on their personal well-being and to experience a deep sense of visceral responsibility toward it (Chinchilla et al., 2022). Strongly fused people also believe that they and the target of fusion synergistically strengthen each other and experience intense feelings of personal agency and mutual invulnerability (Gómez, Brooks et al., 2011). Therefore, strongly fused individuals come across threats to the target of fusion as if they were personal threats and react by augmenting their will to engage in extreme behaviors and costly personal sacrifices to defend and protect the fusion target (e.g., Gómez, Brooks et al., 2011; Swann et al., 2009). One of the most common factors that causes or increases fusion is shared intense dysphoric experiences with in-group members (Whitehouse et al., 2017). Then, for strongly fused people, feelings of exclusion of the group, or themselves as individuals, augment their will to fight.

Identity fusion has been identified as the top risk factor predicting radical intentions by a meta-analysis including dozens of alternative predictors (Wolfowicz et al., 2021). Moreover, our own research with individuals at risk of radicalization, current terrorists, and former terrorists confirms that identity fusion might be a universal driver of behavioral extremism and that the phenomena related to social exclusion might be relevant to understanding its effects and the process of radicalization leading to violence (e.g., Gómez et al., 2017, 2023; Gómez, Atran et al., 2022; Gómez, Bélanger et al., 2021; Gómez, Chiclana et al., 2022).

Identity fusion research with *people at risk of radicalization* includes field studies, lab experiments, and neuroimage investigations. For example, a study with youth from two Moroccan neighborhoods strongly associated with militant jihad showed that participants who considered sharia law as sacred were more willing to make personal sacrifices for it and more supportive of militant jihad if they were fused with a group of friends who shared their ideological convictions – that is, if they were devoted actors (Sheikh et al., 2016). A complementary online study with a WEIRD population showed as well that devoted actors were more willing to self-sacrifice for a different sacred value – democracy – when it was threatened (Sheikh et al., 2016). And a neuroimaging experiment with a sample of supporters of militant global jihadism revealed that ostracizing participants increased the activation of brain areas related to the processing of sacred values – the left interior frontal gyrus – when they thought about nonsacred values and the disposition to fight and die for them (Pretus et al., 2019). Therefore, social exclusion might contribute to the sacralization of values, triggering or accelerating the radicalization process.

Identity fusion research with *current terrorists* also includes members of WEIRD and non-WEIRD populations, and it has been guided by three general aims: (1) unraveling the mechanisms that might motivate extreme actions across groups and cultures; (2) finding the differences that exist between terrorist offenders and other criminal groups; and (3) exploring the psycho-social processes that promote the radicalization, deradicalization, and disengagement of female terrorists.

First, much fusion research on the mechanisms responsible for radicalization leading to violence follows a multicultural and multimethod approach that combines qualitative and quantitative data from field studies with terrorists and online experiments with members of the general population. For example, a field study including face-to-face interviews with IS fighters captured in Iraq and combatants – for example, Peshmerga, members of the Kurdistan Workers' Party – in the first offensive to retake Mosul from IS, and several online studies in Spain, showed that participants were more willing to fight and die for their values when they saw these values as sacred, were fused with a group that shared these values, and envisioned the group as spiritually formidable – that is, strongly convinced in the things they were fighting for, highly resolved, and possessing willpower (Gómez et al., 2017). A series of thirty-one field and online studies in nine countries from the Middle East, Africa, and Europe including different samples – for example, imprisoned jihadists and gang members, people in longstanding conflicts and refugees, US military, Ukrainians before and during the current war with Russia – indicated that fusion was related to the will to fight for groups, leaders, and values through perceptions of spiritual formidability and trust (Gómez, Vázquez & Atran, 2023). And a field study with imprisoned jihadists and several online experiments revealed that feelings of admiration for the sacrifices that other group members make for the group increased fusion and, through this path, augmented endorsement of extreme pro-group actions (Gómez, Bélanger et al., 2021).

Second, a comparative field study in thirty-five Spanish prisons including qualitative and quantitative data from four classes of prisoners – jihadist terrorists, Latino gangs, delinquent bands, and non-jihadist Muslim criminals unconnected to criminal organizations – examined the differences and similarities between jihadists and other types of criminal offenders (Gómez, Atran, et al., 2022). The results showed that jihadists were more fused with their core values and more willing to engage in costly sacrifices for them than other criminal offenders. The results also showed that perceptions of injustice and personal discrimination were positively associated with fusion with their values and negatively associated with fusion with the justice system and, through this process, increased their will to engage in extreme sacrifices. On the other hand, fusion with family was negatively associated with feelings of personal discrimination and injustice.

Third, one investigation explored the mechanisms that might explain the radicalization and disengagement of female jihadists through a field study including female jihadists incarcerated in Spain and a control group of Muslim women imprisoned for offenses unrelated to terrorism (Gómez, Chiclana et al., 2022). The results revealed that crisis in their personal and social identities due to feelings of rejection and ostracism motivated female terrorists to enter radical networks and that feelings of disenchantment for unfulfilled expectancies favored their disengagement from terrorism. In fact, their levels of fusion with religion and the Muslim community dramatically decreased in the present compared to their estimated levels of fusion before entering prison.

Lastly, research with *former terrorists* examining the reasons driving individuals to join two types of violent extremist groups that exhibit differences in ideology and type of radicalization, the Liberation Tigers of Tamil Eelam and Islamist groups associated with the global jihad movement (Gómez, Martínez et al., 2021), indicated that identity processes related to the need to belong, the desire to achieve social recognition, and the motivation to address social injustices were often mentioned by former members of the two types of terrorist groups as reasons for joining. However, they were much more cited for the groups related to the global jihad movement than for the Liberation Tigers of Tamil Eelam, whose members were frequently "forced" to join the group through coercive tactics.

In the following section we discuss several implications of the research on the link between social exclusion and extremism to prevent radicalization leading to violence and promote deradicalization and disengagement.

10.6   Applications for Preventing Radicalization Leading to Violence and Promoting Deradicalization and Disengagement

The previous theoretical models and empirical research indicate that personal- and group-based experiences of social exclusion are common threads that run through the processes of radicalization leading to violence in WEIRD and non-WEIRD contexts and that boosting social inclusion is useful to promote the deradicalization and disengagement of violent extremist offenders and augment social resilience against radicalization. The importance of these phenomena has been acknowledged by the developers of the tools to evaluate the risk of radicalization and the interventions used in prisons, who envision social exclusion and inclusion as risk and protective factors, respectively (for a recent review, see Kruglanski et al., 2019). This knowledge has also crystalized in the United Nations Global Counter-Terrorism Strategy (UN, 2006), which considers that we must urgently address several conditions related to social exclusion that might be conducive to terrorism, such as violations of human rights, social marginalization, political exclusion, or ethnic and religious discrimination. It has deeply influenced the research that we have conducted in the field as well.

Most studies conducted by our team with current terrorists and former terrorists are characterized by the use of face-to-face interviews (e.g., Gómez, Atran et al., 2022; Gómez, Chiclana et al., 2022), which gives us room for extended conversations with the participants and privileged access to their experiences and the meanings that they ascribe to them. We always listen to the interviewees in an objective and nonjudgmental way and try to create a climate of mutual trust and respect (Horgan, 2011). We do not condone violent extremist actions, but we try to convey to the participants that we care about their opinions and value them as human beings; and we offer to them the possibility to collaborate and become active agents in the search for humanitarian solutions to the problems posited by violent extremism. In a considerable number of cases, their response to our approach is highly favorable.

The knowledge and experiences that we have accumulated during our hundreds of interviews have made us see that promoting social inclusion is vital to building bridges to connect people with moderate groups and the values and institutions that make peaceful coexistence possible. For example, our research suggests that fighting rejection and ostracism is important for preventing people from entering the radicalization process (Gómez, Chiclana et al., 2022; Gómez, Martínez et al., 2021); and that avoiding injustices within the prison system and engaging the family and friends of the inmates in the disengagement process might be powerful tools to promote the social reintegration of violent extremists (Gómez, Atran et al., 2022; Gómez, Chiclana et al., 2022).

Promoting social inclusion requires changing the social, cultural, and political norms that perpetuate the social disadvantages experienced by marginalized individuals and groups (e.g., UN, 2016). But it also requires changing people's behaviors, feelings, and thoughts, which can be achieved through educative and sport interventions. Educational programs aimed at facilitating knowledge of the complexities and nuances of sensitive social issues, the importance of taking others' perspective, and the value of diversity and social cohesion might foster mutual understanding and respect among people with different ethnic and religious backgrounds, beliefs, and convictions and increase the resilience of vulnerable communities against terrorism (e.g., European Commission, 2016; Weiss et al., 2023). Sport interventions bring together members of different groups in spaces dominated by fair play, respect, and tolerance (Gerstein et al., 2021), contributing to the development of cross-group friendships and fostering interdependence, mutual trust, social support, and social skills (Mousa, 2020; UNODC, 2015). Sport-based interventions connect people to the wider community and provide space for the cocreation of values and solutions to overcome social tensions and conflicts (UNODC, 2015). They instill a sense of belonging and identity, filling the void created by the lack of fulfilling relationships (Moyano et al., 2022), and can contribute to the development of positive social connections and commitment to prosocial outcomes among individuals at risk, terrorists, and former terrorists (CREST, 2017; UNODC, 2015).

Diversity education programs and sport-based interventions can provide cost-effective and efficient ways of promoting peace. However, the problem of radicalization is exceedingly complex. There are so many types of violent extremist groups and processes of radicalization that we cannot assume that there is a single solution that fits them all (e.g., Feddes et al., 2020; Moskalenko & McCauley, 2020). Preventing radicalization and promoting deradicalization and disengagement are difficult tasks that require interventions tailored at the type of radicalization at hand; and to develop said interventions we still have to do more research. In the following section, we discuss some of the major obstacles faced by researchers interested in the study of violent extremism and provide some suggestions to overcome them.

10.7   Barriers for the Study of Radicalization Leading to Violence, Deradicalization, and Disengagement

In this section we follow Gómez, Vázquez, Chinchilla et al. (2023), who, thanks to their direct experience in the field talking to individuals at different levels of the process of radicalization leading to violence, explain why it is so difficult to investigate radicalization leading to violence. According to them, one of the most pressing barriers for the study of violent extremism is the difficulty of reaching out populations of interest – that is, individuals at risk of radicalization and current and former terrorists. Obtaining the resources, contacts, and trust required to work in partnership with governmental and civil society organizations and to gain access to these populations is almost a herculean task, which explains why the percentage of scientific papers including primary data is minimal (Schuurman, 2020).

Since some aspects of violent extremism are presumably explained by processes shared with normal people who do not engage in violence (Horgan, 2014; Silke, 2009), lack of access to the populations of interest is not an absolute obstacle for conducting research. Doing cross-sectional and experimental studies with the general population is useful to identify the psychosocial mechanisms that matter during the early stages of the radicalization process and to explain why "average" people might become terrorists. However, obtaining data from individuals at risk, current terrorists, and former terrorists is essential to test the ecological relevance of these mechanisms as well as to understand what happens during the latest stages of the radicalization process – when individuals are ready to engage in violence – and during the processes of deradicalization and disengagement. Scientists who do not have the privilege of talking directly to them can analyze the information that they post in forums, on webpages, and in online communities (e.g., Whittaker, 2020) or their manifestos (e.g., Ebner et al., 2022).

Another important barrier is related to the scarcity of comparative studies including different terrorist groups or members of the same terrorist group belonging to different cultures, which precludes that we know how far the similarities and differences between terrorists go. The research at our disposal indicates that social exclusion can motivate people to jump voluntarily into violent extremism across cultures (e.g., Kruglanski et al., 2019, 2020), but that does not mean that there are no differences between them. WEIRD and non-WEIRD populations vary in the extent to which they incorporate their relationship with others in their self-concept (e.g., Markus & Kitayama, 1991), their motivation to restore honor (e.g., Nisbett & Cohen, 1996), their morals (e.g., Haidt, 2012), and their regulation of social relationships (e.g., Fiske & Rai, 2015), among others; it is likely that some of these differences impact the link between social exclusion and extremism.

For example, it is possible that the effect of personal- and group-based experiences of social exclusion varies as a function of culture, such that people from independent cultures are more affected by personal exclusion and less affected by group-based exclusion than people from interdependent cultures (Koomen & van der Pligt, 2016; see also Obaidi et al., 2020). Also, people from non-WEIRD countries might react more extremely to acts of disrespect directed toward their authorities and their purity laws and practices than citizens from WEIRD countries (e.g., Hahn et al., 2019; Haidt, 2012). Furthermore, it is also possible that the behaviors that cause feelings of exclusion within the context of a specific type of relationship – for example, with parents, friends, authorities, out-group members – also varies across cultures, and thus that the paths linking social exclusion and extremism among terrorists from different countries have different points of departure (e.g., Fiske & Rai, 2015). Doing more research to examine these and other differences is essential to understanding how culture shapes the cognitions, emotions, and behaviors of violent extremists across contexts and to developing interventions for countering extremism adapted to their needs. Embracing cumulative science practices and collaboration with researchers working with violent extremists from different communities is one of the most promising avenues to address this (e.g., Brady et al., 2018).

Lastly, Gómez, Vázquez, Chinchilla et al. (2023) also identify another eight major barriers and provide recommendations to cope with each of them: (1) the goals of the research might be blurred due to the lack of cross-fertilization between disciplines – which can be solved by demarcating goals that do not overlap with the goals of other disciplines and conducting interdisciplinary collaborations; (2) the theory that should be used to support the research might be unclear – which can be solved by refining existing theories, creating new theories, or combining theories into new models; (3) the nature of the samples used for the research limits the conclusions that can be reached – which can be solved by including samples of individuals at different levels of radicalization, women, and groups of comparison with the same characteristics as the target groups; (4) fieldwork entails addressing extremely serious ethical risks – which can be minimized by adopting strategies respectful of the rights of the researchers and participants tailored to the populations, contexts, and countries of the research; (5) implementing the best methodology for data collection is complicated – which can be addressed by using triangulation of methods and quantitative measures that are short and easy to understand; (6) developing the skills needed to interview violent extremists requires practice and effort – which can be addressed by establishing training programs and periodical meetings to identify the factors that facilitate or hinder data collection; (7) the data exploitation strategy must be optimized – which can be solved by combining field data with data from the general population and developing strategies to prevent radicalization and promote deradicalization and disengagement based on the results of the research; and (8) advances for science and society should be balanced – which can be solved by disseminating the findings of the research and specifying their possible applications.

10.8 Conclusions

Countering violent extremism requires that we develop and deploy interventions to address its root causes. Social exclusion is one of the factors that consistently appears to provide a fertile ground for the development of violent extremism across different groups and cultures. Research with WEIRD and non-WEIRD populations has repeatedly shown that even singular experiences of social exclusion can enhance the appeal of terrorism and increase the commitment of individuals to their groups and values and their willingness to undertake extreme personal sacrifices on their behalf (see Pfundmair, this volume). Furthermore, chronic and systemic experiences of rejection, marginalization, and injustice might have played a significant role in the rise of jihadist terrorism and other types of extremist violence posing a serious threat to the world today. Therefore, to effectively fight terrorism, it is imperative that we prioritize interventions to promote social inclusion and foster a sense of belonging and cohesion within societies. By increasing our ability to recognize, accept, and celebrate our differences, we can diminish the appeal of violent extremism and contribute to creating a more resilient, peaceful, and harmonious global community.

Acknowledgments

Funding for this chapter was provided by ERC Advanced Grant GA.–101018172.

References

Algan, Y., & Cahuc, P. (2013). Trust and growth. *Annual Review of Economics, 5* (1), 521–549. https://doi.org/10.1146/annurev-economics-081412-102108

Atran, S., Axelrod, R., & Davis, R. (2007). Sacred barriers to conflict resolution. *Science, 317*(5841), 1039–1040. https://doi.org/10.1126/science.1144241

Atran, S., & Medin., D. L. (2008). *The native mind and the cultural construction of nature.* MIT Press.

Barlow, F. K., Paolini, S., Pedersen, A., et al. (2012). The contact caveat: Negative contact predicts increased prejudice more than positive contact predicts reduced prejudice. *Personality and Social Psychology Bulletin, 38*(12), 1629–1643. https://doi.org/10.1177/0146167212457953

Barrele, K. (2015). Pro-integration: Disengagement from and life after extremism. *Behavioral Sciences of Terrorism and Political Aggression, 7*(2), 129–142. https://doi.org/10.1080/19434472.2014.988165

Bélanger, J. J. (2017). The rise and fall of violent extremism. In C. E. Kopetz, & A. Fishbach (Eds.), *The motivation–cognition interface* (pp. 152–177). Routledge

Berman, J. J., Murphy-Berman, V., & Singh, P. (1985). Cross-cultural similarities and differences in perceptions of fairness. *Journal of Cross-cultural Psychology, 16*, 55–67. https://doi.org/10.1177/0022002185016001005

Brady, L. M., Fryberg, S. A., & Shoda, Y. (2018). Expanding the interpretive power of psychological science by attending to culture. *Proceedings of the National Academy of Sciences, 115*(45), 11406–11413. https://doi.org/10.1073/pnas.1803526115

Branscombe, N. R., Schmitt, M. T., & Harvey, R. D. (1999). Perceiving pervasive discrimination among African Americans: Implications for group identification and well-being. *Journal of Personality and Social Psychology, 77*(1), 135–149. https://doi.org/10.1037/0022-3514.77.1.135

Chinchilla, J., Vázquez, A., & Gómez, Á. (2022). Strongly fused individuals feel viscerally responsible to self-sacrifice. *British Journal of Social Psychology, 61*(4), 1067–1085. https://doi.org/10.1111/bjso.12526

Clegg, J. M., Wen, N. J., & Legare, C. H. (2017). Is non-conformity WEIRD? Cultural variation in adults' beliefs about children competency and conformity. *Journal of Experimental Psychology General, 146*, 428–441. https://doi.org/10.1037/xge0000275

Cohen, D., & Gunz, A. (2002). As seen by the other . . . : Perspectives on the self in the memories and emotional perceptions of Easterners and Westerners. *Psychological Science, 13*, 55–59. https://doi.org/10.1111/1467-9280.00409

CREST (2017). *Introductory Guide: Countering Violent Extremism.* Centre for Research and Evidence on Security Threats. https://eprints.lancs.ac.uk/id/eprint/88097/1/17_008_01.pdf

Crisp, R. J., & Abrams, D. (2008). Improving intergroup attitudes and reducing stereotype threat: An integrated contact model. *European Review of Social Psychology, 19*(1), 242–284. https://doi.org/10.1080/14463280802547171

Doosje, B., Loseman, A., & van den Bos, K. (2013). Determinants of radicalization of Islamic youth in the Netherlands: Personal uncertainty, perceived injustice, and perceived group threat. *Journal of Social Issues*, 69(3), 586–604. https://doi.org/10.1111/josi.12030

Ebner, J., Kavanagh, C., & Whitehouse, H. (2022). Is there a language of terrorists? A comparative manifesto analysis. *Studies in Conflict and Terrorism*. https://doi.org/10.1080/1057610X.2022.2109244

Efron, D., Markus, H. R., Jackman, L. M., Muramoto, Y., & Muluk, H. (2018). Hypocrisy and culture: Failing to practice what you preach receives harsher interpersonal reactions in independent (vs. interdependent) cultures. *Journal of Experimental Social Psychology*, 76(5), 371–384. https://doi.org/10.1016/j.jesp.2017.12.009

English, T., & Chen, S. (2011). Self-concept consistency and culture: The differential impact of two forms of consistency. *Personality and Social Psychology Bulletin*, 37(6), 838–849. https://doi.org/10.1177/0146167211400621

European Commission (2016). *Communication from the Commission to the European Parliament, the Council, the European Economic Committee and the Committee of the Regions supporting the prevention of radicalisation leading to violent extremism.* https://eur-lex.europa.eu/legal-content/EN/TXT/PDF/?uri=CELEX:52016DC0379&from=ET

EUROPOL (2019). *EU terrorism situation and trend report.* www.europol.europa.eu/publications-events/main-reports/terrorism-situation-and-trend-report-2019-te-sat

Feddes, A. R., Nickolson, L., Mann, L., & Doosje, B. (2020). *Psychological perspectives on radicalization.* Routledge.

Fehr, E., Fischbacher, U., von Rosenbladt, B., Schupp, J., & Wagner, G. G. (2002). A nation-wide laboratory: Examining trust and trustworthiness by integrating behavioral experiments into representative surveys. *Journal of Contextual Economics-Schmollers Jahrbuch* (4), 529–542. https://doi.org/10.2139/ssrn.385120

Fiske, A. P. (1992). The four elementary forms of sociality: Framework for a unified theory of social relations. *Psychological Review*, 99(4), 689–723. https://doi.org/10.1037/0033-295X.99.4.689

Fiske, A. P., & Rai, T. S. (2015). *Virtuous violence.* Cambridge.

Gerber, J., & Wheeler, L. (2009). On being rejected: A meta-analysis of experimental research on rejection. *Perspectives on Psychological Science*, 4(5), 468–488. https://doi.org/10.1111/j.1745-6924.2009.01158.x

Gerstein, I. H., Blom, L. C., Banerjee, A., Farello, A., & Crabb, L. (2021). Sport for social change: An action-oriented peace education curriculum. *Peace and Conflict: Journal of Peace Psychology*, 27(2), 160–169. https://doi.org/10.1037/pac0000518

Ginges, J., & Atran, S. (2008). Humiliation and the inertia effect: Implications for understanding violence and compromise in intractable intergroup conflicts. *Journal of Cognition and Culture*, 8(3–4), 281–294. https://doi.org/10.1163/156853708X358182

Ginges, J., & Atran, S. (2013). Sacred values and cultural conflict. *Advances in Culture and Psychology*, *4*, 273–301. https://doi.org/10.1093/acprof:osobl/9780199336715.003.0006

Ginges, J., Atran, S., Medin, D., & Shikaki, K. (2007). Sacred bound on rational resolution of violent political conflict. *Proceedings of the National Academy of Sciences*, *104*(18), 7357–7360. https://doi.org/10.1073/pnas.0701768104

Gómez, A. (2002). If my group stereotypes others, others stereotype my group . . . and we know. Concept, research lines and future perspectives of meta-stereotypes. *International Journal of Social Psychology*, *17*, 253–282. https://doi.org/10.1174/02134740260372982

Gómez, A., Atran, S., Chinchilla, J., et al. (2022). Willingness to sacrifice among convicted Islamist terrorists versus violent gang members and other criminals. *Scientific Reports*, *12*(1), 1–15. https://doi.org/10.1038/s41598-022-06590-0

Gómez, Á., Bélanger, J. J., Chinchilla, J., et al. (2021). Admiration for Islamist groups encourages self-sacrifice through identity fusion. *Humanities & Social Sciences Communications*, *8*, 54. https://doi.org/10.1057/s41599-021-00734-9

Gómez, Á., Brooks, M. L., Buhrmester, M. D., et al. (2011). On the nature of identity fusion: Insights into the construct and a new measure. *Journal of Personality and Social Psychology*, *100*(5), 918–933. https://doi.org/10.1037/a0022642

Gómez, A., Chiclana, S., Chinchilla, J., et al. (2022). The mirage of the jihad: Disenchantment as the pathway to disengagement of female jihadists: A case study about radicalization in Spanish prisons. *International Journal of Social Psychology*, *37*(3), 586–617. https://doi.org/10.1080/02134748.2022.2096254

Gómez, A., Chinchilla, J., Vázquez, A., et al. (2020). Recent advances, misconceptions, untested assumptions and future research agenda for identity fusion theory. *Social and Personality Psychology Compass*, *14*(6), e12531. https://doi.org/10.1111/spc3.12531

Gómez, A., López-Rodríguez, L., Sheikh, H., et al. (2017). The devoted actor's will to fight and the spiritual dimension of human conflict. *Nature Human Behavior*, *1*(9), 673–679. https://doi.org/10.1038/s41562-017-0193-3

Gómez, Á., Martínez, M., Martel, F. A., et al. (2021). Why people enter and embrace violent groups. *Frontiers in Psychology*, *11*, 614657. https://doi.org/10.3389/fpsyg.2020.614657

Gómez, Á., Morales, J. F., Hart, S, Vázquez, A., & Swann, W. B. Jr. (2011). Rejected and excluded forevermore, but even more devoted: Irrevocable ostracism intensifies loyalty to the group among identity fused persons. *Personality and Social Psychology Bulletin*, *37*, 1574–1586. https://doi.org/10.1177/0146167211424580

Gómez, Á, Vázquez, A., & Atran, S. (2023). Transcultural pathways to the will to fight. *Proceedings of the National Academy of Science*, *120*(24), e2303614120. https://doi.org/10.1073/pnas.2303614120

Gómez, Á., Vázquez, A., Chinchilla, J., et al. (2023). Why is it so difficult to investigate violent radicalization? *Spanish Journal of Psychology*, *26*, e7. https://doi.org/10.1017/SJP.2023.2

Hahn, L., Tamborini, R., Novotni, E., Grall, C., & Klebig, B. (2019). Applying moral foundations theory to identify terrorist group motivations. *Political Psychology*, *40*(3), 507–522. https://doi.org/10.1111/pops.12525

Haidt, J. (2012). *The righteous mind: How good people are divided by politics and religion*. Penguin Books.

Hales, A. H., & Williams, K. D. (2018). Marginalized individuals and extremism: The role of ostracism in openness to extreme groups. *Journal of Social Issues*, *74* (1), 75–92. https:///doi.org/10.1111/josi.12257

Haslam, N. (2006). Dehumanization: An integrative review. *Personality and Social Psychology Review*, *10*(3), 252–264. https://doi.org/10.1207/s15327957pspr1003_4

Heejung, K., & Markus, H. R. (1999). Deviance or uniqueness, harmony or conformity? A cultural analysis. *Journal of Personality and Social Psychology*, *77*(4), 785–800. https://doi.org/10.1037/0022-3514.77.4.785

Heine, S. J. (2010). Cultural psychology. In S. T. Fiske, D. T. Gilbert, & G. Lindzey (Eds.), *Handbook of social psychology* (pp. 1423–1464). John Wiley & Sons.

Heine, S. J., & Hamamura, T. (2007). In search of East Asian self-enhancement. *Personality and Social Psychology Review*, *11*(1), 4–27. https://doi.org/10.1177/1088868306294587

Heine, S. J., Kitayama, S., Lehman, D. R., et al. (2001). Divergent consequences of success and failure in Japan and North America: An investigation of self-improving motivations and malleable selves. *Journal of Personality and Social Psychology*, *81*, 599–615. https://doi.org/10.1037/0022-3514.81.4.599

Henrich, J. (2021). *The weirdest people in the world. How the West became psychologically peculiar and particularly prosperous*. Penguin Books.

Henrich, J., Heine, S. J., & Norenzayan, A. (2010). The weirdest people in the world? *Behavioral and Brain Sciences*, *33*(2–3), 61–83. https://doi.org/10.1017/s0140525x0999152x

Hogg, M. A. (2021). Uncertain self in a changing world: A foundation for radicalization, populism, and autocratic leadership. *European Review of Social Psychology*, *32*(2), 235–268. https://doi.org/10.1080/10463283.2020.1827628

Hogg, M. A., Meehan, C., & Farquharson, J. (2010). The solace of radicalism: Self-uncertainty and group identification in the face of threat. *Journal of Experimental Social Psychology*, *46*(6), 1061–1066. https://doi.org/10.1016/j.jesp.2010.05.005

Hogg, M., & Wagoner, J. A. (2016). Normative exclusion and attraction to extreme groups: Resolving identity-uncertainty. In K. D. Williams, & S. A. Nida (Eds.), *Ostracism, exclusion, and rejection* (pp. 18–31). Routledge.

Horgan, J. (2008). From profiles to pathways and roots to routes: Perspectives from psychology on radicalization into terrorism. *The Annals of the American Academy of Political and Social Science*, *618*, 80–94. https://doi.org/10.1177/0002716208317539

Horgan, J. (2011). Interviewing the terrorists: Reflections on fieldwork and implications for future research. *Behavioral Sciences of Terrorism and Political Aggression*, *4*(3), 195–211. https://doi.org/10.1080/19434472.2011.594620

Horgan, J. (2014). *The psychology of terrorism* (2nd ed.). Routledge.

IEP (2023). Global Terrorism Index 2023. Institute for Economics and Peace. www .economicsandpeace.org/wp-content/uploads/2023/03/GTI-2023-web.pdf

Iyengar, S. S., & Leeper, M. R. (2002). Choice and its consequences: On the costs and benefits of self-determination. In A. Tesser, D. A. Stapel, & J. V. Wood (Eds.), *Self and motivation: Emerging psychological perspectives* (pp. 71–96). American Psychological Association.

Jasinskaja-Lahti, I., Liebkind, K., & Solheim, E. (2009) To identify or not to identify? National disidentification as an alternative reaction to perceived ethnic discrimination. *Applied Psychology: An International Review, 58*(1), 105–128. https://doi.org/10.1111/j.1464-0597.2008.00384.x

Jin, E. S., & Josephs, R. A. (2016). Acute and chronic physiological consequences of social rejection. In K. D. Williams, & S. A. Nida (Eds.), *Ostracism, exclusion, and rejection* (pp. 81–94). Routledge.

Jones, E. E., Carter-Sowell, A. R., Kelly, J. R., & Williams, K. D. (2009). "I'm out of the loop": Ostracism through information exclusion. *Group Processes & Intergroup Relations, 12*(2), 157–174. https://doi.org/10.1177/1368430208101054

Kamans, E. E. H., Gordijn, E. H., Oldenhuis, H., & Otten, S. (2009). What I think you see is what you get: Influence of prejudice on assimilation to meta-stereotypes among Dutch Moroccan teenagers. *European Journal of Social Psychology, 39*(5), 842–851. https://doi.org/10.1002/ejsp.593

Kashima, Y., Siegal, M., Tanaka, K., & Isaka, H. (1988). Universalism in lay conceptions of distributive justice: A cross-cultural examination. *International Journal of Psychology, 23*, 51–64. https://doi.org/10.1080/00207598808247752

Kim, H. S., & Markus, H. R. (1999). Deviance or uniqueness, harmony or conformity? A cultural analysis. *Journal of Personality and Social Psychology, 77*, 785–800. https://doi.org/10.1037/0022-3514.77.4.785

King, L. A., & Geise, A. C. (2011). Being forgotten: Implications for the experience of meaning in life. *The Journal of Social Psychology, 15*(16), 696–709. https://doi .org/10.1080/00224545.2010.522620

Knapton, H. M., Bäck, H., & Bäck, E. A. (2015). The social activist: Conformity to the ingroup following rejection as a predictor of political participation. *Social Influence, 10*(2), 97–108. https://doi.org/10.1080/15534510.2014.966856

Koomen, W., & van der Plight, J. (2016). *The psychology of radicalization and terrorism*. Routledge.

Kruglanski, A. W., Bélanger, J. J., & Gunaratna, R. (2019). *The three pillars of radicalization: Needs, narratives, and networks.* Oxford University Press.

Kruglanski, A. W., Gelfand, M. J., Bélanger, J. J., et al. (2014). The psychology of radicalization and deradicalization: How significance quest impacts violent extremism. *Advances in Political Psychology, 35*, 69–93. https://10.1111/ pops.12163

Kruglanski, A., Webber, D., & Koehler, D. (2020). *The radical's journey: How German neo-Nazis voyaged to the edge and back.* Oxford University Press.

Lorde, A. (1984). *Sister outsider: Essays and Speeches.* Crossing Press.

Markus, H. R., & Kitayama, S. (1991). Culture and the self: Implications for cognition, emotion, and motivation. *Psychological Review*, *98*, 224–253. https://doi.org/10.1037/0033-295X.98.2.224

McCauley, C., & Moskalenko, S. (2008). Mechanisms of political radicalization: Pathways towards terrorism. *Terrorism and Political Violence*, *20*(3), 415–433. https://doi.org/10.1080/09546550802073367

Mesquita, B. (2001). Emotions in collectivist and individualist contexts. *Journal of Personality and Social Psychology*, *80*, 68–74. https://doi.org/10.1037/0022-3514.80.1.68

Milla, M. N., Yustisia, W., Shadiqi, M. A., & Arifin, H. H. (2022). Mechanisms of 3 N model on radicalization: Testing the mediation by group identity and ideology of the relationship between need for significance and violent extremism. *Studies in Conflict & Terrorism*, 1–15. https://doi.org/10.1080/1057610X.2022.2034231

Moghaddam, F. M. (2005). The staircase to terrorism: A Psychological exploration. *American Psychologist*, *60*(2), 161–169. https://doi.org/10.1037/0003-066X.60.2.161

Molinario, E., Jasko, K., Webber, D., & Kruglanski, A. W. (2021). The social psychology of violent extremism. In A. W. Kruglanski, K. Kopetz, & E. Szumowska (Eds.), *The psychology of extremism: A motivational perspective* (pp. 259–279). Routledge.

Moskalenko, S., & McCauley, C. (2020). *Radicalization to terrorism: What everyone needs to know*. Oxford University Press.

Mousa, S. (2020). Building social cohesion between Christians and Muslims through soccer in post-ISIS Iraq. *Science*, *369*(6505), 866–870. https://doi.org/10.1126/science.abb3153

Moyano, M., Lobato, R. M., Blaya-Burgo, M., et al. (2023). Preventing violent extremism in youth through sports: An intervention from the 3 N model. *Psychology of Sport & Exercise*, *63*, 102283. https://doi.org/10.1016/j.psychsport.2022.102283

Nisbett, R. E., & Cohen, D. (1996). *Culture of honor: The psychology of violence in the South*. Boulder.

Obaidi, M., Anjum, G., Bierwiaczonek, K., et al. (2023). Cultural threat perceptions predict violent extremism via need for cognitive closure. *Proceedings of the National Academy of Sciences*, *120*(20), e2213874120. https://doi.org/10.1073/pnas.2213874120

Obaidi, M., Anjum, G., Lindström, J., et al. (2020). The role of Muslim identity in predicting violent behavioural intentions to defend Muslims. *Group Processes & Intergroup Relations*, *23*(8), 1267–1282. https://doi.org/10.1177/1368430220920929

Obaidi, M., Kunst, J. R., Kteily, N., Thomsen, L., & Sidanius, J. (2018). Living under threat: Mutual threat perception drives anti-Muslim and anti-Western hostility in the age of terrorism. *European Journal of Social Psychology*, *48*(5), 567–584. https://doi.org/10.1002/ejsp.2362

Obaidi, M., Thomsen, L., & Bergh, R. (2018). "They think we are a threat to their culture": Meta-cultural threat fuels willingness and endorsement of extremist violence against the cultural outgroup. *International Journal of Conflict and Violence, 12*(12), 1–13. https://doi.org/10.4119/UNIBI/ijcv.647

Ozer, S., Obaidi, M., & Pfattheicher, S. (2020). Group membership and radicalization: A cross-national investigation of collective self-esteem underlying extremism. *Group Processes & Intergroup Relations, 23*(8), 1230–1248. https://doi.org/10.1177/1368430220922901

Pfundmair, M. (2019). Ostracism promotes a terrorist mindset. *Behavioral Sciences of Terrorism and Political Aggression, 11*(2), 134–148. https://doi.org/10.1080/19434472.2018.1443965

Pfundmair, M., & Mahr, K. A. M. (2022). How group processes push excluded people into a radical mindset: An experimental investigation. *Group Processes & Intergroup Relationships, 26*(6), 1289–1309. http://dx.doi.org/10.1177/13684302221107782

Pfundmair, M., & Wetherell, G. (2019). Ostracism drives group moralization and extreme group behavior. *The Journal of Social Psychology, 159*(5), 518–530. https://doi.org/10.1080/00224545.2018.1512947

Pretus, C., Hamid, N., Sheikh, H., et al. (2019). Ventromedial and dorsolateral prefrontal interactions underlie will to fight and die for a cause. *Social Cognitive and Affective Neuroscience, 14*(6), 569–577. https://doi.org/10.1093/scan/nsz034

Rabasa, A., Pettyjohn, S. L., Ghez, J. J., & Boucek, C. (2010). *Deradicalizing Islamist extremists*. RAND Corporation. www.rand.org/content/dam/rand/pubs/monographs/2010/RAND_MG1053.pdf

Riva, P., & Eck, J. (2016). The many faces of social exclusion. In P. Riva, & J. Eck (Eds.), *Social exclusion: Psychological approaches to understanding and reducing its impact* (pp. ix–xv). Springer International.

Saheed, A. (2021). *Countering Islamophobia/anti-Muslim hatred to eliminate discrimination and intolerance based on religion or beliefs*. Human Rights Council. www.ohchr.org/en/press-releases/2021/03/un-expert-says-anti-muslim-hatred-rises-epidemic-proportions-urges-states

Santana, N. S., Inman, M., & Birnir, J. K. (2013). Religion, government coalitions, and terrorism. *Terrorism and Political Violence, 25*(1), 29–52. https://doi.org/10.1080/09546553.2013.733250

Schultz, J. F., Bahrami-Rad, D., Beauchamp, J. P., & Henrich, J. (2019). The church, intensive kinship, and global psychological variation. *Science, 366*(6466). https://doi.org/10.1126/science.aau5141

Schuurman, B. (2020). Research on terrorism, 2007–2016: A review of data, methods, and authorship. *Terrorism and Political violence, 32*(5), 1011–1026. https://doi.org/10.1080/09546553.2018.1439023

Sheikh, H., Gómez, Á., & Atran, S. (2016). Empirical evidence for the devoted actor model. *Current Anthropology, 57*(13), S204–S209. https://doi.org/10.1086/686221

Shweder, R. A., Munch, N. C., Mahaparta, M., & Park, L. (1997). The "big three" of morality (autonomy, community, divinity) and the "big three" explanations of suffering. In A. M. Brandt, & P. Rozin (Eds.), *Morality and health* (pp. 119–172). Taylor & Francis.

Sidanius, J., Kteily, N., Levin, S., Pratto, F., & Obaidi, M. (2016). Support for asymmetric violence among Arab populations: The clash of cultures, social identity, or counterdominance? *Group Processes & Intergroup Relations, 19*(3), 343–359. https://doi.org/10.1177/1368430215577224

Silke, A. (2009). Contemporary terrorism studies: Issues in research. In R. Jackson, M. B. Smyth, & J. Gunning (Eds.), *Critical terrorism studies: A field research agenda* (pp. 34–48). Routledge.

Silke, A., Morrison, J., Maiberg, G., Slay, C., & Stewart, R. (2021). The phoenix model of disengagement and deradicalization from terrorism and violent extremism. *Monatsschrift Fur Kriminologie and Strafrechtsreform, 104*(3), 310–320. https://doi.org/10.1515/mks-2021-0128

Smart Richman, L., & Leary, M. R. (2009). Reactions to discrimination, stigmatization, ostracism, and other forms of interpersonal rejection: A multimotive model. *Psychological Review, 116*(2), 365–383. https://doi.org/10.1037/a0015250

Smith, H. J., Pettigrew, T. F., Pippin, G. M., & Bialosiewicz, S. (2012). Relative deprivation: A theoretical and meta-analytic review. *Personality and Social Psychology Review, 16*(3), 203–232. https://doi.org/10.1177/1088868311430825

Stephan, W. G., & Stephan, C. W. (2000). An integrated threat theory of prejudice. In S. Oskamp (Ed.), *Reducing prejudice and discrimination* (pp. 23–45). Lawrence Erlbaum Associates.

Swann, W. B. Jr., Buhrmester, M. D., Gómez, A., et al. (2014). What makes a group worth dying for? Identity fusion fosters perception of familial ties, promoting self-sacrifice. *Journal of Personality and Social Psychology, 106*(6), 912–926. https://doi.org/10.1037/A0035809

Swann, W. B. Jr., Gómez, Á., Buhrmester, M. D., et al. (2014). Contemplating the ultimate sacrifice: Identity fusion channels pro-group affect, cognition, and moral decision making. *Journal of Personality and Social Psychology, 106*(5), 713–727. https://doi.org/10.1037/a0035809

Swann, W. B. Jr., Gómez, Á., Seyle, D. C., Morales, J. F., & Huici, C. (2009). Identity fusion: The interplay of personal and social identities in extreme group behavior. *Journal of Personality and Social Psychology, 95*(5), 995–1011. https://doi.org/10.1037/a0013668

Swann, W. B. Jr., Jetten, J., Gómez, Á., Whitehouse, H., & Bastian, B. (2012). When group membership gets personal: A theory of identity fusion. *Psychological Review, 119*(3), 441–456. https://doi.org/10.1037/a0028589

Trompenaars, F., & Hampden-Turner, C. (1998). *Riding the waves of culture: Understanding cultural diversity in global business* (2nd ed.). McGraw-Hill.

UN (2006). The United Nations global counter-terrorism strategy. United Nations: Office of Counter-Terrorism. www.un.org/counterterrorism/un-global-coun ter-terrorism-strategy

UN (2016). Leaving no one behind: The imperative of inclusive development. Report on the world social situation 2016. United Nations: Department of

Economic and Social Affairs. www.un.org/esa/socdev/rwss/2016/full-report
.pdf

UNODC (2015). Preventing violent extremism through sport. United Nations
Office on Drugs and Crime. www.unodc.org/documents/justice-and-prison-
reform/UNODC_Combating_Violence_against_Migrants.pdf

Uskul, A. K., Cross, S. E., Gunsoy, G., & Gul, P. (2019). Cultures of honor. In
S. Kitayama, & D. Cohen (Eds.), *Handbook of cultural psychology* (pp. 793–821).
Guilford Press.

Uskul, A. K., Kirchner-Häusler, A., Vignoles, V. L., et al. (2023). Neither Eastern
nor Western: Patterns of independence and interdependence in the
Mediterranean societies. *Journal of Personality and Social Psychology, 125*(3),
471–495. https://doi.org/10.1037pspa0000342

van Bergen, A. P. L., Wolf, J. R. L. M., Badou, M., et al. (2018). The association
between social exclusion or inclusion and health in EU and OECD countries:
A systematic review. *The European Journal of Public Health, 29*(3), 575–582.
https://doi.org/10.1093/eurpub/cky143

van Bergen, D. D., Feddes, A. F., Doosje, B., & Pels, T. V. M. (2015). Collective
identity factors and the attitude toward violence in defense of ethnicity or
religion among Muslim youth of Turkish and Moroccan descent.
International Journal of Intercultural Relations, 47, 89–100. https://doi.org/
10.1016/j.ijintrel.2015.03.026

van den Boss, K. (2018). *Why people radicalize.* Oxford University Press.

Vergani, M., Iqbal, M., Ilbahar, E., & Barton, G. (2018). The three Ps of radicalization: Push, pull and personal. A systematic scoping review of the scientific
evidence about radicalization into violent extremism. *Studies in Conflict and
Terrorism, 43*(10), 854. https://doi.org/10.1080/1057610X.2018.1505686

Vignoles, V. L., Owe, E., Becker, M., et al. (2016). Beyond the "east–west" dichotomy: Global variation in cultural models of selfhood. *Journal of Experimental
Psychology: General, 145*(8), 966–1000. https://doi.org/10.1037/xge0000175

Webber, D., Chernikova, M., Kruglanski, A. W., et al. (2018). Deradicalizing
detained terrorists. *Political Psychology, 39*(3), 539–556. https://doi.org/
10.1111/pops.12428

Weiss, C. M., Ran, S., & Halperin, E. (2023). Educating for inclusion: Diversity
Education programs can reduce prejudice towards outgroups in Israel.
Proceedings of the National Academy of Sciences, 120(16), e2218621120.
https://doi.org/10.1073/pnas.2218621120

Wesselmann, E. D., Bradley, E., Taggart, R. S., & Williams, K. D. (2022). Exploring
social exclusion: Were we are and where we're going. *Social and Personality
Psychology Compass, 17*, e12714. https://doi.org/10.1111/spc3.12714

Whitehouse, H., Jong, J., Buhrmester, M., et al. (2017). The evolution of extreme
cooperation via shared dysphoric experiences. *Scientific Reports, 7*, 44292.
https://doi.org/10.1038/sreo44292

Whittaker, J. (2020). The online behaviors of Islamic state terrorists in the United States. *Criminology & Public Policy*, *20*, 177–203. https://doi.org/10.1111/1745-9133.12537

Williams, K. D. (2009). Ostracism: A temporal need-threat model. *Advances in Experimental Social Psychology*, *41*, 275–314. https://doi.org/10.1016/S0065-2601(08)00406-1

Wolfovicz, M., Litmanovitz, Y., Weisburd, D., & Hasisi, B. (2020a). Cognitive and behavioral radicalization: A systematic review of the putative risk and protective factors. *Campbell Systematic Reviews*, *17*, e1174. https://doi.org/10.1002/cl2.1102

Wolfovicz, M., Litmanovitz, Y., Weisburd, D., & Hasisi, B. (2020b). A field-wide systematic review and meta-analysis of putative risk and protective factors for radicalization outcomes. *Journal of Quantitative Criminology*, *36*, 407–447. https://doi.org/10.1007/s10940-019-09439

Wong, Y., & Tsai, J. (2007). Cultural models of shame and guilt. In L. Tracy, R. W. Robins, & J. P. Tagney (Eds.), *The self-conscious emotions: Theory and research* (pp. 209–223). Guilford Press.

PART III

Topics Related to the Exclusion–Extremism Link

11

Rejection and Serious Aggression

Hurt People Hurt People

ROBIN M. KOWALSKI AND MARK R. LEARY

If no one turned around when we entered, answered when we spoke, or minded what we did, but if every person we met "cut us dead," and acted as if we were non-existing things, a kind of rage and impotent despair would ere long well up in us, from which the cruelest bodily torture would be a relief.

(William James, 1890, p. 281)

Human beings are highly motivated to be connected to other people – to interact with others, maintain supportive social relationships, and belong to social groups. Indeed, people are rarely indifferent to whether they are being accepted or rejected by others, and the motivation to be accepted and to belong influences a great deal of human cognition, emotion, and behavior (Baumeister & Leary, 1995; Leary & Gabriel, 2022). When people believe that they are not being valued and accepted as much as they desire – through social exclusion, devaluation, marginalization, or feeling like they do not matter to those around them – they generally respond in one of three ways: by behaving prosocially in order to be accepted, withdrawing to avoid further hurt, or responding aggressively, as suggested in the opening quote by William James (Maner et al., 2007; Richman & Leary, 2009). Our focus in this chapter is on aggressive responses to social rejection.

Experimental studies on the effects of rejection on aggression have found that people who have been rejected often become angry and aggress against others in large and small ways. For example, they evaluate other people more negatively (e.g., Bourgeois & Leary, 2001; Leary et al., 1995; Twenge et al., 2001) and are more likely to administer noxious stimuli (such as shock, loud noise, and hot sauce) to other participants, sometimes even if those other individuals were not directly involved in rejecting them (e.g., Kirkpatrick et al., 2002; Twenge et al., 2001; Warburton et al., 2003). Although the forms of aggression studied in experimental studies are, by necessity, relatively innocuous, rejection has also been linked to more extreme forms of aggression, including school and mass shootings, intimate partner violence, hazing, retaliative suicide, and cyberbullying. The current chapter focuses on these extreme forms of aggression.

11.1   The Psychological Underpinnings and Consequences of Interpersonal Rejection

Before examining the link between rejection and extreme forms of aggression, we must clarify key terms used throughout the chapter. Many of the constructs used by researchers in this field involve everyday terms – such as rejection, exclusion, ostracism, and (not) belonging – that are often imprecise or inadequately defined, making it difficult to know whether studies purporting to study the same phenomenon actually do. Each of these terms has a different connotation, as well as its own conceptual shortcomings. For example, people do not experience mere "exclusion" as rejection (Leary et al., 1995); people can feel rejected even when they are not objectively "rejected" in any sense (Bourgeois & Leary, 2001; Leary et al., 1998), and people can feel that they are rejected from or that they do not belong to groups of which they are actually a member (Bourgeois & Leary, 2001). In addition, many of these terms – such as acceptance/rejection, inclusion/exclusion, belonging/not belonging, and mattering/anti-mattering – are typically treated as dichotomous when, in fact, feelings of rejection clearly lie on a continuum.

To avoid confusion, we will use the term "rejection" to refer to all experiences in which people perceive that they are inadequately accepted or do not belong because people invariably feel rejected in all these phenomena. For example, people feel rejected when they perceive that they are explicitly rejected, intentionally excluded or isolated, ostracized, marginalized, dismissed, avoided, discriminated against, and denied group membership, and when they do not matter or fit in (Leary, 2001; Richman & Leary, 2009). To be clear, these phenomena differ in important ways, but they all involve the sense of being rejected.

In addition, we use the concept of "relational value" to integrate findings across terms and phenomena that involve the experience of rejection. Several years ago, Leary (2001) suggested that acceptance and rejection may be fruitfully conceptualized in terms of relational value. In this view, people who seek acceptance are fundamentally interested in establishing, maintaining, or increasing their relational value to other people – that is, the degree to which others value having a relationship with them. Being relationally valued means not only that the person is "accepted" (in the everyday use of the term), but also that the person is likely to receive an array of desirable outcomes from those who value them.

Like feelings of acceptance and rejection, relational value lies on a continuum: people may believe that their relational value to another person in a particular context ranges from zero to a high level. In this view, people feel rejected when they perceive that their relational value to a certain person (or group of people) in a particular context is not as high as they want it to be. Conversely, people who feel that their relational value to others in a particular context is sufficiently high feel that they are accepted.

Rejection (or, equivalently, perceiving that one's relational value is unacceptably low) invariably involves both emotional and motivational outcomes. An array of negative emotions can arise from rejection experiences, including hurt feelings (which is perhaps the primary emotional reaction to rejection), sadness (when a valued relationship is lost), anger (when rejection is viewed as unjustified), guilt or shame (when one's own misbehavior leads to actual or potential relational devaluation), and jealousy (when one's relational value to another person seems to be eroded by a third party; Leary, 2021; Leary et al., 2001).

Although these emotional reactions can be accompanied by a variety of behavioral reactions, our interest here is on aggressive behaviors. As we will explore throughout the chapter, many explanations have been offered to account for the link between rejection and aggression (Leary et al., 2006). For example, rejection is a source of pain and frustration, both of which can elicit aggression in human beings and other animals. Some aggression is explicitly motivated by retribution, an effort to inflict suffering on someone who has rejected us. In other instances, aggression seems to be motivated by a desire to influence another person's behavior, as when someone deters a romantic partner from ending a relationship through violence or threats of violence. Sometimes, people use aggression as a self-presentational effort to influence observers' impressions of them to deter other people from treating them in a dismissive or rejecting manner. Others have suggested that some aggression reflects an effort to reestablish a sense of control when social situations go awry or an effort to boost self-esteem following rejection. Aggression may also occur from disinhibition or loss of self-control.

Regardless of the precise mechanism or motivation underlying aggression in a particular case, one fact is clear: A good deal of aggression and violence is perpetrated by people who feel that other people inadequately value having relationships with them. In such cases, the perpetrator feels rejected, is invariably hurt and angry, and behaves aggressively, often for reasons that are known only to them. In the following sections, we examine five varieties of extreme aggression that result from rejection – school and mass shootings, intimate partner violence, hazing, suicide, and cyberbullying. Common to all these forms of aggression is the fact that, when people are hurt, they desire to hurt others.

11.2   School and Mass Shootings

One of the clearest examples of the link between social rejection and aggression can be found in school (K–12) and mass shootings (Peterson & Densley, 2021). Statistics for the number of K–12 and mass shootings vary a great deal depending on the criteria used to define types of shootings. For example, in the Violence Project mass shooter database (Peterson & Densley, 2023), a mass shooting is defined as

> a multiple homicide incident in which four or more victims are murdered with firearms – not including the offender(s) – within one event, and at least some of the murders occurred in a public location or locations in close geographical proximity (e.g., a workplace, school, restaurant, or other public settings), and the murders are not attributable to any other underlying criminal activity or commonplace circumstance (armed robbery, criminal competition, insurance fraud, argument, or romantic triangle).

According to this definition, 190 mass shootings were perpetrated between 1966 and 2023. In contrast, the Gun Violence Archive, which defines mass shootings as an incident in which there is "a minimum of four victims shot, either injured or killed, not including any shooter," puts the number of mass shootings at 611 in 2020 alone.

In examining the relationship between social rejection and general aggressiveness, the direction of causality is often unclear: Does social rejection lead to aggressive behavior, or are aggressive people more likely to be socially rejected (Hales et al., this volume)? However, in the case of school and mass shootings, the direction seems clearer, showing that rejection precedes the violent behavior. Evidence for the link between rejection and school shootings can be found in both research on the topic and the verbiage of the shooters themselves. To examine empirical evidence for the role of rejection in school shootings, we conducted a study that examined predictors of K–12 shootings that occurred between January 1995 and March 2001 (Leary et al., 2003). To be included in our study, the shooting had to occur at school during the school day, someone had to be killed or injured, and the shooter had to be a student at the school. Evidence for interpersonal rejection was found in thirteen of the fifteen shootings that met these criteria. In some cases, the shooter had experienced a long-term history of rejection, often bullying. In other instances, the rejection was acute, such as the recent breakup of a close relationship. Dylan Klebold, one of the two Columbine shooters, wrote in his journal that "the lonely man strikes with absolute rage." Another shooter who sexualized his weapons stated that "weapons are not like people … They don't reject you. They need you. I wanted something that could not reject me" (Peterson & Densley, 2021: 21). Of course, many youths in K–12 are bullied or experience romantic breakups yet do not shoot anyone. Additional risk factors were also present in most shootings, including a history of psychological problems, a fascination with death, and a fascination with guns and violence.

In 2021, we built on our 2003 study by examining the extent to which these same predictors applied to K–12 shootings that had occurred since March 2001 as well as to mass shootings (in which four or more individuals excluding the shooter were killed; Peterson & Densley, 2023) that occurred outside of school (Kowalski et al., 2021). For K–12 shootings, we modified the criteria slightly from Leary et al. (2003) to include that the shooter could be a current *or former* student. Of the fifty-seven K–12 shootings that met the criteria, 63 percent of the shooters had experienced a long-term and/or acute rejection. Fifty-three percent of the mass shooters had experienced an acute rejection experience, most commonly a romantic breakup or being fired from work. For example, in 2019, a 36-year-old man who had been fired from his job with a trucking company opened fire in the west Texas towns of Odessa and Midland, killing seven people (Karimi & Lavandera, 2019). In addition, 20 percent of the mass shooters in the Kowalski et al. study reported a long-term history of rejection.

As with K–12 shootings, rejection was not the only factor involved in mass shootings. A history of psychological problems, a fascination with violence, and a fascination with guns were also associated with mass shootings (Kowalski et al., 2021, Study 3). According to Peterson and Densley (2021), who have studied mass shooters extensively, "Mass shooters are angry and lonely, and many of them fixate on specific people or groups they can blame for their own miserable circumstances. . . . Mass shooters not only research other perpetrators of mass shootings but also spend time in online communities where they become more radicalized towards violence" (p. 17).

The rejections experienced by K–12 and mass shooters can take many forms, two of which have already been mentioned: firings from work and romantic breakups. In other instances, however, the rejection seems to have involved adverse childhood experiences such as physical or sexual abuse at the hands of their parents or bullying at the hands of their peers. In our study, 49 percent of the mass shooters had experienced some type of adverse childhood experience (Kowalski et al., 2021, Study 3). People who experience repeated rejection, particularly in childhood, often come to expect ongoing rejection (Sjåstad et al., 2021), leading them to behave in "protective" ways that might help them deter or avoid future rejection, such as behaving aggressively toward others or avoiding social interactions and relationships. Ironically, these behaviors push other people away and lead them to exclude the individual, creating a vicious cycle of exclusion and rejection sometimes followed by aggression.

Rejection can also take the form of workplace discrimination. Although K–12 school shooters are almost exclusively White, Blacks represent 20 percent of mass shooters, making them disproportionately represented among mass shooters (Blacks compose only 13 percent of the population of the United States; Peterson & Densley, 2021). According to Peterson and Densley, most shootings perpetrated by Black individuals occur in the workplace where they felt they were subject to racism, discriminated against by being paid lower wages and receiving fewer benefits, and generally marginalized. For example, the Molson Coors shooter in Milwaukee, Wisconsin, shot and killed five coworkers and himself in 2020. Although reports indicated that he experienced psychological problems, these reports also suggested that he had experienced racism on the job, including a noose being placed either in or on his locker (Lutheran & Barton, 2020). Although not classified as a mass shooting (because only two people were killed), similar circumstances surround the shooting of two news reporters in Virginia in 2015 (Cox et al., 2015). The gunman, also a news reporter, had been fired from multiple television stations prior to the shooting and had filed multiple reports of racism and discrimination, including the claim that his colleagues sometimes left a watermelon in the office to taunt him (Robertson, 2015) and that he had been called a "monkey" by a news producer in Tallahassee (Robertson, 2015). Prior to the shooting, he stated "I've been a human powder keg for a while . . . just waiting to go BOOM!" (Robertson, 2015).

Social rejection can also arise from how people perceive that their national, ethnic, or racial group is being treated. For example, some mass shooters believed that the position of Whites within the United States is being usurped by Blacks and immigrants (Graupmann & Wesselmann, this volume). Along those lines, the shooter who killed nine at Mother Emanuel AME Church in Charleston, South Carolina, wanted to start a "race war" (Peterson & Densley, 2021, p. 129), believed that Blacks should be enslaved again, and praised the Ku Klux Klan. Similarly, incels (young men who are involuntarily celibate because they can't attract women) think that they have been excluded from romantic and sexual relationships that everyone else seems to have (Rousis & Swann, this volume). The 22-year-old who shot and killed six people in Isla Vista, California, stated in his autobiography that

> It was society's fault for rejecting me. It was women's fault for refusing to have sex with me . . . women's rejection of me was a declaration of war . . . I will destroy all women because I can never have them. I will make them suffer for rejecting me. I will arm myself with deadly weapons and wage a war against *all women and the men they are attracted to.* And I will slaughter them like the animals they are.   (Dalrymple, 2014)

Some shooters, such as the Charleston shooter and the Isla Vista shooter, go on deep dives into the Internet to find support for the positions they hold. In keeping with the confirmation bias, they search selectively, finding support for their beliefs that then, with validation, become more extreme. Among those who already believe that they and/or their national, ethnic, or racial group are being marginalized and rejected, these feelings and perceptions become even more extreme. Indeed, according to Peterson and Densley (2021, p. 131), "in the internet age, even 'lone wolves' are never truly alone, and it is ideology that helps them feel part of the pack. In fact, extremism is less an ideological movement and more of a social one. It offers people with shared deficits a sense of collective identity and belonging that previously did not exist."

Some shooters also search the Internet for information about previous shooters. Unsure how to handle the rejection and isolation they are experiencing, they may look to shooters, such as Dylan Klebold and Eric Harris, the Columbine shooters, who also experienced rejection and isolation. They not only receive validation for their own feelings but also obtain information on how to respond to the personal crisis that they are experiencing (Peterson & Densley, 2021).

In some cases, violence becomes a means for shooters who have been told or made to feel that they do not matter, that they are invisible, to become known. Referring to the shooter who killed the two news reporters in Virginia in 2016, a 26-year-old man who killed nine at an Oregon community college stated in his blog, "I have noticed that so many people like him are all alone and unknown, yet when they spill a little blood, the whole world knows who they are. A man who was known by no one, is now known by everyone" (Sidner et al., 2015). He also stated in his manifesto, "And here I am, 26, with no friends, no job, no girlfriend, a virgin. I long ago realized that society likes to deny people like me these things" (Anderson, 2017).

COVID-19 brought a temporary respite to school and mass shootings in the United States because schools were closed. No mass shootings occurred within the United States between March 15, 2020, when four were killed and three injured in Springfield, Missouri, and January 9, 2021, when five were killed and three injured in Chicago, Illinois (Peterson & Densley, 2023). Even though the feelings of potential shooters may not have abated, the opportunities to act on those feelings were certainly reduced (Schildkraut & Turanovic, 2022). However, COVID also increased potential shooters' isolation and gave them time to spend on the Internet seeking information about previous shooters and finding validation for their beliefs. Thus, when society reopened, a spate of mass shootings erupted, including shootings at three spas in Atlanta and one at King Soopers grocery store in Boulder, Colorado, where ten people lost their lives (Peterson & Densley, 2023).

11.3 Intimate Partner Violence

Intimate partner violence (IPV) encompasses a broad array of behaviors that involve physical, psychological, or sexual aggression by a current or former intimate partner, such as a spouse, dating partner, or ongoing sexual partner (Breiding et al., 2015). IPV occurs in response to many factors – including heated arguments, perceived disrespect, and failure to behave as one's partner demands – but many instances of IPV stem directly from events that cause one partner to feel rejected by the other. In many cases, the rejection is explicit, as when a partner ends or threatens to end a relationship, but, often, feelings of rejection arise from mundane events that cause people to perceive that their partner is ignoring, dismissing, or criticizing them. Whether explicit or inferred, at their core, these kinds of events may lead people to perceive that their relational value to their partner is low.

Even the most extreme form of IPV, homicide, can result from perceived rejection. In an analysis of 551 cases in which men had killed their wives, Crawford and Gartner (1992) concluded that 45 percent of the murders occurred in response to a real or imminent separation (see also Barnard et al., 1982), and the event that directly precipitated the murder was most often one in which the man felt rejected. Not only was the couple typically separated at the time, but the men explicitly reported being unable to deal with the rejection or their lack of control over their wives. Interestingly, perceived rejection seems to provoke homicide more for men than women; Barnard et al. (1982) found that events that led women to murder their husbands more often involved some form of physical or verbal abuse by the husband.

The link between perceived rejection and IPV is substantiated by a good deal of research, although not all this research has explicitly identified "rejection" as the cause. For example, in an early study of IPV among dating couples, Makepeace (1989) found that rejection accounted for 15 percent of the violent episodes among people who were dating steadily and 11 percent of the episodes for those who were living together. But these figures greatly underestimated the role of rejection in dating violence because sexual refusal and jealousy, both of which can convey low relational value and elicit feelings of rejection, accounted for large numbers of additional cases of violence.

Jealousy, in particular, figures prominently in IPV (Dobash & Dobash, 2015). Many studies have linked IPV to jealousy seemingly without recognizing that jealousy inherently involves concerns with rejection. Specifically, jealousy arises when people believe that their relationship with another person is being undermined by the presence or intrusion of a third party (Guerrero et al., 2004). Wilson and Daly (1996) found that both women who are victims of IPV and the men who abuse them report jealousy as the most common precursor to violence. Similarly, a meta-analysis of studies of IPV in Latin American countries revealed that jealousy was the second most common trigger of IPV after alcohol consumption (Bott et al., 2012). Jealousy is also related to IPV among gay and bisexual men (Stephenson et al., 2023).

IPV is also provoked by real or imagined infidelity (Barnard et al., 1982; Conroy, 2014; de Weerth & Kalma, 1993; Nemeth et al., 2012; Shackelford et al., 2005), which obviously involves perceived rejection. Crawford and Gartner's (1992) analysis showed that, in 15 percent of the cases in which men killed their wives, the husbands suspected that their wives were having an extramarital affair (see also, Barnard et al., 1982).

Several theorists have suggested that aggression, including homicide, in response to infidelity may arise from an evolved mechanism (Arnocky et al., 2022; Buss & Duntley, 2014). From an evolutionary perspective, partner infidelity is a serious threat to an animal's reproductive success. A partner's involvement with another mate can lead them to leave the relationship; possibly defect from caring for current offspring; result in the loss of material, social, and emotional benefits; and cause reputational damage. As a result, many animals, including human beings, appear to possess adaptations that function to prevent, curtail, and punish a partner's infidelity, and, among humans, these adaptations may result in IPV.

Given the role of perceived rejection in IPV, people who are particularly worried about being rejected are predisposed to respond strongly to signs that their relational value in a partner's eyes is low or declining, and attachment theory provides one framework for understanding individual differences in IPV (McClellan & Killeen, 2000). People who score high in attachment anxiety tend to have insecurities about their close relationships and are excessively dependent on their partners and friends for support and reassurance. As a result, they are especially vigilant to potential relationship threats and prone to jealousy (Dutton et al., 1994; Kim et al., 2018; Mauricio et al., 2007) and, importantly, more likely to engage in IPV (Babcock et al., 2000; Barbaro & Shackelford, 2019; Holtzworth-Munroe et al., 1997; Jackson et al., 2015; Mauricio et al., 2007). See Velotti and colleagues (2018) for an extensive review of the research on attachment style and IPV.

IPV is also related to borderline personality disorder which, among other things, involves deep concerns about rejection and abandonment (Jackson et al., 2015). A meta-analysis of 207 studies showed a robust link between borderline personality disorder and IPV (Spencer et al., 2019). In their frantic efforts to avoid real or imagined abandonment, people with borderline personality disorder tend to monitor and control their partners' activities and may become aggressive when they believe, often unjustly, that their partner is behaving in ways that undermine the relationship. To make matters worse, people with borderline personality disorder also display strong emotional reactions and have difficulty controlling their anger. In intimate relationships, concerns about abandonment paired with strong emotions manifests in unpredictable, uncontrollable outbursts of anger that may include aggression.

In sum, violence in intimate relationships often arises from concerns with how one is regarded and valued by one's partner. Real and imagined rejection often underlies IPV, including a large proportion of homicides in which one partner kills the other. The World Health Organization's analysis of global data from sixty-six countries found that, on average, intimate partner homicides accounted for about 40 percent of all killings of women and 6 percent of the murders of men (Stockl et al., 2013).

11.4   Hazing

Hazing – also referred to as ragging (Garg, 2009), initiation rites (Kirby & Wintrup, 2002), or rites of passage (Waldron & Kowalski, 2009) – is a broad term that refers to a variety of behaviors that are required to be accepted into a group but that involve embarrassment, humiliation, and sometimes physical pain. The behaviors included under the umbrella of hazing range from mild, acceptable initiation rites, such as attending a skit night or team roast, to severe, unacceptable initiation activities that involve being kidnapped and abandoned, publicly ridiculed, or physically hurt. Hazing occurs in many different types of groups, but most research has focused on the hazing of initiates into fraternities and sororities (Nuwer, 2001), sports teams (Hoover, 1999; Swingle & Salinas, 2018; Waldron & Kowalski, 2009), marching bands (Harris, 2011; Silveira, 2018; Silveira & Hudson, 2015), and the military (Keller et al., 2015; Knight & Boettcher, 2018).

Researchers have defined hazing differently depending on the organization in which it occurs, which has unnecessarily complicated analyses of hazing across various settings. For example, in the context of fraternities, the Fraternity Executives Association has defined hazing as "any action taken or situation created intentionally, whether on or off fraternity premises, to produce mental or physical discomfort, embarrassment, harassment, or ridicule" (Nuwer, 2018, p. 26). Applied to sports teams, hazing has been defined as

> any potentially humiliating, degrading, abusive, or dangerous activity expected of a junior-ranking athlete by a more senior team-mate, which does not contribute to either athlete's positive development, but is required to be *accepted* as part of a team, regardless of the junior-ranking athlete's willingness to participate. This includes, but is not limited to, any activity, no matter how traditional or seemingly benign, that sets apart or alienates any team-mate based on class, number of years on team, or athletic ability.   (Crow & MacIntosh, 2009, p. 449)

Despite differences in the criteria specified, definitions of hazing converge on a few common features. Hazing is typically perpetrated by senior or superior individuals against junior or inferior individuals (e.g., pledges, rookies, new employees), although hazing of senior members occasionally occurs (Knight & Boettcher, 2018). Sometimes, the newcomers are not yet members of the group, and hazing is used to test their suitability for group membership. More often, though– as with sports teams, bands, army recruits, new employees, and club initiates – newcomers are already members of the group, and the purpose of hazing is to make the rookies "real," full-fledged members in good standing.

A national survey of hazing among 11,482 college students (Allan & Madden, 2008) showed that 47 percent of students had experienced hazing before attending college. Although 55 percent (61 percent male; 52 percent female) of the students had experienced hazing victimization based on their responses to a checklist of behaviors, 90 percent of these did not label the behaviors as hazing. Hazing occurred most frequently on varsity athletic teams (74 percent), followed by fraternities/sororities (73 percent), club sports teams (64 percent), performing arts groups (56 percent), service groups (50 percent), and intramural teams (49 percent). Across all groups, the most common hazing behaviors involved drinking games (26 percent), singing or chanting by themselves or with select others in public (17 percent), associating with certain people but not others (12 percent), and consuming excessive amounts of alcohol leading to sickness or unconsciousness (12 percent).

We see three points of connection between hazing and the effects of social rejection on aggression. First, from the initiate's perspective, hazing often conveys that one has low relational value because, although one may be a nominal member of the group, one is not fully accepted until hazed. So, the hazing-related aggression is essentially due to the person's low status or relational value. Second, in everyday life, being mistreated usually conveys that one's relational value to the perpetrator is low, at least at the moment of the mistreatment. We don't typically humiliate, harass, or physically harm people whose relationships we value highly. Third, both perpetrating and tolerating hazing is motivated, in part, by a desire for social acceptance. Not only do victims typically endure whatever is demanded to be accepted by current group members, but perpetrators often inflict aggression on initiates because other group members expect them to and because they might suffer a loss of status or acceptance if they refuse to execute their hazing responsibilities. They may also justify the behavior, both now and in the future, which explains why victims often become perpetrators (Jost & Banaji, 1994; Oliff, 2002; Thomas & Meglich, 2018).

Although not limited to a specific age or demographic group, hazing manifests a developmental trend as prevalence rises from middle school through high school and young adulthood, declining as people enter their 30s. The need to belong, which peaks in adolescence and young adulthood (Graupensperger et al., 2018), may lead people to engage in behaviors they might otherwise not do in an attempt to be a member of a desired group (Baumeister & Leary, 1995; Joyce & Nirh, 2018; Owen et al., 2008). In reflecting on being hazed as a fraternity pledge, one man explicitly noted the link between hazing and concerns about acceptance and rejection, stating "From the college a capella group to a local fraternity house, students live in anxiety as they eagerly seek acceptance and some semblance of a sense of belonging. Unfortunately, some of today's organizations take advantage of that desperate need to belong" (Boettcher & Salinas, 2018, p. 19).

11.5 Suicide

Freud (1930) viewed depression as aggression turned inward, and many other theorists have suggested that a common factor underlying suicide is a feeling of social disconnection, as manifested in rejection, marginalization, thwarted belonging, social exclusion, and other experiences that convey low relational value (e.g., Durkheim, 1897/1951; Joiner, 2005; Mueller et al., 2021). One of the first to draw a connection between suicide and feelings of marginalization was Durkheim (1897/1951). In his sociological perspective on suicide, Durkheim proposed four types of suicide: egoistic, altruistic, anomic, and fatalistic. Egoistic suicide occurs among people who feel that they are poorly integrated in society; in other words, they do not belong (Moore, 2017). Altruistic suicide occurs among people who feel they fail to live up to the high standards held by those in their community and, therefore, no longer deserve to live. Anomic suicide occurs during times of economic turmoil, and fatalistic suicide stems from feelings of hopelessness and a lack of control over one's life (Moore, 2017). More recently, these four forms of suicide have been subsumed within a social capital framework, where social capital is defined in terms of people's social connections with others (Moore, 2017). In this view, low feelings of social capital are a major risk factor for suicide.

Along these lines, Joiner et al. (2009; see also Chu et al., 2017) suggested that thwarted belonging, perceived burdensomeness to other people, and hopelessness lead to suicidal ideation. Whether people with suicidal ideation attempt suicide is then moderated by the "capacity for suicide," for example, whether the person has the means to carry out the act or has a high tolerance for pain (Joiner et al., 2021). Whereas early research focused on general and/or trait hopelessness, more recently researchers have suggested that the hopelessness that predisposes people to suicide is specifically related to perceiving that one's current lack of belonging and/or perceived burdensomeness is not likely to change in the future (e.g., Chu et al., 2017; Klonsky & May, 2015).

Deas et al. (2023) recently found additional evidence of the link between rejection, anti-mattering, and suicide in their examination of suicide posts in the subreddit SuicideWatch. They found that nearly 70 percent of the posts contained sentiments of anti-mattering, defined as feeling insignificant and that no one cares. One poster in Deas et al.'s study stated:

> I am 38, past eight years I had over 1000 rejections from women telling me I was ugly, disgusting, worth less, use less, told me I had nothing to offer, would ignore me, laugh at me, mock me. guys would make comments on my pics and make comments like omfg, fat ugly pos and then barf emojis … I can't take life anymore and I can't take being single and alone and lonely. I am done. it ends tonight. its over.

Another stated:

> im just tired of being worthless. im not good enough for anyone ... was
> going to school for a while until i came out to my parents and they cut me
> off ... never had any job and ive been just whittling away at the money
> i had. im tired of being gay. im going to hell no matter what i do and even
> if thats wrong its not like i can be happy in this life- constant rejection. im
> ugly and fat and i get laughed at by even people i consider ugly. i have
> never and will never fit into their culture and obviously im not fitting into
> straight stuff either. my family hates me, i dont have friends, im going ot
> be homeless in a week, im out of money and ive been eating nothing but
> a bowl of plain rice a day for weeks ... dont tell me to go on welfare. id
> very seriously rather die.

Although this research highlights the link between rejection, belonging, mattering, and suicide, some may question whether suicide is, indeed, a form of aggression and, thus, relevant to the current chapter. The literature on aggressive or moralistic suicide (e.g., Manning, 2015) provides clarification. This form of suicide is motivated by a desire to permanently avoid interaction with other people as well as the desire to punish those whom the suicidal person perceives as a "wrongdoer," particularly those who have rejected them (Manning, 2015). Viewed this way, the person who commits aggressive or moralistic suicide does so (1) because of hopelessness regarding their relational value and social acceptance, and (2) explicitly as an act of aggression to inflict pain and suffering on those whom they perceive to have wronged them.

Manning (2015) found that most cases of aggressive or moralistic suicide occur because the suicidal person experienced some type of interpersonal rejection, such as divorce or infidelity, leading them to desire to induce guilt, remorse, or general suffering in the person (or people) left behind. For example, in one of Manning's case files, the person wrote:

> If you are reading this something has happened, you should have took my
> calls. All we needed to do was talk. You have always had a problem dealing
> [with] things. Now how are you going to deal [with] this. You should have
> kept your legs closed ... I don't care if you hate me now [because] each
> time you see our children you will see me ... What are you going to do?
> I hope you feel as bad as I have the past 4 weeks (Case #247).
>
> (Manning, 2015, p. 332)

Another suicide note stated:

> Katie, Maybe you are happy now. I thought about taking you [i.e.,
> committing homicidesuicide] but I don't think its worth while for
> I don't believe God will let you live to [sic] long. For you no good as
> they come. Take care of [daughter] I don't see how she could ever love you
> again. I can't understand why you left for there sure wasn't any one else if
> there was I wouldn't do this. Tell that doll I love her and to always be good.

> I wanted to talk to her but you made me so mad and I new [sic] I would cry. I have set here and cryed [sic] for an hour now. I hope you are happy. I don't see how you can stand to live ... You should frame this where you can read it wonse [sic] and a while you no good bitch (Case #493).(p. 332)

Interestingly, people who engage in moralistic suicide seem to believe that, on some level, they mattered to the individual against whom they are seeking revenge. If they did not matter to the surviving individual to some extent, then their suicide would have no effect.

In a twist on aggressive, retaliative suicide, in some tribal societies, suicide is used as a form of revenge in which the ghost of the dead individual is believed to come back to harass the person they desire to avenge (Jeffreys, 1952). For example, people who have been marginalized and rejected by being unjustly accused of crimes they didn't commit or of sorcery (Hurault, 1961) will sometimes commit suicide so that their spirit can seek revenge against those who made the false accusations or their descendants. Suicide in such tribal societies may also be used to rally tribal members against certain individuals. For example, battered wives may commit suicide to mobilize family members against a husband who repeatedly abused them (Manning, 2015). In all these cases, suicide is used to aggress against other people. Importantly, however, most suicides are not of this aggressive subtype.

11.6   Cyberbullying

Compared to the behaviors discussed thus far, the link between rejection and cyberbullying has received less research attention. However, there are clear relationships that warrant additional research, four of which we will examine in this section. Cyberbullying, or online bullying, involves bullying through electronic communication technologies (Kowalski et al., 2012). It can take a number of forms, including outing and trickery (e.g., getting someone to disclose information they would prefer others not to know and sharing that information), flaming (e.g., an online fight), harassment (e.g., repeatedly sending rude and/or offensive communications to others online), denigration (e.g., putting others down online), impersonation (e.g., pretending to be someone else online and disseminating negative information to others as that person), cyberstalking (e.g., online harassment that includes threats), and, most importantly for this chapter, exclusion (e.g., intentionally blocking or excluding people from online forums, platforms, chatrooms, and the like; Willard, 2007).

A related behavior, cybertrolling, has been defined as "the practice of behaving in a deceptive, destructive, or disruptive manner in a social setting on the internet with no apparent instrumental purpose" (Buckels et al., 2014, p. 97). Although similar, cyberbullying and cybertrolling are distinguished from one another by the seemingly aimless motivation of cybertrolls compared to the intentional nature of cyberbullying (Buckels et al., 2014; Wright, 2017). Seemingly motivated by sadistic desires, cybertrolls seek fun at others' expense.

One topic that has linked rejection to cyberbullying perpetration involves rejection sensitivity. As will be discussed in detail later, rejection sensitivity is "the disposition to anxiously expect, readily perceive. and intensely react to rejection by significant others" (Downey et al., 2000, p. 45; see also Romero-Canyas et al., 2010). Rejection sensitivity has been linked to social media use, with people high in rejection sensitivity more likely to use social media than people lower in rejection sensitivity (Demircioglu & Goncu-Kose, 2021; Farahini et al., 2011). Two types of rejection sensitivity have been identified that have relevance to cyberbullying perpetration, specifically angry rejection sensitivity and anxious rejection sensitivity. Angry rejection sensitivity is associated with aggressive behavior in general (Bondu & Krahe, 2015; Jacobs & Harper, 2013) as well as with cyberbullying perpetration in particular (Demircioglu & Goncu-Kose, 2022). However, anxious rejection sensitivity is associated with lower cyberbullying perpetration.

Second, people who have been cyberbullied often feel rejected and marginalized. In a study of cyberbullying experiences among youth 16 to 20 years of age (Kowalski & Toth, 2018), one student reported "Another student at my middle school cyberbullied me because I am gay. While I was raised knowing that there was nothing wrong with homosexuality, it hurt to feel the rejection from another student." Another said "My friend sent me messages on facebook telling me that everyone hated me and that I'd be better off dead." Some people grapple with the negative psychological effects of marginalization, such as low self-esteem, depression, and suicidal ideation. For example, in the Kowalski and Toth study, one participant's reaction to the cyberbullying was "I tried to kill myself." Others retaliate. These individuals are cyber bully/victims. In some instances, the online retaliation is not for having been victimized virtually but having been a victim of traditional, face-to-face bullying. Unable to retaliate in person, perhaps because they fear being harmed or are not in close physical proximity with the target, they seek revenge via online bullying (Kowalski et al., 2014).

Third, research has indicated that peer rejection may magnify the effects of cybervictimization on subsequent cyber aggression. Specifically, Wright and Li (2013), in a longitudinal examination of sixth, seventh, and eighth graders, found that both peer rejection and cyber victimization at Time 1 independently predicted cyber aggression six months later at Time 2. Importantly, however, peer rejection and cyber victimization at Time 1 interacted such that the effects of cyber victimization on cyber aggression were stronger among youth who had experienced high levels of peer rejection (see, however, Calvete et al., 2010). Although additional research is needed in this area, Wright and Li's findings suggest that peer rejection can lead to anger, frustration, and a desire to retaliate online.

Fourth, research has found that perceived parental rejection is also linked to cyberbullying perpetration (Seyoung & Bong, 2022), suggesting a displacement effect of perceived rejection by the parents onto others in the virtual world. Perhaps children and youth who feel that they have been rejected or neglected by their parents feel powerless to stand up to the parents and, thus, redirect their frustration and anger toward other people online.

11.7   Sensitivity to Rejection

Many people experience social rejection yet do not respond aggressively. In some cases, such as with the school and mass shootings, people may have reached a tipping point where a compilation of factors that include rejection led to an aggressive response. In other cases, however, personality characteristics may moderate the link between rejection and aggression, leading people to respond to the same provocation in different ways.

One particularly important characteristic is rejection sensitivity, which we mentioned briefly earlier in this chapter (see also Renström & Bäck, this volume). People higher in rejection sensitivity are more inclined to respond aggressively to feelings of rejection than those lower in rejection sensitivity. In one study of college men who were invested in a close relationship, rejection sensitivity predicted the incidence of dating violence (Downey et al., 2000), and, as noted earlier, angry rejection sensitivity is associated with aggressive behavior (Bondu & Krahe, 2015; Jacobs & Harper, 2013) and cyberbullying (Demircioglu & Goncu-Kose, 2022).

Feldman and Downey (1994) noted that parental rejection can cause children to become more sensitive to rejection. Parental rejection, while not common to all shootings, has been found to be present in many of the school and mass shootings. Additionally, low parental monitoring, which could be perceived by some youth as a sign of parental rejection, has been linked to cyberbullying involvement. Rejection sensitivity also correlates with depression and loneliness (Gao et al., 2017).

People higher in rejection sensitivity are more likely to perceive ambiguous stimuli as indicative of rejection than those lower in rejection sensitivity (Romero-Canyas et al., 2010). Downey, Lebolt, et al. (1998) observed aggressive behavior and reduced academic performance among minority middle school students who were high in rejection sensitivity. Ironically, the hostile and aggressive responses that often follow real or imagined rejection often elicit the very rejection that was feared initially (Downey, Freitas, et al., 1998).

11.8   Conclusion: Hurt People Hurt People

Few, if any, people can say that they have never experienced rejection. Indeed, most of us have been rejected, dismissed, avoided, marginalized, and treated in other ways that convey that we have low relational value again and again. People's responses to rejection vary, however, from passive responses, such as withdrawing from social situations, to more active responses, such as behaving aggressively toward those who rejected them. The five forms of aggressive responses to rejection discussed in this chapter – school and mass shootings, intimate partner violence, hazing, suicide, and cyberbullying – are increasingly frequent in today's society. People who perceive that others do not value their relationship as much as they want feel angry and hurt and often desire to make the rejector suffer as well. So, they aggress – in retribution, to deter future rejection, to exert control – and their aggression is sometimes extreme, causing the rejector to experience physical injury, emotional trauma, or even death.

References

Allan, E. J., & Madden, M. (2008). *Hazing in view: College students at risk*. Stop Hazing. www.stophazing.org/hazing-view/

Anderson, R. (2017). "Here I am, 26, with no friends, no job, no girlfriend": Shooter's manifesto offers clues to 2015 Oregon college rampage. *LA Times*. www.latimes.com/nation/la-na-school-shootings-2017-story.html

Arnocky, S., Davis, A., Locke, A., McKelvie, L., & Vaillancourt, T. (2022). Violence and homicide following partner infidelity. In T. DeLecce, & T. K. Shackelford (Eds.), *The Oxford handbook of infidelity* (pp. 516–554). Oxford University Press.

Babcock, J. C., Jacobson, N. S., Gottman, J. M., & Yerington, T. P. (2000). Attachment, emotional regulation, and the function of marital violence: Differences between secure, preoccupied, and dismissing violent and nonviolent husbands. *Journal of Family Violence*, 15, 391–409.

Barbaro, N., & Shackelford, T. K. (2019). Environmental unpredictability in childhood is associated with anxious romantic attachment and intimate partner violence perpetration. *Journal of Interpersonal Violence*, 34, 240–269.

Barnard, G. W., Vera, H., Vera, M. I., & Newman, G. (1982). Till death do us part: A study of spouse murder. *Bulletin of the American Academy of Psychiatry & the Law*, 10, 271–280.

Baumeister, R. F., & Leary, M. R. (1995). The need to belong: Desire for interpersonal attachment as a fundamental human motivation. *Psychological Bulletin*, 117, 497–529.

Boettcher, M. L., & Salinas, C., Jr. (2018). Testimonies. In C. Salinas, Jr., & M. L. Boettcher (Eds.), *Critical perspectives on hazing in colleges and universities: A guide to disrupting hazing culture* (pp. 14–23). Routledge.

Bondu, R., & Krahe, B. (2015). Links of justice and rejection sensitivity with aggression in childhood and adolescence. *Aggressive Behavior*, 41(4), 353–368. https://doi.org/10.1002/ab.21556

Bott, S., Guedes, A., Goodwin, M. M., & Mendoza, J. A. (2012). *Violence against women in Latin America and the Caribbean: A comparative analysis of population-based data from 12 countries*. Pan American Health Organization.

Bourgeois, K. S., & Leary, M. R. (2001). Coping with rejection: Derogating those who choose us last. *Motivation & Emotion*, *25*, 101–111.

Breiding, M. J., Basile, K. C., Smith, S. G., Black, M. C., & Mahendra, R. (2015). *Intimate partner violence surveillance: Uniform definition and recommended data elements* (Ver. 2). Centers for Disease Control and Prevention.

Buckels, E. E., Trapnell, P. D., & Paulhus, D. L. (2014). Trolls just want to have fun. *Personality and Individual Differences*, *67*, 97–102. https://doi.org/10.1016/j.paid.2014.01.016

Buss, D. M., & Duntley, J. D. (2014). Intimate partner violence in evolutionary perspective. In T. K. Shackelford, & R. D. Hansen (Eds.), *The evolution of violence* (pp. 1–22). Springer.

Calvete, E., Orue, I., Estévez, A., Villardón, L., & Padilla, P. (2010). Cyberbullying in adolescents: Modalities and aggressors' profile. *Computers in Human Behavior*, *26*(5), 1128–1135. https://doi.org/10.1016/j.chb.2010.03.017

Chu, C., Buchman-Schmitt, J. M., Stanley, I. H., et al. (2017). The interpersonal theory of suicide: A systematic review and meta-analysis of a decade of cross-national research. *Psychological Bulletin*, *143*(12), 1313–1345. https://doi.org/10.1037/bul0000123

Conroy, A. (2014). Marital infidelity and intimate partner violence in rural Malawi: A dyadic investigation. *Archives of Sexual Behavior*, *43*, 1303–1314.

Cox, J. W., Hedgpeth, D., & Jouvenal, J. (2015, August 26). Two Roanoke journalists killed on live television by angry former colleague. Washington Post. www.washingtonpost.com/local/crime/two-roanoke-journalists-killed-on-live-television-by-angry-former-colleague/2015/08/26/8e534e0e-4c0c-11e5-902f-39e9219e574b_story.html

Crawford, M., & Gartner, R. (1992). *Woman killing: Intimate femicide in Ontario, 1974–1990*. Women We Honour Action Committee.

Crow, R. B., & Macintosh, E. W. (2009). Conceptualizing a meaningful definition of hazing in sport. *European Sport Management Quarterly*, *9*(4), 433–451. https://doi.org/10.1080/16184740903331937

Dalrymple, J. (2014, May 25). *The bizarre and horrifying autobiography of a mass shooter*. Buzzfeed News. www.buzzfeednews.com/article/jimdalrympleii/the-bizarre-and-horrifying-autobiography-of-a-mass-shooter

Deas, N., Kowalski, R. M., Finnell, S., et al. (2023). I just want to matter: Examining the role of anti-mattering in online suicide support communities using natural language processing. *Computers in Human Behavior*, *139*, 107499. https://doi.org/10.1016/j.chb.2022.107499

Demircioğlu, Z. I., & Göncü-Köse, A. (2021). Effects of attachment styles, dark triad, rejection sensitivity, and relationship satisfaction on social media addiction: A mediated model. *Current Psychology*, *40*(1), 414–428. https://doi.org/10.1007/s12144-018-9956-x

Demircioğlu, Z. I., & Göncü-Köse, A. (2022). Antecedents of problematic social media use and cyberbullying among adolescents: Attachment, the dark triad and

rejection sensitivity. *Current Psychology*, 2, 31091–31109. https://doi.org/
10.1007/s12144-022-04127-2

De Weerth, C., & Kalma, A. P. (1993). Female aggression as a response to sexual jealousy: A sex role reversal? *Aggressive Behavior*, 19, 265–279.

Dobash, R. E., & Dobash, R. P. (2015). *When men murder women*. Oxford University Press.

Downey, G., Feldman, S., & Ayduk, O. (2000). Rejection sensitivity and male violence in romantic relationships. *Personal Relationships*, 7(1), 45–61.

Downey, G., Freitas, A. L., Michaelis, B., & Khouri, H. (1998). The self-fulfilling prophecy in close relationships: Rejection sensitivity and rejection by romantic partners. *Journal of Personality and Social Psychology*, 75(2), 545–560. https://doi.org/10.1037/0022-3514.75.2.545

Downey, G., Lebolt, A., Rincon, C, & Freitas, A. L. (1998). Rejection sensitivity and children's interpersonal difficulties. *Child Development*, 69, 1074–1091.

Durkheim, E. (1897/1951). *Suicide: A study in sociology*. Free Press. Translated by J. A. Spaulding and G. Simpson.

Dutton, D. G., Saunders, K., Starzomski, A., & Bartholomew, K. (1994). Intimacy-anger and insecure attachment as precursors of abuse in intimate relationships. *Journal of Applied Social Psychology*, 24, 1367–1386.

Farahani, H. A., Aghamohamadi, S., Kazemi, Z., Bakhtiarvand, F., & Ansari, M. (2011). Examining the relationship between sensitivity to rejection and using Facebook in university students. *Procedia Social and Behavioral Sciences*, 28, 807–810. https://doi.org/10.1016/j.sbspro.2011.11.147

Feldman, S., & Downey, G. (1994). Rejection sensitivity as a mediator of the impact of childhood exposure to family violence on adult attachment behavior. *Development and Psychopathology*, 6(1), 231–247.

Freud, S. (1930). Civilization and its discontents. *Standard Edition*, 21, 64–145.

Gao, S., Assink, M., Cipriani, A., & Lin, K. (2017). Associations between rejection sensitivity and mental health outcomes: A meta-analytic review. *Clinical Psychology Review*, 57, 59–74. https://doi.org/10.1016/j.cpr.2017.08.007

Garg, R. (2009). Ragging: A public health problem in India. *Indian Journal of Medical Science*, 63(6), 263

Graupensperger, S. A., Benson, A. J., & Evans, M. B. (2018). Everyone else is doing it: The association between social identity and susceptibility to peer influence in NCAA athletes. *Journal of Sport and Exercise Psychology*, 40, 117–127. https://doi.org/10.1123/jsep.2017-0339

Guerrero, L. K, Spitzberg, B. H., & Yoshimura, S. M. (2004). Sexual and emotional jealousy. In J. H. Harvey, A. Wenzel, & S. Sprecher (Eds.), *Handbook of sexuality in close relationships* (pp. 311–345). Lawrence Erlbaum.

Gun Violence Archive (2023, May 3). Explainer. www.gunviolencearchive.org/explainer

Harris, L. V. (2011, March). Behind the music: Hazing or brotherhood? www.ebony.com

Holtzworth-Munroe, A., Stuart, G. L., & Hutchinson, G. (1997). Violent versus nonviolent husbands: Differences in attachment patterns, dependency, and jealousy. *Journal of Family Psychology*, *11*(3), 314–331. https://doi.org/ 10.1037/0893-3200.11.3.314

Hoover, N. (1999). *Initiation rites and athletics: A national survey of NCAA sports teams: Final report*. Alfred University and Reidman Insurance Co Inc.

Hurault, J. W. (1961). *The Boni refugee Blacks of French Guiana*. Ifan.

Jackson, M. A., Sippel, L. M., Mota, N., Whalen, D., & Schumacher, J. A. (2015). Borderline personality disorder and related constructs as risk factors for intimate partner violence perpetration. *Aggression and Violent Behavior*, *24*, 95–106.

Jacobs, N., & Harper, B. (2013). The effects of rejection sensitivity on reactive and proactive aggression. *Aggressive Behavior*, *39*, 3–12. https://doi.org/10.1002/ ab.21455

James, W. (1890). *The principles of psychology*. Encyclopedia Brittanica.

Jeffreys, M. D. W. (1952). Samsonic suicide or suicide of revenge among Africans. *African Studies*, *6*(3), 118–122.

Joiner, T. (2005). *Why people die by suicide*. Harvard University Press

Joiner, T. E., Jeon, M. E., Lieberman, A., et al. (2021). On prediction, refutation, and explanatory reach: A consideration of the Interpersonal Theory of Suicidal Behavior. *Preventive Medicine*, *152*(Pt 1), 106453. https://doi.org/10.1016/j .ypmed.2021.106453

Joiner, T. E., Jr., Van Orden, K. A., Witte, T. K., et al. (2009). Main predictions of the interpersonal–psychological theory of suicidal behavior: Empirical tests in two samples of young adults. *Journal of Abnormal Psychology*, *118*(3), 634–646. https://doi.org/10.1037/a0016500

Jost, J. T., & Banaji, M. R. (1994). The role of stereotyping in system-justification and the production of false consciousness. *British Journal of Social Psychology*, *33*, 1–27.

Joyce, S. B., & Nirh, J. (2018). Fraternity and sorority hazing. In C. Salinas, Jr., & M. L. Boettcher (Eds.), *Critical perspectives on hazing in colleges and universities: A guide to disrupting hazing culture* (pp. 52–64). Routledge.

Karimi, F., & Lavandera, E. (2019, September 1). *Report: Gunman in West Texas shooting rampage was fired hours before*. CNN. www.cnn.com/2019/09/01/us/ odessa-texas-shooting-sunday/index.html

Keller, K. M., Matthews, M., Curry Hall, K., et al. (2015). *Hazing in the U.S. Armed Forces: Recommendations for hazing prevention policy and practice*. RAND.

Kim, K. J., Feeney, B. C., & Jakubiak, B. K. (2018). Touch reduces romantic jealousy in the anxiously attached. *Journal of Social and Personal Relationships*, *35*, 1019–1041.

Kirby, S. L., & Wintrup, G. (2002). Running the gauntlet: An examination of initiation/hazing and sexual abuse in sport. *Journal of Sexual Aggression*, *8*, 49–68. https://doi.org/10.1080/13552600208413339

Kirkpatrick, L. A., Waugh, C. E., Valencia, A., & Webster, G. D. (2002). The functional domain specificity of self-esteem and the differential prediction of aggression. *Journal of Personality and Social Psychology, 82,* 756–767.

Klonsky, E. D., & May, A. M. (2015). The Three-Step Theory (3ST): A new theory of suicide rooted in the "ideation-to-action" framework. *International Journal of Cognitive Therapy, 8*(2), 114–129. https://doi.org/10.1521/ijct.2015.8.2.114

Knight, S., & Boettcher, M. L. (2018). Military hazing in university programs. In C. Salinas, Jr., & M. L. Boettcher (Eds.), *Critical perspectives on hazing in colleges and universities: A guide to disrupting hazing culture* (pp. 65–74). Routledge.

Kowalski, R. M., Giumetti, G., Schroeder, A., & Lattanner, M. (2014). Bullying in the digital age: A critical review and meta-analysis of cyberbullying research among youth. *Psychological Bulletin, 140,* 1073–1137. https://doi.org/10.1037/a0035618

Kowalski, R. M., Leary, M., Hendley, T., et al. (2021). K–12, college/university, and mass shootings: Similarities and differences. *Journal of Social Psychology, 161* (6), 753–778. https://doi.org/10.1080/00224545.2021.1900047

Kowalski, R. M., Limber, S., & Agatston, P. W. (2012). *Cyber bullying: Bullying in the digital age* (2nd ed.). Wiley.

Kowalski, R. M., & Toth, A. (2018). Cyberbullying among youth with and without disabilities. *Journal of Child & Adolescent Trauma, 11,* 7–15. https://doi.org/10.1007/s40653-017-0139-y

Leary, M. R. (2001). Toward a conceptualization of interpersonal rejection. In M. R. Leary (Ed.), *Interpersonal rejection* (pp. 3–20). Oxford University Press.

Leary, M. R. (2021). Emotional reactions to threats to acceptance and belonging: A retrospective look at the big picture. *Australian Journal of Psychology, 73,* 4–11.

Leary, M. R., & Gabriel, S. (2022). The relentless pursuit of acceptance and belonging. *Advances in Motivation Science, 9,* 135–178.

Leary, M. R., Koch, E., & Hechenbleikner, N. (2001). Emotional responses to interpersonal rejection. In M. R. Leary (Ed.), *Interpersonal rejection* (pp. 145–166). Oxford University Press.

Leary, M. R., Kowalski, R. M., Smith, L., & Phillips, S. (2003). Teasing, rejection, and violence: Case studies of the school shootings. *Aggressive Behavior, 29,* 202–214.

Leary, M. R., Springer, C., Negel, L., Ansell, E., & Evans, K. (1998). The causes, phenomenology, and consequences of hurt feelings. *Journal of Personality and Social Psychology, 74,* 1225–1237.

Leary, M. R., Tambor, E. S., Terdal, S. K., & Downs, D. L. (1995). Self-esteem as an interpersonal monitor: The sociometer hypothesis. *Journal of Personality and Social Psychology, 68,* 518–530.

Leary, M. R., Twenge, J. M., & Quinlivan, E. (2006). Interpersonal rejection as a determinant of anger and aggression. *Personality and Social Psychology Review, 10*(2), 111–132.

Lee S., & Mun I. B. (2022) How does perceived parental rejection influence cyberbullying by children? A serial mediation model of children's depression and smartphone addiction. *The Social Science Journal.* https://doi.org/10.1080/03623319.2022.2070826

Lutheran, A., & Barton, G. (2020, November 25). A gun collector's paranoia, a wrong suspect and the role of racism. What the Molson Coors mass shooting records reveal. Milwaukee Journal Sentinel. www.jsonline.com/story/news/crime/2020/11/25/milwaukee-molson-coors-shooting-miller-brewery-shooter-motive-unknown/6422187002/

Makepeace, J. (1989). Dating, living together, and courtship violence. In M. A. Pirog-Good, & J. E. Stets (Eds.), *Violence in dating relationships: Emerging social issues* (pp. 94–107). Praeger.

Maner, J. K., DeWall, C. N., Baumeister, R. F., & Schaller, M. (2007). Does social exclusion motivate interpersonal reconnection? Resolving the "porcupine problem." *Journal of Personality and Social Psychology, 92*(1), 42–55. https://doi.org/10.1037/0022-3514.92.1.42.

Manning, J. (2015). Aggressive suicide. *International Journal of Law, Crime, and Justice, 43*, 326–341.

Mauricio, A., Tein, J., & Lopez, F. G. (2007). Borderline and antisocial personality scores as mediators between attachment and intimate partner violence. *Violence and Victims, 22*, 139–157.

McClellan, A. C., & Killeen, M. R. (2000). Attachment theory and violence toward women by male intimate partners. *Journal of Nursing Scholarship, 32*, 353–360.

Moore, M. D. (2017). Durkheim's types of suicide and social capital: A cross-national comparison of 53 countries. *International Social Science Journal, 66*, 151–161. https://doi.org/10.1111/issj.12111

Mueller, A. S., Abrutyn, S., Pescosolido, B., & Diefendorf, S. (2021). The social roots of suicide: Theorizing how the external social world matters to suicide and suicide prevention. *Frontiers in Psychology, 12.* https://doi.org/10.3389/fpsyg.2021.621569

Nemeth, J. M., Bonomi, A. E., Lee, M. A., & Ludwin, J. M. (2012). Sexual infidelity as trigger for intimate partner violence. *Journal of Women's Health, 21*, 942–949.

Nuwer, H. (2001). *Wrongs of passage: Fraternities, sororities, hazing, and binge drinking.* Indiana University Press.

Nuwer, H. (2018). Hazing in fraternities and sororities: A primer. In H. Nuwer (Ed.), *Hazing: Destroying young lives* (pp. 24–41). Indiana University Press.

Oliff, H. (2002, April). Lifting the haze around hazing. *Education Digest, 67*(8), 21–27.

Owen, S. S., Burke, T. W., & Vichesky, D. (2008). Hazing in student organizations: Prevalence, attitudes, and solutions. *Oracle: The Research Journal of the Association of Fraternity Advisors, 3*(1), 40–58.

Peterson, J., & Densley, J. (2021). *The violence project: How to stop a mass shooting epidemic.* Abrams Press.

Peterson, J., & Densley, J. (2023). The Violence Project database of mass shootings in the United States (Version 6). www.theviolenceproject.org

Richman, L. S., & Leary, M. R. (2009). Reactions to discrimination, stigmatization, ostracism, and other forms of interpersonal rejection: A dynamic, multi-motive model. *Psychological Review, 116,* 365–383.

Robertson, G. (2015, August 26). Virginia TV journalists killed by suspect with "powder keg" of anger. *Reuters.* www.reuters.com/article/us-usa-shooting-vir ginia/virginia-tv-journalists-killed-by-suspect-with-powder-keg-of-anger-idUSKCN0QV1HY20150826

Romero-Canyas, R., Downey, G., Berenson, K., Ayduk, O., & Kang, N. J. (2010). Rejection sensitivity and the rejection–hostility link in romantic relationships. *Journal of Personality, 78,* 119–148. https://doi.org/10.1111/j.1467-6494.2009.00611.x

Schildkraut, J., & Turanovic, J. J. (2022). A new wave of mass shootings? Exploring the potential of COVID-19. *Homicide Studies, 26*(4), 362–378. https://doi.org/10.1177/10887679221101605

Shackelford, T. K., Goetz, A. T., Buss, D. M., Euler, H. A., & Hoier, S. (2005). When we hurt the ones we love: Predicting violence against women from men's mate retention. *Personal Relationships, 12,* 447–463.

Sidner, S., Lah, K., Almasy, S., & Ellis, R. (2015, October 2). *Oregon shooting: Gunman was student in class where he killed 9.* CNN. www.cnn.com/2015/10/02/us/oregon-umpqua-community-college-shooting/index.html

Silveira, J. M. (2018). Tradition or torment: Examining hazing in the college marching band. In C. Salinas, Jr., & M. L. Boettcher (Eds.), *Critical perspectives on hazing in colleges and universities: A guide to disrupting hazing culture* (pp. 40–51). Routledge.

Silveira, J. M., & Hudson, M. W. (2015). Hazing in the college marching band. *Journal of Research in Music Education, 63*(1), 5–27. https://doi.org/10.1177/0022-429415569064

Sjåstad, H., Zhang, M., Masvie, A. E., & Baumeister, R. (2021). Social exclusion reduces happiness by creating expectations of future rejection. *Self and Identity, 20*(1), 116–125. https://doi.org/10.1080/15298868.2020.1779119

Spencer, C., Mallory, A. B., Cafferky, B. M., et al. (2019). Mental health factors and intimate partner violence perpetration and victimization: A meta-analysis. *Psychology of Violence, 9,* 1–17.

Stephenson, R., Darbes, L. A., Rosso, M. T., et al. (2023). Perceptions of contexts of intimate partner violence among young, partnered gay, bisexual and other men who have sex with men in the United States. *Journal of Interpersonal Violence, 37.*

Stockl, H., Devries, K., Rotstein, A., et al. (2013). The global prevalence of intimate partner homicide: A systematic review. *Lancet, 382,* 859–865.

Swingle, E., & Salinas, C., Jr. (2018). Hazing in intercollegiate athletics. In C. Salinas, Jr., & M. L. Boettcher (Eds.), *Critical perspectives on hazing in colleges and universities: A guide to disrupting hazing culture* (pp. 27–39). Routledge.

Thomas, B. J., & Meglich, P. (2018). Justifying new employees' trials by fire: Workplace hazing. *Personnel Review, 48*(2), 381–399. https://doi.org/10.1108/PR-01-2018-0025

Twenge, J. M., Baumeister, R. F., Tice, D. M., & Stucke, T. S. (2001). If you can't join them, beat them: Effects of social exclusion on aggressive behavior. *Journal of Personality and Social Psychology, 81*, 1058–1069.

Velotti, P., Beomonte Zobel, S., Rogier, G., & Tambelli, R. (2018). Exploring relationships: A systematic review on intimate partner violence and attachment. *Frontiers in Psychology, 9*, 1–42.

Waldron, J. J., & Kowalski, C. L. (2009). Crossing the line: Rites of passage, team aspects, and ambiguity of hazing. *Research Quarterly for Exercise and Sport, 80*, 291–302.

Warburton, W., Williams, K. D., & Cairns, D. (2003, April). Effects of ostracism and loss of control on aggression. Paper presented at the 32nd meeting of the Society of Australian Social Psychology, Sydney, Australia.

Willard, N. (2007). *Cyberbullying and cyberthreats. Responding to the challenge of online social aggression, threats, and distress.* Research Press.

Wilson, M., & Daly, M. (1996). Male sexual proprietariness and violence against wives. *Current Directions in Psychological Science, 5*, 2–7.

Wright, M. F. (2017). Parental mediation, cyberbullying, and cybertrolling: The role of gender. *Computers in Human Behavior, 71*, 189–195. https://doi.org/10.1016/j.chb.2017.01.059

Wright, M. F., & Li, Y. (2013). The association between cyber victimization and subsequent cyber aggression: The moderating effect of peer rejection. *Journal of Youth & Adolescence, 42*(5), 662–674. https://doi.org/10.1007/s10964-012-9903-3

Chronic Social Exclusion, Radicalization, and Extremism

MARCO MARINUCCI AND PAOLO RIVA

12.1 Introduction

As this book illustrates, while numerous factors contribute to the complex phenomenon of radicalization, one aspect that has gained significant attention in recent years is the link between social exclusion and the propensity for individuals to embrace extremist ideologies and engage in acts of violence. This chapter examines a specific form of social exclusion, *chronic* social exclusion, that is, exclusion that persists over time and across situations.

Examining some news reports and real-life cases that have gained particular media and public attention, several striking examples highlight the intersection between the chronicity of social exclusion and pathways to radicalization.

One such instance is the story of Chad Escobedo, the mass shooter of Springwater Trail High School, Oregon, USA. In 2007, he was a 15-year-old adolescent who shot through his school window, injuring ten students. In a recent interview, Escobedo stated the following:

> I think they're ignored, not listened to. There are many cases besides mine ... but I wasn't trying to kill anybody; I was trying to instil fear into the public. I felt trapped, like I was in a cage. . ... There was this teacher who was always on my case about certain things . . .. I started failing his classes. I liked soccer but they wouldn't let me play on the team. It was getting to the point where it was a burden to get up in the morning to go to school. I felt like no one cared what I wanted in life. (Hannaford, 2018)

This short extract offers various starting points to elaborate on the role of chronic social exclusion in extreme behaviors. First, Escobedo considers social exclusion, mainly ostracism (being ignored), as a common condition afflicting mass shooters. Second, the social exclusion situation oppressing him was not a single, acute event of rejection or ostracism. Instead, it seemed like a more pervasive scenario where social exclusion originated from multiple contexts (i.e., the teacher, the soccer team, and general others). Third, his action sprang from the urge to exert control over the environment and seek recognition (i.e., instill fear) and from a condition of seeming depression (i.e., feeling trapped and a burden to get up) and unworthiness (i.e., no one cared). The chronic lack of control, depression, and unworthiness characterizing Chad's state before the assault overlaps with the components of the *resignation stage* that, as we review in this chapter, is theorized to be the most significant psychological repercussion of chronic and pervasive social exclusion (Williams, 2009).

The case of Chad Escobedo is just one of many examples emphasizing how a background characterized by pervasive and persistent social exclusion can fuel radicalization and extreme behaviors. Anders Breivik, who killed seventy-seven people in Norway in 2011, was pictured as persistently excluded and rejected (Graf, 2016; Pfundmair, Wood, et al., 2022). Brenton Tarrant, the anti-Muslim terrorist who killed fifty-one people in the Christchurch, New Zealand, attack in 2019, justified his crimes by presenting himself as a victim of bullying who felt ostracized and sought revenge against society (Cave & Saxton, 2021).

Aside from journalistic reports, the few empirical studies focusing on radicalized individuals, terrorists, and mass shooters highlight chronic exclusion as a biographic factor boosting extreme violence. Leary et al. (2003) analyzed fifteen school shootings in the United States between 1995 and 2001. They showed that acute or long-term episodes of social exclusion – including ostracism, rejection, or bullying – were present in nearly all of the perpetrators. The follow-up project from Kowalski et al. (2021) looking at 158 attacks, including school, college, and mass shootings between 2001 and 2018, showed that at least one-fifth of all of the shooters experienced a history of long-term social exclusion (Kowalski & Leary, this volume). Pfundmair, Aßmann, et al. (2022) coded case files of subjects under investigation by the German police and found that episodes of short-term exclusion and a history of persistent and pervasive exclusion were highly prevalent in the early stages of the radicalization process.

The previous chapters of this book and the evidence described showed how social exclusion might be one of the critical factors that can initiate a chain of processes and events that culminate in extremely aggressive behaviors like terroristic attacks and mass shootings. However, most of the studies reviewed focused on the short-term effects of brief episodes of social exclusion in sensitizing individuals to a radical ideology (e.g., Hales & Williams, 2018; Pfundmair, 2019) and fostering membership with radical groups (Pfundmair & Mahr, 2022). This chapter will focus on *chronic social exclusion* as a crucial igniter catalyzing extremism.

12.2   Defining Chronic Social Exclusion

In attempting to define chronic social exclusion, we believe focusing on two key dimensions is essential. The first is the temporal dimension. By definition, the attribute "chronic" qualifies a stable and persisting experience over time.

The second is the contextual dimension. Humans live within complex networks with multiple group affiliations (e.g., family, friends, colleagues). To be defined as such, chronic exclusion must also be pervasive, characterizing multiple areas of existence.

Based on this line of reasoning and building on previous definitions (Riva & Eck, 2016), we define chronic social exclusion as the experience of being separated from others physically or emotionally through episodes of rejection, ostracism, and social isolation that persist over time and are pervasive across social contexts.

12.2.1   *Persistent and Pervasive: The Temporal and Contextual Dimensions of Chronic Exclusion*

The definition of chronic social exclusion we provided considers a temporal dimension – repeated exclusion persisting over time – and a contextual dimension – social exclusion that occurs pervasively across multiple social domains. We developed the definition of chronicity along these two dimensions as they are those considered by the major theoretical models of social exclusion, namely the temporal need-threat model of ostracism (Williams, 2009) and the multimotive model of interpersonal rejection (Smart Richman & Leary, 2009). Focusing on the temporal dimension, however, the theoretical models do not offer a clear temporal framework defining how long exclusion must last to display its chronic implications. The literature framed the chronicity of social stressors without any temporal delimitation. According to Zhang et al. (2017), social adversity can be chronic when it occurs "repeatedly, continuously, or accumulatively" (p. 2). In Williams (2009), chronic ostracism is plainly conceptualized as "persistent" (p. 320), and similarly, Smart Richman and Leary (2009) connote chronic rejection when manifesting "over a prolonged period of time" (p. 370). Differently, medical sciences define more precisely the temporal extension of chronic pathologies. For example, fatigue is chronic when lasting for at least six months (Wessely et al., 1996), and chronic pain when lasting for at least three months (Merskey et al., 1979). Despite the scarcity of a clear definition of chronic social exclusion, a few studies operationalized it more precisely. Based on the pain overlap theory (Eisenberger & Lieberman, 2004; Riva, Wesselmann, et al., 2014), Riva et al. (2017) considered social pain chronic if it lasted for at least three months. They showed that experiencing social exclusion during the previous three months predicted the long-term psychological repercussions of chronic exclusion as theoretically conceived by Williams (2009). In a longitudinal study on marginalized asylum seekers and refugees, Marinucci and Riva (2021a) showed that the perception of social exclusion and its impact on well-being became stable and chronic between three and six months, but not earlier. Therefore, the empirical research on the temporal chronicity of social exclusion suggests that its onset and long-term psychological repercussions might develop in three to six months.

The contextual dimension of chronic exclusion – the pervasiveness – was primarily addressed by the multimotive model (Smart Richman & Leary, 2009) concerning behavioral responses to interpersonal rejection. Accordingly, if people perceive the experienced rejection as coming from multiple people or domains of social life, they are likely to withdraw from social relationships and stop seeking connections with others. Persistent and pervasive exposure to rejection could lead people to expect further hurt from future interactions. Such expectations would push people to avoid social interaction, driven by the motive to protect themselves from further pain (Ren et al., 2020; Vangelisti, 2001). The fear of being hurt would lead people to distance themselves from those who previously hurt them and from others whose acceptance is not secure (Vangelisti et al., 2005). The research has not systematically investigated pervasive exclusion's behavioral and psychological implications; however, some emerging studies have started considering it. For instance, concerning radicalism and extremism, Pfundmair and Mahr (2022) considered pervasiveness as an indicator of radicalized Islamists' levels of social exclusion.

Next to the temporal and contextual dimensions of the chronicity of exclusion, an additional focus that helps to understand the features of chronic exclusion is the many forms it can take in daily life.

12.2.2   Rejection, Ostracism, and Social Isolation

In episodes of rejection, people receive direct negative attention from others and experience a relational devaluation, suggesting they are not wanted (Wesselmann et al., 2016). Cues of rejection do not necessarily consist of explicit communication indicating that one is not wanted, and people can feel rejected even when someone addresses them with hurtful laughter (Klages & Wirth, 2014) or in an angry manner (Wesselmann et al., 2010). Harassment at work and in schools through bullying and mobbing are also forms of rejection explicitly directed against a victim (Schuster, 1996). Furthermore, discrimination and stigmatization at both the interpersonal and intergroup levels can be included among the broad categories of rejection-based exclusion conveying relational devaluation (Smart Richman & Leary, 2009). People belonging to stigmatized social groups can also experience rejection daily via *microaggressions*, which can be subtle, rude, and invalidating comments or even direct insults targeting the stigmatized persons' social group (Wesselmann et al., 2019). DeSouza et al. (2019) found that sexual minorities recognized events from subtle neglect to explicit hostility as microaggressions frequently happening in their lives.

When ostracized, people experience being ignored by others. Ostracism occurs when one's presence is not acknowledged, and people are treated as if they do not exist, leading to a profoundly upsetting experience (Williams, 2009). The perception of being ignored may arise from verbal and nonverbal cues like being forgotten (King & Geise, 2011), not being given eye contact (Nezlek et al., 2012), or being part of a conversation with people talking in an unspoken language (i.e., linguistic ostracism; Dotan-Eliaz et al., 2009). Also, using smartphones while interacting face-to-face with others – being *phubbed* (Roberts & David, 2016) – can make people feel ostracized, as individuals recalling being phubbed reported feeling excluded and devalued (Hales et al., 2018).

Social isolation, especially when forced, is an additional phenomenon that might evoke exclusion-related feelings, although not necessarily involving a source actively rejecting or ignoring a victim – like rejection and ostracism. Drawing from the literature about loneliness and social connectedness (Baumeister & Leary, 1995; Cacioppo et al., 2011; Holt-Lunstad et al., 2010), social isolation can be generally defined as a lack or poorness of quantity and quality of social connections and operationalized as physical separation from others. Recent literature highlighted the strong intertwinement between ostracism with its psychological repercussions and social isolation (Williams & Nida, 2022), showing how people tend to feel excluded even when they are left out incidentally, resulting in being isolated from others due to the casual course of events (Lindström & Tobler, 2018). People from the general population might eventually become isolated due to accidental circumstances like separation, loss, relocation, and unemployment (Pohlan, 2019; Williams & Nida, 2022). Due to the COVID-19 outbreak in recent years, the population worldwide underwent strict and prolonged social isolation imposed by nation-level lockdowns to prevent the virus from spreading. Researchers worldwide produced a vast corpus of research investigating the psychological conse-quences of forced social isolation, often applying the theoretical framework of social exclusion to social isolation (Hales et al., 2021) and finding the same psychological repercussions (e.g., Marinucci, Pancani, et al., 2022; Pancani et al., 2021). Beyond circumstances, specific populations are more exposed to forced isolation. Social isolation among older people is a growing concern in WEIRD (Western, educated, industrialized, rich, and democratic) societies as it is thought to contribute to increased morbidity and mortality rates (Cacioppo et al., 2011). People in institutionalized care also face social isolation (Goffman, 1961). Prison is another institution that aims to isolate detained people from the rest of society. The explicit isolation experienced by prisoners can turn into feelings of social exclusion, and this condition might be further aggravated by solitary confinement (Wesselmann et al., 2021).

In our definition of chronic social exclusion, we comprehensively consider the related yet different exclusion phenomena of rejection, ostracism, and forced isolation for three reasons. First, from a theoretical and empirical standpoint, these phenomena evoke similar adverse psychological responses (e.g., negative emotions and need-threats; Lutz & Schneider, 2021). The overlap between the psychological consequences suggests that people might consider and process these events similarly (Wesselmann et al., 2019), although they might still present nuances and elements of distinction in their behavioral and psychological repercussions (e.g., Molden et al., 2009). Second, the research often considered these different phenomena within the same theoretical framework (Gerber & Wheeler, 2009; Willimas & Nida, 2022; Williams & Zadro, 2001). Third, especially in biographic factors fostering extremism, ostracism, rejection, and social isolation are often hard to distinguish in real-world situations, and they all were shown to be similarly tightly related to extreme behaviors and radicalized group affiliations (Gómez et al., 2011; Kowalski et al., 2021; Wood, 2020).

12.3   Psychological and Behavioral Consequences of Chronic Social Exclusion

The temporal need-threat model of ostracism (Williams, 2009) is the most comprehensive theoretical framework outlining the psychological and behavioral consequences of social exclusion. The model emphasizes two specific features of individuals' responses to ostracism. The first, central one is that individuals' reactions to ostracism develop over time. Individuals' responses can be categorized into three subsequent stages describing immediate, short-term, and chronic responses to social exclusion (i.e., the *reflexive, reflective,* and *resignation* stages). The second is that social exclusion threatens four fundamental needs: belonging, self-esteem, control, and meaningful existence, with a more recent consideration of the threat to the need for certainty (Hales et al., 2021).

As discussed in early theoretical models (Baumeister & Leary, 1995; Leary et al., 1995), social exclusion threatens the need for belonging and self-esteem as it disrupts social connections with others, often with interpersonal messages conveying relational devaluation. In addition, Williams's (2009) model considered exclusion's impact on the need for control and meaningful existence. Control is threatened because social exclusion is unilateral, and victims can only passively experience it. The need for recognition and meaning is frustrated by the lack of acknowledgment implied in being ignored, and people are treated as if they were invisible or did not exist. According to the model, after the prompt detection of ostracism and the experience of social pain and need-threat in the first *reflexive* stage, individuals enter the *reflective* stage, where they appraise the meaning, the motives, and the relevance of the exclusion and enact behavioral coping strategies seeking to recover the most threatened needs. The research showed that people might cope with exclusion by behaving prosocially and pursuing re-inclusion or affiliation into novel social groups (e.g., Maner et al., 2007), especially if the victims are most threatened in the inclusionary cluster need (i.e., self-esteem and belonging). Alternatively, if most threatened in the power need cluster (i.e., control and significance), people can respond aggressively, trying to reestablish a sense of control over and agency in the events (e.g., Twenge et al., 2001).

Aside from the prosocial and aggressive responses, research also highlighted that a third behavioral response (i.e., social withdrawal) might help individuals cope with social exclusion. People might seek solitude after social exclusion and opt for social withdrawal (Ren et al., 2020) and avoidant behavior patterns. Social withdrawal is also the direct behavioral consequence of pervasive and chronic exclusion envisioned by the other theoretical framework that accounted for the chronicity of exclusion, the multimotive model (Smart Richman & Leary, 2009). Social withdrawal might be a strategy to prevent further social pain from social interactions learned to be rejecting (Vangelisti et al., 2005) or to leave the place to contemplative behaviors that can help the cognitive coping of exclusionary events (Long & Averill, 2003).

Suppose the behavioral coping strategies from the reflective stage failed to recover the threatened needs and cease ostracism. If exclusion persists over time despite the individual's attempts to cope with the situation, people enter the last stage of Williams's (2009) model, the resignation stage, which is a psychological state characterized by chronic feelings of depression, alienation, helplessness, and unworthiness. When episodes of social exclusion persist over time and situations, people's resources necessary to fortify the continuously threatened needs become depleted, and the thwarted need for belonging develops into alienation, self-esteem into depression, reactance into learned helplessness, and attempts to prove one's meaningful existence into unworthiness. In other words, chronically excluded individuals are extremely deprived of social acceptance and desperately eager for relatedness and social inclusion. However, their failed attempts for affiliation and persistent and pervasive exclusion relegated them to a resigned surrender to social isolation, rejection, and ostracism.

Perhaps due to the challenges of empirically investigating chronic social exclusion and its long-term consequences, the resignation stage remains the less articulated part of Williams's model, which has received little, although growing, empirical attention (Wesselmann & Williams, 2017). The first evidence substantiating the theoretical proposition of the resignation stage came from the qualitative study by Zadro (2004), who interviewed people experiencing long-term ostracism. A corpus of research on the resignation stage has been emerging only recently. Focusing on the general population, Riva et al. (2017) showed that chronically excluded people reported higher levels of the four outcomes of the resignation stage than the control groups (including people with experiences of chronic physical pain). Rudert et al. (2021) provided longitudinal support that ostracism predicted a diagnosis of depression three years later. A longitudinal study conducted during the COVID-19 lockdown showed that people presented a significantly higher resignation during the lockdown phases imposing stricter physical distancing and social isolation than during the less restrictive phase (Marinucci, Pancani, et al., 2022). Büttner et al. (2023) showed that people reporting more pervasive and chronic social exclusion in their daily lives also reported higher resignation. Zamperini et al. (2020) provided qualitative evidence that people exposed to pervasive ostracism in different contexts reported higher resignation. Aside from these studies on the general population, the empirical research on the resignation stage focused on individuals from marginalized social groups. Due to their group membership, people from marginalized social groups are exposed to social exclusion persistently in multiple life domains, considering the foundational level of political and civil rights, macro-social discrimination in the housing and job market, intergroup prejudice, interpersonal ostracism and rejection, and isolation.

12.3.1   Challenging the Exclusion–Resignation Link: The Role of Intervening Factors

In recent years, our research group has started a strand of research investigating the exclusion-related processes leading to the development of the resignation stage in people belonging to marginalized social groups like prisoners, immigrants, and homeless people. The evidence we provided, while validating the resignation stage as a possible outcome of chronic exclusion, challenges the assumption that resignation is the inescapable outcome of it.

In a longitudinal study on asylum seekers, we found that experiences of ostracism and rejection were associated with an increase in the resignation stage after six months but not after three months, highlighting how the chronicity of social exclusion and its long-term repercussions on the resignation stage might develop in a temporal arch of three to six months (Marinucci & Riva, 2021a). In related works, besides providing cross-sectional and quasi-experimental evidence of the chronic exclusion–resignation link, we focused on the intervening factors that can moderate and mediate the relationship between chronic exclusion and resignation. A research project highlighted a cross-sectional association between the experiences of rejection and ostracism and the outcomes associated with the resignation stage in a sample of asylum seekers and refugees. The research also found a similar association between peer-reported social exclusion and the resignation outcomes in first-generation immigrant adolescents involved in a large-scale research project from different European countries. In both studies, we found that intergroup social connections with the majority national group (i.e., the host social group) and other immigrants were crucial moderators of the exclusion–resignation link. Indeed, higher levels of quantity and quality of social connections with the national majority group reduced the impact of social exclusion on resignation. In contrast, higher connections with other immigrants aggravated it. We reasoned that social connections with the high-status national group could trigger positive identification processes buffering against the impact of social exclusion. In contrast, connections with other immigrants could influence stigmatized identification processes, amplifying the perception of segregation within a marginalized social group and aggravating the impact of chronic exclusion (Marinucci & Riva, 2021b). We replicated the same pattern of results in experimental and longitudinal studies, confirming and establishing the role of intergroup social connections with the national group and other immigrants as moderators of the link between exclusion and its negative impact. In detail, we found that social connections with the national group reduced both the negative immediate emotional impact of an experimental exposure to social exclusion and the long-term resignation stage. In contrast, social bonds with other immigrants amplified them (Marinucci, Mazzoni, et al., 2022). In a research project more squarely centered on identification processes, Mazzoni et al. (2020) showed that first-generation immigrants' identification with the national majority group was negatively associated with resignation, whereas identification with other immigrants did not affect resignation.

Similarly, a research project on homeless people found replicated evidence that unhoused people had higher resignation than housed people, and the difference was due to the higher occurrences of ostracism, rejection, and isolation experienced by homeless people. Similar to the findings related to identification with other stigmatized immigrants, the studies on homeless people showed that the perception of inequality and the stigmatized identification with the homeless group amplified the perception of being excluded, ultimately increasing the resignation. Differently, identity ties with other homeless were not an efficient source of social support against social exclusion and resignation (Marinucci et al., 2023).

A quasi-experimental study showed that incarcerated people presented higher resignation than free citizens due to the persistent and pervasive exclusion enacted by the prison system (Aureli et al., 2020). The study investigated the impact of a support group within the prison implemented to provide social and emotional support and build social connections with other inmates and free citizens. The support group was composed of free citizens who volunteered within the prisons, coordinated by trained psychologists. By making the participants cooperate in joint tasks, the support group aimed to promote and consolidate relationships among the prisoners and between them and the group of volunteers. For example, one of the activities was organizing a theater play, where the volunteers and the inmates acted for an audience of both volunteers and prisoners. Activities like the one described fostered new social relationships between prisoners, the volunteers, and the audience. In addition to such social activities, the group also actively provided psychological support through structured moments of emotional sharing. The volunteers encouraged prisoners to share their experiences related to their imprisonment and to support each other emotionally. In these moments, the psychologists, prisoners, and volunteers discussed the feelings, thoughts, and events related to detention. Through these actions, the support group promoted the acceptance of the condition of imprisonment, supporting prisoners in exploring their feelings and fostering their sense of worthiness, thus alleviating inmates' emotional suffering. The research results showed that the inmates who joined the support group had significantly lower levels of resignation than those who did not participate, and their resignation levels did not differ from a control group of free citizens. The support groups within prisons reduced the gap between inmates' and free citizens' overall resignation, and the effect was explained by an increased sense of social support and improved psychological flexibility in dealing with the challenging and painful experience of incarceration.

Some studies investigated the factors related to interpersonal connections and group affiliation that could influence the development of the resignation stage among the general population in specific circumstances. Zamperini and colleagues (2020) showed that people could recover from the resignation stage by affiliating with new social groups, such as religious ones. A longitudinal study conducted during the massive COVD-19 lockdown in 2020 found that people had higher levels of resignation during the most restrictive isolation phases. Furthermore, the resignation stage induced by the persistent lack of face-to-face interactions was reduced by the availability of online social connections (Marinucci, Pancani, et al., 2022).

Therefore, the research on resignation and the factors that could influence its development depicts the resignation stage as a rather malleable psychological condition that could be both reduced and aggravated by individual and situational factors, including specific social connections. In particular, the emerging literature suggests that interpersonal and group relationships can reduce the long-term feelings of depression, alienation, helplessness, and unworthiness induced by chronic exclusion. However, this is true unless those social connections occur with other stigmatized and chronically excluded group members, as the social identity research tradition similarly suggests (e.g., see the *amplification hypothesis*; Rubin & Stuart, 2018). Chronically excluded individuals who have entered the resignation stage seem highly sensitive to novel or available social relationships as these constitute an extremely precious (and rare) source of social acceptance and inclusion that puts an end to long-lasting social exclusion and helps the recovery of the chronically threatened needs of belonging, self-esteem, control, and meaningfulness, ultimately reducing resignation and improving their well-being. This interpretation is supported by longitudinal experimental data showing that repeatedly excluded participants were hypersensitive to novel episodes of social inclusion, as their basic needs were more nourished by the novel inclusion compared to repeatedly included people (Büttner et al., 2023). Hence, chronic social exclusion and the derived persistent frustration of the basic needs resulting in the resignation stage make people exceptionally starved for social inclusion and need recovery, which can have both positive implications and downsides. As a positive implication, the hypersensitivity to social inclusion makes people attuned to new social interactions and possibilities for exiting the resignation stage, also advocating from a theoretical perspective that the resignation stage could be a reversible psychological condition. As a downside, it might expose chronically excluded people to an increased risk of affiliating with detrimental social groups, further aggravating resignation and the sense of social exclusion (as in the case of other stigmatized groups) or even leading to extremism and radicalization. Within this lens, these detrimental affiliations would, at the same time, reestablish inclusion and acceptance while leading to adverse psychological and social repercussions, converging with the counterfinal view of radicalization proposed by Kruglanski et al. (2014).

12.4   Linking Chronic Social Exclusion, Resignation, and Radicalization

As discussed in the previous chapters of this book, the exclusion researchers highlighted that the need-threat posed by acute social exclusion and the behavioral responses to exclusion interestingly parallels the motivations for terrorism and the behavioral dynamics involved (Pfundmair, 2019; Pfundmair, this volume). Social exclusion can make people more vulnerable to various forms of social influence and obedience (Riva, Williams, et al., 2014) and promote aggressive behaviors (e.g., Twenge et al., 2001; Warburton et al., 2006; Wesselmann et al., 2010) in the forms of provocation and retaliation (Williams, 2009), which are also known motives for terrorism (Kydd & Walter, 2006). Furthermore, the need for certainty and control are considered roots of extremism (Hogg et al., 2013; Wagoner & Hogg, this volume). Similarly, the quest for significance, encompassing the needs for self-esteem and meaningfulness, is a crucial motivation for extremism and terrorism (Kruglanski et al., 2014; Ellenberg & Kruglanski, this volume). Lastly, the need to belong plays a pivotal role in motivating terrorism and building group membership with extremist groups (Doosje et al., 2016; Doosje et al., this volume). The overlap between the needs threatened by acute experiences of social exclusion and that motivating extremism is among the strongest theoretical argument driving the research linking social exclusion with radicalization processes. Research has listed episodes of rejection and ostracism among the biographical factors creating the optimal preconditions for radicalism to flourish (Kowalski et al.,

2021; Pfundmair, Aßmann, et al., 2022). In this sense, research has predominantly investigated the link between exclusion and radicalism, focusing on acute episodes of social exclusion, for instance, by showing that a brief manipulation of ostracism can increase openness toward extreme groups (Hales & Williams, 2018; Pfundmair, 2019; Pfundmair & Mahr, 2022).

However, if an acute experience of social exclusion can be enough to increase extremism, chronic social exclusion is likely to influence radicalization even more strongly. We argue that acute exclusion is only a distal or incidental antecedent of extremism that might have only a little influence on radicalization processes if not intersecting with more proximal risk processes linked to other bio-psychosocial factors and group processes (e.g., see Kowalski et al., 2021; Pfundmair, Aßmann, et al., 2022). Indeed, social exclusion is a universal phenomenon, and people experience its acute episodes worldwide and daily. People possess a broad set of coping behaviors that help to recover from acute social exclusion and, generally, those normative coping strategies are effective in ending social exclusion and healing from its wounds. For instance, Riva (2016) categorized the most common coping strategies along the cognitive–behavioral and approach–avoidance axis. Such a conceptual model distinguished between most (e.g., positive reappraisal, prosocial behaviors) and least (e.g., rumination, alcohol use) adaptive strategies. Leary et al. (2003) and successively Kowalski et al. (2021) found that alongside other risk factors like fascination with guns and mental health problems, acute or chronic social exclusion was particularly dominant in individuals committing school shootings. However, these extreme acts of aggression have been related more to persistent rather than acute exclusion, as in the case of victims of bullying or being isolated from the peer group (Anderson et al., 2001).

The consequences of both acute and chronic exclusion can overlap with the early stages of radicalization. However, chronic exclusion is considerably closer to radicalization as all the normative coping strategies and alternatives to extremism have failed, and affiliation with extreme groups might be the only way out of the absolute social vacuum surrounding the chronically excluded.

12.4.1   The Conceptual Overlap between Resignation and the Early Stage of Radicalization

The central theoretical proposition of this chapter is that the psychological condition of the resignation stage might expose people to an exceptional risk – more powerful and direct than acute exclusion – of affiliating with extremist groups. Indeed, the absolute deprivation by chronic exclusion weakens individuals, making them hypersensitive and eager for social inclusion and acceptance and to exit the resignation stage. This hypersensitivity adds to the fact that the characteristics of chronic exclusion and the resignation stage overlap with the features of the early stage and motives for radicalization according to the most relevant theoretical models on the topic, namely the staircase to terrorism (Moghaddam, 2005), the "3-N" approach (Webber & Kruglanski, 2016), and the three phases of radicalization (Doosje et al., 2016).

The staircase to terrorism (Moghaddam, 2005) describes the terrorist act as a gradual process divided into five steps. Most of the population occupies the first step, the foundational ground floor. The starting point leading to ascending the staircase is the perception of injustice and deprivation. High levels of perceived deprivation compared to others and perception of the unfairness of such deprivation matter most for the rise of terrorism. People who are chronically excluded from others and society by definition perceive a deprivation in their fundamental need for social connections, and such deprivation might also be perceived as unfair. Although literature already emphasized that social exclusion comes with the perception of unfairness (Kimel et al., 2017), we are unaware of research about chronically excluded individuals' appraisal of their marginalized condition. In one of the pieces of research we described earlier, we found that homeless people considered unfairness as an indivisible facet of the economic inequality they experience (Marinucci et al., 2023). These results are only partial indicators of how chronically excluded people might consider their situation; however, they provide empirical, albeit slightly related, support for the reasonable assumption that marginalized individuals might feel unfairly deprived compared to others.

The "3-N" approach (i.e., need, narrative, and network; Webber & Kruglanski, 2016) identifies the quest for significance as the most foundational need motivating terrorism. The need for a meaningful existence is a universal human motivation that, according to Kruglanski et al. (2014), includes various basic motivations, including self-esteem, control, and belonging (Baumeister & Leary, 1995). The model theorizes that the quest for significance motivating radicalization needs to be activated by individual or group events that threaten the loss of significance or constitute an opportunity to gain meaning. According to the model, personal humiliation is the most prototypical instance of significance loss, but any personal failure or transgression can also be a starter of the quest. Episodes of social exclusion are events threatening the need for meaningfulness (Williams, 2009), and chronic social exclusion and the derived resignation stage exasperate the threat to the need for a meaningful existence. As already detailed, the resignation stage is characterized by lasting depression, alienation, helplessness, and unworthiness. Therefore, chronically excluded individuals are exaggeratedly frustrated in their needs, enclosed in the need for significance, and this motivational overlap makes them at the utmost risk of entering the radicalization process. Lyons-Padilla et al. (2015) found that Muslim immigrants' experiences of social exclusion amplified the consequences of marginalization and cultural identity loss on significance loss, in turn predicting a radical interpretation of Islam and support for fundamentalist groups.

The "3-N" approach is tightly connected with the three phases radicalization model (Doosje et al., 2016). The latter postulates that feelings of insignificance strongly influence the first stage of radicalization, the sensitivity phase, where people become cognitively open to radical ideologies. In addition, the model postulates that individuals have a shield of resilience that makes them resistant to radical messages. Chronically excluded individuals' shields against radicalism might be weakened by the severe threat to their basic needs and psychological well-being, and their craving for social inclusion and acceptance might make them hypersensitive to radical ideologies and groups, which pledge belonging, acceptance, and the coveted inclusion in a novel social group.

Another fundamental element of overlap between resignation and radicalization lies in alienation. Alienation is defined as the sense of isolation and perceived separation from significant other individuals and groups arising from the perception of being socially excluded (Jessor et al., 1973). Alienation is a central feature of the resignation stage, and it derives from the chronic and repeated threat to the need to belong that occurs when social exclusion lasts over time and comes from multiple sources (Williams, 2009). Alienation is a construct of interest for its theoretical and empirical influence on radicalization and violent extremism (Vergani et al., 2021). Anecdotal evidence suggests that alienation was in the personal background of radicalized individuals who committed extreme acts of violence in the name of ideological causes (Kluger, 2016; McAuley, 2016). Empirical evidence suggests that alienation might be implied in extremist acts from loners, as research shows that alienated youth tended to respond with aggression following acute rejection from the peer group (Reijntjes et al., 2010). Also, alienation was positively associated with violent extremist and criminal attitudes, and it amplified the influence of existential and significance threat on support for extremist views (Vergani et al., 2021). Researchers theorized that alienation could relate to violence as persistent and pervasive exclusion from society weakens the bonds with prosocial and normative sources of support like school and family, and this might create room for radicalized affiliation and the rejection of social norms inhibiting violence (Reijntjes et al., 2010). Also, alienation is theoretically associated with powerlessness and meaninglessness, converging with the significance quest theory from the "3-N" radicalization model (Kruglanski et al., 2014).

Hence, based on the models of radicalization, chronically excluded individuals are at risk of entering radicalization processes for four reasons. First, they experience a situation of deprivation and injustice that can kickstart the ascent of the staircase of terrorism. Second, they experience the resignation stage, consisting of the chronic frustration of the basic needs and feelings of alienation, depression, unworthiness, and helplessness that intrinsically motivate them toward radicalism to gain significance, belonging, esteem, and certainty. Third, the state of resignation makes chronically excluded people become hypersensitive to the influence of radical groups. Finally, chronically excluded people's disruption of normative ties with prosocial institutions in the societal network creates room for affiliation with radical, unconventional groups embracing violent attitudes. These factors describe how chronically excluded individuals might become attuned to radicalization. However, the link between chronic exclusion and radicalism is not at all definitive. Whether people within the resignation would radicalize or not depends on many bio-psychosocial factors, including the occasional encounter with a radicalized network.

12.4.2   Resurrect or Radicalize?

The literature about the resignation stage underlines that chronically excluded people might eventually be welcomed in a caring context where they can reexperience reconnection and acknowledgment. Hales (2018) defined this possibility as a "miraculous feat" (p. 376), a *social resurrection* opposite to the *social death* and oblivion of social exclusion. However, such experiences might be rare, and people come to these revitalizing experiences randomly, through residual shared social networks or occasional encounters. For instance, Zamperini et al. (2020) describe the cases of random encounters with the House of Tenderness, a religious group offering novel affiliations to people banned and excluded from their original religious communities. Ideally, social resurrection would lead to prosocial and lasting social inclusion in a normative and conventional context. However, radical groups might appeal to chronic-ally excluded people as an opportunity for social resurrection. Stranahan (2000) describes how displaced refugees who had become homeless due to the battle of Shanghai in 1937 became the perfect target for the Chinese Communist Party's radical mobilizing. Similarly, Tunisian marginalized slums characterized by social exclusion, vulnerability, crime, and protests became the perfect ground for the spread of the Salafi-Jihadi movement leading youth radicalization to jihadist extremism (DAAM, 2020).

However, both resurrection and radicalization require an encounter with a network channeling the novel group affiliation. Sageman (2004) describes that the entrance into radicalized Islamist networks often occurs in mosques channeled by firebrand Imams. Gustafson (2021) maintained that the recruit-ment in radicalized groups might occur via the Internet and social media, through in-person meetings, and small fractions of key individuals coordinat-ing the affiliation. Schmid (2013) highlighted the existence of radical milieus, physical or virtual social spaces constituting points of attraction toward the radical group, where in particular vulnerable and marginalized people can find a new role and identity, breaking with past experiences of chronic exclusion and oppression.

Local circumstances and random encounters might constitute the last turning point toward radicalization or resurrection. For this reason, we believe it is essential to provide people from marginalized groups and contexts with institutional occasions for social resurrection. The novel affiliation within normative groups would help chronically excluded people to recover their threatened needs and resignation, defusing a dangerous trigger that could push toward radical groups. The creation of prosocial occasions of affiliation might take away the space for radical antisocial affiliations. For example, take the prison context as a venue of chronic exclusion and marginalization where radicalization might develop. Khosrokhavar (2013) discusses how the most psychologically fragile people in jail can take refuge in radicalization, guided by radicalizers (i.e., those coordinating the recruiting process). The radicalization processes would be counteracted if the prison provided inmates with alternative institutional encounters providing support and affiliation. This could be the case in the study by Aureli et al. (2020), where inmates who joined the support group within the prison had the same resignation levels as free citizens, lower than those who did not participate. The support group reduced the resignation, built prosocial connections offering a social resurrection – even if still within the prison context – and neutralized the possible risks of affiliation with antisocial groups of prisoners. Relatedly, we found that experiences of social exclusion led to lower longitudinal resignation over time for immigrants who developed more frequent and closer connections with people from the Italian national group. In contrast, higher development of connections with other immigrants increased the longitudinal consequences of social exclusion on resignation. In other words, establishing relationships with the local population constituted a resilient social factor counteracting the development of the resignation stage, as against the segregated relationships within immigrant niches. In addition to increasing the sense of exclusion and resignation, the segregation within marginalized niches constitutes a risk factor for political radicalism (Varady, 2008). In the immigration context, creating the opportunity for bridging connections with the local communities might help to reduce the risk of radicalization.

Chronically excluded people are not entirely at the mercy of their encounters with radicalized individuals and social networks. As Doosje et al. (2016) pointed out, people possess a resilience shield against radicalization, which is true also for the most persistently excluded people. Some research on homeless people found that personal factors like resilience, particularly the concept of tenacity – the sense of power and adherence to one's values and goals in the face of adversities – might help to cope against chronic social exclusion and sustain well-being. Similar individual factors might help to counteract the sensitization to radicalized groups among the most excluded.

12.5 Conclusion

This chapter defined the characteristics of chronic social exclusion and its psychological repercussions and reviewed the psychological processes that might push chronically excluded individuals to affiliate with radicalized and extreme groups. We provided a comprehensive definition of the chronicity of social exclusion, considering persistence over time and pervasiveness across situations as its main features. We reviewed the theoretical and empirical literature on the psychological repercussions of social exclusion, describing the resignation stage characterized by depression, alienation, unworthiness, and helplessness as the primary consequences of chronic exclusion. The empirical literature investigating the resignation stage in marginalized social groups and the general population questions the theoretical assumption that conceives the resignation stage as the only and unavoidable consequence of chronic exclusion. Rather, the literature suggests that interpersonal and group social connections might influence the resignation, reducing or further aggravating its development. Therefore, we theorized that chronically excluded individuals amid the resignation stage might be hypersensitive and eager for novel social connections and, from there, at risk of becoming sensitive to radicalism, bridging the literature about chronic exclusion and radicalization processes. Lastly, we discussed social circumstances applied in marginalized contexts that can determine whether chronically excluded people would resurrect through affiliation with normative social groups or radicalize with antisocial ones. In doing so, we primarily focused on the first stages of the radicalization process, related to the sensitivity phase to radical ideologies and groups. However, the influence of chronic social exclusion and resignation might also extend to later stages of radicalization. Once affiliated with the radical network, the person stops being chronically excluded and becomes accepted in the radicalized system. However, the past experienced social exclusion and resignation might constitute a risk factor, pushing toward the act of violence and thus reaching the top of the staircase to terrorism. It could be that the previously excluded people, mindful of the social pain and resignation derived from being chronically excluded, would conform and comply even more with the radical group and ideology to avoid being banned from the group and risking reentering the condition of chronic exclusion. Indeed, the possible novel exclusion after being finally reincluded and resurrected through the radicalized group might constitute such a terrifying threat that the person would do everything to preserve the affiliation (i.e., avoiding the significance loss; Kruglanski et al. (2014); Ellenberg & Kruglanski, this volume) and therefore pursue the violent act. This argument is only possible theoretical speculation on how chronic exclusion could further drive extreme violence and calls for future research and theoretical models accounting for the relevance of chronic exclusion throughout all the radicalization stages.

References

Anderson, M., Kaufman, J., Simon, T. R., et al. (2001). School-associated violent deaths in the United States, 1994–1999. *Jama*, *286*(21), 2695–2702. https://doi.org/10.1001/jama.286.21.2695

Aureli, N., Marinucci, M., & Riva, P. (2020). Can the chronic exclusion–resignation link be broken? An analysis of support group in prisons. *Journal of Applied Social Psychology*, *50*(2), 638–650. https://doi.org/10.1111/jasp.12701

Baumeister, R. F., & Leary, M. R. (1995). The need to belong: Desire for interpersonal attachments as a fundamental human motivation. *Psychological Bulletin*, *117*(3), 497–529.

Büttner, C. M., Jauch, M., Marinucci, M., et al. (2023). It will (never) stop hurting: Does chronic social exclusion lead to hyper- or hypo-sensitive psychological responses? *Group Processes & Intergroup Relations*. Advance online publication. https://doi.org/10.1177/13684302221140002

Cacioppo, J. T., Hawkley, L. C., Norman, G. J., & Berntson, G. G. (2011). Social isolation. *Annals of the New York Academy of Sciences*, *1231*(1), 17–22. https://doi.org/10.1111/j.1749-6632.2011.06028.x

Cave, D., & Saxton, A. (2021). New Zealand gives Christchurch killer a record sentence. *New York Times*. www.nytimes.com/2020/08/26/world/asia/christchurch-brenton-tarrant-sentenced.html

DAAM (2020, September 18). The paths of Jihadist extremism and experiences of daily exclusion among the youth of the popular neighborhoods: An attempt at understanding. https://daamdth.org/archives/11945?lang=en

DeSouza, E. R., Wesselmann, E. D., Taschetto, L. R., et al. (2019). Investigating ostracism and racial microaggressions toward Afro-Brazilians. *Journal of Black Psychology*, *45*(4), 222–268. https://doi.org/10.1177/0095798419864001

Doosje, B., Moghaddam, F. M., Kruglanski, A. W., et al. (2016). Terrorism, radicalization and de-radicalization. *Current Opinion in Psychology*, *11*, 79–84. https://doi.org/10.1016/j.copsyc.2016.06.008

Dotan-Eliaz, O., Sommer, K. L., & Rubin, Y. S. (2009). Multilingual groups: Effects of linguistic ostracism on felt rejection and anger, coworker attraction, perceived team potency, and creative performance. *Basic and Applied Social Psychology*, *31*(4), 363–375. https://doi.org/10.1080/01973530903317177

Eisenberger, N. I., & Lieberman, M. D. (2004). Why rejection hurts: A common neural alarm system for physical and social pain. *Trends in Cognitive Sciences*, *8*(7), 294–300.

Gerber, J., & Wheeler, L. (2009). On being rejected: A meta-analysis of experimental research on rejection. *Perspectives on Psychological Science*, *4*(5), 468–488.

Goffman, E. (1961) *Asylums*. Doubleday/Anchor.

Gómez, Á., Morales, J. F., Hart, S., Vázquez, A., & Swann Jr., W. B. (2011). Rejected and excluded forevermore, but even more devoted: Irrevocable ostracism intensifies loyalty to the group among identity-fused persons. *Personality and Social Psychology Bulletin*, *37*(12), 1574–1586.

Graf, J. (2016, July 22). Er wurde zuruckgewiesen – uberall. Wie Breivik zum Massenmorder wurde. [He got rejected – everywhere. How Breivik became a mass murderer.] N-tv. www.n-tv.de/politik/Wie-Breivik-zum-Massenmoerder-wurde-article18245816.html

Gustafson, E. (2021). Jihadist terrorist organization usage of foreign fighters: An analysis of the factors surrounding the recruitment, motivation, and usage of foreign fighters. *TCU Digital Repository*. https://repository.tcu.edu/handle/116099117/49052

Hales, A. (2018). Death as a metaphor for ostracism: Social invincibility, autopsy, necromancy, and resurrection. *Mortality*, *23*(4), 366–380. https://doi.org/10.1080/13576275.2017.1382462

Hales, A. H., Dvir, M., Wesselmann, E. D., Kruger, D. J., & Finkenauer, C. (2018). Cell phone-induced ostracism threatens fundamental needs. *The Journal of Social Psychology*, *158*(4), 460–473. https://doi.org/10.1080/00224545.2018.1439877

Hales, A. H., & Williams, K. D. (2018). Marginalized individuals and extremism: The role of ostracism in openness to extreme groups. *Journal of Social Issues, 74* (1), 75–92. https://doi.org/10.1111/josi.12257

Hales, A. H., Wood, N. R., & Williams, K. D. (2021). Navigating COVID-19: Insights from research on social ostracism. *Group Processes & Intergroup Relations*, *24*(2), 306–310. https://doi.org/10.1177/1368430220981408

Hannaford, A. (2018, September 12). We asked 12 mass killers: "What would have stopped you?" *GQ Magazine: British GQ.* www.gq-magazine.co.uk/article/mass-shootings-in-america-interviews

Hogg, M. A., Kruglanski, A., & Van den Bos, K. (2013). Uncertainty and the roots of extremism. *Journal of Social Issues, 69*(3), 407–418.

Holt-Lunstad, J., Smith, T. B., & Layton, J. B. (2010). Social relationships and mortality risk: A meta-analytic review. *PLoS Medicine*, *7*(7), e1000316. https://doi.org/10.1371/journal.pmed.1000316

Jessor, R., Jessor, S. L., & Finney, J. (1973). A social psychology of marijuana use: Longitudinal studies of high school and college youth. *Journal of Personality and Social Psychology*, *26*(1), 1–15.

Khosrokhavar, F. (2013). Radicalization in prison: The French case. *Politics, Religion & Ideology, 14*(2), 284–306.

Kimel, S. Y., Mischkowski, D., Kitayama, S., & Uchida, Y. (2017). Culture, emotions, and the cold shoulder: Cultural differences in the anger and sadness response to ostracism. *Journal of Cross-Cultural Psychology*, *48*, 1307–1319. https://doi.org/10.1177/0022022117724900

King, L. A., & Geise, A. C. (2011). Being forgotten: Implications for the experience of meaning in life. *The Journal of Social Psychology*, *151*(6), 696–709. https://doi.org/10.1080/00224545.2010.522620

Klages, S. V., & Wirth, J. H. (2014). Excluded by laughter: Laughing until it hurts someone else. *The Journal of Social Psychology*, *154*(1), 8–13. https://doi.org/10.1080/00224545.2013.843502

Kluger, J. (2016, June 14). This is what drove the Orlando killer. *Time*. http://time.com/4368275/mateen-orlando-why-he-killed/

Kowalski, R. M., Leary, M., Hendley, T., et al. (2021). K–12, college/university, and mass shootings: Similarities and differences. *The Journal of Social Psychology*, *161*(6), 753–778. https://doi.org/10.1080/00224545.2021.1900047

Kruglanski, A. W., Gelfand, M. J., Bélanger, J. J., et al. (2014). The psychology of radicalization and deradicalization: How significance quest impacts violent extremism. *Political Psychology*, *35*, 69–93. https://doi.org/10.1111/pops.12163

Kydd, A. H., & Walter, B. F. (2006). The strategies of terrorism. *International Security*, *31*(1), 49–80. https://doi.org/10.1162/isec.2006.31.1.49

Leary, M. R., Kowalski, R. M., Smith, L., & Phillips, S. (2003). Teasing, rejection, and violence: Case studies of the school shootings. *Aggressive Behavior: Official Journal of the International Society for Research on Aggression*, *29*(3), 202–214.

Lindström, B., & Tobler, P. N. (2018) Incidental ostracism emerges from simple learning mechanisms. *Nature Human Behaviour*, *2*, 405–414. https://doi.org/10.1038/s41562-018-0355-y

Long, C. R., & Averill, J. R. (2003). Solitude: An exploration of benefits of being alone. *Journal for the Theory of Social Behaviour*, *33*(1), 21–44. https://doi.org/10.1111/1468-5914.00204

Lutz, S., & Schneider, F. M. (2021). Is receiving dislikes in social media still better than being ignored? The effects of ostracism and rejection on need threat and coping responses online. *Media Psychology*, *24*(6), 741–765. https://doi.org/10.1080/15213269.2020.1799409

Lyons-Padilla, S., Gelfand, M. J., Mirahmadi, H., Farooq, M., & Van Egmond, M. (2015). Belonging nowhere: Marginalization & radicalization risk among Muslim immigrants. *Behavioral Science & Policy*, *1*(2), 1–12.

Maner, J. K., DeWall, C. N., Baumeister, R. F., & Schaller, M. (2007). Does social exclusion motivate interpersonal reconnection? Resolving the "porcupine problem." *Journal of Personality and Social Psychology*, *92*(1), 42–55. https://doi.org/10.1037/0022-3514.92.1.42.

Marinucci, M., & Riva, P. (2021a). Surrendering to social emptiness: Chronic social exclusion longitudinally predicts resignation in asylum seekers. *British Journal of Social Psychology*, *60*(2), 429–447. https://doi.org/10.1111/bjso.12410

Marinucci, M., & Riva, P. (2021b). How intergroup social connections shape immigrants' responses to social exclusion. *Group Processes & Intergroup Relations*, *24*(3), 411–435. https://doi.org/10.1177/1368430219894620

Marinucci, M., Mazzoni, D., Pancani, L., & Riva, P. (2022). To whom should I turn? Intergroup social connections moderate social exclusion's short- and long-term psychological impact on immigrants. *Journal of Experimental Social Psychology*, *99*. https://doi.org/10.1016/j.jesp.2021.104275

Marinucci, M., Pancani, L., Aureli, N., & Riva, P. (2022). Online social connections as surrogates of face-to-face interactions: A longitudinal study under Covid-19 isolation. *Computers in Human Behavior*, *128*, 107102. https://doi.org/10.1016/j.chb.2021.107102

Marinucci, M., Riva, P., Lenzi, M., et al. (2023). On the lowest rung of the ladder: How social exclusion, perceived economic inequality and stigma increase homeless people's resignation. *British Journal of Social Psychology.* Advance online publication. https://doi.org/10.1111/bjso.12657

Mazzoni, D., Pancani, L., Marinucci, M., & Riva, P. (2020). The dual path of the rejection (dis)identification model: A study on adolescents with a migrant background. *European Journal of Social Psychology, 50,* 799–809. https://doi.org/10.1002/ejsp.2672

McAuley, J. (2016, July 16). New details suggest attacker in Nice was alienated, troubled man. *Washington Post.* www.washingtonpost.com/world/new-details-suggest-attacker-in-nice-was-alienated-troubled-man/2016/07/16/d53caab4-4af7-11e6-8dac-0c6e4accc5b1_story.html

Merskey, H., Albe-Fessard, D. G., Bonica, J. J., et al. (1979). The need of a taxonomy. *Pain, 6*(3), 247–252. https://doi.org/10.1016/0304-3959(79)90046-0

Moghaddam, F. M. (2005). The staircase to terrorism: A psychological exploration. *American Psychologist, 60*(2), 161–169.

Molden, D. C., Lucas, G. M., Gardner, W. L., Dean, K., & Knowles, M. L. (2009). Motivations for prevention or promotion following social exclusion: Being rejected versus being ignored. *Journal of Personality and Social Psychology, 96* (2), 415–431.

Nezlek, J. B., Wesselmann, E. D., Wheeler, L., & Williams, K. D. (2012). Ostracism in everyday life. *Group Dynamics: Theory, Research, and Practice, 16*(2), 91–104. https://doi.org/10.1037/a0028029

Pancani, L., Marinucci, M., Aureli, N., & Riva, P. (2021). Forced social isolation and mental health: A study on 1,006 Italians under COVID-19 lockdown. *Frontiers in Psychology, 12,* 663799.

Pfundmair, M. (2019). Ostracism promotes a terroristic mindset. *Behavioral Sciences of Terrorism and Political Aggression, 11*(2), 134–148. https://doi.org/10.1080/19434472.2018.1443965

Pfundmair, M., Aßmann, E., Kiver, B., et al. (2022). Pathways toward jihadism in Western Europe: An empirical exploration of a comprehensive model of terrorist radicalization. *Terrorism and Political Violence, 34*(1), 48–70.

Pfundmair, M., & Mahr, L. A. (2022). How group processes push excluded people into a radical mindset: An experimental investigation. *Group Processes & Intergroup Relations,* 13684302221107782.

Pfundmair, M., Wood, N. R., Hales, A., & Wesselmann, E. D. (2022). How social exclusion makes radicalism flourish: A review of empirical evidence. *Journal of Social Issues,* 1–19. https://doi.org/10.1111/josi.12520

Pohlan, L. (2019). Unemployment and social exclusion. *Journal of Economic Behavior & Organization, 164,* 273–299. https://doi.org/10.1016/j.jebo.2019.06.006

Reijntjes, A., Thomaes, S., Bushman, B. J., et al. (2010). The outcast-lash-out effect in youth: Alienation increases aggression following peer rejection. *Psychological Science, 21*(10), 1394–1398.

Ren, D., Wesselmann, E. D., & van Beest, I. (2020). Seeking solitude after being ostracized: A replication and beyond. *Personality and Social Psychology Bulletin*, *47*(3), 426–440. https://doi.org/10.1177/0146167220928238

Riva, P. (2016). Emotion regulation following social exclusion: Psychological and behavioral strategies. In P. Riva, & J. Eck (Eds.), *Social exclusion: Psychological approaches to understanding and reducing its impact* (pp. 199–225). Springer International. https://doi.org/10.1007/978-3-319-33033-4_10

Riva, P., & Eck, J. (2016). The many faces of social exclusion. In P. Riva, & J. Eck (Eds.), *Social exclusion: Psychological approaches to understanding and reducing its impact* (pp. ix–xv). Springer International. https://doi.org/10.1007/978-3-319-33033-4

Riva, P., Montali, L., Wirth, J. H., Curioni, S., & Williams, K. D. (2017). Chronic social exclusion and evidence for the resignation stage: An empirical investigation. *Journal of Social and Personal Relationships*, *34*(4), 541–564. https://doi.org/10.1177/0265407516644348

Riva, P., Wesselmann, E. D., Wirth, J. H., Carter-Sowell, A. R., & Williams, K. D. (2014). When pain does not heal: The common antecedents and consequences of chronic social and physical pain. *Basic and Applied Social Psychology*, *36*, 329–346.

Riva, P., Williams, K. D., Torstrick, A. M., & Montali, L. (2014). Orders to shoot (a camera): Effects of ostracism on obedience. *The Journal of Social Psychology*, *154*, 208–216.

Roberts, J. A., & David, M. E. (2016). My life has become a major distraction from my cell phone: Partner phubbing and relationship satisfaction among romantic partners. *Computers in Human Behavior*, *54*, 134–141. https://doi.org/10.1016/j.chb.2015.07.058

Rubin, M., & Stuart, R. (2018). Kill or cure? Different types of social class identification amplify and buffer the relation between social class and mental health. *The Journal of Social Psychology*, *158*(2), 236–251.

Rudert, S. C., Janke, S., & Greifeneder, R. (2021). Ostracism breeds depression: Longitudinal associations between ostracism and depression over a three-year-period. *Journal of Affective Disorders Reports*, *4*, 100118.

Sageman, M. (2004) *Understanding terror networks*. University of Pennsylvania Press.

Schmid, A. P. (2013). Radicalisation, de-radicalisation, counter-radicalisation: A conceptual discussion and literature review. *ICCT Research Paper*, *4*(2), 1–97.

Schuster, B. (1996). Rejection, exclusion, and harassment at work and in schools. *European Psychologist*, *1*(4), 293–317. https://doi.org/10.1027/1016-9040.1.4.293

Smart Richman, L., & Leary, M. R. (2009). Reactions to discrimination, stigmatization, ostracism, and other forms of interpersonal rejection: A multimotive model. *Psychological Review*, *116*(2), 365–383.

Stranahan, P. (2000). Radicalization of refugees: Communist Party activity in wartime Shanghai's displaced persons camps. *Modern China*, *26*(2), 166–193.

Twenge, J. M., Baumeister, R. F., Tice, D. M., & Stucke, T. S. (2001). If you can't join them, beat them: Effects of social exclusion on aggressive behavior. *Journal of Personality and Social Psychology, 81*(6), 1058–1069. https://doi.org/10.1037/0022-3514.81.6.1058

Vangelisti, A. L. (2001). Making sense of hurtful interactions in close relationships: When hurt feelings create distance. In V. Manusov, & J. H. Harvey (Eds.), *Advances in personal relations: Attribution, communication behavior, and close relationships* (pp. 38–58). Cambridge University Press.

Vangelisti, A. L., Young, S. L., Carpenter-Theune, K., & Alexander, A. L. (2005). Why does it hurt? The perceived causes of hurt feelings. *Communication Research, 32*, 443–477. https://doi.org/10.1177/0093650205277319

Varady, D. (2008). Muslim residential clustering and political radicalism. *Housing Studies, 23*(1), 45–66.

Vergani, M., Iqbal, M., O'Brien, K., Lentini, P., & Barton, G. (2021). Examining the relationship between alienation and radicalization into violent extremism. In S. Bonino & R. Ricucci (Eds.), *Islam and Security in the West* (pp. 115–138). Palgrave Macmillan. https://doi.org/10.1007/978-3-030-67925-5_6

Warburton, W. A., Williams, K. D., & Cairns, D. R. (2006) When ostracism leads to aggression: The moderating effects of control deprivation. *Journal of Experimental Social Psychology, 42*(2), 213–220. https://doi.org/10.1016/j.jesp.2005.03.005

Webber, D., & Kruglanski, A. W. (2016). Psychological factors in radicalization: A "3 N" approach. In G. LaFree, & J. D. Freilich (Eds.), *The handbook of the criminology of terrorism* (pp. 33–46). Wiley. https://doi.org/10.1002/9781118923986.ch2

Wesselmann, E. D., Butler, F. A., Williams, K. D., & Pickett, C. L. (2010). Adding injury to insult: Unexpected rejection leads to more aggressive responses. *Aggressive Behavior, 36*(4), 232–237. https://doi.org/10.1002/ab.20347

Wesselmann, E. D., Grzybowski, M. R., Steakley-Freeman, D. M., et al. (2016). Social exclusion in everyday life. In P. Riva, & J. Eck (Eds.), *Social exclusion: Psychological approaches to understanding and reducing its impact* (pp. 3–23). Springer International. https://doi.org/10.1007/978-3-319-33033-4_1

Wesselmann, E. D., Michels, C., & Slaughter, A. (2019). Understanding common and diverse forms of social exclusion. In S. Rudert, R. Greifeneder, & K. Williams (Eds.), *Current directions in ostracism, social exclusion, and rejection research* (pp. 1–17). Routledge.

Wesselmann, E. D., & Williams, K. D. (2017). Social life and social death: Inclusion, ostracism, and rejection in groups. *Group Processes & Intergroup Relations, 20*(5), 693–706. https://doi.org/10.1177/1368430217708861

Wesselmann, E. D., Williams, K. D., Ren, D., & Hales, A. H. (2021). Ostracism and solitude. In R. J. Coplan, J. C. Bowker, & L. J. Nelson (Eds.) *The handbook of solitude: Psychological perspectives on social isolation, social withdrawal, and being alone* (pp. 209–223). Wiley. https://doi.org/10.1002/9781119576457.ch15

Wessely, S., Chalder, T., Hirsch, S., Wallace, P., & Wright, D. (1996). Psychological symptoms, somatic symptoms, and psychiatric disorder in chronic fatigue and chronic fatigue syndrome: A prospective study in the primary care setting. *American Journal of Psychiatry, 153*, 1050–1059. https://doi.org/10.1176/ajp.153.8.1050

Williams, K. D. (2009). Ostracism: A temporal need-threat model. *Advances in Experimental Social Psychology, 41*, 275–314. https://doi.org/10.1016/S0065-2601(08)00406-1

Williams, K. D., & Nida, S. A. (2022). Ostracism and social exclusion: Implications for separation, social isolation, and loss. *Current Opinion in Psychology, 47*, 101353. https://doi.org/10.1016/j.copsyc.2022.101353

Williams, K. D., & Zadro, L. (2001). Ostracism: On being ignored, excluded, and rejected. In M. R. Leary (Ed.), *Interpersonal rejection* (pp. 21–53). Oxford University Press.

Wood, N. (2020). Adventures in solitude: The link between social isolation and violent extremism [Unpublished master's thesis]. University of Pittsburgh.

Zadro, L. (2004). *Ostracism: Empirical studies inspired by real-world experiences of silence and exclusion* [Unpublished doctoral dissertation]. University of New South Wales, Sydney, Australia.

Zamperini, A., Menegatto, M., Mostacchi, M., Barbagallo, S., & Testoni, I. (2020). Loss of close relationships and loss of religious belonging as cumulative ostracism: From social death to social resurrection. *Behavioral Sciences, 10*(6), 99.

Zhang, J., Ding, C., Tang, Y., Zhang, C., & Yang, D. (2017). A measure of perceived chronic social adversity: Development and validation. *Frontiers in Psychology, 8*, 2168. https://doi.org/10.3389/fpsyg.2017.016

13

Connecting Conspiracy Beliefs and Experiences of Social Exclusion

ROLAND IMHOFF

13.1 Introduction

It is one of the core tenets of ostracism research that being socially excluded deprives basic human needs on several levels. It threatens individuals' need to belong, need to feel good about themselves, need to perceive having control, and need for recognition (Williams, 2009). Conspiracy beliefs, in contrast, are frequently theorized to be a response to deprived social needs, often the very same ones: the need to have clear and definitive explanations (epistemic needs), to exert agency and control (existential needs), and to feel good about oneself and connected to others (social needs; Douglas et al., 2017). Against this background, it seems unsurprising that various connections have been made between social exclusion experiences on the one hand and the endorsement of conspiracy theories on the other hand. Potentially less intuitive, research has also explored the reverse direction: experiencing social exclusion due to the public endorsement of conspiracy theories. In the following, I will review this literature by starting with the direct intuitive examples (ostracism leading to conspiracy beliefs), as well as indirect connections via the respective deprived needs. I will end with the reverse directions as well as open research questions. Before doing so, however, I will briefly summarize some basic tenets of psychological research into the antecedents and consequences of conspiracy beliefs and their relevance for radicalization processes.

13.2 Conspiracy Beliefs and Radicalization

Conspiracy beliefs range from curious ideas (like the one that the earth is flat, but an elite group of scientists and politicians tries to make us buy the globe hoax) to dangerous worldviews associated with some of the most extreme forms of intergroup atrocities (like the one that Jews secretly control the fate of the world via string puppets). Starting with a seminal paper by Goertzel (1994) and robustly replicated again and again (e.g., Bruder et al., 2013; Frenken & Imhoff, 2021; Swami et al., 2011; Williams et al., 2022), social scientists have shown that despite the apparent diversity of conspiracy beliefs, their endorsement seemingly clusters tightly together. Virtually any one conspiracy belief seems to be positively correlated with virtually any other. This has led authors to conclude either that individual conspiracy theories mutually reinforce each other to form a monological belief system (Goertzel, 1994) or that there is a latent disposition to belief that the world is governed by plots hatched in secret, a conspiracy mentality (Imhoff & Bruder, 2014; Imhoff et al., 2022a). From this latter perspective, the exact content of a conspiracy theory does not matter a lot, as the schematic representation of the world governed by malevolent hidden forces that leaves little room for randomness (a conspiracy theory of society; Popper, 1966) serves as a foil to make sense of any new event or phenomenon. Information is then not processed in a bottom-up way of collecting relevant information, but the core belief – that anything is the result of the direct design of a ruthless elite – prompts selective information processing in a top-down manner (for the ubiquity of such confirmatory information processing, see Oeberst & Imhoff, 2023).

Importantly, there is nothing inherently wrong about this. We all engage in confirmatory information processing and it is part of the human behavioral arsenal to coordinate secretly with others for their own benefit (i.e., to conspire). It is thus not outrageous to suspect this. And indeed, a general conspiracy mentality seems largely normally distributed around the midpoint of the scale (Imhoff et al., 2022a), even in large representative samples (Imhoff, 2015). Adding further support for the idea that conspiracy beliefs may contain adequate perceptions of reality, it has been repeatedly found that general conspiracy mentality tends to be more pronounced in contexts that have a higher likelihood of conspiracies being present. Examples include countries with higher levels of corruption (Alper, 2023; Alper & Imhoff, 2023; Hornsey et al., 2018) or a lower democracy index (Hornsey & Pearson, 2022; for a discussion of using such objective measures to tear apart cultural from sociostructural antecedents, see Imhoff, 2022).

Despite this, several authors have noted social costs associated with such beliefs, particularly on the extreme ends of the conspiracy belief spectrum (Jolley et al., 2020). Being extremely low on the conspiracy mentality spectrum might have costs for oneself because one almost naively trusts, even in the presence of untrustworthy others (Frenken & Imhoff, 2023; Meuer & Imhoff, 2021). Although this may entail risks for the individual to naively trust anyone, from a societal perspective, it is not problematic per se. This is markedly different for a very pronounced conspiracy mentality. Being extremely high on the conspiracy mentality spectrum implies social costs and a threat to the social fabric.

Specifically, conspiracy beliefs (specific or generalized) have been associated with reduced compliance with infection-curbing behaviors in a pandemic (Imhoff & Lamberty, 2020), also longitudinally (Bierwanowicz et al., 2020; for a meta-analytic overview of pandemic associations of conspiracy beliefs, see Bierwanowicz et al., 2022). More generally, they have been associated with reduced compliance with social norms (Pummerer et al., 2023) and opposition to necessary infrastructure projects to limit climate change (Winter et al., 2022). Pointing toward one of the key components of radicalized behavior, German and US participants who were experimentally manipulated to adopt a high (vs. low) conspiracy mentality perspective deemed it less likely to engage in normative political action (like signing petitions or protesting) and more likely to engage in nonnormative and violent political action (like assaulting a political representative or manipulating election results; Imhoff et al., 2021). Likewise, endorsement of coronavirus-related conspiracy statements was positively associated with the self-reported intention to engage in acts of political vandalism against 5G technology (Jolley & Paterson, 2020). In a nationally representative sample of Germans, respondents who scored high on conspiracy mentality showed greater violent extremism (measured as radicalism intentions), particularly if they were low on self-control (Rottweiler & Gill, 2022). Looking at the phenomenon from the end result of full radicalization, Bartlett and Miller (2010) could show that most violent terrorist groups operate with conspiracy-laden rhetoric (for a more recent analysis with similar results, see Rousis et al., 2022).

On the level of political orientation, conspiracy mentality has been robustly established as being more pronounced on the political extremes, particularly among supporters of opposition parties on the right (Imhoff et al., 2022b; for the US American example of such views being only present at the right end of the political spectrum, see van der Linden et al., 2021). In addition to self-reported symbolic political orientation, conspiracy beliefs have also been associated with a number of problematic ideological fragments of extremist worldviews. Even the endorsement of conspiracy beliefs that do not explicitly blame Jews is typically associated with anti-Semitic attitudes (Bilewicz & Imhoff, 2022). Conspiracy theories often portray the world as a conflict between forces of good and evil, with the side characterized as evil typically demonized and portrayed as worthy of inhumane treatment. It is thus not surprising that conspiracy theories have been identified as tools to dehumanize discriminated out-groups (as in the case of Asians during the COVID-19 pandemic; Sakki & Castrén, 2022).

13.3 Conspiracy Beliefs as Consequences of Ostracism

Conspiracy beliefs have been theorized to be an intergroup phenomenon that follows more or less directly from the perception of social rejection by a powerful group (van Prooijen & van Lange, 2014). Not all conspiracy theories can be meaningfully framed as intergroup phenomena, however. Many take the form of intragroup speculations about one's own elected representatives secretly following a different agenda than they publicly claim. Nevertheless, even when we ignore the intergroup aspect of conspiracy beliefs (or a corresponding worldview), it makes sense to connect it to ostracism experiences. Ostracism has been postulated to deprive a whole range of basic needs (Hales et al., this volume; Williams, 2009), and conspiracy beliefs are (independent of their intergroup nature) sense-making reactions to deprived needs. Experimental approaches have shown that recalling an experience of being ostracized led to an increased endorsement of conspiracy beliefs compared to recalling an episode of physical pain or a neutral episode (Poon et al., 2020; Studies 2 & 4). A different manipulation of ostracism, receiving bogus feedback about the (low) number of likes one's profile had received by other participants (Wolf et al., 2015), also led to a greater agreement with political conspiracy theories (Poon et al., 2020; Study 3). Although conceptually not identical, research on workplace bullying might also be relevant for the general idea. Self-reported experiences of workplace bullying were associated with conspiracy beliefs, and imagining being bullied at a new workplace led to higher endorsements of conspiracy theories than imagining being supported (Jolley & Lantian, 2022).

Weaker, correlational evidence points in the same direction; the extent to which participants reported feeling socially excluded in a recent social event was positively correlated with their endorsement of three specific conspiracy theories (Graeupner & Coman, 2017). In the same vein, experiences of ostracism (as measured by the scale by Gilman et al., 2013) showed positive correlation with various political conspiracy theories (Poon et al., 2020; Study 1) as well as with COVID-19 conspiracy beliefs among a UK-based sample stratified across age, sex, and ethnicity ($N = 895$; Gkinopoulos & Uysal, 2021).

Thus, although there is some experimental and correlational support for the idea that being ostracized evokes a greater willingness to explain the state of the world with conspiracies by a powerful elite, this direct evidence is relatively modest (particularly in the case of experimental evidence for directly experiencing rather than remembering ostracism; for a counterintuitive finding that belongingness increases conspiracy beliefs among self-uncertain individuals, see van Prooijen, 2016). The bulk of research provides indirect support by connecting conspiracy beliefs to the deprivation of a need that has also been postulated to be negatively affected by experiences of ostracism.

13.4   Conspiracy Beliefs and Need Deprivation

The influential temporal need-threat model of ostracism (Williams, 2009) posits that experiences of ostracism trigger an initial reflexive phase characterized by social pain in response to the frustration of four fundamental needs: the need to belong, the need for a positive self-esteem, the need for control, and the need for a meaningful existence. More recently, a fifth need has been added to this list: the need for certainty – both in oneself and the world around oneself (Hales & Williams, 2021; Hales et al., this volume). All these deprived needs will then lead to a reflection on the experience and coping efforts to fortify them. A similar reasoning has been applied to conspiracy beliefs, whereby these are adopted as a response to deprived needs, as a coping response (Douglas et al., 2017). Different from the ostracism literature that has at least partially focused on effective ways to fortify the needs (e.g., Molet et al., 2013; Pfundmair et al., 2015; Waldeck et al., 2017), most of the psychological literature on conspiracy beliefs takes a skeptical stand on whether adopting conspiracy beliefs is actually functional in quenching the needs it arose from. Independent of this question, I will briefly summarize the literature that connects conspiracy beliefs to the five classes of needs mentioned previously.

13.4.1   Need to Belong

Lacking social connection deprives the need to belong (Leary & Baumeister, 1995) and results in compensatory action: increasing connection. People who do not feel not sufficiently socially integrated will seek company and connection. A similar homeostatic principle has been postulated on the level of group identification: People seek social identities that offer an optimal distinctiveness by balancing the need to belong and the need to be different (Brewer, 1991). While ostracism is one of the more blatant and obvious sources of not feeling connected, it is less clear how believing in conspiracy theories could be functional in coping with this.

One way to think about it might be that joining groups or communities of conspiracy believers can address the need to belong by creating a sense of connection to like-minded others. This, however, does not really provide a specific explanation, as the same might be true for virtually any other community of like-minded others. This would then allow the prediction that any of one's previously held beliefs is strengthened (as any form of social proof by others is actively sought and will start a process of confirmatory information processing). A specific explanation for the connection from a heightened need to belong to the endorsement of conspiracy beliefs requires additional assumptions. These could take the form that nowadays most people seek connections online and online communities have a particularly high risk of leading down a conspiracy rabbit hole, either because of the disproportionately large number of conspiracy communities specifically or because conspiracy content is privileged by social media algorithms, or because conspiracy communities are more explicit in their expression of providing community for people feeling deprived of connections (in contrast to official news sites). It is also conceivable of course that it is not just the lure to feel connected that makes conspiracy beliefs attractive, but its combination with a sense-making opportunity: providing an explanation for why one feels lonely, ostracized, and disconnected.

Conspiracy theories typically provide explanations that shift blame for negative outcomes from the individual to the secret plots of powerful others. Not having friends, then, could be attributed to a malicious plan to socially isolate the individual. Thus, it is theoretically not pressingly necessary but at least conceivable that feeling less socially connected than preferred might increase the adoption of conspiracy beliefs. Is there reliable evidence of such a pattern?

Several cross-sectional studies provide some support for at least an association between conspiracy beliefs and loneliness. It is important to note that these studies typically do not try to quantify social connectedness in an objective way but assess subjective feelings of being lonely (typically measured with the UCLA scale; Russell et al., 1980). This makes sense as it is not necessarily the (objective) lack of contacts but rather the subjective feeling of loneliness that indicates a need for compensation to the individual (Hawkley & Cacioppo, 2010).

In a large sample representative for the German population between the age of 14 and 95 in terms of age, gender, and education, Hettich and colleagues (2022) observed positive correlations between self-reported loneliness on the one hand and conspiracy mentality (Imhoff & Bruder, 2014; short version by Imhoff, 2015), $r = .19$, and respectively specific conspiracy theories about the coronavirus pandemic, $r = .15$, on the other hand. Both associations were not significant any longer once other variables (demographics, personality functioning) were controlled for in multiple regression analyses.

Another large study among German adolescents conducted during the coronavirus pandemic (Neu et al., 2023) reports an association of loneliness with conspiracy mentality and the acceptance of political violence, both $rs = .22$, also after controlling for shared variance with demographic variables.

Connecting experiences of ostracism, feelings of loneliness, conspiracy beliefs, and nonnormative political intentions, Jolley and colleagues (2023) reported three studies that consistently provide support for an association of conspiracy beliefs with experiences of feeling ostracized (Rudert et al., 2020; Study 1: $r = .17$; Study 2: $r = .23$) as well as feeling lonely (Hughes et al., 2004; Study 1: $r = .18$; Study 2: $r = .16$; Study 3: $r = .14$). Self-reported nonnormative political intentions and actual behavior (refusing to pay taxes on the received participation fee) were less consistently related at the level of zero-order correlations but corroborated as potential consequences in serial mediation analyses (for the causal ambiguities regarding correlational mediation analyses, see Fiedler et al., 2011; Lemmer & Gollwitzer, 2017).

Importantly, however, such cross-sectional analyses do not allow for causal inferences. Using two comparatively large multi-wave surveys, Bertlich and colleagues (in prep) replicated the finding that individual differences in self-reported loneliness were robustly associated with general conspiracy mentality and COVID-19 conspiracy beliefs, but failed to find support for a longitudinal association in random intercept crossed-lagged models. Thus, the data supported neither the notion that loneliness leads to increases in conspiracy beliefs nor the opposite effect that heightened conspiracy beliefs increase loneliness. The cross-sectional association might thus not indicate a causal mechanism between the two but merely shared variance with a third variable (e.g., negative reporting bias; control deprivation). Alternatively, it might be that it is not the temporally fluctuating transient loneliness that could be modeled in such a study, but the long-lasting persistent loneliness (captured by the stable between-subject) variance that causes conspiracy beliefs. This would allow a connection to the resignation phase postulated for enduring experiences of ostracism (Williams, 2009).

In summary, there is some data in support of a connection between a deprived need to belong and the endorsement of conspiracy theories, but these are typically not very strong or reliable. More work is thus required both empirically and theoretically to clarify this connection.

13.4.2   Self-worth

Being ostracized compromises one's self-esteem as it may signal that the self is a person not worthy of inclusion. Individuals should thus be motivated to reestablish a sense of self-worth. How could the endorsement of conspiracy theories help in that regard? From a theoretical angle, two routes are conceivable. First, as with attributing loneliness to evil forces, conspiracy theories are potent for providing an explanation for virtually any self-deficit. Explaining these by powerful forces having shifted the odds against oneself protects the self from negative emotional consequences. Second, holding a conspiracy belief might be seen as an achievement to be proud of in and of itself, as only a few "enlightened" individuals see through the smokescreen created to keep the majority of "sheeple" ignorant.

The available data compatible with this general reasoning mostly consists of correlations between conspiracy beliefs and an exaggerated self-view (narcissism) on the one hand and the need to feel special and unique on the other hand.

Based on the reasoning that a fragile sense of self-worth requiring constant external validation and that is easily threatened by critique is at the core of (collective) narcissism, and that conspiracy theories deflect blame from the self or one's own group, some studies have reported associations of conspiracy beliefs and narcissism – at the individual or collective level. Narcissistic self-views were associated with beliefs in conspiracy theories about COVID-19 (Ahadzadeh et al., 2023; Siem et al., 2021) and a variety of measures of general conspiracy mentality (Kay, 2021), particularly when statistically controlling for non-defensive self-positivity (Cichocka et al., 2016a; replicated by Siem et al., 2021). Likewise, collectively narcissistic beliefs (conviction about one's group's superiority and entitlement to special treatment) were associated with conspiracy beliefs about gender relations (Marchlewska et al., 2019), vaccinations (Cislak et al., 2021), COVID-19 (robustly across fifty-six countries; Sternisko et al., 2023), and the political sphere (Cichocka et al., 2016b; for a meta-analytic integration, see Golec de Zavala et al., 2022). During the 2016 US presidential election, collective narcissism longitudinally predicted an increase in general conspiracist thinking controlling for a lagged measure of conspiracist thinking at an earlier measurement wave (Golec de Zavala & Frederico, 2018).

Speaking to the second route mentioned earlier, Cichocka and colleagues (2022) argued in a recent overview paper that not only fragile and vulnerable narcissism is associated with conspiracy beliefs. They argue the same is true for grandiose narcissism via a heightened need for uniqueness. Conspiracy theories can be attractive for individuals with such a need as they are by definition exclusive knowledge: If everyone knew about a conspiracy it would not be secret anymore, thus eliminating one of the cardinal criteria of a conspiracy theory (the *secret* coordination of a group of people to their own benefit and the public's disadvantage). Claiming to see through this secret plot thus makes the person claiming so special. And indeed, the self-reported need for uniqueness is a reliable predictor of general conspiracy mentality (Imhoff & Lamberty, 2017, 2018; Lantian et al., 2017), also meta-analytically (Biddlestone et al., 2022; Bowes et al., 2023). Some experimental evidence suggests that manipulating need for uniqueness (slightly) increases the endorsement of conspiracy theories, but this effect was small and significant by conventional standards only if meta-analytically aggregated (Lantian et al., 2017).

In conclusion, some evidence is compatible with the notion that the adoption of conspiracy beliefs is an effort to cope with threats to self-worth, but it is not clear whether this is indeed functional in the sense that it does help boost self-esteem. One of the problems in achieving a more complete understanding of this is the field's overreliance on cross-sectional correlations (van Prooijen & Imhoff, 2022). With such data and a dynamic model of coping with need deprivation, any correlation can be interpreted as supportive of the theory: A positive correlation of self-esteem and conspiracy beliefs would speak to the effectiveness of conspiracy beliefs to regain a sense of self-worth, whereas a negative correlation (as it has been observed meta-analytically; $r = -.08$; Bowes et al., 2023; $r = -.06$; Stasielowicz, 2022) could be seen as support for the notion that low self-esteem drives conspiracy belief.

13.4.3   Control/Agency

Another need deprived when ostracized is the need for control and agency, to be in control of one's own outcomes and surroundings. This kind of control deprivation is arguably most robustly associated with conspiracy beliefs in the literature. There is a plethora of experimental as well as correlational findings linking feelings and situations of low control to greater endorsements of conspiracy theories.

The reasoning behind the notion that conspiracy beliefs help compensate for the lack of control are twofold. First, seeing through things, understanding an enigmatic phenomenon lends the illusion of control. This function is closely tied to the idea of aversion to randomness and an increased need for epistemic control or: certainty. Pure randomness is not only unpredictable and uncertain but also uncontrollable. Given the conceptual overlap, I will elaborate on this idea of predictability and other epistemic when talking about the deprived need for certainty. The second function is closely related but more concrete. If conspiracies are behind a pandemic or a health threat a loved one is experiencing, actual control and agency is possible. Like in a classical Greek tragedy or Hollywood movie, it just takes a hero (or several) to put a stop to the conspirators' game. The loved one would be well again, the pandemic over, and everybody's life could go back to normal – a tempting promise conspiracy theories offer in times of acute control deprivation. If my social exclusion is due to a secret sinister plan, I just have to expose and defeat that conspiracy to end my pain, saving me from effortful social servility to re-achieve social inclusion.

At the level of associations, frequently reported correlates of conspiracy beliefs are powerlessness (e.g., Abalakina-Paap et al., 1999; Imhoff & Bruder, 2014), anomia (e.g., Abalakina-Paap et al., 1999; Goertzel, 1994), or directly (low) control (e.g., Imhoff & Lamberty, 2018) with meta-analytical estimates of $r = .28$, $r = .34$, $r = -.17$, respectively (Bowes et al., 2023). Furthermore, people with a general disposition to believe in conspiracy theories more readily interpret even mundane actions as intentional (Frenken & Imhoff, 2022), readily attribute intentionality to geometrical shapes (Douglas et al., 2016) and nonliving entities like the wind (Imhoff & Bruder, 2014), and they are more likely to detect patterns in random noise (van Prooijen et al., 2018). These cross-sectional correlations, however, are less interesting than the relatively numerous studies testing the effect of control deprivation on conspiracy beliefs experimentally.

In one of the earliest demonstrations of this effect, participants who recalled a threatening episode over which they had no control agreed more with conspiracy theories about a fictitious scenario than those who recalled a threatening episode over which they did have control (Whitson & Galinsky, 2008, Study 4; note though that the sample was extremely small, the effect just significant, and the conspiracy scenarios relating to rather mundane examples of not receiving promotion). Reminding people of chaotic hazards beyond their control like diseases or natural disaster by asking them how much control they have over them (vs. asking them how much control they have over watching TV or not) increased their endorsement of election-related conspiracy theories (Sullivan et al., 2010, Study 2; again, with a small sample and just significant). Despite frequent replications of this general effect (e.g., van Prooijen & Acker, 2015), this effect seems less robust than often assumed. A meta-analysis reported only weak support, not surpassing what would be expected by chance in the presence of no effect (Stojanov & Halberstadt, 2020). A closer look at this data, however, suggests that there is evidence for an effect of control deprivation on specific conspiracy beliefs, but not reliably on the more trait-like conspiracy mentality (Imhoff et al., 2022a). Adding further fuel to the fire of skepticism, however, even the COVID-19 pandemic as a real-world example of drastic control deprivations on a large scale (not being able to see friends, go to work, being under a health regime to curb infections) did not seem to increase the endorsement of conspiracy theories in large-scale surveys (Imhoff, 2023), although it did increase the visibility of conspiracy theories.

What is more, however, is that even *if* control deprivation does increase conspiracy belief, evidence for the functionality of these beliefs is lacking. In other words, there is currently no evidence that adopting a conspiracy belief or worldview will help people regain a sense of control over important outcomes in their life, let alone provide them with actual control over their outcomes. This of course does not speak against the possibility that experiences of ostracism might evoke conspiracy beliefs via experienced control deprivation. It just suggests that this way of coping may not be particularly effective in regaining a sense of control.

13.4.4   Recognition/Meaningful Existence

The fourth need deprived by experiences of ostracism is the need to feel recognized for existence and worthy of attention (Ellenberg & Kruglanski, this volume). Arguably, this connects well to background variables discussed as increasing the vulnerability to conspiracy theories. Several data point to the role of demographic variables signaling status (as a proxy for being meaningful in the eyes of other) as close associates of conspiracy beliefs. Conspiracy beliefs are more prevalent among individuals in unemployment (Imhoff, 2015), low in subjective social class (van Prooijen, 2017), low in formal education (Imhoff et al., 2022b; van Prooijen, 2017), and members of marginalized religious, ethnic (van Prooijen et al., 2018), and racial (Crocker et al., 1999) groups.

Although the conceptual leap covers a greater distance here, it seems highly plausible that the aversive experience of feeling invisible and neglected reported by ostracized individuals is similar to the chronic experience of low status and marginalized individuals. Not being included in mainstream society due to educational, language, or economic barriers might undermine not just one's sense of agency, self-worth, and social connection but also one's very identity. Conspiracies theories, then, offer an explanation for one's own underprivileged position and deflect blame from oneself to a corrupt system – arguably a healthy reaction.

13.4.5   Need for Certainty

As already alluded to earlier, conspiracy theories have been prominently posited to arise from epistemic needs (Douglas et al., 2017). Humans prefer to live in a predictable environment and predictability might be spelled out as certainty about what will happen. Rather than accepting that some things (e.g., earthquakes, pandemics, assassinations by lone gunmen) just happen, people willingly attribute intentionality, agency, and systematicity. Conspiracy theories offer an ideal combination of these qualities, as a small group of people planned (intentionally) to bring about a certain event (agency), and knowing about this makes one realize that many seemingly unrelated events and phenomena are intrinsically connected (systematicity). Perceiving the world in such a way reassures one's feeling of control as it increases predictability. As predictability implies not only certainty about what will happen next but also controllability over it, a large chunk of the empirical evidence speaking to this need is already mentioned under the passage on control deprivation.

Not all certainty, however, implies controllability. In fact, although attributing the fate of the world to the sinister campaign of a small group of villains introduces the hypothetical possibility of regaining control by exposing them and their plot, in most cases this will not happen. Instead, the idea of an almighty cabal of political and economic elites might deprive one's feeling of (political) control even further. The same is not true for certainty. Knowing (or believing to know) who did it will create certainty and provide a definite answer. Conspiracy theories may thus provide closure as long as the official explanation is lacking (Marchlewska et al., 2018) or non-conspiracist explanations do not seem proportional in light of the consequences they seek to explain (Leman & Cinnirella, 2007; Radnitz & Underwood, 2017; Van Prooijen & Van Dijk, 2014). Pitting uncertainty (a sense-making deficit) and lack of control (an agency deficit) directly against each other, however, Kofta and colleagues (2020) demonstrated across cross-sectional, longitudinal, and experimental studies that the latter provides a more potent explanation for increases in (anti-Semitic) conspiracy beliefs. Adding to that – and paralleling the available evidence for lack of control – despite some evidence that lack of certainty may make conspiracy beliefs attractive, there is very little evidence that adopting a conspiracy belief will successfully satisfy the need for certainty.

13.5   Ostracism as a Consequence of Conspiracy Beliefs

Up until this point, I have elaborated on how the deprivation of fundamental needs through experiences of ostracism may increase the likelihood of adopting conspiracy beliefs to cope with this need deprivation (even if this way of coping will not prove functional in fortifying those needs). The connection between ostracism and conspiracy beliefs, however, may not be unidirectional. Indeed, at least in most Western societies, conspiracy theories are stigmatized beliefs, potentially leading to social exclusion (for a discussion of conspiracy theories as accurate detection of valid cues to corruption and intransparency in other contexts, see Imhoff, 2022).

Conspiracy theories, that is, suspicions about others having conspired to their advantage and the public's disadvantage, are not right or wrong prima facie. The extent of their accuracy is a function of how well they are compatible with the available evidence. Against this truism, many authors have defined conspiracy theories in a way that they are inherently wrong (Napolitano & Reuter, 2023) or at least "epistemically risky" (Douglas & Sutton, 2023). This strategy has been criticized by others who argue that the very use of the label "conspiracy theory" is a routinized strategy of exclusion (Husting & Orr, 2007). This resonates with the finding that people use the label conspiracy theory to denote something they disbelieve (Douglas et al., 2021), even though labeling something as a conspiracy theory does not reduce belief in it (Wood, 2016).

Compatible with such a view of conspiracy theories as stigmatized beliefs is not only the notion that people understand that expressing conspiracy theories will entail social costs of being negatively evaluated (Green et al., 2023). Experimental evidence also shows that people fear being ostracized for endorsing conspiracy theories (Lantian et al., 2018). Participants were instructed to write a text of three arguments in favor of (or opposing) a popular conspiracy theory behind the terrorist attacks on a satire magazine in Paris with the goal to convince readers. Afterwards, participants who argued in favor of the conspiracy theory anticipated more negative evaluation from the audience and were more concerned about being socially excluded. Connecting this to extremism, participants who were asked to judge the extent to which they would be willing to exclude others, reporting greater willingness to exclude members of groups who engage in extreme forms of activism (Hales & William, 2020).

As an important limitation, these studies rely on hypothetical expectations. It is not clear that expressing conspiracy beliefs will indeed foster episodes of ostracism. It is also not clear how to evaluate this. Although explaining ostracism with target characteristics (Rudert et al., 2020) can easily have a flavor of victim blaming, conspiracy worldviews have the potential to undermine virtually any rational discourse. Coherent conspiracy belief systems undermine the epistemic social contract that the world is as we have been told by politicians, experts, and mass media (Imhoff et al., 2018). In such a situation, it is challenging to find common ground to talk about virtually any topic if one cannot even agree on basic premises (e.g., that anthropogenic climate change exists or that the earth is not flat). Sometimes it may thus be tempting and seemingly in the best interest of a discussion to separate the spheres or – put more bluntly – exclude conspiracy believers.

There is, however, a danger. Not only may such exclusion add fuel to a fire of an escalating cycle of becoming less and less open to a balanced weighting of available evidence, but even subtle sources of feeling left out like overly complex wording of health advice also led people high in conspiracy mentality to feel socially excluded and hence less trustful in both the message and science in general, as well as less willing to comply with health recommendations (in the context of the COVID-19 pandemic; Schnepf et al., 2021).

13.6   Conclusion and Future Directions

Conspiracy beliefs have gained public attention as justification devices for nonnormative actions in several contexts, giving rise to worries about their potential as radicalization multipliers. Likewise, ostracism and lack of social connections has been discussed as a risk factor for radicalized identities and action.

Ostracism deprives fundamental needs, for which conspiracy beliefs offer a way to cope. In most cases, however, this coping does not deliver on its promise to successfully satisfy those needs (Liekefett et al., 2023). As a caveat, however, some of these connections between deprived needs and the increased endorsement of conspiracy theories rest on weak data – predominantly cross-sectional correlations and underpowered experiments.

Future research may also explore new avenues of how the two concepts are connected. As only one example, some scholars have suggested that an over-looked active ingredient in being socially excluded is that it is boring not to be included (e.g., never receiving the ball in Cyberball games; Jacoby & Sassenberg, 2009). Likewise, recent research in the field of conspiracy beliefs suggests that people consume conspiracy theories also for their entertainment value (van Prooijen et al., 2022) – conspiracy theories typically tell better and more captivating stories of villains being exposed by virtuous heroes.

Endorsing and publicly expressing conspiracy beliefs may expose one to the risk of being ostracized. Here, too, the database could be stronger, as the available experimental studies rest on hypothetical anticipations rather than observed behavior. Nevertheless, taking this possibility of a bidirectional influence seriously may suggest the danger of a vicious cycle of radicalization processes: people who feel ostracized feel drawn to conspiracy theories as they offer an explanation for their social pain and an opportunity to regain a feeling self-worth, agency, and connection. Adopting and expressing such beliefs, however, will make it harder to be socially accepted and integrated by most others, again further adding to feelings of social exclusion. It thus is worthwhile to invest time and effort to better understand the intricate relationship between ostracism and escalating conspiracy belief to keep people from falling into the proverbial "rabbit hole" (Sutton & Douglas, 2022).

References

Abalakina-Paap, M., Stephan, W. G., Craig, T., & Gregory, W. L. (1999). Beliefs in conspiracies. *Political Psychology, 20,* 637–647. https://doi.org/10.1111/0162-895X.00160

Ahadzadeh, A. S., Ong, F. S., & Wu, S. L. (2023). Social media skepticism and belief in conspiracy theories about COVID-19: The moderating role of the dark triad. *Current Psychology, 42*(11), 8874–8886.

Alper, S. (2023). There are higher levels of conspiracy beliefs in more corrupt countries. *European Journal of Social Psychology, 53*(3), 503–517.

Alper, S., & Imhoff, R. (2023). Suspecting foul play when it is objectively there: The association of political orientation with general and partisan conspiracy beliefs as a function of corruption levels. *Social Psychological and Personality Science, 14,* 610–620.

Bartlett, J., & Miller, C. (2010). *The power of unreason: Conspiracy theories, extremism and counter-terrorism.* Demos.

Bertlich, T., Bräscher, A., Germer, S., Witthöft, M., & Imhoff, R. (2024). Owners of a lonely heart? Investigating the longitudinal relationship between loneliness and conspiracy beliefs. [Manuscript under review].

Biddlestone, M., Green, R., Cichocka, A., Douglas, K., & Sutton, R. M. (2022, April 8). A systematic review and meta-analytic synthesis of the motives associated with conspiracy beliefs. https://doi.org/10.31234/osf.io/rxjqc

Bierwiaczonek, K., Gundersen, A. B., & Kunst, J. R. (2022). The role of conspiracy beliefs for COVID-19 health responses: A meta-analysis. *Current Opinion in Psychology, 46,* 101346.

Bierwiaczonek, K., Kunst, J. R., & Pich, O. (2020). Belief in COVID-19 conspiracy theories reduces social distancing over time. *Applied Psychology: Health and Well-Being, 12*(4), 1270–1285.

Bilewicz, M., & Imhoff, R. (2022). Political conspiracy beliefs and their alignment on the left–right political spectrum. *Social Research: An International Quarterly, 89,* 679–706.

Bowes, S. M., Costello, T. H., & Arber, T. (2023). The conspiratorial mind: A meta-analytic review of motivational and personological correlates. *Psychological Bulletin, 149*(5–6), 259–293. https://doi.org/10.1037/bul0000392

Brewer, M. B. (1991). The social self: On being the same and different at the same time. *Personality and Social Psychology Bulletin, 17*(5), 475–482.

Bruder, M., Haffke, P., Neave, N., Nouripanah, N., & Imhoff, R. (2013). Measuring individual differences in generic beliefs in conspiracy theories across cultures: Conspiracy mentality questionnaire. *Frontiers in Psychology, 4,* 225.

Cichocka, A., Marchlewska, M., & Biddlestone, M. (2022). Why do narcissists find conspiracy theories so appealing? *Current Opinion in Psychology, 47,* 101386.

Cichocka, A., Marchlewska, M., & Golec de Zavala, A. (2016a). Does self-love or self-hate predict conspiracy beliefs? Narcissism, self-esteem, and the endorsement of conspiracy theories. *Social Psychological and Personality Science, 7*(2), 157–166.

Cichocka, A., Marchlewska, M., Golec de Zavala, A., & Olechowski, M. (2016b). "They will not control us": In-group positivity and belief in intergroup conspiracies. *British Journal of Psychology, 107*, 556–576. https://doi.org/10.1111/bjop.12158

Cislak, A., Marchlewska, M., Wojcik, A. D., et al. (2021). National narcissism and support for voluntary vaccination policy: The mediating role of vaccination conspiracy beliefs. *Group Processes & Intergroup Relations, 24*(5), 701–719.

Crocker, J., Luhtanen, R., Broadnax, S., & Blaine, B. E. (1999). Belief in US government conspiracies against blacks among black and white college students: Powerlessness or system blame? *Personality and Social Psychology Bulletin, 25*(8), 941–953.

Douglas, K. M., & Sutton, R. M. (2023). What are conspiracy theories? A definitional approach to their correlates, consequences, and communication. *Annual Review of Psychology, 74*, 271–298.

Douglas, K. M., Sutton, R. M., Callan, M. J., Dawtry, R. J., & Harvey, A. J. (2016). Someone is pulling the strings: Hypersensitive agency detection and belief in conspiracy theories. *Thinking & Reasoning, 22*(1), 57–77.

Douglas, K. M., Sutton, R. M., & Cichocka, A. (2017). The psychology of conspiracy theories. *Current Directions in Psychological Science, 26*(6), 538–542.

Douglas, K. M., van Prooijen, J.-W., & Sutton, R. M. (2021). Is the label "conspiracy theory" a cause or a consequence of disbelief in alternative narratives? *British Journal of Psychology, 113*(3), 575–590. https://doi.org/10.1111/bjop.12548

Fiedler, K., Schott, M., & Meiser, T. (2011). What mediation analysis can (not) do. *Journal of Experimental Social Psychology, 47*(6), 1231–1236.

Frenken, M., & Imhoff, R. (2021). A uniform conspiracy mindset or differentiated reactions to specific conspiracy beliefs? Evidence from latent profile analyses. *International Review of Social Psychology, 34*(1), 1–15.

Frenken, M., & Imhoff, R. (2022). Malevolent intentions and secret coordination. Dissecting cognitive processes in conspiracy beliefs via diffusion modeling. *Journal of Experimental Social Psychology, 103*, 104383.

Frenken, M., & Imhoff, R. (2023). Don't trust anybody: Conspiracy mentality and the detection of facial trustworthiness cues. *Applied Cognitive Psychology, 37*, 256–265.

Gilman, R., Carter-Sowell, A., DeWall, C. N., Adams, R. E., & Carboni, I. (2013). Validation of the ostracism experience scale for adolescents. *Psychological Assessment, 25*, 319–330. https://doi.org/10.3389/fpsyg.2013.00379

Gkinopoulos, T., & Uysal, M. (2021, October 7). Ostracism and conspiracy beliefs about COVID-19: Personality and existential underlying mechanisms in a quote sampling study during the first wave of the pandemic. https://doi.org/10.31234/osf.io/q4hkn

Goertzel, T. (1994). Belief in conspiracy theories. *Political Psychology, 15,* 731–742.

Golec de Zavala, A., Bierwiaczonek, K., & Ciesielski, P. (2022). An interpretation of meta-analytical evidence for the link between collective narcissism and conspiracy theories. *Current Opinion in Psychology, 47,* 101360.

Golec de Zavala, A., & Federico, C. M. (2018), Collective narcissism and the growth of conspiracy thinking over the course of the 2016 United States presidential election: A longitudinal analysis. *European Journal of Social Psychology, 48,* 1011–1018. https://doi.org/10.1002/ejsp.2496

Graeupner, D., & Coman, A. (2017). The dark side of meaning-making: How social exclusion leads to superstitious thinking. *Journal of Experimental Social Psychology, 69,* 218–222.

Green, R., Toribio-Flórez, D., Douglas, K. M., Brunkow, J. W., & Sutton, R. M. (2023). Making an impression: The effects of sharing conspiracy theories. *Journal of Experimental Social Psychology, 104,* 104398.

Hales, A. H., & Williams, K. D. (2020). Extremism leads to ostracism. *Social Psychology, 51*(3), 149–156. https://doi.org/10.1027/1864-9335/a000406

Hales, A. H., & Williams, K. D. (2021). Social ostracism: Theoretical foundations and basic principles. In P. A. M. Van Lange, E. T. Higgins, & A. W. Kruglanski (Eds.), *Social psychology: Handbook of basic principles* (3rd ed., pp. 337–349). Guilford.

Hawkley, L. C., & Cacioppo, J. T. (2010). Loneliness matters: A theoretical and empirical review of consequences and mechanisms. *Annals of Behavioral Medicine, 40*(2), 218–227.

Hettich, N., Beutel, M. E., Ernst, M., et al. (2022). Conspiracy endorsement and its associations with personality functioning, anxiety, loneliness, and sociodemographic characteristics during the COVID-19 pandemic in a representative sample of the German population. *PLoS ONE, 17*(1), e0263301.

Hornsey, M. J., Harris, E. A., & Fielding, K. S. (2018). Relationships among conspiratorial beliefs, conservatism and climate scepticism across nations. *Nature Climate Change, 8*(7), 614–620.

Hornsey, M. J., & Pearson, S. (2022). Cross-national differences in willingness to believe conspiracy theories. *Current Opinion in Psychology, 47,* 101391.

Hughes, M. E., Waite, L. J., Hawkley, L. C., & Cacioppo, J. T. (2004). A short scale for measuring loneliness in large surveys: Results from two population-based studies. *Research on Aging, 26*(6), 655–672. https://doi.org/10.1177/0164027504268574

Husting, G., & Orr, M. (2007). Dangerous machinery: "Conspiracy theorist" as a transpersonal strategy of exclusion. *Symbolic interaction, 30*(2), 127–150.

Imhoff, R. (2015). Beyond (right-wing) authoritarianism: Conspiracy mentality as an incremental predictor of prejudice. In M. Bilewicz, A. Cichocka, & W. Soral (Eds.), *The psychology of conspiracy* (pp. 122–141). Routledge.

Imhoff, R. (2022). Conspiracy theories through a cross-cultural lens. *Online Readings in Psychology and Culture, 5*(3).

Imhoff, R. (2023). The psychology of pandemic conspiracy theories. In M. Butter, & P. Knight (Eds.) *Covid conspiracy theories in global perspective* (pp. 15–25). Taylor & Francis.

Imhoff, R., Bertlich, T., & Frenken, M. (2022a). Tearing apart the "evil" twins: A general conspiracy mentality is not the same as specific conspiracy beliefs. *Current Opinion in Psychology*, *46*, 101349.

Imhoff, R., & Bruder, M. (2014). Speaking (un-)truth to power: Conspiracy mentality as a generalized political attitude. *European Journal of Personality*, *28*, 25–43.

Imhoff, R., Dieterle, L., & Lamberty, P. (2021). Resolving the puzzle of conspiracy worldview and political activism: Belief in secret plots decreases normative but increases non-normative political engagement. *Social Psychological and Personality Science*, *12*, 71–79.

Imhoff, R., & Lamberty, P. (2017). Too special to be duped: Need for uniqueness motivates conspiracy beliefs. *European Journal of Social Psychology*, *47*, 724–734.

Imhoff, R., & Lamberty, P. (2018). How paranoid are conspiracy believers? Towards a more fine-grained understanding of the connect and disconnect between paranoia and belief in conspiracy theories. *European Journal of Social Psychology*, *48*, 909–926.

Imhoff, R., & Lamberty, P. (2020). A bioweapon or a hoax? The link between distinct conspiracy beliefs about the Coronavirus disease (COVID-19) outbreak and pandemic behavior. *Social Psychological and Personality Science*, *11*, 1110–1118.

Imhoff, R., Lamberty, P., & Klein, O. (2018). Using power as a negative cue: How conspiracy mentality affects epistemic trust in sources of historical knowledge. *Personality and Social Psychology Bulletin*, *44*, 1364–1379.

Imhoff, R., Zimmer, F., Klein, O., et al. (2022b). Conspiracy mentality and political orientation across 26 countries. *Nature Human Behavior*, *6*, 392–403.

Jacoby, J., & Sassenberg, K. (2009). Is being excluded boring? Paper presentation. The 10th Annual Society for Personality and Social Psychology Conference, Tampa, FL.

Jaiswal, J., Singer, S. N., Siegel, K., & Lekas, H. M. (2019). HIV-related "conspiracy beliefs": Lived experiences of racism and socio-economic exclusion among people living with HIV in New York City. *Culture, Health & Sexuality*, *21*(4), 373–386.

Jolley, D., & Lantian, A. (2022). Bullying and conspiracy theories: Experiences of workplace bullying and the tendency to engage in conspiracy theorizing. *Social Psychology*, *53*, 198–208. https://doi.org/10.1027/1864-9335/a000492.

Jolley, D., Mari., S., & Douglas, K. M. (2020). Consequences of conspiracy theories. In M. Butter, & P. Knight (Eds.), *Routledge handbook of conspiracy theories* (pp. 231–241). Routledge.

Jolley, D., & Paterson, J. L. (2020). Pylons ablaze: Examining the role of 5G COVID-19 conspiracy beliefs and support for violence. *British Journal of Social Psychology*, *59*(3), 628–640.

Jolley, D., Paterson, J., & Thomas, R. (2023). Refusing to pay taxes: Loneliness, conspiracy theorising and non-normative political action. *Social Psychology*, *54*(5), 308–319.

Kay, C. S. (2021). The targets of all treachery: Delusional ideation, paranoia, and the need for uniqueness as mediators between two forms of narcissism and conspiracy beliefs. *Journal of Research in Personality*, *93*, 104128.

Kofta, M., Soral, W., & Bilewicz, M. (2020). What breeds conspiracy antisemitism? The role of political uncontrollability and uncertainty in the belief in Jewish conspiracy. *Journal of Personality and Social Psychology*, *118*(5), 900–918.

Lantian, A., Muller, D., Nurra, C., & Douglas, K. M. (2017). "I know things they don't know!": The role of need for uniqueness in belief in conspiracy theories. *Social Psychology*, *48*(3), 160–171. https://doi.org/10.1027/1864-9335/a000306

Lantian, A., Muller, D., Nurra, C., et al. (2018). Stigmatized beliefs: Conspiracy theories, anticipated negative evaluation of the self, and fear of social exclusion. *European Journal of Social Psychology*, *48*(7), 939–954.

Leary, M. R., & Baumeister, R. F. (1995). The need to belong. *Psychological Bulletin*, *117*(3), 497–529.

Leman, P. J., & Cinnirella, M. (2007). A major event has a major cause: Evidence for the role of heuristics in reasoning about conspiracy theories. *Social Psychological Review*, *9*(2), 18–28.

Lemmer, G., & Gollwitzer, M. (2017). The "true" indirect effect won't (always) stand up: When and why reverse mediation testing fails. *Journal of Experimental Social Psychology*, *69*, 144–149.

Liekefett, L., Christ, O., & Becker, J. C. (2023). Can conspiracy beliefs be beneficial? Longitudinal linkages between conspiracy beliefs, anxiety, uncertainty aversion, and existential threat. *Personality and Social Psychology Bulletin*, *49*(2), 167–179.

Marchlewska, M., Cichocka, A., Łozowski, F., Górska, P., & Winiewski, M. (2019). In search of an imaginary enemy: Catholic collective narcissism and the endorsement of gender conspiracy beliefs. *The Journal of Social Psychology*, *159*(6), 766–779.

Meuer, M., & Imhoff, R. (2021). Believing in hidden plots is associated with decreased behavioral trust: Conspiracy belief as greater sensitivity to social threat or insensitivity towards its absence? *Journal of Experimental Social Psychology*, *93*, 104081.

Molet, M., Macquet, B., Lefebvre, O., & Williams, K. D. (2013). A focused attention intervention for coping with ostracism. *Consciousness and Cognition*, *22*(4), 1262–1270.

Napolitano, M. G., & Reuter, K. (2023). What is a conspiracy theory? *Erkenntnis*, *88*(5), 2035–2062.

Neu, C., Küpper, B., Luhmann, M., Deutsch, M., & Fröhlich, P. (2023). Extrem einsam? Die demokratische Relevanz von Einsamkeitserfahrungen unter Jugendlichen in Deutschland *[Extremely lonely? The democratic relevance of loneliness experiences among adolescents in Germany]*. Das Progressive Zentrum. www.progressives-zentrum.org/wp-content/uploads/2023/02/Kollekt_Studie_Extrem_Einsam_Das-Progressive-Zentrum.pdf

Oeberst, A., & Imhoff, R. (2023). Towards parsimony in bias research: Proposing a common framework of belief-consistent information processing. *Perspectives on Psychological Science, 18*(6), 1464–1487.

Pfundmair, M., Eyssel, F., Graupmann, V., Frey, D., & Aydin, N. (2015). Wanna play? The role of self-construal when using gadgets to cope with ostracism. *Social Influence, 10*(4), 221–235.

Poon, K. T., Chen, Z., & Wong, W. Y. (2020). Beliefs in conspiracy theories following ostracism. *Personality and Social Psychology Bulletin, 46*(8), 1234–1246.

Popper, K. (1966). *The open society and its enemies* (5th ed.). Princeton University Press.

Pummerer, L., Ditrich, L., Winter, K., & Sassenberg, K. (2023). Think about it! Deliberation reduces the negative relation between conspiracy belief and adherence to prosocial norms. *Social Psychological and Personality Science, 14*(8), 952–963.

Radnitz, S., & Underwood, P. (2017). Is belief in conspiracy theories pathological? A survey experiment on the cognitive roots of extreme suspicion. *British Journal of Political Science, 47*(1), 113–129.

Rottweiler, B., & Gill, P. (2022). Conspiracy beliefs and violent extremist intentions: The contingent effects of self-efficacy, self-control and law-related morality. *Terrorism and Political Violence, 34*(7), 1485–1504. https://doi.org/10.1080/09546553.2020.1803288

Rousis, G. J., Richard, F. D., & Wang, D. D. (2022). The truth is out there: The prevalence of conspiracy theory use by radical violent extremist organizations. *Terrorism and Political Violence, 34*(8), 1739–1757. https://doi.org/10.1080/09546553.2020.1835654

Rudert, S. C., Keller M. D., Hales A. H., Walker M., & Greifeneder R. (2020). Who gets ostracised? A personality perspective on risk and protective factors of ostracism. *Journal of Personality and Social Psychology, 118*, 1247–1268. https://doi.org/10.1037/pspp0000271

Russell, D., Peplau, L. A., & Cutrona, C. E. (1980). The revised UCLA Loneliness Scale: Concurrent and discriminant validity evidence. *Journal of Personality and Social Psychology, 39*(3), 472–480. https://doi.org/10.1037/0022-3514.39.3.472

Sakki, I., & Castrén, L. (2022). Dehumanization through humour and conspiracies in online hate towards Chinese people during the COVID-19 pandemic. *British Journal of Social Psychology, 61*, 1418–1438. https://doi.org/10.1111/bjso.12543

Schnepf, J., Lux, A., Jin, Z., & Formanowicz, M. (2021). Left out: Feelings of social exclusion incite individuals with high conspiracy mentality to reject complex scientific messages. *Journal of Language and Social Psychology*, *40*(5–6), 627–652.

Siem, B., Kretzmeyer, B., & Stürmer, S. (2021). The role of self-evaluation in predicting attitudes toward supporters of COVID-19-related conspiracy theories: A direct and a conceptual replication of Cichocka et al. (2016). *Journal of Pacific Rim Psychology*, *15*, 18344909211052587.

Stasielowicz, L. (2022). Who believes in conspiracy theories? A meta-analysis on personality correlates. *Journal of Research in Personality*, *98*, 104229.

Sternisko, A., Cichocka, A., Cislak, A., & Van Bavel, J. J. (2023). National narcissism predicts the belief in and the dissemination of conspiracy theories during the COVID-19 pandemic: Evidence from 56 countries. *Personality and Social Psychology Bulletin*, *49*(1), 48–65.

Stojanov, A., & Halberstadt, J. (2020). Does lack of control lead to conspiracy beliefs? A meta-analysis. *European Journal of Social Psychology*, *50*(5), 955–968.

Sullivan, D., Landau, M. J., & Rothschild, Z. K. (2010). An existential function of enemyship: Evidence that people attribute influence to personal and political enemies to compensate for threats to control. *Journal of Personality and Social Psychology*, *98*(3), 434–449. https://doi.org/10.1037/a0017457

Sutton, R. M., & Douglas, K. M. (2022). Rabbit Hole Syndrome: Inadvertent, accelerating, and entrenched commitment to conspiracy beliefs. *Current Opinion in Psychology*, *48*, 101462.

Swami, V., Coles, R., Stieger, S., et al. (2011). Conspiracist ideation in Britain and Austria: Evidence of a monological belief system and associations between individual psychological differences and real-world and fictitious conspiracy theories. *British Journal of Psychology*, *102*(3), 443–463.

Van der Linden, S., Panagopoulos, C., Azevedo, F., & Jost, J. T. (2021). The paranoid style in American politics revisited: An ideological asymmetry in conspiratorial thinking. *Political Psychology*, *42*(1), 23–51.

van Prooijen, J. W. (2016). Sometimes inclusion breeds suspicion: Self-uncertainty and belongingness predict belief in conspiracy theories. *European Journal of Social Psychology*, *46*(3), 267–279.

Van Prooijen, J. W. (2017). Why education predicts decreased belief in conspiracy theories. *Applied Cognitive Psychology*, *31*(1), 50–58.

Van Prooijen, J. W., & Acker, M. (2015). The influence of control on belief in conspiracy theories: Conceptual and applied extensions. *Applied Cognitive Psychology*, *29*(5), 753–761.

Van Prooijen, J. W., Douglas, K. M., & De Inocencio, C. (2018). Connecting the dots: Illusory pattern perception predicts belief in conspiracies and the supernatural. *European Journal of Social Psychology*, *48*(3), 320–335.

Van Prooijen, J. W., & Imhoff, R. (2022). The psychological study of conspiracy theories: Strengths and limitations. *Current Opinion in Psychology*, *48*, 101465. https://doi.org/10.1016/j.copsyc.2022.101465

Van Prooijen, J. W., Ligthart, J., Rosema, S., & Xu, Y. (2022). The entertainment value of conspiracy theories. *British Journal of Psychology, 113*(1), 25–48.

Van Prooijen, J. W., Staman, J., & Krouwel, A. P. (2018). Increased conspiracy beliefs among ethnic and Muslim minorities. *Applied Cognitive Psychology, 32* (5), 661–667.

Van Prooijen, J. W., & Van Dijk, E. (2014). When consequence size predicts belief in conspiracy theories: The moderating role of perspective taking. *Journal of Experimental Social Psychology, 55*, 63–73.

Van Prooijen, J. W., & Van Lange, P. A. (2014). The social dimension of belief in conspiracy theories. In J. W. van Prooijen, & P. A. van Lange (Eds.) *Power, politics, and paranoia: Why people are suspicious of their leaders* (pp. 237–253). Cambridge University Press.

Waldeck, D., Tyndall, I., Riva, P., & Chmiel, N. (2017). How do we cope with ostracism? Psychological flexibility moderates the relationship between everyday ostracism experiences and psychological distress. *Journal of Contextual Behavioral Science, 6*(4), 425–432.

Whitson, J. A., & Galinsky, A. D. (2008). Lacking control increases illusory pattern-perception. *Science, 322*, 115–117. https://doi.org/10.1126/science.1159845

Williams, K. (2009). Ostracism: A temporal need threat model. *Advances in Experimental Social Psychology, 41*, 275–314.

Williams, M. N., Marques, M. D., Hill, S. R., Kerr, J. R., & Ling, M. (2022). Why are beliefs in different conspiracy theories positively correlated across individuals? Testing monological network versus unidimensional factor model explanations. *British Journal of Social Psychology, 61*(3), 1011–1031.

Winter, K., Hornsey, M. J., Pummerer, L., & Sassenberg, K. (2022). Anticipating and defusing the role of conspiracy beliefs in shaping opposition to wind farms. *Nature Energy, 7*(12), 1200–1207.

Wolf W., Levordashka A., Ruff J. R., et al. (2015). Ostracism online: A social media ostracism paradigm. *Behavior Research Methods, 47*, 361–373. https://doi.org/ 10.3758/s13428-014-0475-x

Wood, M. J. (2016). Some dare call it conspiracy: Labeling something a conspiracy theory does not reduce belief in it. *Political Psychology, 37*(5), 695–705.

INDEX

Milton Keynes UK
Ingram Content Group UK Ltd.
UKHW020206040624
443535UK00019B/137